IMPLEMENTING AND AUDITING THE INTERNAL CONTROL SYSTEM

Also by Dimitris N. Chorafas

MANAGING RISK IN THE NEW ECONOMY
NEW REGULATION OF THE FINANCIAL INDUSTRY
MANAGING CREDIT RISK: 1. Analysing, Rating and Pricing the Profitability of Default
MANAGING CREDIT RISK: 2. The Lessons of VAR Failures and Imprudent Exposure
RELIABLE FINANCIAL REPORTING AND INTERNAL CONTROL: A Global Implementation Guide
CREDIT DERIVATIVES AND THE MANAGEMENT OF RISK
SETTING LIMITS FOR MARKET RISK
HANDBOOK OF COMMERCIAL BANKING: Strategic Planning for Growth and Survival in the New Decade
UNDERSTANDING VOLATILITY AND LIQUIDITY IN FINANCIAL MARKETS
THE MARKET RISK AMENDMENT: Understanding Marking-to-Model and Value-at-Risk
COST EFFECTIVE IT SOLUTIONS FOR FINANCIAL SERVICES
AGENT TECHNOLOGY HANDBOOK
TRANSACTION MANAGEMENT
INTERNET FINANCIAL SERVICES: Secure Electronic Banking and Electronic Commerce?
NETWORK COMPUTERS VERSUS HIGH-PERFORMANCE COMPUTERS
VISUAL PROGRAMMING TECHNOLOGY
HIGH-PERFORMANCE NETWORKS, PERSONAL COMMUNICATIONS AND MOBILE COMPUTING
PROTOCOLS, SERVERS AND PROJECTS FOR MULTIMEDIA REAL-TIME SYSTEMS
THE MONEY MAGNET: Regulating International Finance, Analyzing Money Flows and Selecting a Strategy for Personal Hedging
MANAGING DERIVATIVES RISK
ROCKET SCIENTISTS IN BANKING
HOW TO UNDERSTAND AND USE MATHEMATICS FOR DERIVATIVES: 1. Foreign Exchange and the Behaviour of Markets
HOW TO UNDERSTAND AND USE MATHEMATICS FOR DERIVATIVES: 2. Advanced Modelling Methods
AN INTRODUCTION TO COMMUNICATIONS NETWORKS AND THE INFORMATION SUPERHIGHWAY (*with Heinrich Steinmann*)
DERIVATIVE FINANCIAL INSTRUMENTS: Managing Risk and Return
FINANCIAL MODELS AND SIMULATION: Concepts, Processes and Technology

Implementing and Auditing the Internal Control System

Dimitris N. Chorafas

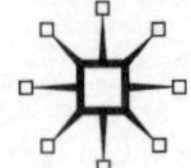

First published 2001 by
PALGRAVE
Houndmills, Basingstoke, Hampshire RG21 6XS and
175 Fifth Avenue, New York, N.Y. 10010
Companies and representatives throughout the world

PALGRAVE is the new global academic imprint of
St. Martin's Press LLC Scholarly and Reference Division and
Palgrave Publishers Ltd (formerly Macmillan Press Ltd).

ISBN 0–333–92936–5

This book is printed on paper suitable for recycling and made from fully managed and sustained forest sources.

A catalogue record for this book is available from the British Library.

Library of Congress Cataloging-in-Publication Data

Chorafas, Dimitris N.
Implementing and auditing the internal control system / Dimitris N. Chorafas.
p. cm.
Includes bibliographical references and index.
ISBN 0–333–92936–5
1. Auditing, Internal. I. Title.

HF5668.25 .C523 2000
657'.458—dc21 00–049149

10 9 8 7 6 5 4 3 2 1
10 09 08 07 06 05 04 03 02 01

Printed in Great Britain by
Antony Rowe Ltd, Chippenham, Wiltshire

Contents

PART II MANAGEMENT APPRAISAL OF AND ACCOUNTABILITY FOR THE INTERNAL CONTROL SYSTEM

List of Figures

List of Tables

Preface

Written on the threshold of the twenty-first century – a time that is increasingly marked by globalization of products and services, rapid progress in financial analytics, and technological breakthroughs – this text addresses itself to managers and professionals. Typically, its readers have, or are about to have, fiduciary responsibilities and/or an immediate and deep interest in assuring the evolution of internal control for reasons of good governance.

The International Organization for Securities Commissions (IOSCO) says that a control structure can only be as effective as the people who operate it. Therefore, strong commitment by the board as well as by all managers and professionals working for a financial institution, a manufacturing enterprise, or any other organization, is a prerequisite to the good functioning of *internal control* – that is, the intelligence necessary to ascertain that an entity functions effectively, according to ethical standards, board policies, and regulatory rules.

One of the lessons managers should learn very early in their careers is that they have to deal with the world as they find it, not as they might wish it to be. From this derives the need for interpretation of information internal control provides, looking for presence or absence of compliance and asking why and how there are deviations, and what that means for their company's present and future. Here are, in a nutshell, the five basic principles of an effective internal control.

- Internal control is a dynamic system covering all types of risk, addressing fraud, assuring transparency, and making possible reliable financial reporting.
- The chairman of the board, the directors, the chief executive officer (CEO), and senior management are responsible and accountable for internal control.
- Beyond risks, internal control goals are preservation of assets, account reconciliation, and compliance. Laws and regulations impact on internal control.
- The able management of internal control requires policies, organization, technology, open communications, access to all transactions, real-time operation, quality control, and corrective action.
- Internal control must be regularly audited by internal and external auditors to ensure its rank and condition, and to see to it there is no cognitive dissonance at any level.

Cognitive dissonance is the name for the organizational phenomenon whereby people ignore something that does not fit their view of the world and pretend it does not exist. This is distinct from outright fraud, or the intentional falsification of events and records. But, like fraud, cognitive dissonance is anathema to the proper functioning of an internal control system, and therefore internal auditors and external auditors must be on the alert.

An organizational issue to attract the auditor's attention in examining the lines of authority and accountability for internal control purposes is the separation of responsibility for the measurement, monitoring, and supervision of exposure from that of day-to-day operations. Auditors are, or at least should be, well aware that the execution of any transaction and the inventorying of any position are giving rise to risk. Risk has to be monitored and managed, but this must independent of trading, lending, and other revenue sidelines.

Auditing is part of senior management duties. The role of internal audit is to analyze and reconcile accounts, test the dependability of financial statements, evaluate qualitative business aspects, detect fraud, and master internal control details. The internal auditing function must be staffed with first-class people, be supported by the best technology, and report directly to the board or the Audit Committee. In executing their functions, auditors should form a view on the correctness and efficiency of the way in which the company is managed.

* * *

With globalization, deregulation, and the advent of derivatives, credit institutions, as well as the treasury operations of manufacturing, merchandising, and service companies, are finding that their traditional tools for management control no longer suffice. They must develop more efficient processes able to measure and monitor their risks in real-time. They must also have tools that permit to exercise timely and accurate control.

This is well known to national and international regulators who have issued a number of directives to enhance existing means for compliance, and promote risk management systems – including the use of Audit Committees and the redefining of internal control functions. Regulatory authorities are also seeing to it that both the members of the board of directors and external auditors are responsible for the company's system of internal checks and balances, and for the implementation of rigorous solutions able to provide assurance against material misstatement or loss.

The book the reader has on hand addresses the need for a direct confirmation that senior management and the auditors have reviewed the effectiveness of the system of internal financial and operational controls. This text is divided into three parts. Part 1 defines both auditing and internal control, then explains why internal control *must* be audited and in which way this should be done to improve upon the quality of deliverables.

Chapter 1 addresses the role of auditing in an organization. It demonstrates that auditing is an indispensable instrument of management, and documents that rigorous auditing can provide value-added services. This chapter also outlines the functions and responsibilities of the *Auditing Committee*, at the level of the board of directors. Its existence has been strongly recommended by the Basle Committee on Banking Supervision of the Bank for International Settlements (BIS).

Chapter 2 focuses on internal control. After defining the internal control functions and the senior management policies on which these should rest, it presents to the reader the successive steps necessary for implementing a rigorous internal control system, demonstrating why properly studied and applied internal controls can be instrumental in curbing not only fraud but as well credit risk, market risk, operational risk, and other major exposures.

Chapter 3 examines the need for internal controls from the viewpoint of globalization of financial markets. It brings home the point that important differences in accounting systems handicap internal control and auditing, and it documents how conflicts of interest work to the detriment of internal control – and therefore of the company's ability to take hold of itself.

The theme of Chapter 4 is new standards for auditing internal controls and risk management systems. Practical examples range from the more classical auditing of cash flow to risk-based auditing. A methodology for auditing the internal control system is presented in Chapter 5. Internal control information is compared to military intelligence, and applications examples are taken from trading in derivative financial instruments.

Accurate information passed in a timely fashion to decision-makers can enable them to take appropriate steps whether these focus on new business opportunities or on control action. The latter is the role of *internal control intelligence*. However, numbers and statistics are only a small part of the game. Much of the risk taken by a company because of trading and inventoried positions is inherently unqualified. Yet, we try not only to qualify it but also, whenever possible, to quantify it – because this is the only way to control it.

On these premises rests Part II, which addresses top management's accountability for internal control. The line of responsibilities starts at the chairman of the board, and though authority is delegated responsibility is not; it always stays at the top. This is precisely Chapter 6's subject. The text explains why effective internal control requires trustworthy people all the way down the line of command. It also brings into perspective the need for restructuring, and makes the point that it is wise to keep away from creative accounting practices.

The synergy between internal controls and core functions is the next important theme examined. Chapter 7 looks into core functions from the perspective of a credit institution. Emphasis is placed on both *a priori* and *a posteriori* studies as well as on compliance. Attention is also paid to management intent and on why transparency is practically synonymous with market discipline.

Transparency requires both appropriate board policies and an efficient internal control structure. This is explained in Chapter 8, which takes as an example of necessary policies those of a better-known brokerage in the United States. The reader is also presented with advice on useful tests on the way internal controls works, tips on improvements, and a discussion on the role of advanced technology in making the internal control system so much more efficient.

Technology can be instrumental in distilling data streams and in mining databased events, but as Part III explains through case studies for information to become intelligence there is no substitute for sound and well informed analysis. On the bottom line, internal control intelligence is the interpretation of facts and figures and educated guesswork on management intent at all levels of the organization.

The practical examples in Chapter 9 revolve around applying internal control to *our* institution's limits system, and to other prudential benchmarks put in place by top management. The text presents the reasons why setting limits is a business requiring know-how and imagination, as well as a feedback which makes possible dynamic limits management. The latter is the theme of Chapter 10, which elaborates further on the role of auditing in controlling the calculation of prices and risk premiums, estimating the amount of leveraging, and identifying a range of risks from equity trading to currency positions.

Chapter 11 changes the frame of reference by examining the role of internal control in engineering and manufacturing. Starting with long-termism and short-termism in research and development (R&D), it proceeds with internal control applied to engineering design. Practical examples are taken from project management and design reviews, as well as from prototyping and quality assurance. Unavoidably, this leads to a discussion on information technology.

Effective internal control and high technology are inseparable, particularly so in a very dynamic, globalized market. Chapter 12, therefore, focuses its attention on the services information technology provides in connection to the auditing of internal controls. It also explains why the use of advanced technology is not a fad but an obligation. The cutting edge of technology is never a bleeding edge unless we don't know what we are doing. But falling behind in technology has often proved to be *the* bleeding side of an internal control system.

While much can be done by way of supporting an internal control structure through human resources employed by *our* firm, external auditors can also play a major role. This is the theme of Chapter 13, which addresses both classical and modern duties of external auditors, in connection with scrutiny and verification of *our* company's internal controls. Part of this discussion is outsourcing, its strengths and weaknesses; another part is the responsibilities of all players involved in auditing internal controls.

* * *

The careful reader who considers all of the points which have been made will appreciate that internal control should be examined from different angles to assure the appropriateness of policies and procedures. Among the issues to which attention should be paid is auditing staff qualifications. Is the staff experienced in analyzing an internal control system and its effectiveness? Is a training programme in effect? Are members of the staff experienced in specialized areas such as risk management and information technology?

Other questions, too, are key to the interpretation of intelligence. Does the depth coverage of the audits appear to be sufficient? Is the chief auditor member of an executive system planning committee? Is he or she reporting directly to the chairman or the auditing committee? Behind these queries are the reasons why from Chapter 1 auditing procedures have been brought under a magnifying glass. Do these procedures employ statistically valid sampling techniques, with acceptable reliability and precision? Is the content of auditing independent of adverse influences by different interests? Has the auditing of internal control been formally established by the board of directors?

It worth practically nothing to audit internal controls if the intelligence being collected is distorted by self-imposed limitations and deliberate misconceptions. Distortions of factual and documented discoveries in the auditing of internal control is a very dangerous business for any company, no matter how senior and how clever its board, CEO, and top management may be. This has been the conclusion of the research which led to this book.

Acknowledgements

I am indebted to a long list of knowledgeable people, and of organizations, for their contribution to the research which made this book possible. Also to several senior executives and experts for constructive criticism during the preparation of the manuscript. The complete list of the senior executives and organizations who participated to this research is shown in the Appendix.

Let me take this opportunity to thank Stephen Rutt and Zelah Pengilley for suggesting this project and seeing it all the way to publication, and Keith Povey and Barbara Docherty for the editing work. To Eva-Maria Binder goes the credit for compiling the research results, typing the text, and making the camera-ready artwork and index.

Valmer and Vitznau DIMITRIS N. CHORAFAS

The author and publishers are grateful to the Crédit Suisse Group for permission to reproduce copyright material from the *Crédit Suisse Annual Report of 1998*.

List of Abbreviations and Acronyms

AICPA	American Institute of Certified Public Accountants
ALM	Assets and Liabilities Management
ASB	Accounting Standards Board (UK)
BAI	Bank Administration Institute
BIS	Bank of International Settlements
BNE	Bank of New England
BWG	Bankwesengesetz (Austrian Banking Act)
CAD	Computer-Aided Design
CAM	Computer-Aided Manufacture
CAR	Capital-at-Risk
CEO	Chief Executive Officer
CFO	Chief Financial Officer
CFTC	Commodities Futures Trading Commission
CMO	Collateralized Mortgage Obligation
COSO	Committee of Sponsoring Organizations (Treadway Commission)
CPA	Certified Public Accountant
CRMO	Chief Risk Management Officer
DSP	Digital Signal Processing
ECB	European Central Bank
EMI	European Monetary Institute (now ECB)
ESCB	European System of Central Banks
FASB	Financial Accounting Standards Board (US)
FCPA	Foreign Corrupt Practices Act (US)
FDIC	Federal Deposit Insurance Corporation (US)
FDICIA	Federal Deposit Insurance Corporation Improvement Act (US)
FIRREA	Financial Institutions Reform, Recovery, and Enforcement Act (US)
FSA	Financial Services Authority (UK)
G-10	Group of Ten (US, UK, Japan, Germany, France, Italy, Canada, Holland, Belgium, Sweden, Switzerland and Luxemburg as observer)
G-30	Group of Thirty (a Washington Think Tank)

GAAP	Generally Accepted Accounting Principles (US)
GAAP	Generally Accepted Accounting Practice (UK)
GAAS	Generally Accepted Accounting Standards.
GOA	General Accounting Office (US)
GIGA	Giga Instructions per Second
HFFD	High-Frequency Financial Data
IAS	International Accounting Standard
IASC	International Accounting Standards Committee
IIA	Institute of Internal Auditors
IC	Internal Control
ICS	Internal Control System
IMF	International Monetary Fund
IOSCO	International Organization for Securities Commissions
ISDA	International Derivatives Dealers Association
IT	Information Technology
KWG	German Banking Act
LTCM	Long-Term Capital Management
MIPS	Million Instructions per Second
MITI	Ministry of International Trade and Industry (Japan)
MOU	Memorandum of Understanding
NASD	National Association of Securities Dealers
NASDAQ	National Association of Securities Dealers Automated Quotation
NPV	Net Present Value
NYSE	New York Stock Exchange
OCC	Office of the Comptroller of the Currency (US)
OTC	Over the Counter
OTS	Office of Thrift Supervision
QA	Quality Assurance
R&D	Research and Development
RICO	Racketeer Influenced and Corrupt Practices Act (US)
ROI	Return on Investment
RV	Replacement Value
S&L	Savings & Loan
SEC	Securities and Exchange Commission (US)
SFAS	Statement of Financial Accounting Standards (US)
SQC	Statistical Quality Control
STRG	Statement of Total Recognized Gains and Losses (UK)
TQM	Total Quality Management
VAR	Value-at-Risk

Part I
Why Internal Control Systems Must be Audited

1 The Role of Auditing in an Organization

INTRODUCTION

When he became warden of the Mint, Sir Isaac Newton stepped away from tradition and began to question what he was taught. This is today the task of auditing. Newton also provides a good paradigm for another reason. Once he said to a famous crook: 'I shall only tell you in general that I understand your way and therefore sue you.' Auditors usually don't sue the company, but the regulators may.

Etymologically, the term *auditing* comes from a Latin word whose meaning is 'hearing'. Listening or hearing is an important part of the auditing practice, but not the whole of it. Auditors must do research, analysis, and evaluation. They must be led in their professional practice by a proactive concept of examination and review. In this book we will be particularly concerned about the auditing of an internal control system (see Chapter 2 for the definition of internal control).

Whether performed by internal auditors or external certified public accountants (CPA, chartered accountants), the original mission of an audit function has been to assure accounting reconciliation and compliance, as well as reliable financial reporting. As we will see in this and subsequent chapters, however, this mission has been extended in recent years to cover *internal control*.

The difficulty of spotting the real facts on whether the rules established by the law of the land, the regulators, and the company's own board are observed is neither minor nor passing. Internal auditors and external auditors must now examine *if* ethical values are observed and *if* credit policy, trading policy, limits policy, and so on are being followed to the letter. There are tools for accomplishing this mission. The check-up on credit policy can be assisted by:

- Statistical sampling of credits
- Reviews of credit ratings and
- Interviews with account managers and credit officers.

As shown in Figure 1.1, there is indeed an expanding auditing landscape. The results of investigations are typically summarized into process ratings,

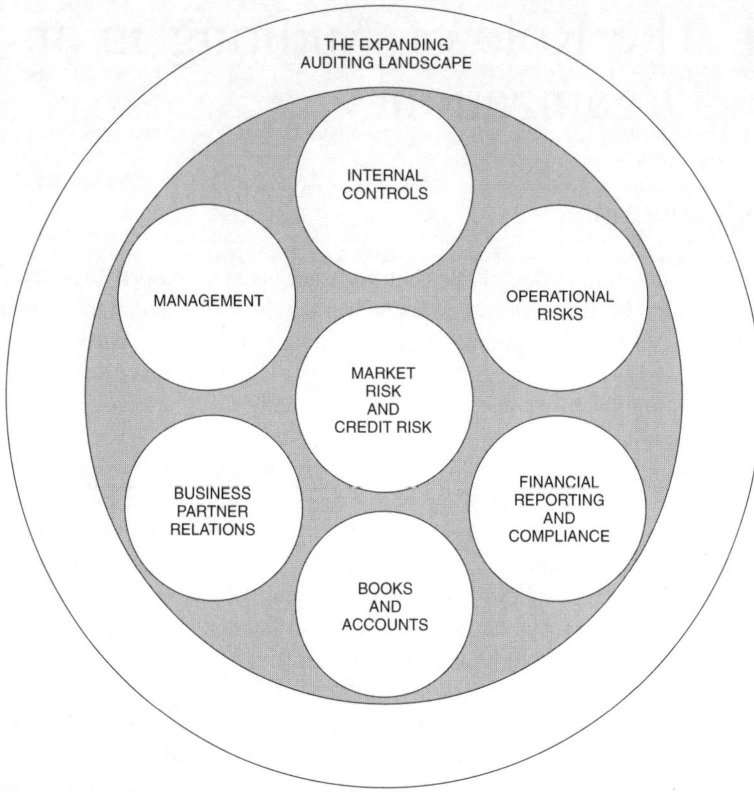

Figure 1.1 The domains where auditing functions are necessary if modern business continues to expand

which are essentially quality ratings. An auditing report might reflect failure to comply with established rules and regulations, that the company is dealing in instruments not allowed by its charter, or that it has been ordered by regulators to pay a heavy penalty for non-compliance.

While auditing a company's books and its management control system, internal and external auditors are essentially producing something akin to military information, or more precisely *internal control intelligence*. This process is basically looking for presence or absence of what is 'normal' and 'expected'. Is anyone deliberately suppressing control data streams? Is anyone falsifying records? Are financial reports dependable? Is there any disaster brewing?

If 'yes', rigorous measures must be taken by senior management to redress the situation. This, too, is part and parcel of a valid system of internal control. As Chapter 2 will explain, internal control should be proactive, with the result that corrective action by management not only immediately follows audits but also looks into the future, aiming to ensure that at all times an entity can pass the tests of good financial health administered by supervisory authorities.

Internal auditing should be given free reign in its inspection of internal control, because the rigorous examination of information from many sources is one of the key instruments for detecting, analyzing, and documenting undesirable developments relatively quickly. Audit's findings should be reported directly to the *Audit Committee* (see Chapter 6) and the board. If certain operations are not in control, action must be taken before deficiencies cause greater damage.

AUDITING DEFINED

Auditing started as the systematic verification of books and accounts, including vouchers and other financial or legal records of a physical or juridical person. The lion's share of this work was in accounting, but as we will see below, this function of verification has been extended to cover internal controls – and therefore organizational and operational issues. Internal control and auditing should not be confused even if, as Figure 1.2 shows, they tend to overlap in some of the notions underpinning them. (For a definition of internal control see the Preface and Chapter 2.)

Whether auditing is seen from the more confined perspective of books and accounts or in the broader landscape of a thorough examination contributing to prudent management of an organization, which includes internal control and operational functions, its purpose is that of determining integrity and compliance of the activities under investigation. In the case of accounting, for instance, the an aim of auditing is to show the true financial condition and certify the statements rendered. An audit may be done by internal agents, external agents or both.

Auditing is no general review and survey. It must perform a detailed analysis of every business transaction. While some experts say that an audit is completely analytical, the fact remains that it consists of both analysis and interpretation of facts, and figures. Through the audit, the entity receives a report which contains opinion(s), facts and figures as well as information and reactions that may not be otherwise available – or may not be duly appreciated at the level of the board, the chief executive officer (CEO), and his immediate assistants.

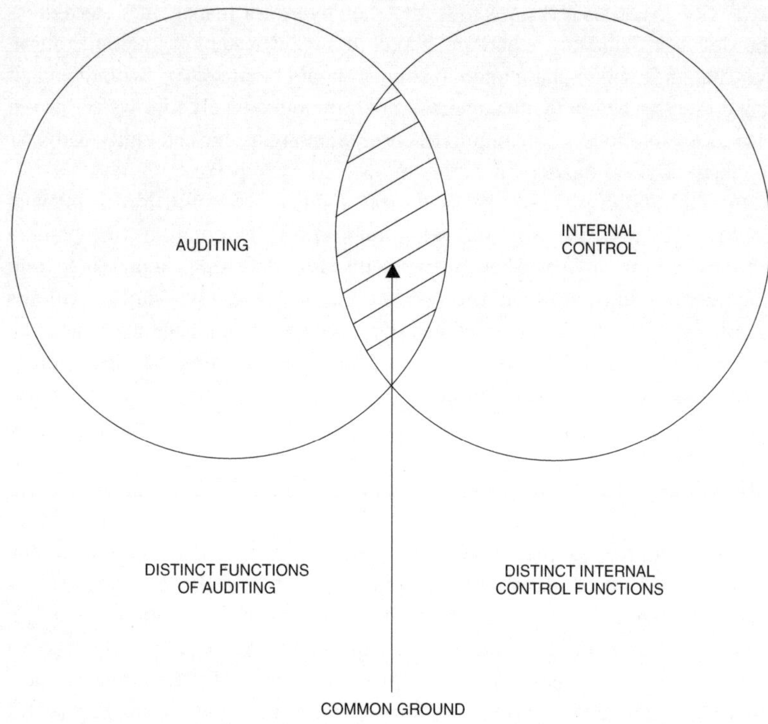

Figure 1.2 The concepts underpinning internal control and audit tend, up to a point, to overlap

Precisely because auditing offers top management and the regulators the benefits of an independent review, its principles and conduct have to be beyond reproach. The domain in which auditing is exercised has expanded beyond accounting statements and financial operations into other complex ramifications of management practice. Over the last 30 years auditors have become involved way beyond books and accounts; the purpose of their work has come to cover a far wider scope than it formerly did. Also, the auditor must keep pace with a fast expanding business field which is characterized by:

- Globalization
- Product innovation
- Deregulation and reregulation and
- A fast-advancing technology.

Audits may be divided into several classes or kinds, but in practically each one the auditor must exercise plenty of talent. Often, his or her work obliges them to disregard some sort of limit of demarcation between 'this' or 'that' auditing type or auditing tool. What, however, should under no condition be disregarded by the auditor is ethics, legal responsibility, and personal accountability.

The ethics and ethical code of the profession of auditing are comparable to those of other, much older professions like accounting. Over the years, the attitude of individual practitioners has done much to promote a high level of ethical practice. Auditors need to abide by what Aristotle called *moral virtue*, which he said was taught and learned, if at all, at a very early age.

Regarding the nuts and bolts of the trade, the auditor's work should be guided by a good sense of professional conduct, with a perception of moral responsibility present in every facet of the work being done. The professional conduct of every auditor falls naturally into four major classes:

- Relationship to the client
- Responsibility to peers,
- Responsibility to supervisory authorities and
- Accountability to professional bodies and to the public at large.

At the conclusion of every audit, the board, Audit Committee or generally the legal representative of the client, receives a report and a certificate (see Chapter 13 on types of reports). The report is prepared by the auditor from his or her working papers accumulated during the audit, interviews, and general observations. Increasingly, audits involve technical issues, therefore being mastery of technology – not just of accounting rules and principles – has become a requirement. All information contained in an auditing report is of a confidential nature.

An auditing programme is a planned procedure for an audit, including the value-added services which may be required. Knowledge, imagination, and initiative must be brought into play at all times during an audit. Regardless of how well planned the work seems to be, contingency plans should be on hand to guide the auditor into alternative paths in accomplishing his or her mission. Another important ingredient is a checklist towards the close of the audit, to make sure that nothing has been overlooked or remains obscure in the final report.

Some auditors use the term *model* for a prepared framework which guides their activities and assists in improving their performance. Whether or not it is considered as a model, a reference framework should be regularly done before going into an audit and updated during its execution. A good framework should be flexible, permitting revision of an auditing programme in response to:

- Changing conditions and/or findings of the client's business and
- The evolution of auditing principles and technology, which is continuous.

Based on this work, the auditor must develop and safeguard a complete illustrative set of working papers. These used to be kept on hard copy, as proof of audit findings and conclusions. Though hard copy is still necessary for legal reason, its contents should also be databased and mined through expert systems (Chorafas and Steinmann, 1991). Throughout his work the auditor will need to constantly refer to these databased elements in an effort to completely master partial findings, integrating them into the final report:

- Working papers include all data and other references collected during the course of the audit.
- Their content must be full, detailed, and explicit, as working papers are a valuable type of documentation.

On the bottom line, a thorough and analytical internal check is an indispensable part of any operation. This is true where the work of one employee is verified by another employee or by an outside independent agency. The operational people and the examiners should be working independently of one another, and reporting to a different line of command. The auditor should always determine whether or not the company's internal controls are in force, and are effective. As we will see in Chapter 2, internal control is integral part of any well managed business.

AUDITING AS AN INDISPENSABLE ELEMENT OF A MANAGEMENT SYSTEM

The fact that auditors are responsible for assessing the soundness and adequacy of an entity's accounting, operating, and administrative functions as well as its day-to-day controls, makes them a crucial element of a management system. Audit reports must be presented to all members of the board, the CEO and senior executives, identifying defects which must be remedied systematically and promptly. Follow-up audits should describe:

- Weaknesses which are not yet remedied and
- Recommendations not yet implemented.

In the United States, the Federal Reserve instructs its examiners that they should review documents taking into account the reporting process followed by the auditor, in order to subsequently evaluate the nature and efficiency of tasks the internal auditing has performed. The central bank's examiners also look into whether or not internal auditors have been given the authority necessary to perform a dependable job, including free access to any records needed for the proper conduct of their investigation.

As Figure 1.3 suggests, auditing is a metalayer (higher level) of day-to-day functions. Some organizations look at internal control as part of daily ongoing activities (see also Chapter 8), while they assign to auditing the independent examination function which must show if financial reporting is reliable or the assets are oversold.

Many interesting things can come out of a carefully crafted audit. In December 1999, for example, the first independent audit ever of Bank Indonesia (the central bank of the country) revealed that $7 billion in funds earmarked for emergency loans had disappeared. Auditors suspect some of the money was rerouted to an affiliate bank in Amsterdam (*Business Week*, 31 January 2000). Others think some busybodies in high places of the old regime took the money and ran.

Because auditing procedures are an indispensable part of the evaluation of internal controls, it is important for the auditor to conduct activities in a way permitting the interpretation of *management intent*. This deeper aspect of an examination will assist in evaluating the effectiveness of:

- The way in which top management directives are being issued (and followed)
- Compliance with designated laws and regulations
- Financial reporting procedures and practices and
- Internal control policies and supporting structure.

A rigorous approach to fulfilling the requirements described by these four bullet points can permit us to investigate whether people, departments or branches are doing their job or are attempting to erect a bureaucratic smoke screen. The aim might be to hide management's intentions, or obscure errors existing in the books at a given point in time.

Intelligence provided through an audit is nothing more than the information that has been systematically and professionally collected, analyzed, distilled, and reported. Typically, this needs to be done in a way enabling the persons receiving it to take appropriate action. In any professional intelligence operation it is important:

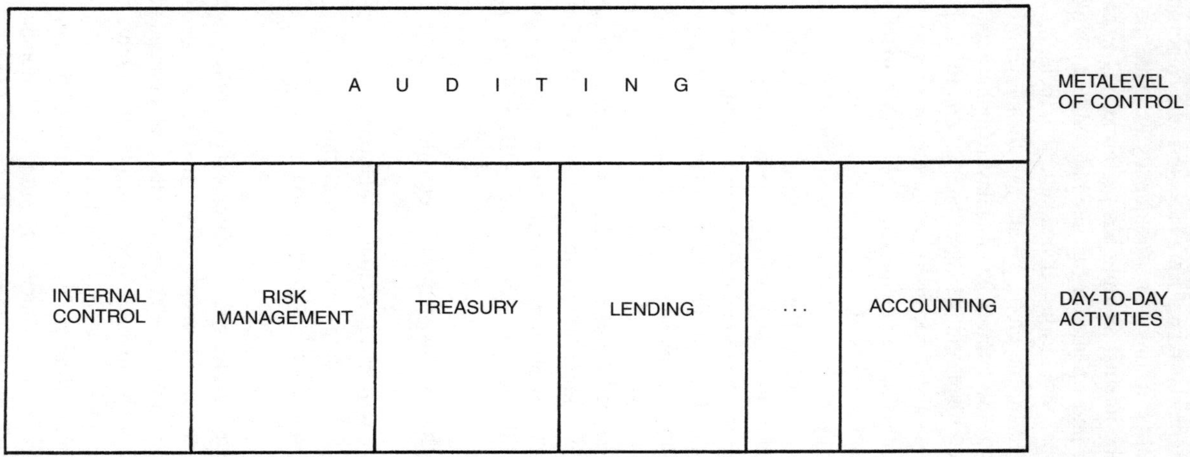

A U D I T I N G

METALEVEL OF CONTROL

INTERNAL CONTROL

RISK MANAGEMENT

TREASURY

LENDING

. . .

ACCOUNTING

DAY-TO-DAY ACTIVITIES

Figure 1.3 It is wise to make a distinction between the functions of auditing and those of internal control

- To look for *collateral*, that is reports from other sources able to validate the information in the books and
- To have a collection system with a rapid retrieval and dissemination – i.e. with *fast-response capability*.

To perform their functions in an able manner, auditors must objectively determine the accuracy of assertions on compliance with laws and regulations of policies, procedures, accounting rules, and other practices. They must ensure that the entity has an Audit Committee composed solely of outside directors and that this committee has access to outside legal counsel.

The way British, Swiss, German, and American regulators look at the internal and external auditors' responsibility in connection with an institution's internal controls is that their steady assessment is intended to ensure that these controls promptly and accurately safeguard assets against loss, and can provide intelligence based on recorded transactions. Evidential matter includes the presence of adequate safeguards and audit trails available at all times. Additional responsibilities of auditors in regard to internal controls are:

- Evaluating the effectiveness of administrative controls and procedures and
- Examining whether the efficiency of operations meets the board's standards.

To reach conclusions in a factual and documented manner internal auditors must perform tests as part of their work programme. This is helped by detailed standards promulgated by professional associations – in America, the Institute of Internal Auditors (IIA) and the Bank Administration Institute (BAI), for instance.

Both the IIA and the BAI underline that the ability of an internal auditing function to achieve its objectives depends, in large part, on the independence maintained by audit personnel. Frequently, internal auditing's independence can be determined by its reporting lines within the organization and the person or level to whom auditing results are reported. A top-level relationship enables the internal audit function to assist the directors in fulfilling their responsibilities.

Since auditing is an indispensable element of a properly functioning management system, the auditors' responsibilities should be explained in a position description, with reporting lines delineated in terms both of organization and structure, and in personnel policy. Sound procedures would require that audit results be documented in the Audit Committee and board of directors' minutes.

Auditors cannot afford to be subject to what psychologists call *cognitive dissonance*, a phenomenon whereby people ignore something that does not fit their view of the world, and pretend that it does not exist or is of a totally different magnitude. The search for cognitive dissonance is for an practical purposes connected with internal control activities, and therefore a broadening of the auditor's mission.

This extension of auditing perspectives into operational functions (see the discussion on operational risk in Chapter 2) means that internal the discussion on operational risk) and external auditors must go beyond reviewing the reliability and integrity of financial and operating information connected with uncovering fraud and into the means used to identify, measure, classify, and report. Specifically auditors must examine whether:

- Financial and operating records and reports indeed contain accurate, timely, complete, and useful information and
- Record-keeping and data processing reporting are really adequate and effective in a material sense.

Some regulators, as well as the best managed companies, include in the auditors' mission the safeguarding of assets. They want to see that internal auditors review ways and means for safeguarding assets from a pragmatic viewpoint, and, as appropriate, verify that such assets exist and are correctly reported; evaluate various types of losses such as those resulting from theft, fire, improper or illegal activities; and examine whether the use of resources is economical and efficient. This is part of what I mentioned in the Preface as accurate information passed in timely fashion to decision-makers to enable them to take corrective action.

SENIOR MANAGEMENT RESPONSIBILITIES IN CONNECTION WITH AUDITING AND INTERNAL CONTROLS

Internal audit is in essence a process of self-assessment. Members of the board, the CEO, and senior managers have responsibility for establishing not only an appropriate system of internal control but also the means for auditing it and for reporting on its effectiveness. Many executives taking part in the research which led to this book made the point that in a modern company:

- The level of assurance provided by testing traditional financial compliance is significantly less than should be expected
- An orderly control of all aspects of operations is most vital, and auditing should have direct access to all operational channels.

The concept is shown in Figure 1.4, and this is only an example. Lack of transparency to internal auditors and external auditors is a dangerous nonsense, which invariably has serious consequences. Somebody has to ask awkward questions, and that is the mission of the auditors – who have to think about those who intent to commit fraud and have to put themselves in their adversaries' mind.

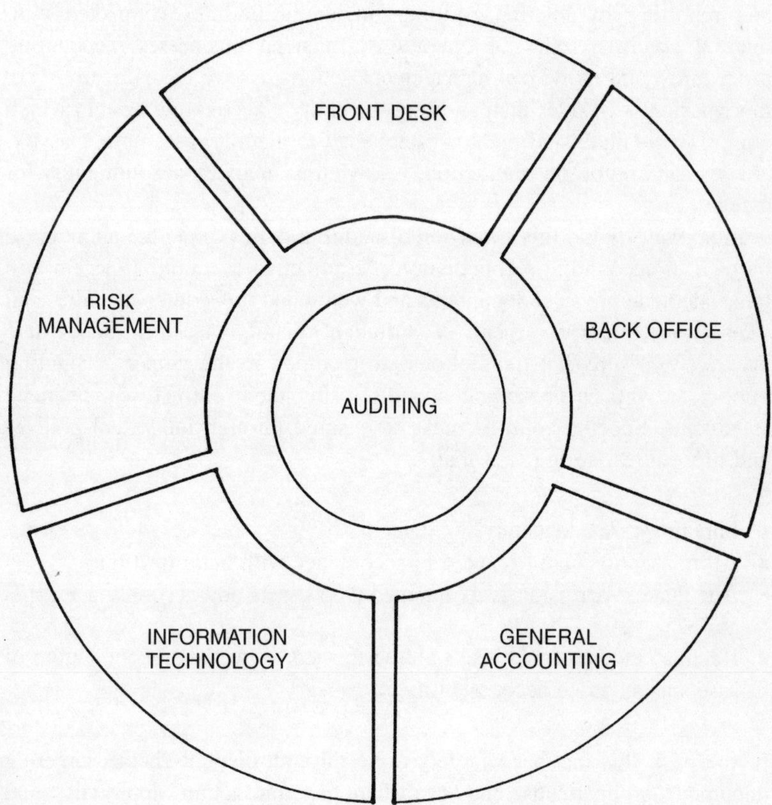

Figure 1.4 Front desk and back office should be separated, and the same is true of other functions, but all must be transparent to auditing

A steady and focused assessment and self-assessment requires a framework for reviewing and evaluating business areas, analyzing the design and execution of operations, evaluating necessary control means and methods, and achieving evaluation of ongoing activities in a way characterized by the quality of results. The more recent trend is towards:

- Empowering auditing with a growing range of control responsibilities
- Continuously improving quality goals and expected quality results,
- Providing the audit functions with focus, so that it becomes top management's primary feedback element.

The internal company environment impacts upon the process of analysis and reporting by internal auditing, including findings connected with internal controls, types of operations, financial businesses, accounting procedures, and individual management actions. As we have already seen, this mission is broader than auditing the entity's accounting system which comprises methods and records established to identify, assemble, classify, analyze, and report on transactions – as well as maintain accountability for assets.

In no way should this extension of auditing duties dilute the attention to be paid to accounting reconciliation. An effective accounting system will have adequate physical documents and well tuned procedures to address all transactions, describe them in sufficient detail, measure their value accurately, assure that transactions are recorded in the proper accounting period, as well as presenting and disclosing them correctly in financial statements. Specific controls must be ensured through individual policies and procedures, seeing to it that:

- Functions are adequately segregated
- All transactions are executed in accordance with authorizations
- Adequate supervision is maintained over assets and accounting records and
- Regular, independent checks are performed, as well as reconciliation of assets to recorded accountability.

In the past, this has been largely done through clerical checks targeting document comparisons and cancellations, transaction approvals, and review of data used to prepare financial reports as well as management reports. But the volume of transactions and the worth embedded in them mean that predominantly manual auditing methods are no longer efficient.

Technology can provide significant assistance; high technology is a direct responsibility of top management. Since the mid-1980s, tier-1 organizations have successfully implemented expert systems and agents (interactive knowledge artefacts, Chorafas, 1998a) for auditing purposes, including screening tests, compliance checks, and reconciliation of accounts. Interestingly enough, in many cases these applications were selected and promoted by the auditors rather than the data processors, because the users saw more clearly the advantages offered to their work by advanced technology solutions.

All auditing programmes should employ a significant amount of knowledge engineering. To appreciate the role of knowledge-based tools and methods one should understand that a company's control environment is the corporate atmosphere in which financial statements are prepared. A strong control environment reflects management's consciousness of and commitment to an effective system of internal control which is audited according to a plan of normal, tightened and reduced inspection according to the results obtained.

Technology should be used to amplify the value of what auditors produce for management, as well as help to investigate many areas in the organization which are still not being fully addressed. Globalization, greater competition, deregulation, cost containment, proliferation of instruments, the control of exposure, and the heavy burden being imposed on work units by all types of missions require:

- A new, thoroughly analytical but also fully integrated auditing strategy and
- A methodology able to minimize overlaps, duplications, and gaps.

Software can be both friend and foe to the auditors. Computer software is very important to the support of business operations, but also it can be relatively easily manipulated by personnel. An audit programme should therefore ensure the availability of independently prepared computer programs that not only employ the computer as an audit tool but also audit the business software which is being used (see also Chapter 13).

A modern company cannot afford a weak control environment, which is practically synonymous with one which is not regularly audited, because this undermines the effectiveness of internal controls. It also creates a predisposition toward misrepresentations in financial statements, an inordinate amount of assumed exposure, and other types of fraud. Each one of these variables can be effectively tracked through statistical quality control (SQC) charts which help in visualizing if tolerances are being observed and if the process is in control (Chorafas, 2000a). A weak control environment where tolerances are disregarded suggests flaws in the entity's philosophy and operating style, including:

- Fault lines in organization and structure
- Failures in enforcing of responsibility and
- Deficient personnel management methods.

A company's organizational philosophy and operating style encompass a broad range of characteristics, starting with board of directors' attitudes and actions toward financial reporting, ethics, and business risks; the CEO's and senior management's emphasis on meeting the budget, profit targets, risk limits, and other financial or operating goals; and the extent to which one or a few individuals dominate the control environment.

These are core areas and each one of them must be subject to internal control procedures. By its very existence in a company's mainstream activities, this polyvalence of missions leads to the bifurcation of auditing functions, which is shown in Figure 1.5. Reporting lines leading to the board and auditing committee emphasize the strategic aspects of self-assessment as a whole. By contrast, the feedback to middle management is tactical, characterized by:

- Analyzing and interpreting the pattern of specific operations, particularly those which are not in control
- Assessing necessary corrective measures and their timing
- Defining the nature of immediate action at a tactical level of reference.

Activity reports should be submitted to the board, the CEO and senior management, both at regular intervals and ad hoc. These reports should flush out weak points, compare performance of an audited department's goals to accomplished work, explain the reason for major variances from the auditor's viewpoint and indicate any action taken or needed. Such reports should also suggest necessary improvements documented through the assessment of source material and hands-on inspections.

VALUE-ADDED SERVICES TO BE PROVIDED BY AUDITING

Nowadays, the regulators require internal and external auditors to be particularly attentive in analyzing a company's internal controls and its organizational structure, because this can give an overall opinion about

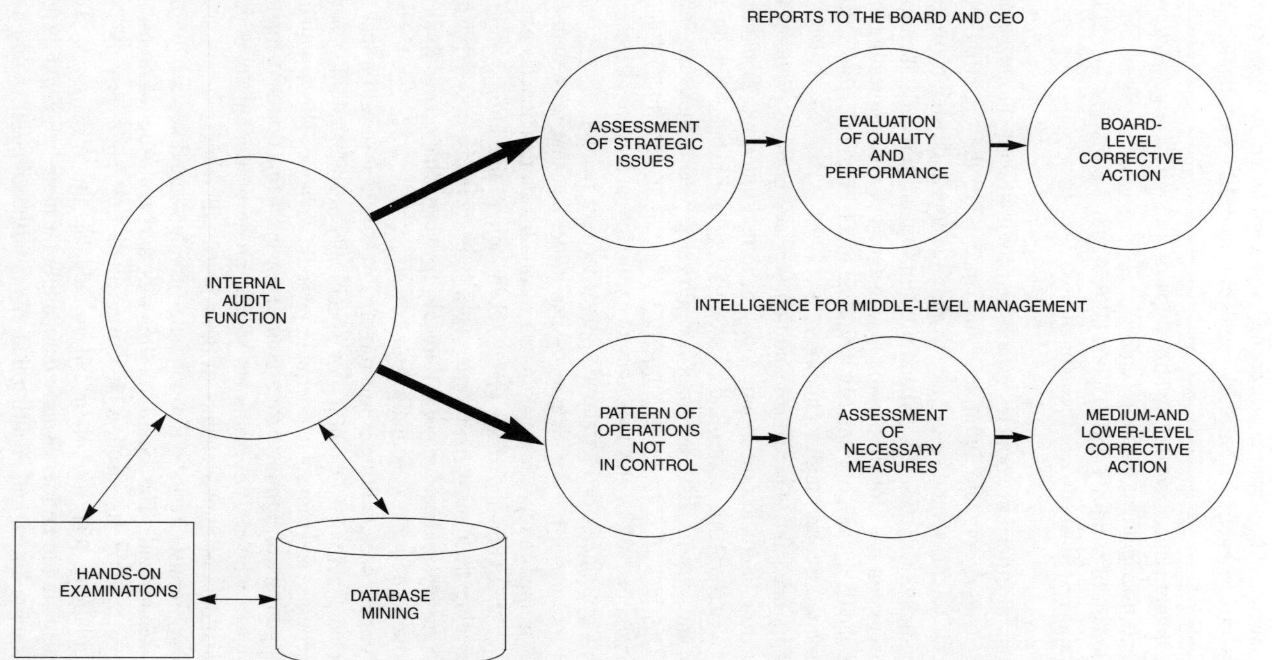

Figure 1.5 The bifurcation in self-assessment through internal control and auditing

how management is planning, directing, and controlling its operations. Attention paid to internal control by regulators considers such matters as:

- Form, nature, and, reporting relationships of an entity's organizational units and management positions and
- Assignment of authority and responsibility to these positions, including constraints established over their functioning.

For reasons of efficiency, policies established by the board should clarify the understanding of, and improve compliance with, the organization's objectives. Systems should be in place to alert auditors to deviations so that these are immediately investigated and brought to management's attention. As the discussion has already pointed out, methods of communicating and enforcing the delegation of authority would be much more effective if they were supported through high technology.

While the need for value-added auditing services is more pronounced than ever, few internal audit groups today have real-time tools to monitor the effectiveness of the controls they exercise, or use agents to audit all accounts and ensure that resources are allocated where they are most needed. This lack of appropriate support was a reason why internal audit was criticized in 1987 by the Treadway Commission, and again in 1999 by the Basle Committee, for ineffective approaches (see below).

Part of the reason for this deficiency lies in the fact that most auditors have been trained in reporting accounting reconciliation deficiencies not in *analyzing the significant* risks being taken across the entity, and in prognosticating their most likely aftermath. It is therefore not surprising that some surveys indicate major differences between what boards think is being audited and what is actually being done.

In my experience, auditing is much more effective if it sees to it that all service-related activities, even if not specifically manifested in general ledger accounts, are subject to adequate periodic reviews. This is equally true of appraisals of administrative control for each function and for the company as a whole. The examiners should produce auditing comments and suggestions for improvements of operational efficiency.

On these premises rest the development of value-added services by the auditing department. The board of directors and the Audit Committee should be the first to disallow reactive, tired, dull audit reports and recommendations that too often fail to address the real issues. Top management should be increasingly demanding far more value and insight from internal auditors, and ensuring that this is forthcoming. It should also emphasize the need for value-added services:

- Traditional-type internal audit involves after-the-fact inspection, but offers little by way of inciting continuous improvement
- Continuous improvement can be assisted through a new auditing culture supported through an entity-wide monitoring and control system.

This system should benefit from input from all work units and target quality assurance, with activities under control monitored throughout the company and interactively reported. All documentation must be databased for further analysis when necessary, and knowledge artefacts used to derive intelligence from this information.

A battery of critical queries can help in guiding the chief auditors' hand. Does the frequency and scope of management control action comply with statutory requirements of internal audits? How sophisticated are *our* auditing standards? Is each auditor preparing a time budget? Are plan versus actual time analyzes used as a guide in forward planning? Does the depth of coverage appear to be sufficient? Is each auditor periodically reporting his or her progress in completing the frequency and scope schedule? Does the board's auditing committee approve significant deviations, if any, from the original programme?

In order to improve overall efficiency, and add value to auditing work, the audit methodology should itself come under scrutiny. Are different entry dates and time periods between reviews scheduled so as to frustrate anticipation of entry dates by auditees? Are controls on opening and closing general ledger and other accounts adequate? Is auditing formally advised of any changes? Is the company's possession of *all* assets owned or managed in fiduciary capacities subjected to verification?

Other queries, too, are important. Given that the auditing function itself is – or at least should be – subject to administrative controls, does the audit manual contain the scope and objective of each audit function? Does it provide for certain deviations from audit procedures, done for the sake of adaptability to changing conditions? Are these procedures approved by the Audit Committee? Do audit procedures provide for the follow-up of exceptions noted in previous audits?

The use of statistical and other tools should also be investigated. Do audit procedures employ statistical sampling techniques with acceptable reliability and precision? Is there available a method for resolution of exceptions and deficiencies? Are statistical quality control charts available to show trends in demerits and help ascertain whether the audited processes are in control? Are there provisions for an expression of the opinion of the auditor regarding the adequacy and efficiency of internal controls?

Some of the queries pertaining to the efficiency of the auditing function necessarily relate to the personality of the chief auditor, their status in the organization and the definition of their duties. The director of internal auditing should be given by the board a statement of purpose which clearly defines the authority and responsibility for the job to be done. The planning process which he or she establishes must include:

- Goals
- Work schedules
- Staffing and financing plans
- The use of technology
- A steady improvements schedule and
- Activity reports.

In my postgraduate studies at the University of California, I had a professor who taught his students that the goals of the internal auditing department should not only be spelled out but should also be measurable. Therefore, they should be accompanied by measurement criteria, yardsticks, quality assurance standards, and targeted dates of accomplishment.

Whether or not value-added functions are included, work schedules must outline what activities are to be audited; when they will be audited; and what are the time and cost estimates. Auditing programmes should take into account the scope of the work planned as well as the nature and extent of previous audit work. Work schedules should be sufficiently flexible to cover unanticipated demands for a more rigorous internal auditing job.

Staffing plans and financial budgets must include specifications which help in computing the number of auditors, the technology to be put at their disposal, and the knowledge, skills, and disciplines required to perform assigned work. This leads to the definition of education and training requirements, as well as auditing research and development efforts and the sophistication of technological supports:

- Today, research and development is the necessary supplement to any business activity worth its salt, and auditing is no exception.
- Every function can be done better if we pay enough attention to improving it, as well as to shortening the timetables of deliverables by bettering the means used in its execution.

The discussion above mentioned the use of expert systems as an example. This is a mid-to-late 1980s' solution, which has itself been subject to steady improvement. For instance, instead of expert systems resident at a workstation we are now using *agents*, or interactive knowledge artefacts which are mobile and proactive – flushing out inconsistencies, violations of compliance, inordinate risks, and other weak points, and therefore alerting their master to take the required action. But while technology is a welcome supplement to the auditor's functions, the No. 1 criterion is organizational: to where exactly does the auditing department report?

THE ROLE OF AN INDEPENDENT AUDIT COMMITTEE AND THE CONTRIBUTION OF THE TREADWAY COMMISSION

The concept of an independent *Audit Committee* composed of outside directors and reporting directly to the board has been briefly introduced above. In the United States, the Audit Committee is general practice in all companies of a certain importance. In Europe, too, its role is growing in importance. Because among its most vital duties is overseeing of internal control and of the audit function, the Audit Committee must be characterized by a significant degree of independence.

For instance, in the United States regulators insist that the Audit Committee does not include individuals who are large customers of the company. For US credit institutions, this requirement is a rule established by the Federal Deposit Insurance Corporation (FDIC), one of the four main regulators. As I have already mentioned, the Audit Committee should be composed of outside directors.

The concept of an independent Audit Committee is not new, but it has been significantly strengthened by the seminal work done by the Treadway Commission. This Commission, which was active in the mid- to late 1980s is named after its chairman James C. Treadway, Jr, formerly a commissioner of the Securities and Exchange Commission (SEC). Officially in the United States this is known as the National Commission on Fraudulent Financial Reporting – and it is in fact a milestone in financial reporting and auditing practices:

- Individually, most of the Treadway Commission's recommendations filtered into the Statement of Financial Accounting Standards (SFAS) by the Financial Accounting Standards Board (FASB).
- As a pattern, the implementation of the Treadway Commission's recommendations was promoted by the Committee of Sponsoring Organizations (COSO) of the Treadway Commission (Chorafas, 2000a).

Today COSO is used as a term to identify the pattern of these recommendations and their application for reliable financial reporting. In 1998 the Federal Reserve Banks of New York, Boston, and Chicago were the first to implement COSO. This has been followed by the other Fed banks and, according to a 1998 decision by the Federal Reserve Board, by all credit institutions with $500 million or more in assets.

COSO has been instrumental in seeing to it that credit institutions are also now concerned about internal controls. Companies which have focused on value-added auditing services assert that traditional approaches to audit are no more able to deliver because they are not self-sufficient in assessing the growing range of issues which add up to organizational and operational deficiencies. These companies are also seeing to it that they have an Audit Committee at the level of their board of directors, and that the independence of this committee is ensured at all times.

True enough, there is no unique definition of the duties an Audit Committee should perform other than receiving and examining the confidential report of the internal auditors. However, from meetings with companies with an Audit Committee, I have compiled a list of other responsibilities. These include:

- Approving salary, hiring and firing related to senior staff of internal auditing
- Providing the opportunity for auditors to meet and discuss findings without internal directors and line management being present
- Recommending or approving appointment of external auditors and the scope of their services
- Reviewing with senior management and external auditors the year-end findings and
- Meeting with regulatory authorities to sort out problems, if any.

Within the scope of these references, the Audit Committee can play an important role in preventing, or at least in detecting, fraudulent financial reporting. The Treadway Commission highlighted important aspects of the Audit Committee's oversight function – stating, for example, that senior management and the Audit Committee should ensure the internal auditors' uninhibited involvement in examining the company's entire financial reporting process. This, the Treadway Commission said, should:

- Be done in an appropriate, rigorous and detailed way and
- Be co-ordinated with the work by independent, certified public accountants.

Some sources suggest that, in the absence of a universal definition of goals and mission, in the current state of affairs there are certain gaps in the Audit Committee's work. For instance, a Treadway Commission-sponsored study found that internal auditors often concentrate on the review of controls at the division, subsidiary, or other business component level, rather than at corporate level. Independent public accountants, on the other hand, are generally responsible for audit examination at corporate level.

The Treadway Commission has also highlighted other important Audit Committee functions, such as the need to review the company's process of assessing the risk of fraudulent financial reporting. It also pressed the point that the Audit Committee should evaluate the fitness of the programme established to monitor compliance with the code of corporate conduct. According to these guidelines the Audit Committee should:

- Oversee the quarterly or more frequent reporting process, with particular emphasis on financial statements and finding of misconduct and
- Keep at all times open lines of communication, not only with the chief internal auditor but also with the chief accounting officer.

The Treadway Commission developed this set of recommended Audit Committee duties and responsibilities from a review and consideration of practices many well managed companies follow, the extensive guidance the public accounting and legal professions have published on the subject, and necessary improvements suggested by the results of its own research. In the years which followed the publication of the recommendations, most of the suggested improvements have been incorporated into the definition of the mission of an Audit Committee. In order to provide for integration of auditing reports the auditing committee must ensure:

- A greater awareness of audit results by the chief financial officer, who usually has responsibility for the preparation of financial statements and
- A steadily improved co-ordination between internal auditors and independent public accountants, all the way from the supervision of fraudulent financial reporting to internal control.

The Audit Committee should appreciate that organizational status and independence of action are essential in insulating internal auditors from compromising with different organizational influences and political pressures. This role is further enhanced by helping to establish an ethical environment throughout the company's operations and management functions.

The Basle Committee on Banking Supervision, too, has looked into audit commission functions and responsibilities. In early 1998 it recommended that all credit institutions of a certain size should have an Audit Committee. The Bank for International Settlements (BIS) immediately put in to practice this recommendation, choosing a former governor of the Bank of England as chairman of its newly instituted Audit Committee.

GOOD PRACTICE GUIDELINES REGARDING AUDITING COMMITTEE FUNCTIONS AND RESPONSIBILITIES

An Audit Committee should normally consist of not fewer than three independent (external) directors. The maximum size may vary, but the committee should be small enough so that each member is an active participant. To my book, if three is the minimum membership five may well be the maximum. The term of appointment is at the discretion of the board of directors, but often ranges in the three–five years timeframe with or without renewal.

The question of an Audit Committee's size relates to another query: how many members should the board feature? There is no unique answer, but there exists good practice. Cisco Systems says:

> The number of authorized directors shall not be less than eight nor more than fifteen, with the exact number of directors to be fixed from time to time within such range by a duly adopted resolution of the board or shareholders in accordance with the company's bylaws.

Many companies look favourably at Audit Committee duties. At Marsh & McLennan, CFO Frank J. Borelli says:

> The Audit Committee of the corporate board of directors must take a strong leadership role. We rated the different units and those that were not up to par, [they] were summoned to an Audit Committee meeting and [were] asked for a report and then follow-up reports. That gets attention.
>
> (*Business Week*, 13 July 1998)

Most of the companies I met in this research emphasized the positive influence, both current and potential, of an effective Audit Committee. In terms of implementation statistics I was told that while 85 per cent of all publicly quoted companies in the United States have Audit Committees. It is interesting to notice that companies with Audit Committees represent a significantly smaller percentage of public entities involved in fraudulent financial reporting cases than those which have no Audit Committee.

The statistics to which I make reference are based on the number of fraudulent cases brought to justice by the SEC. Indeed, the SEC has long recognized the importance of independent Audit Committees to the integrity of financial reporting, and this shows up in the policies followed by exchanges under its authority:

- The New York Stock Exchange (NYSE) requires that all its listed companies have Audit Committees composed *solely* of independent directors.
- The National Association of Securities Dealers (NASD) also requires that all national market system companies establish and maintain Audit Committees that have a majority of independent directors.

Companies participating to my research pressed the point that considerable attention should be paid to accounting tools and methodology for accounting controls, including records established to identify, record, assemble, classify, analyze, and report the entity's transactions and portfolio positions. A similar statement is valid about maintaining accountability for the company's assets. The Audit Committee must ensure that an effective system solution is in place and that the procedures are adequate. Through internal and external auditors, the Audit Committee should make sure that:

- Front desk, back office and other functions are properly segregated
- All transactions are executed in accordance with management's general or specific authorization
- Proper physical and logical control is maintained over assets and
- Any discrepancy in reconciliation of assets leads to direct assignment of accountability.

It would, however, be difficult to make the point that there is a global pattern on how auditing committees should be composed to fulfil these tasks in the most effective way. Even if there is more or less a convergence of opinions on the definition of 'core duties', differences do exist because of cultural, structural, and other reasons. Even central banks do not follow the recommendation by the Basle Committee that an independent Audit Committee is a 'must':

- Some of the 11 central banks of euroland have an auditing committee. Others don't, though they have an auditing department. That's not at all the same thing.

- The European Central Bank (ECB) itself has an *Auditors Committee* formed by the heads of the 11 central banks – who are in a way internal directors of the system of European Central Banks (ESCB).

In my book this sort of solution is not satisfactory, and for a variety of reasons. First of all, independence of opinion; the relation of the ECB to the 11 central banks sees to it that the governors of central banks of member states can by no stretch of the imagination be taken as 'independent'. Then the question of numbers; 11 members, a number to be increased as euroland expands, is too big for an Audit Committee. This looks rather like a small parliament.

Also, the kind of 'old chaps' club' has structural defects. The deliberations of every Audit Committee must be characterized by independence of opinion and a questioning attitude: Is this true? Is it credible? Is there something missing? It is different to see this type of questioning coming from the heads of 11 central banks who arc also governors of Euroland's reserve banks.

Line duties should disqualify the governors of the 11 central banks from membership in ECB's Audit Committee. The structural defects go even deeper. Contrary to what is currently done, it is the ECB which *should audit* Euroland's central banks through a body of its own examiners – its auditing department, if you wish. This is precisely what the Federal Reserve Board is doing for the 12 Federal Reserve Banks, as we will see in Chapter 13.

Let me summarise in a few paragraphs the principles on which the institution of an Audit Committee rests. In every entity there should be a rule mandating an *independent* Audit Committee because, as the discussion has already documented, the Audit Committee's role is important to the financial reporting process all the way to the assessment of independence of CPAs. In turn, the independence of CPAs is most critical to the review of the adequacy of, and compliance with, internal controls. These issues contribute significantly to the establishment of a reliable business environment.

Companies should consider good practice guidelines in exercising their judgement. To entities that already have auditing committees, the guidelines reviewed in this text can serve as a standard for self-assessment. Companies just establishing auditing committees, or those seeking to improve their committees' effectiveness, may find the discussion to be helpful in suggesting practical ways for auditing committees as well as means to strengthen their own responsibilities. What has been explained in connection to the practice of auditing highlights the need for the auditing committee:

- To be fully informed and vigilant
- To have thoroughly described duties and responsibilities and
- To be able to review management's business behaviour based on independent opinions.

Every well managed company has in place a system to monitor compliance with a high code of conduct. Senior management should advise the auditing committee when it seeks a second opinion on a significant issue, whether this is connected with accounting and finance or any other domain which has to do with internal control. And all reports commissioned by the board, the CEO, and top executives having to do with management control should reach the Audit Committee.

This chapter has described in general terms the auditing committee's responsibilities as seen by cognisant people and entities with experience in this function. A more detailed delineation and description of responsibilities is best left to the discretion of an individual company's top management and its board of directors. It is always advisable to consider individual conditions, in order to tailor a solution to the needs and circumstances of each organization.

2 What is Meant by 'Internal Control'?

INTRODUCTION

Knowledge is not synonymous with reliable financial reporting and to the proper management of exposure, but it is a basic ingredient of both. Without knowledge we will not be able to reconcile accounts, comply with regulations, or find a solution in controlling the risks we are taking – unless we stumble on it. Without timely and accurate information, the board, the CEO, and senior management will not be in a position to steer the company towards the right course.

Information and knowledge have to be upkept all the time, because they decay very fast. Therefore in well managed companies the board, the CEO, and senior executives are keen to upkeep their skills and know-how, ensure the channels of communication are open, and provide themselves with a dynamic, proactive system which allows them to know everything that needs to be known on the way the company functions. This is the role of *internal control.*

The reader will find in the appendix to this chapter the definitions by the American Institute of Certified Public Accountants (AICPA), which is the oldest on record; the Basle Committee on Banking Supervision; the European Monetary Institute (EMI), now the European Central Bank (ECB); the Institute of Internal Auditors (IIA); and COSO:

- The proper functioning of the company's internal control is part of the accountability of the board and of top management.
- In principle, the internal control system is affected by, and affects, all levels of personnel, because it brings transparency.

Internal control intelligence enables senior executives to track exposure from credit risk, market risk, operational risk, settlement risk, legal risk, and other risks relating to transactions, to assets, and to liabilities – as well as to fraud and security issues. The goals characterizing the internal control of a credit institution and of a manufacturing or merchandising company do not differ markedly from one another. The aim is to:

- Safeguard business assets
- Assist in compliance and accounting reconciliation

- Promote personal accountability and
- Lead to timely corrective action.

The establishment of an appropriate internal control system is a demanding business. A sound application and proper functioning of internal controls require both external supports such as laws, regulations, and rigorous supervision; and internal developments such as corporate policies, clear objectives, organization and structure, reliable information, and advanced technology.

A comprehensive pattern is presented in Figure 2.1 which presents a snapshot of focal areas entering into the internal control orbit. These should attract senior management's attention. Internal control is for a company what Socrates used to call his *demon* – the inner voice that whispers: 'Take care.' A key ingredient to successful implementation of Socrates' demons is a relentless self-discipline.

To enhance their internal control system, companies should use a wide range of tools and techniques, supported by real-time computers, sophisticated software, online mining of transactional and other databases, quality control charts, simulation models, and interactive visualization of financial and other reports. Furthermore, because all systems can malfunction and they degrade with time, internal control must be regularly audited (see Chapter 1) by competent persons who have no incompatible or conflicting duties.

All employees must be subject to internal control, even if they have no financial responsibilities. The internal control system should be primarily concerned with those positions that have the ability to influence the records and that have access to assets. Everybody should contribute to internal control. The question is not whether each individual is honest, but rather whether situations exist that:

- Might permit an intentional error or other bias to be concealed or
- Make it possible for unintentional errors to remain undetected, hence unknown to top management.

As a rule, sound internal control exists when no one is in a position to make significant deviations from rules and regulations, or perpetrate irregularities, without timely detection. For this reason, a system of internal controls should include procedures necessary to ensure transparency in accounts and other business functions, as well as rapid monitoring of failures – whether these concern books and accounts or other matters.

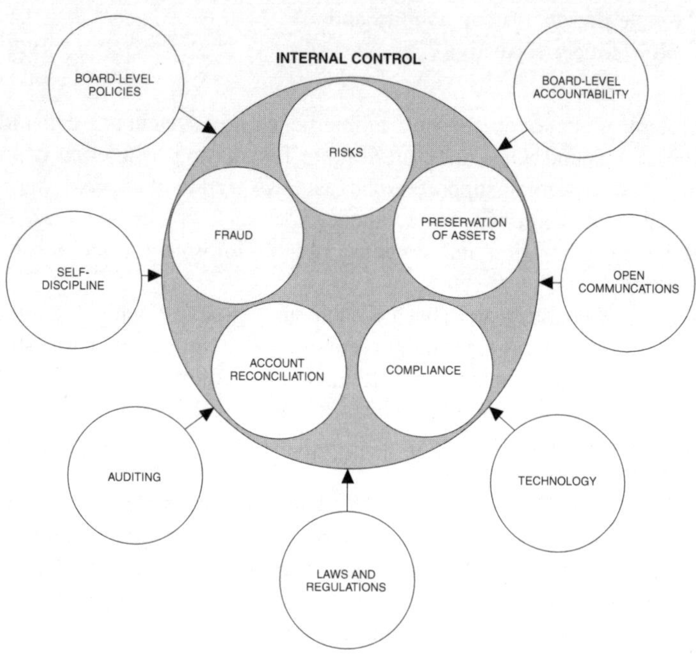

Figure 2.1 Focal areas of internal control and the impact of internal and external key factors

'INTERNAL CONTROL' DEFINED

The goal behind increased emphasis on internal controls is to limit the losses from operational failures by recognizing that reliable financial reporting, the safeguarding of capital, and effective risk management are most important issues in synergy with one another, and must be served through focused management attention. To make internal control approaches more effective, it is necessary to identify and correct weak practices with some form of sanction to people and departments supporting them – while rewarding correct practices through a system of merits. This is a top management duty. Here in five bullet points is my definition of internal control (IC) and its responsibilities:

- IC is a dynamic system covering all types of risk, addressing fraud, assuring transparency, and making possible reliable financial reporting.

- The chairman of the board, the directors, the chief executive officer, and senior management are responsible and accountable for IC.
- Beyond risks, internal control goals are the preservation of assets, account reconciliation, and compliance. Laws and regulations impact on IC.
- The able management of IC requires policies, organization, technology, open communications channels, access to all transactions, real-time operation, quality control, and corrective action.
- IC must be regularly audited by internal and external auditors to ensure its rank and condition, and see to it there is no cognitive dissonance at any level.

'This is consistent with the COSO model of efficiency and effectiveness', said David L. Robinson of the Federal Reserve Board in Washington, DC. 'The definition of internal control should not be limited to banks', observed Robert A. Sollazzo of the Securities and Exchange Commission (SEC) in New York. 'Since this definition underlines that internal control is a process effected by the board and senior management to ensure adequacy and accuracy, we agree with it. It is COSO-based', suggested Bill Morris and Gene Green, of the Office of the Comptroller of the Currency (OCC).

Hans-Dietrich Peters and Hans Werner Voth, of the Deutsche Bundesbank, stated that the first level responsible for internal control is the board. They added that all levels of management must be acutely aware of the need for internal control – and must be accountable for exercising it in an effective manner.

Practically all senior executives who participated in this research were of the opinion that internal control responsibilities start at the board level and they affect the way people operate in every department of the institution. Well tuned internal control helps to ensure that information senior management receives is accurate. Expert opinions have converged on two facts:

- Internal controls are valid only as far as the people working for the organization observe them and
- Controls should be designed not only to prevent failures like Barings and Orange County, but also to underline the accountability of every person.

'It is the responsibility of senior management to define the internal control structure', said Claude Sivy, of the Bank for International Settlements (BIS). 'If internal control is going to work, management must be committed to it', added Edward A. Ryan, Jr of the SEC in Boston. John B. Caouette, of MBIA Insurance Corporation, concurred: 'Internal controls are only successful if embedded in a strict risk management culture.'

One of the consistent themes of good management is the ability to know what is happening in all corners of the organization. 'Internal control is a concept which reaches all levels of management and the activities pertinent to those levels', said Jonathan E.C. Grant, of the Auditing Practices Board in London. 'To do the proper service to internal control we should not confuse:

- Monitoring, and
- The basic concept.'

Jonathan Grant also underlined the danger that line management might leave internal control duties to somebody else down the line of command. Therefore, he suggested that the definition must specifically emphasize management's accountability – as internal control is everybody's business and every employee, from top to bottom, should care for it and for its deliverables.

Speaking of deliverables, the report on risk management and control guidance for securities firms by the Technical Committee of the International Organization for Securities Commissions (IOSCO) (1998) has helped in establishing a rigorous approach to capturing non-measurable risks by primarily relying on qualitative assessments. This, IOSCO says, is a key ingredient of internal control. The report sets out a dozen elements of a risk management and control system, intended as benchmarks which can be used by supervisors to measure the adequacy of a company's internal control system.

Other entities emphasize the role played by organization. The search for an effective organizational solution has in the background the need to make internal control concrete and enforceable. In a study which treated issues involving fraud, the SEC made *specific* references to lack of internal control – knowing quite well that, all by itself, an abstract statement regarding the presence or absence of internal control will not be enforceable. It has to be substantiated by measurements.

The evaluation of internal control should also include consideration of other existing accounting and administrative measures and take into consideration circumstances that might counteract or mitigate apparent weaknesses; or might impair an established control procedure. An example is a formal part of the company's operational system, such as budget procedures, that includes a careful comparison of budgeted and actual amount by competent management personnel.

An essential factor of an internal control examination is being alert to indications about adverse circumstances which might lead company officers or employees into courses of action they normally would not pursue. An adverse circumstance to which internal auditors' control should be especially sensitive exists when the personal financial interests of managers or employees depend directly on:

- Operational results
- Sales quotas or
- Other financial incentives.

As Figure 2.2 suggests, there is a common core between the functions of internal control and other major organizational activities. Many financial industry executives who participated in this research underlined the need for powerful tools to make internal control proactive. 'Most current tools are post-event', said Clifford Griep, of Standard & Poor's in New York,

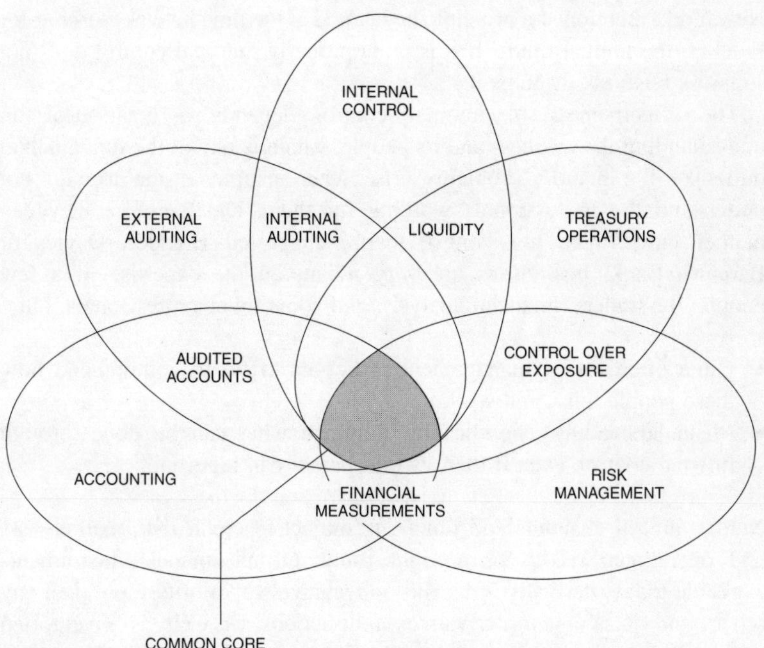

Figure 2.2 The functions of internal control, auditing, accounting, treasury, and risk management overlap, but also have a common core

'but internal control must be proactive. It must deal with pre-transaction approval'.

In the opinion of David L. Robinson, internal control must in principle be content-neutral, but a system designed to serve this purpose should be commensurate with the complexity of the business which it supports. This is true of banking and finance as it is of any other industry. A content-neutral approach is a sound principle to follow in regard to organization and structure – particularly when it is enriched with measurable objectives, which is COSO's goal.

WHAT CONSTITUTES A SOUND INTERNAL CONTROL POLICY?

A good system of internal control is synonymous with taking the longer view on how the business should be planned, conducted, and controlled. This has been the majority opinion of the cognizant executives who contributed to this study. Is a tough internal control policy working against growth in the business? Lev Borodovski, of Crédit Suisse First Boston in New York, mentioned a principle he learned at the time he was working for Fidelity, the mutual fund: 'If it is done properly, internal control does not suppress business. It helps it.'

The effectiveness of internal control depends a great deal on understanding the business and its people, which is one of the fundamental duties of the board. 'Problems arise when people at the top do not understand the professionals working for them, and therefore they can neither guide them nor control them', suggested Brandon Davies of Barclays Bank. Institutions are very reliant on the expertise of a few people: the traders, financial analysts, and some other professionals, but:

- Quite often senior management makes no effort to comprehend how these people think and work.
- Misunderstandings significantly diminish what can be done through internal control, even if there is transparency in reporting.

Neither are all channels and functions subject to credit risk, market risk, and operational risk – or outright fraud. Of all financial instruments available today, derivatives depend on technical superiority more than any other; and it is again derivatives transactions as well as inventoried positions that may lead to an inordinate amount of exposure. Therefore, other things being equal, derivative financial instruments should attract greater internal control attention.

In an organizational sense, a crucial question is who should have overall responsibility for the internal control function. Timothy Stier of the Office of Thrift Supervision (OTS) said that: 'If you have an accounting system like two-entry bookkeeping, you have to have internal control.' But in a broader definition of controlling exposure, Stier sees internal control under risk management: 'Compliance, too, makes sense under risk management, because there is regulatory risk.'

'We view internal control as the process that makes up for risk management, by providing the nuts and bolts', said Curtis Wong of the Federal Insurance Deposit Corporation (FDIC). For this reason, FDIC today places greater emphasis than ever on internal and on external reviews which it considers to be part of internal control functions. Audits of internal controls, Wong suggests, contribute to better risk management.

'The role of bank managers is not only to assure the proper functioning of their institution, but also see to it that auditors obtain a consistent and coherent image of status and results', stated Alain Coune of the International Monetary Fund (IMF), adding that: 'This is true of the quantification side of internal control and of audit. The qualification aspects, particularly those concerning internal controls, have not been till now tightly coupled to audit – though this might change.'

'As a general remark I will state that we don't see internal controls as a separate field. Instead we look at them as a very integrated part of all activities connected with any substantial risk of any kind', wrote Bernt Gyllenswärd of Skandinaviska Enskilda Banken. The opinion of another senior audit executive has been that: 'A well-studied internal control puts a saddle on a horse that never had one.'

Beata Stelmach of the Polish Securities Commission wrote that: '[Internal] control is overseen by the banks' management boards and executive committees as a part of their daily activities. It is controlled by the departments monitoring the activities of the entity.' As the careful reader will observe, a positive characteristic of these opinions is that they are not cloning one another. Among themselves they define a whole spectrum of internal control policies and activities – which is why they are so valuable.

For a long time in my professional practice I have come to appreciate that learned opinions which complement one another help in opening one's perspective. They also define among themselves a sound control environment in which some functions like accounting operate today, and where reliable financial statements can be prepared. A strong control environment reflects management's consciousness of and commitment to transparency in accounts and transactions – which is a different way of looking at a sound system of internal control:

- A strong control culture does not guarantee the absence of fraudulent financial reporting or inordinate risks, but reduces the chance that management will override internal controls.

The overriding of internal controls is a dangerous nonsense which can lead to disasters so shameful that people think they are best ignored. Wise men, however, know disasters should not be forgotten but serve as lessons for not to repeat the same mistakes again:

- A weak control culture undermines the effectiveness of a company's internal control system, if there is one. It may also reflect a predisposition toward misinterpretations in financial statements.

A company's organizational philosophy and operating style are evidently reflected into its internal control system. The fact has been brought to the reader's attention that this encompasses a broad range of characteristics like the board's and senior management's attitudes and actions toward financial reporting, ethics, business opportunities, and business risks. Under no condition should internal control be seen as a matter of applying easy labels to complex subjects. A system of internal controls is inherently complex but as the next section demonstrates, after the concept is in place solutions can be developed in an reliable manner step-by-step.

STEPS IN IMPLEMENTING AN INTERNAL CONTROL SYSTEM

There exist no hard and fast rules on how an internal control system should be designed and implemented. The answer to the question 'how to' go about its application and, in the case where one is already in place, 'how to' provide improvements, depends largely on the company, its culture, organization, product line, quality of personnel, extent of operations, and other management controls in existence. But there are some more general rules which should be brought to the reader's attention. The pattern in Figure 2.3 presents the infrastructure and the pillars on which a valid solution rests. The pillars are:

- Internal control procedures
- Effectiveness and performance

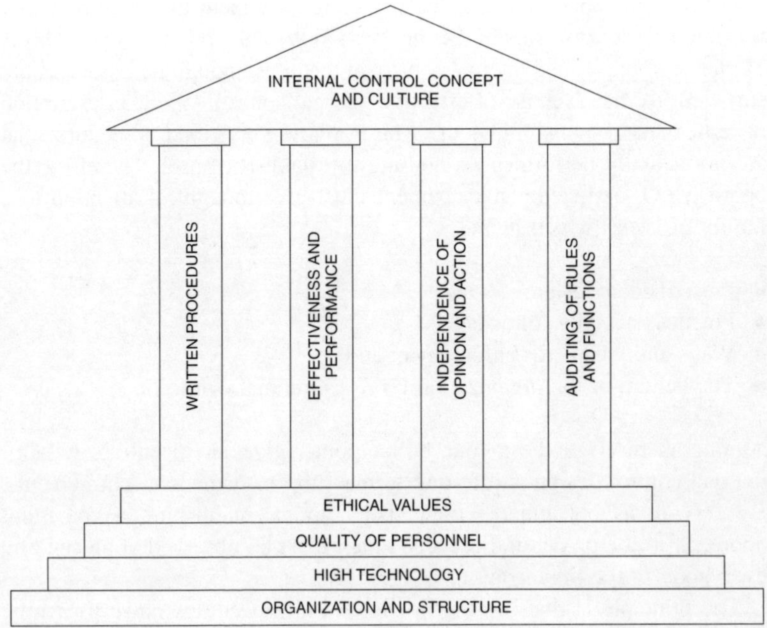

Figure 2.3 Infrastructure and pillars supporting a valid solution to internal control

- Independence of opinion and action
- Auditing of internal control rules and functions.

Part II and Part III elaborate in greater detail on these issues by focusing on a company's core functions and the type of internal control that serves them best. Chapter 9 explains how to establish an efficient internal control structure; Chapters 10 and 11 concentrate on the implementation of internal control in a credit institution, taking the limits system as an example. Chapter 12 examines how to apply internal control concepts in manufacturing – particularly in engineering design, product development, and quality assurance.

A case can, however, be made that fundamental concepts concerning the methodology and the most basic procedures should be explained at this point in time because in this way they become a framework on which all subsequent discussion is based. This would allow us to tackle the harder job of *internal control intelligence* before getting involved into specific implementation cases and the best practices these might involve.

Let me immediately add to the preceding statement that accountability for internal control should be in every job description – even if the existence of prescribed internal control procedures, though necessary, is not sufficient for the exercise of effective internal control. While a description of duties and responsibilities must be in place, prescribed procedures that are not actually performed do nothing to establish control. Therefore, the board, CEO, and senior management must give thoughtful attention to a family of issues which includes:

- Prescribed set of procedures
- Practices actually followed
- Ways and means for enforcement and
- The culture of the organization *vis-à-vis* internal control.

Among themselves these four bullet points give an incentive to tailor internal control design and testing to meet top management requirements. By serving as benchmarks they also help in establishing a consistent approach to the procedural aspects which must be observed at all time by everybody in the organization.

The principle is that rules, guidelines, and procedures must always be tested. Evaluation of competence in carrying them out requires some degree of subjective judgement because attributes such as intelligence, knowledge, and attitude are not exactly quantifiable. Therefore, senior management should be alert for indications that:

- Employees have failed consistently or substantially to perform their internal control duties
- Or, a serious question has been raised concerning their business behaviour and their abilities.

To be in a position to reach such conclusions, the auditing department and/or managers themselves must review reports and responses emanating from internal control chores; examine written evidence on merits and demerits concerning the company's system of management controls; find out what each department does in internal control practice; and elaborate on the functions of personnel within each department. An analytical approach requires posing as many focused questions as possible during person-to-person meetings.

Because independence of opinion is fundamental to the correct functioning of an internal control system, in judging the independence of a person, senior management must avoid looking at that person strictly as an individual. It should also examine the functions the person performs within the context of company operations, as well as the way in which he or she responds in a given situation. For example, an individual may be the sole cheque signer while an assistant may prepare monthly statements. This is a weak spot in internal control.

For obvious reasons I never tire of emphasizing the need for independence of opinion and action by people responsible for internal control activities. The same is true about separation of duties. *If* employees who have access to assets also have access to accounting records, perform related review operations, or immediately supervise the activities of other employees who maintain the records, *then*, they may be able to both perpetrate and conceal defalcations:

- Duties concerned with the custody of assets are incompatible with record-keeping for those assets
- Duties concerned with the performance of business activities are incompatible with authorization or review of those activities.

Not only should such organizational glitches not be allowed to happen, and must be immediately corrected where they exist, but full attention should also be given by the board to the way internal controls are audited. An effective way to begin an on-site review of internal control is to identify the various key functions applicable to the area under review. For each position, a number of questions should be asked:

- Is this a critical position?
- Can a person in this position do something unethical?
- How will this act affect the recording of transactions?
- Can an error perpetrate material irregularities of some type?

Not only fraud but also plain errors must be brought under the magnifying glass. If an error can be made or irregularity perpetrated, senior management and/or the auditors should examine the likelihood that normal routines could disclose it on a timely basis: Do controls exist that would prevent or detect significant errors or the perpetration of irregularities? What are the specific opportunities open to the individual to conceal any irregularity? Are there any mitigating controls that will reduce or eliminate such opportunities?

As the concepts behind these queries document, there are no miracles to be made through internal control policies and procedures. What there is, is a systematic approach turning over every stone in the organization and in its procedures, with the objective of uncovering weaknesses in the structure, in the individual fulfilling a given job, or in both. Anything short of a methodological approach and a penetrating mind able to challenge the obvious is guaranteed to give substandard results.

IMPROVING THE STATUS OF INTERNAL CONTROL IN BUSINESS AND INDUSTRY

An implementation plan addressed to internal control, as well as the method chosen for its upkeep, should be tailored to a company's conditions without violating the basic principles I have outlined and the definitions given in the Appendix. For instance, that responsibility and accountability for internal control starts at the level of the board of directors, the CEO, and senior managers. This is necessary because, as a rule, successful execution of internal control depends on leadership, not only on the collaboration of lower levels of supervision.

A question I am often asked in my seminars is the relation which exists between general management duties, internal control and the functions of bank supervision. Figure 2.4 provides the answer in a nutshell. This response is specific to a banking environment, using limits and compliance as an example. A meaningful discussion on current status and future perspectives of internal control can be made only with reference to specifics. Therefore, in this section and the next I take credit institutions as a reference, even if the evidence accumulating in new forms of risk suggests that most banks are behind what is required by a prudent internal control policy.

For instance, if its system of internal controls was in good shape, the Bayerische Landesbank would not have had DM400 million in unwarranted losses. Bayerische Landesbank is a big institution, but it is not alone in this plight. In the large number of cases, even major banks do not have in place the system of checks and balances which permits them to immediately control the type of exposure that took place at Barings and Daiwa Bank in 1995, or National Westminster Bank and Union Bank of Switzerland in 1997.

The concept underlying internal control functions must promote in the most explicit manner the supervision and compliance requirements set by the board for conducting business activities. These must be observed at all time in order to safeguard *our* bank's future. Controlling the observance of clearly stated guidelines is the job of internal auditing, and as we saw in

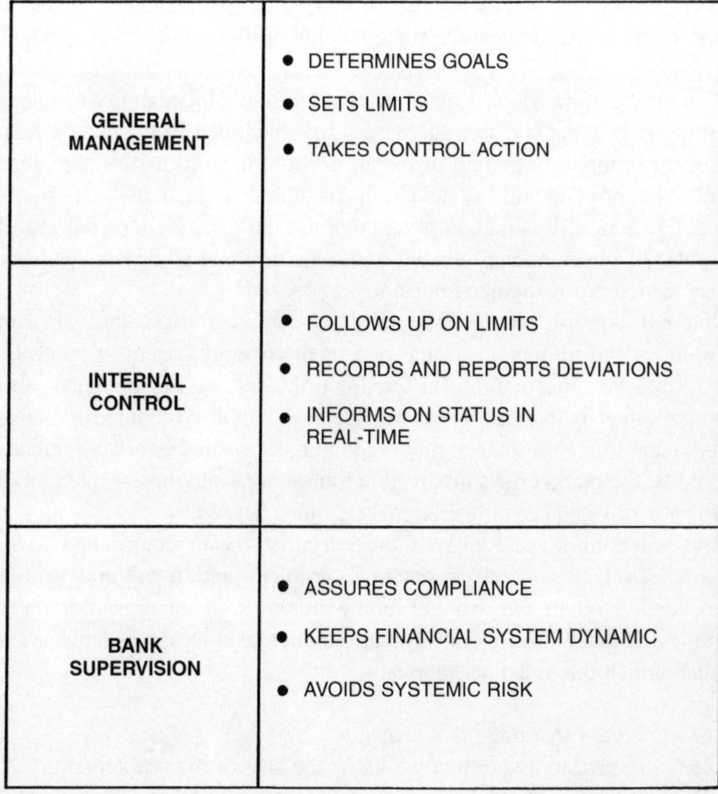

Figure 2.4 Roles and responsibilities of different agents concerned by the control of risk

Chapter 1 internal audit should be assisted by intelligent knowledge artefacts:

- These agents must be designed by the institution, not bought as a commodity, and
- They should be implemented in collaboration between internal auditing and the technologists.

Chapter 1 also brought to the reader's attention the fact that a bank's system of internal controls, and the technology supporting it, must cover all transactions by channel of activity and by desk: money market, capital market (securities and debt instruments), foreign exchange, loans and other interest rate exposure, traded commodities, and, most evidently derivatives.

One of the tests which I make to ascertain the dependability of internal controls is whether transactions which are concluded in the bank's name, either for proprietary trading or for the account of third parties, are always carefully controlled and any deviations from rules immediately reported for corrective action. It is a good policy that not only transactions but also the portfolio of positions is evaluated both regularly and ad hoc for gains and losses which are recognized but not yet realized.

Internal control has a great deal to do with exposure, yet some institutions fail to appreciate that part of the overall system of controls is not only the information on creditworthiness to be obtained about counterparties by independent rating agencies, but also the internal analysis to be made in regard to each major counterparty. Another area of attention should be the market risks involved in transactions and those existing in the portfolio; still another is operational risk (see below).

Internal control, said one of the executives who contributed to this research project, is both a practical problem and a cultural problem embedded deep in our way of doing business. Another senior banker commented that to find a valid solution to internal control problems one has to distinguish three distinct phases:

- *Identification* that there is a problem
- *Measurement* to assure that we know the size of the problem
- The *Solution*, or alternative solutions, needed to end that problem, at least in its current form.

Identification, measurement and solution(s) are three giant steps in both personal life and business life that pervade our thinking, decisions, and actions. There is an important link here with the world of military intelligence. The tangible is given greater value than the intangible. Intangibles are harder to identify and measure; yet, sometimes, this is unavoidable.

Both for tangibles and for intangibles senior management must rely on analytical information. A great deal will be obtained by mining the bank's own database(s). Quite often, internal control is deficient because it is not formally established as both a concept and a practice, and financial institutions do not monitor every transaction in a rigorous manner. Also managers make judgements, implicitly or explicitly, which ignore some types of risk or lack detail. The discussion above also pressed home the point that the internal control solution which is good for one institution can serve another in only an average way:

- A sound internal control system must be designed in accordance with the scale, complexity, and risk content of the lending, trading, investing, and other activities conducted or projected.

What this bullet point essentially states is the principle of *materiality*, so dear to the accounting profession. We do not wish to either overshoot or undershoot the right level of internal control:

- A company's business strategy, its clients, its suppliers, its practices, and the market(s) in which it operates should be taken into account in designing the internal control system.

At the foundation of the control environment lies the fact that an effective organizational structure can provide an overall framework for forecasting, planning, staffing, organizing, directing, and controlling operations. Reliable solutions consider such matters as the reporting relationships of organizational units; the assignment of authority and responsibility; and the constraints established over day-to-day and longer-term funding as well as functioning.

Efficient methods of communicating and enforcing the assignment of authority and the watch over accepted responsibility, are those which clarify the understanding of, and improve compliance with, the organization's policies and objectives. For instance, the policies regarding acceptable business practices and conflicts of interest. Job descriptions are necessary, and they should delineate specific duties and associated accountability.

Technology plays a key role in connection with communications methods. But while technology should be used to assist internal control, it does not substitute management's responsibility for establishing and maintaining an interactive supervisory system designed to provide reasonable assurance regarding the integrity and reliability of financial statements – including prevention and detection of fraudulent financial reporting as well as protection of assets and their value.

WHAT IS MEANT BY A 'RIGOROUS INTERNAL CONTROL SOLUTION'?

A rigorous internal control solution is an integral part of overall risk monitoring, and it is embedded in the management structure covering *all* of a company's areas of business. But what is meant by *rigorous*? *Webster's Dictionary* says the term means: 'Severe, exact, strict, scrupulous, accurate, allowing no abatement or mitigation':

- All these definitions apply to an internal control solution, and the way it should be executed
- The mechanics of this solution should facilitate the identification and analysis of risks, from both trading and non-trading activities.

Here is how three different institutions look at this issue. At Bank J. Vontobel, internal controls focus on limits (private and institutional); all types of derivatives trades; credit lines; risk policies (clients and correspondent banks); brokerage operations; and assets/liabilities management. A quantitative and qualitative risk analysis done by internal auditing involves 11 weighted queries, the highest weight being given to internal control.

In the case of Bank Leu, the most important mission given to internal control is compliance. Bank Leu gave a good reason why internal control should be self-standing and should not be a part of auditing. According to its policy, auditing is a supervisory metalayer (see also Chapter 1). On the contrary, internal control, risk management, treasury, lending, accounting, and other departments are concerned with day-to-day activities.

Lars O. Grönstedt, of Handelsbanken, suggested that at his institution credit risk and market risk are two distinct disciplines, and for practical reasons monitoring of these two risk classes is more efficient if they are kept in different organizations than integrated in the same one. However, Grönstedt added, internal control is over all business activities and the credit risk department is involved in setting market risk relevant limits, in so far as they concern market risk parameters used in establishing counterparty limits.

A few of the technologically most advanced banks pressed the point that internal control can also be seen as a system supported through networks, computers, and sophisticated software, which is at the service of all authorized managers and professionals in the bank – from board members to the lower level of supervision. And as we have seen in Chapter 1, high technology can also help in increasing the efficiency of auditing internal control.

Whether sophisticated software is or is not used to make more efficient internal control functions, a well designed system will be flexible enough to enable the company to respond at short notice to changes in the market and in operational conditions. But flexibility does not mean lack of standards. On the contrary, the internal control and its individual components, methods, parameters, and computational procedures have to be documented in detail and reviewed regularly (at least annually). Also, they must be continuously developed to become more focused than they have been.

This task is doable, provided the bank not only uses high technology rather than classical and obsolete data processing software and hardware, but also invests its information technology where it counts: at the top of the hierarchical pyramid rather than at the bottom. As Figure 2.5 suggests:

- The information environment at the top of the organizational pyramid is unstructured. There is also where the intangibles exist.
- By contrast, at the bottom of the organizational pyramid the information environment is structured, and therefore it is easier to control it.

We will be talking in more detail about information technology issues and investments in Chapter 13, but in a world of interdisciplinary activities a preview of issues which are further out in a discussion always helps in better appreciating the subject on hand. The point is that because organization-wise internal control belongs to the top of the pyramid, it should benefit from the most advanced technological solutions.

A rigorous internal control approach would pay full attention to the information technology being used, from networks and databases, to data-mining, models, and interactive reporting through visualization (turning tables into graphs). Not only the channels of communications must operate in real-time and the modelling of all types of exposure effectively done, but also market-related parameters must be adjusted immediately to changes in financial conditions and/or board decisions with an impact on the management of risk:

- Risk figures derived from risk-based audits (see Chapter 4) must be continuously compared with actual market data, as well as trends indicating a change in direction.
- In the event of major discrepancies between model-based projections and actual figures, senior management must be immediately informed.

A reference valid for all transactions, as well as for marking to market the bank's assets and liabilities, is that significant attention should be paid to the level of detail which can be reached through internal control. For instance, it is a relatively common practice that what are considered to be related securities are aggregated together in the same bucket. Yet not only does each of these instruments have its own risks, but exposure also varies

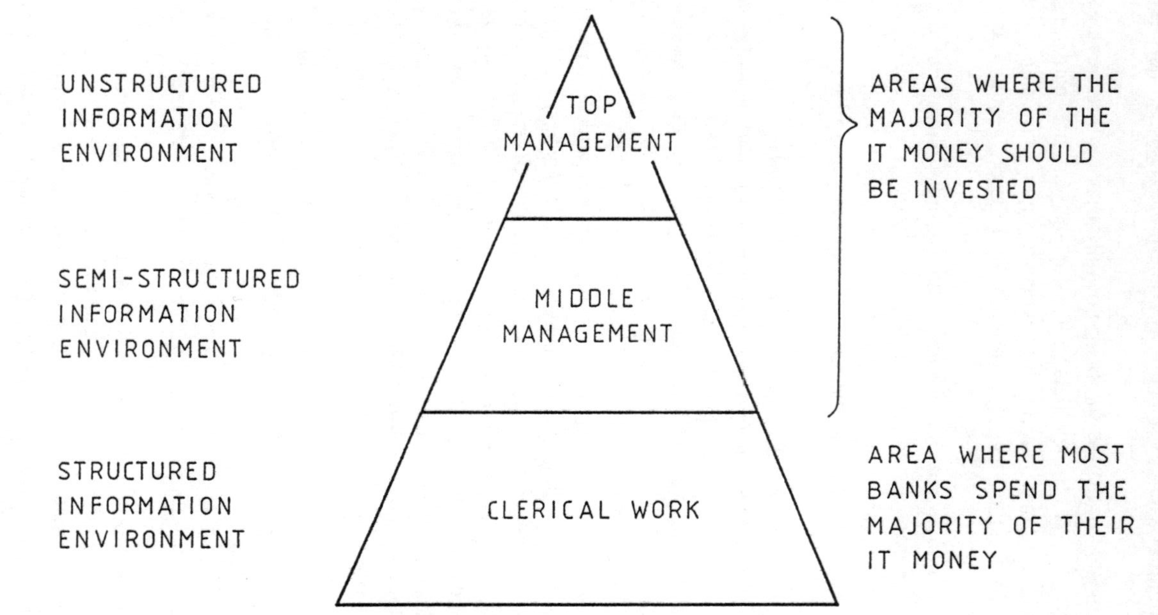

Figure 2.5 Technological solutions addressed to high-grade professionals must be positioned in an unstructured information environment

in connection with the counterparty and its leverage. As a senior British banker was to suggest:

- A bank's internal controls have failed if it suffers a substantial loss from an event which was anticipated but not monitored
- Or, an event which was not anticipated by *our* bank while there is evidence in the financial industry about its occurrence and its perils.

An even greater peril is that people who have assumed risky positions in the hope of making some good profits for the bank (and commissions for themselves) may deliberately suppress or falsify records. This happens when they feel that their own career or that of their friends and supporters is in danger as red ink flows left and right.

Internal controls must also reflect the prevailing regulatory requirements by type of financial institution, country of operations, nature of instruments being handled, and other criteria. They must ensure that there is compliance with the rules set by regulators, for any transaction, anywhere in the world – and they should evolve to match the change, or anticipated change, in regulations.

For instance, an interesting part of German regulations regarding internal control is that traders should not permit brokers to run their own positions, and should not accept deals of 'name-to-follow' type. They must insist that brokers name the counterparty immediately, the only exception being when brokers are allowed to enter into such a deal within the scope of exchange regulations. This is also a case which has to do with operational risk.

A PRACTICAL EXAMPLE WITH INTERNAL CONTROL APPROACHES TO OPERATIONAL RISK

Operational risks are as old as business, but awareness about the need to keep them under lock and key, and built up reserves for them, is relatively new. The leading opinion in business and industry today is that operational risk is a complex issue which has not yet been analyzed in a detailed manner. Ways and means for controlling operational risk cannot be put in place until and unless we identify all factors of an operational nature that can go wrong. This is done in Table 2.1, based on the findings of research which I did in 1999.

Several aspects of operational risk might be dealt with by means of an explicit disclosure regime covering all exposures to and losses arising from operational problems. While these disclosures would realistically be made to the board, the CEO, and senior executives, a regime specifically

Table 2.1 The top dozen operational risks

1. Mismanagement at all levels, starting with the board and CEO
2. Quality of professional personnel (staffing) and lack of skills
3. Organization, including separation between front office and back office
4. Execution risk, including the handling of transactions, debit/credit confirmations
5. Fiduciary and trust activities, as well as reputational risk
6. Legal risk, under all jurisdictions in which the bank operates, and compliance to regulations
7. Documentation – a cross between operational risk and legal risk
8. Payments and settlements, including services provided by clearing agents, custody agents, and major counterparties
9. IT risks: software, computer platforms, databases, networks
10. Security, including ways and means to unearth rogue traders and other fraudulent people – internal or external
11. Infrastructural services including utilities: power, telecoms, water
12. Risks associated with less known or appreciated factors, present and future, because of novelty and globalization

designed to control operational risk might be coupled with public disclosure of information describing the pattern of a company's operational risk profile.

Attention to operational risk was boosted by the fact that the 1999 New Capital Adequacy Framework of the Basle Committee on Banking Supervision makes a distinct reference to 'operational risk' and the fact that its background reasons can lead to capital requirements in excess of those already existing for credit risk and market risk. Financial institutions started to look at their operations and the exposure they assume because of them, as well as ways and means for bending the operational risks curve.

As the careful reader will observe in Table 2.1, mismanagement is the No. 1 factor in the constellation of operational risks, followed by inadequate professional staffing, substandard organization and the ever-present execution risk. The dozen operational risks shown in Table 2.1 can be supplemented by others which are less important or specific to a certain environment or entity. Operational risks are not independent from one another. There is a synergy particularly among the top four. Figure 2.6 emphasises this point.

Sometimes it is possible to insure against some elements of operational risk. To be effective, this approach should be market-based as well as focused. Such insurance would shift risk to a group of instruments designed to cope with a special kind of exposure, and use external skills competent in assessing operational problems. But at the same time, external consultants may be lenient and give a false sense of security to *our* institution.

Quantification of each operational risk characteristics and range of variation will provide useful data both for immediate corrective action, and for preventing its repetition. For instance, properly studied and implemented preventive measures help to reduce reputational risk; but it is no less true that the very existence of reputational risk applies a market discipline to our company's management:

- Information is crucial in operational risk. Reporting trends can act as an early warning signal of growing operational exposure, and the reason(s) behind it.

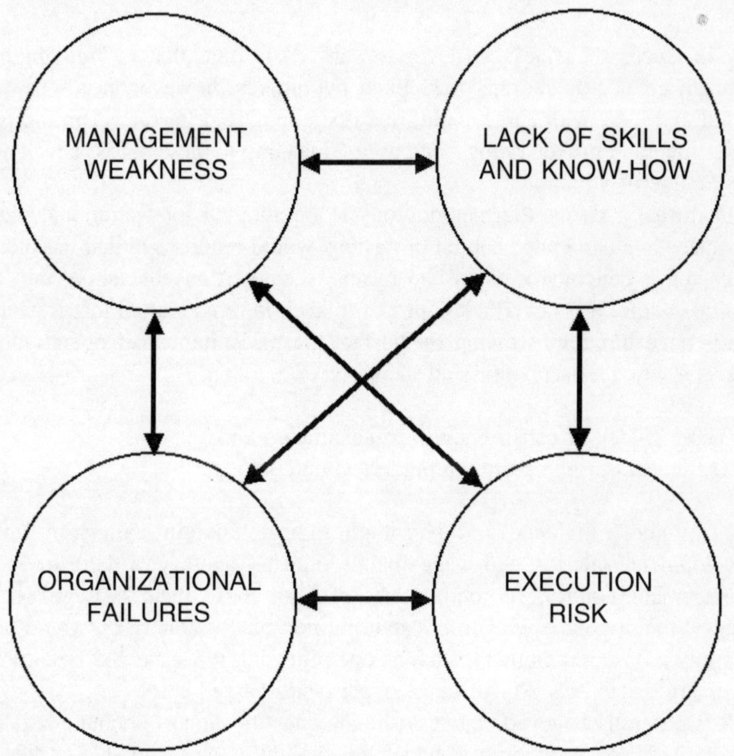

Figure 2.6 The top four operational risks influence one another in a significant way

- But reporting must observe the materiality of the losses to be disclosed, and the timing of disclosure. It must also reflect appropriate sanctions.

As a rule, a company's operational risk will not necessarily bear a significant relationship to its market risk or credit risk. It would therefore make sense to move away from market risk and credit risk calculations and compute an operational risk capital charge related to data that reflect the scale and frequency of this exposure. Regulators advise that practical operational risk examples might be:

- Significant variability in earnings
- Fluctuations in business turnover
- Statistics and trends in staff turnover
- Staff costs divided between frontdesk and back office
- Prevailing error rates and
- Return on technology investments.

For instance, a business turnover to staff costs ratio that is *high* might indicate greater operational risk. Such hypotheses, however, needs to be tested and used with care, scaling the operational risk factor according to experimentally proven ratios – and giving meaning to these ratios as well as their range of variation.

In different terms, the methodology to be adopted for operational risk estimates and associated capital provisions would require detailed research to establish benchmark ratios and means to convert any overshoot into a capital charge. It is nevertheless proper to keep in mind that all metrics and ratios have limitations owing to the fact the measurement of operational risk is a new preoccupation and therefore:

- There is lack of consistency in its calculation and
- Difficulties in interpreting a numerical outcome.

For example, a high staff turnover might indicate underinvestment in staff development, salaries, and wages below industry average, a hard driving management control, or the product of both these factors. Regulators suggest that a good approach in capturing non-measurable risks, would be to apply a base requirement, such as one reflecting the scale and type of a company's activities. For instance, x per cent of fixed costs.

It is generally believed that as a rule the quantification of operational risk should be based on algorithms which are straightforward, and able to relate capital to the size of some factor. If so, this has to be done on the basis of a certain logic. The metrics to be chosen should never be of a nature which could be interpreted as a penalty on success. Neither should they encourage entities to modify their structure in in vain hopes of meeting 'this' or 'that' type of needs, rather than following rigorous risk management requirements.

In conclusion, internal control should be very sensitive to operational risk, but also to present-day opportunities and limitations of metrics applied to operational risk. Such measures should not be developed for quantification's sake alone, but in order to serve specific operational goals. They should therefore be realistic, able to provide effective assistance in management control and/or as prognosticators. They must avoid false alarms, and be auditable by internal and external auditors.

APPENDIX: DEFINITIONS OF INTERNAL CONTROL BY AICPA, BASLE COMMITTEE, EMI, IIA AND COSO

American Institute of Certified Public Accountants' (AICPA) Committee on Working Procedures

Internal control comprises the plan of organization and all of the coordinate methods and measures adopted within the business to safeguard its assets, check the accuracy and reliability of its accounting data, promote operational efficiency, and encourage adherence to subscribed managerial policies.

This definition dates back to 1949 and is broad, recognizing that the system of internal control extends beyond those matters which relate directly to the functions of the accounting and financial departments to include budgetary control, standard costs, periodic operating reports, statistical analyses and dissemination thereof, a training programme designed to aid personnel in meeting their responsibilities, and an internal audit staff to provide additional assurance to management as to the adequacy of its outlined procedures and the extent to which they are being effectively carried out.

A later definition by the AICPA divided internal control into two components:

1. Administrative control, which includes, but is not limited to, the plan of organization and the procedures and records that are concerned with the decision processes leading to the management's authorization of transactions. Such authorization had been defined as a management function directly associated with the responsibility for achieving the objectives of the organization, and as starting point for establishing accounting control of transactions.
2. Accounting control, comprising the plan of organization and the procedures and records concerned with the safeguarding of assets and the reliability of financial statements, designed to provide reasonable assurance that:

   - Transactions are executed in accordance with management's general or specific authorization

- Transactions are recorded as necessary to permit preparation of financial statements in conformity with generally accepted accounting principles or any other criteria applicable to such statements and to maintain accountability for assets
- Access to assets is permitted only in accordance with management's authorization and
- Recorded accountability for assets is compared with existing assets at reasonable intervals, with appropriate action taken with respect to any differences.

Basle Committee on Banking Supervision

Internal control is a *process* effected by the board of directors, senior management and all levels of personnel. It is *not solely a procedure or policy* that is performed at a certain point in time, but rather it is *continually operating* at all levels within the bank.

Historically, the internal control process has been a mechanism for reducing instances of *fraud, misappropriation*, and *errors*, but it has recently become *more extensive*, addressing *all risks* faced by banking organizations. Internal control consists of five interrelated elements:

- *Management oversight* and the *control culture*
- *Risk assessment*
- *Control activities*
- *Information* and *communication*
- *Monitoring activities.*

The effective functioning of these elements is essential to achieving a bank's *operational, information*, and *compliance objectives.*

European Monetary Institute (EMI), Predecessor to the European Central Bank (ECB)

An internal control system (ICS) can be regarded as the process (including all the controls, financial or otherwise) effected by a credit institution's *board of directors, senior management*, and other personnel to provide reasonable assurance that the following objectives are achieved:

- Accomplishment of established *goals and objectives*
- Economical and efficient use of *resources*
- Adequate control of the *various risks* incurred and the *safeguarding of assets*
- Reliability and integrity of *financial and management information*
- Compliance with *laws and regulations* as well as *policies, plans, internal rules, and procedures.*

(EMI underlines that regardless of how well designed it may be and how well it may function, an ICS can only provide reasonable assurance that the above-mentioned objectives have been attained.)

Institute of Internal Auditors (IIA)

Internal control is actions taken by management to plan, organize, and direct the performance of sufficient actions so as to provide reasonable assurance that the following objectives will be achieved:

- The accomplishment of established objectives and goals for *operations and programs*
- The economical and efficient use of *resources*
- The safeguarding of *assets*
- Reliability and *integrity of information*
- Compliance with *policies, plans, procedures, laws, and regulations.*

Committee of Sponsoring Organizations of the Treadway Commission (COSO)

Internal control is a process effected by the board, management and other personnel designed to provide reasonable assurance regarding the achievement of the following objectives:

- Effectiveness and efficiency of operations, i.e. basic business objectives: *performance and profitability* goals, safeguarding of *resources*
- Reliability of *financial reporting*
- Compliance with applicable *laws and regulations.*

3 Internal Control and the Globalization of Financial Markets

INTRODUCTION

One of the missing links in effective globalization of financial markets is the ability of internal control systems to span the whole network of a company's operations – for any transaction or position, anywhere in the world, at any time. Steady tracking is important because fully or partly controlled instruments and subsidiaries abroad represent a major part of the risk taken by the parent company, contrary to the generally held opinion that they only represent 'added income'.

The statement I just made is as valid for credit institutions as it is for manufacturing and merchandising concerns. Regulators, too, have problems with globalization, regarding the inspection of the foreign subsidiaries of institutions under their control. Co-ordination between bank supervisors is crucial, and it has been obtained among the Group of Ten (G-10) countries through the Basle Committee. But such co-ordination is still wanting when it requires collaboration by supervisory authorities of emerging countries.

A different way of making this statement is that co-ordination among supervisors is at its best in the G-10. For instance, the German Federal Banking Supervision Bureau has a Memorandum of Understanding (MOU) with the French and British regulatory authorities. Such facilities do not exist, for example, with Singapore. This lack of universal supervisory standards and exchanges of regulatory intelligence in an environment of globalization does not allow the agents of the Federal Banking Supervisory Bureau to check the accounts of a German bank's affiliate in many parts of the world – though in an indirect way certified public accountants' (CPA) firms can be commissioned to do this job.

'We depend on assessment by private accountants', said a senior executive of the German Federal Banking Supervisory Bureau during our meeting in Berlin. Then he added that the intention of the Banking Supervisory Bureau authority is to intensify the relationship with all other supervisory authorities in the globalized market with an MOU similar to those existing with G-10 regulators. This is seen as an urgent matter because the rapid evolution of institutions, products and markets is increasingly challenging the effectiveness of:

- Management oversight
- Market discipline and
- Official supervision.

In 1997, that concern prompted the creation of a study group on the global supervision of financial institutions and markets by the Washington-based Group of Thirty (G-30), a think tank. Managing an expanding range of complex products and services around the globe and around the clock is a daunting challenge, and it is in no way business as usual for internal control systems of the type known till the late 1990s. The global operating environment places a premium on understanding, implementing, and managing a sophisticated system of global internal controls.

A difficult task faces a company's board, its CEO, and senior executives, as well as national supervisors who are charged with setting requirements for global operations of complex conglomerates, while being constrained by the current limits of national legal jurisdiction and regulatory charters. Even as progress is being made in strengthening the international supervisory framework for banking, securities, and insurance, the restrictions of institutional and geographic boundaries that define the existing framework is still present – even if the walls separating bank supervisors tend to diminish.

Regulatory authorities are particularly concerned by the potential for systemic risk arising from gaps between the global operations of institutions and markets, and nationally-based systems of accounting, reporting, law, and supervision. Corporate executives, on the other hand, are most concerned about the heterogeneity of accounting standards (see below) which makes it difficult for a global company to create a factual and documented consolidation of its books. The auditing of accounts which follow heterogeneous accounting standards is also that much more complicated.

THE IMPACT OF GLOBALIZATION ON INTERNAL CONTROL

Demand has never been greater for services that internal control can or could provide to globalized companies, but to appreciate the issues involved we should start from fundamentals. The classical types of internal controls have been authorization for transactions, safeguards over assets and records, segregation of duties, and documentation standards. Also, verification duties, which over the years had tended to integrate internal control responsibilities with auditing.

Traditionally, internal accounting control for banks and other companies included books and records of the firm's assets and liabilities, as well as segregated entries of customer property. From this perspective, the duty of a day-to-day manager or chief operating executive 'was not to sign every check' as one analyst put it, but to be on the feedback line of internal control intelligence focusing on:

- Capital protection and
- Sound risk management.

This more classical type of activity, and of associated responsibility, has been extended in recent years to cover accountability for making judgements on the degree of independence of different organizational functions, including their relationships with corporate governance and with compliance activities; observance of rules and regulations; and all the other subjects we studied in Chapter 2. Among tier-1 companies, these enlarged responsibilities are supported by sophisticated technology.

However, while the existence of state-of-the-art technology is definitely a major 'plus', it is not an assurance that there exists an adequate internal control environment. The lack of it is an indication of insufficient management attention paid to globally expanding operations – and what this means in terms of preservation of assets and reputation of the firm. Therefore, the board and senior management must ask for mechanisms able to verify that internal controls, once established, are being followed and deviations immediately corrected.

This is not a one-off task but a permanent one, and it cannot be performed manually in the long run. Let me take a globally operating credit institution as an example, to explain the meaning of this statement. While in its home country this institution may have retail banking operations, one can bet that abroad it concentrates on trading and asset management. Therefore, global internal control should focus on the frame of reference shown in Figure 3.1. Factors behind this real-time framework are:

- Intraday valuation required in all dynamic markets
- Performance premiums which create risk incentives and
- A clear distinction to be made in accounting by axis of reference.

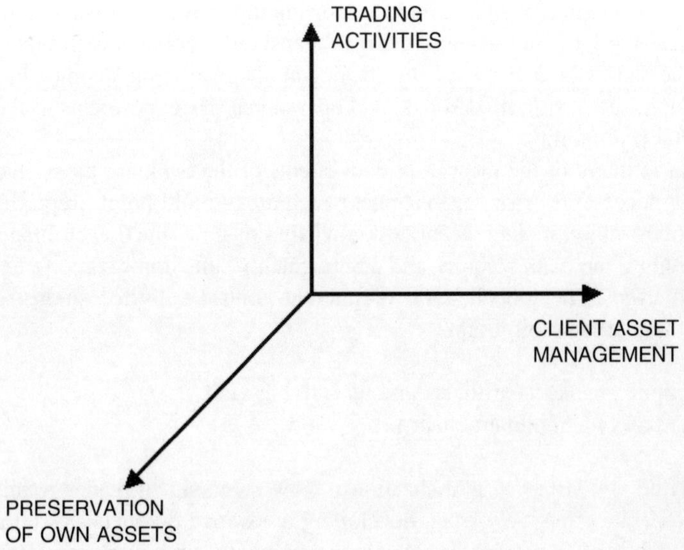

Figure 3.1 A real-time framework for focusing internal control by country and in a global setting

Institutions with first-class internal control have paid full attention to real-time reporting. The Boston-based State Street Bank, for example, is able to produce a *virtual balance sheet* within less than 30 minutes, and the next goal is 5 minutes. This is doable with advanced technology provided senior management has the will to get commendable results. (A virtual balance sheet permits us to map assets and liabilities with 96 per cent or better accuracy, which is plenty for a real-time management information system.)

Particularly in connection with global operations, the integrative frame of reference presented by a virtual balance sheet can be a major competitive advantage. Another reason real-time feedback is so important is that very few of the global credit institutions work as a network. The large majority lack the necessary integration of internal knowledge across borders. Yet, with today's dispersed markets, with their:

- Financial hot spots,
- Choosy clients and
- Dynamic market players

a thorough integration of internal control intelligence is necessary if the board and the CEO are to be in charge. Transborder collaboration among all of the bank's branches is vital to managing the institution's competitive position, its credit risk, market risk, and operational risk exposure as well as its global profitability.

Because many of the most important clients of the bank are themselves global, successful risk management requires multi-point reporting capabilities which include accurate knowledge of how much each branch is leveraging the bank's equity and assets. Such results don't come free of cost or effort. The globalization of internal control calls for studies of organizational learning, both:

- About *our* bank, its affiliates and its activities and
- About all *our* important client firms.

One of the key issues in globalization is how independent business units can co-operate effectively when developing innovative products as well as when evaluating exposure to clients, instruments, and markets. Headquarters should play a critical role in supporting risk-oriented co-operation. Because a great deal of credit and market information is developed in subsidiaries, companies must through special task forces specialize in facilitating shared developments and making possible knowledge transfers – eliminating complacency and bringing full management attention to troubled spots.

REGULATORS LOOK AT INTERNAL CONTROL AS A FOUNDATION OF SOUND MANAGEMENT

Regulatory authorities are keen to provide internal and external auditors with guidance on how to assess an entity's internal control structure during an audit of financial statements. This must in principle be done in accordance with Generally Accepted Auditing Standards (GAAS), which are not to be confused with the Generally Accepted Accounting Principles (GAAP) discussed below. An assessment of a company's internal control system helps the auditor to better evaluate assertions set forth in financial statements. It also helps to determine the extent of testing to be done.

The Office of Thrift Supervision (OTS) underlined that institutions should not only have in place an adequate system of internal controls but also that internal control should be an integral part of the bank's risk management system. Superficially, a reference to the OTS might look out of place in a discussion on globalization, but in reality this is a pretty good example if we make the assumption that OTS is comparable to the headquarters of a large global entity with about 1100 independent business units, of which 70 are of a reasonably large size. (That is the number of thrifts supervised by OTS.)

Working on this hypothesis of a well managed global headquarters function which exercises prudential supervision of the entities over which it has authority, let me bring into our perspective some of the OTS directives for retail banks (savings and loans, S&L, thrifts). These directives explicitly state that internal control should promote:

- Efficient operations within established risk limits
- Reliable financial and regulatory reporting procedures and
- Compliance with relevant laws, regulations, and institutional policies.

Exporting this paradigm to a global scale, the headquarters should expect that local management policies will pay adequate attention to prudential limits; assure a timely and accurate process for measuring, evaluating, and reporting exposure; put a premium on a strong control environment; and make certain that each independent business unit, as well as the institution as a whole, abides by ethical values. This framework engages the accountability of board directors, the CEO, and all senior managers in the affiliates.

Along with the emulation of a well tuned headquarters function, the OTS also provides a practical example of the focused, technology-based approach which it has adopted. As Timothy Stier, its chief accountant, has shown, OTS pays a great amount of attention to interest rate risk taken on by the regulated 1100 S+Ls. The larger of these institutions file a report with interest rate risk information using a model of compliance developed by OTS.

I have been favourably impressed by this model. Even the big banks, at least their majority, do not possess such a sophisticated approach. The model integrates *What If* hypotheses on the movement of interest rates with the effect of changes in maturity. OTS runs simulations based on real-life statistics submitted by the S&Ls through the Monte Carlo model (Chorafas, 1994a). The internal control fact to remember is that the relatively small US thrifts have learned *how to do*:

- Sensitivity measurements
- Worst-case scenarios

- Capital before-shock calculations and
- Capital after-shock reporting.

This thorough experimental approach to internal control takes current commitments and market interest rates and computes possible exposure by changing the interest rates 100, 200, 300, and 400 basis points up and down. The benchmark adverse condition is the 200 basis points shock level. This is one of the best examples I have found on using technology to strengthen an institution's internal control. Timothy Stier explained that the OTS has also developed a lot of other models which assist the S&Ls' senior management in handling interest rate risk and other risks.

The choice of the OTS advanced applications is intentional because today accountability for internal control is at board level, a statement equally true in several European countries. 'Pursuant to the first sentence of Paragraph 1 of Article 39 of the Austrian Banking Act [Bankwesengesetz, BWG] it is the executive board's responsibility to establish, keep up and revise the internal control. This responsibility is seen as part of their duty of diligence', wrote Dr Martin Ohms of the Austrian National Bank.

'The internal control system covers market risk, credit risk, settlement risk, operations risk and legal risk', said Heinz Frauchiger of Bank J. Vontobel who, as chief auditor, reports directly to the bank's CEO. Typically well managed institutions have underlined the fact that internal control functions are driven from the governing body down to operational levels which identify, quantify, report, and manage the risks of the business.

The solution that both supervisory authorities and some of the credit institutions themselves have suggested is that of a risk management group independent of risk generating functions, such as trading activities, reporting to the executive committee but audited by internal auditing. This risk management function, which some institutions see as the *alter ego* of internal control, is charged with day-to-to responsibility for:

- Risk monitoring
- Measurement and
- Analytical evaluation.

Evidently, its efficiency depends on the development and use of risk and performance measures able to ensure that all business activities are being run in accordance with defined top management strategies; that operational controls exist over front desk and back office regarding authorization for and reporting of transactions, and a real-time information system is on hand to process and visualize the results of risk analysis.

There has, however, been some divergence of opinion on how the implementation of what I have just stated should take place, though there was no visible discord on the need for a clear concept underlying internal control activities. Such divergence was particularly present in terms of organization. Figure 3.2 presents the four different organizational solutions which I have most frequently encountered in my research. I don't see it necessary to comment which one of these is 'better', because:

- All of them have strengths and weaknesses both in an absolute and a relative sense.
- Most often the organizational solution chosen by an entity is situational, fitting its culture, structure, and business environment.

In a general sense, both for global and for national activities institutions assign internal control duties sometimes to auditing, sometimes to risk management, and in other, more rare cases, to accounting, operations or the legal counsel. This is not surprising because, as we saw in Chapter 2, the areas covered by accounting, auditing, risk management, and internal control overlap, while each also has its own sphere of interest.

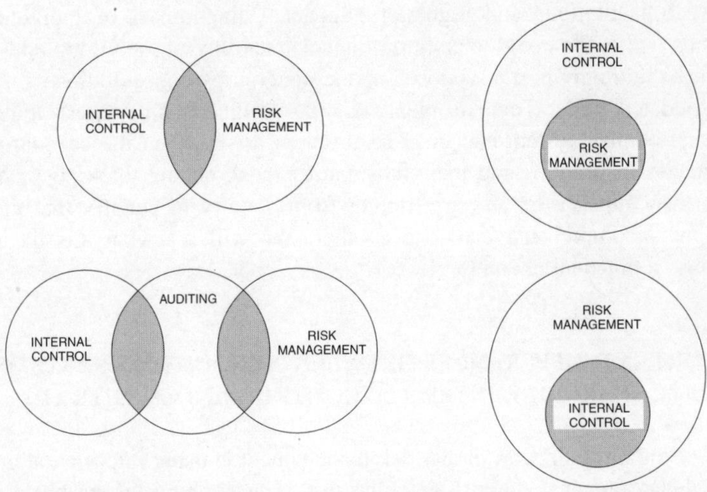

Figure 3.2 Four different organizational approaches followed by credit institutions with regard to internal control and risk management

Because organizational responsibilities are not so well settled in an industry-wide sense, and each institution has adopted more or less its own solution, it is appropriate to have a written definition of duties for internal control. In connection with both local and global operations, this should describe the needs of auditors, risk managers, and other professionals in performing duties which assist the internal control system.

Prior to closing this subject on organization challenges associated with internal control for global operations, as an introduction to the theme of the next section on important differences in accounting principles existing in a globalized economy, let me briefly bring to the reader's attention some issues concerning the supervision of financial conglomerates. Published in July 1995, by the Tripartite Group of Bank, Securities and Insurance Regulators, 'The Supervision of Financial Conglomerates' was a seminal paper addressing particular problems in any group of companies under common control whose exclusive or predominant activities consist of providing significant services in at least two out of three financial sectors:

- Banking
- Securities and
- Insurance.

This report suggested that the five main areas of interest to supervisors involve capital adequacy, co-operation and exchange of information between institutions and regulatory agencies, the impact of individual entities within the conglomerate on financial stability of the Group and of markets, intragroup transactions, and counterparty concentrations on a consolidated basis. There is plenty a well designed and properly tuned internal control system can do. The problem arises when the accounting languages institutions and their subsidiaries speak among themselves and with their supervisors are so different from country to country that they become incomprehensive to one another. We will see what this means through a practical example.

IMPORTANT DIFFERENCES BETWEEN ACCOUNTING SYSTEMS HANDICAP GLOBAL INTERNAL CONTROL AND AUDITING

One of the difficulties in global risk management is using information and knowledge out of context. Something that is understood in one business environment, may not be easily appreciated in another, or may even be distorted. Knowledge exchange is too often simplistically equated with codifying information, writing it in a spreadsheet, inputting it into computers, and shifting it around. In contrast to this near-sighted approach, true knowledge integration is the outgrowth of:

- Financial
- Technical and
- Social processes.

Global risk management is not possible by applying easy labels, because control activities usually require a significant paradigm shift. Few companies have established a track record of mastering the diverse cultural approaches and incompatible accounting rules prevailing in different countries. The result of using incompatible accounting systems is a significant operational risk exposure.

In my postgraduate studies at the University of California, in the early 1950s, I had a professor of accounting who taught his students that if one is free to choose the system in which one makes one's accounts one can prove practically anything. A very profitable enterprise could show deficits, while one which is in the red could parade itself as star performer.

These minor miracles in financial reporting are usually done through *creative accounting* (see the next section), but big differences in national accounting systems can be just as confusing. A truly International Accounting System (IAS) does not seem to be around the corner. It has been years in development, but universal rules are not yet hammered out because of basic disagreements (Chorafas, 2000a).

Not only does internal control currently operate at reduced speed because of diversity in accounting rules, and because auditors require training in different incompatible systems, but also investors unaware of major differences fall into the crevasses existing between one financial reporting scheme and another, learning about the existence of these crevasses in a very painful way. Failure to know the fine print of the law is not excusable, neither is it excusable not to master the financial instruments in which our company trades, and the counterparty with which it enters into contracts.

Financial plans and control procedures which do not pay full attention to the fact that accounting rules and reporting systems are incompatible from one country to the other, mislead senior management into believing the situation is in control. Diversity in accounting rules and principles makes it impossible to do a first-class job in leveraging analytical knowledge across a variety of environments.

Therefore, well managed companies try to unify their accounting procedures. This is what Crédit Suisse has done by adopting on a global basis the US Generally Accepted Accounting Principles (GAAP). In the spring of 1998 Crédit Suisse Group embarked on a project to reconcile its financial statements to US GAAP in a phased process lasting until 2001. Reconciliation to US GAAP is expected to bring the Group a number of benefits, including:

- Easier access to the international capital markets
- Better benchmarking with competitors and
- An improved ability to make acquisitions in the United States.

Don't be misled by easy labels. US GAAP, British GAAP, Canadian GAAP, and others using the same anagram are not the same thing. To better appreciate the important differences between US GAAP and accounting rules prevailing in Italy, an accounting system known as 'Italian GAAP', let us keep in mind that while the laws of physics are the same in all countries, accounting rules and laws of financial reporting vary. Indeed, in the majority of cases prevailing differences between countries are quite important – and they are also misleading.

Takes as an example the differences, and even contradictions, between Italian and American laws regulating financial reporting. A case in point is the determination of shareholders' equity as well as net income. Even the label 'Italian GAAP' is tricky because its rules have no relation to those of US GAAP – what the label actually means is that a financial statement has been prepared and presented in conformity with accounting principles generally accepted in Italy, including:

- Legislative Decree 87 of 27 January 1992, which implemented European Commission Directive 56/635 and Bank of Italy regulations of 16 January 1995 and
- A supplement on accounting principles issued by the Italian Accounting Profession (Consiglio Nazionale dei Dottori Commercialisti e dei Ragionieri), or in the absence thereof, those issued by the International Accounting Standards Committee (IASC).

In other words, what is collectively called 'Italian GAAP' is a set of rules which, though valid in Italy, give no assurance that net income and shareholders' equity as determined in accordance to its rules would not be higher or lower than financial reporting through another system – for example US GAAP. There is absolutely no assurance that financial statements would not differ from what they would have been *if* determined in accordance to other financial reporting frameworks.

Table 3.1 explains the most important outstanding differences between US GAAP and 'Italian GAAP'. As the reader will appreciate from this description, financial results reported by an entity in Italian GAAP would be misleading to the American financial analyst or auditor who is not aware of differences existing in the letter of the law. Such differences have nothing to do with creative accounting (see the next section) but rather with the fact that even in a globalized economy different jurisdictions have incompatible rules governing financial statements.

INTERNAL CONTROL DEFICIENCIES, CONFLICTS OF INTEREST, AND THE MASSAGING OF ACCOUNTING DATA

Many banks think they have a superb system of internal control, only to find out the hard way that it is full of weak spots and that it has many deficiencies which do not permit top management to know what happens down the line. Furthermore, because in dynamic financial markets even the best systems get obsolete fast, internal control solutions which were super five years ago, or even three years ago, may today be inadequate. It is therefore advisable that written directives by the board specify that:

- Internal control principles, tools and systems are audited regularly regarding their validity
- Internal control deficiencies are reported in a timely manner to senior management and
- Weak spots are addressed promptly by qualified people who do not have direct operating responsibilities, and hence potential conflicts of interest.

Banks which have the policy of critically reviewing their internal controls system often find that some deficiencies are structural, while others are the result of ill-studied or ineffective policies and procedures whose consequences eventually show up. Or, policies and procedures which became inadequate because market conditions and/or the internal structure changed. Deficiencies may also be the outgrowth of past practices which were inflexible and with time became ineffectual. A question frequently asked, when I make this statement in my lectures, is: 'Who should be responsible for flushing out internal control deficiencies?' An evident answer is the internal auditors (see Chapter 1) whose examination can identify and document gaps and loopholes – both during regular inspection and in the course of special investigations requested by the supervisors, top management, or one of the divisions.

Table 3.1 Comparison of some of the outstanding differences between US GAAP and Italian GAAP

US GAAP	Italian GAAP
Provision for General Banking Risks	
Allowance for general banking risks are not permitted under US GAAP	But in accordance with Italian GAAP, banks can provide for general banking risks
Extraordinary Items	
Extraordinary items must be: material, unusual in nature, and rare in occurrence. Therefore, extraordinary items are seldom presented in US GAAP financial statements. If they are presented, • The related income tax effects are disclosed and • Extraordinary items are presented net of such tax effects	Italian GAAP criteria for the classification of certain items as extraordinary are generally much less restrictive than US GAAP; their related income tax effects are not separately measured in the statement of income
Investments in Subsidiaries and Consolidation	
Consolidation is generally required for all majority-owned subsidiaries with investments greater than 50 per cent of the outstanding voting stock – except when control is likely to be temporary or control is not held by majority owner	The consolidated financial statement comprises the accounts of the entity and those banking and financing companies in which it controls, directly or indirectly, the majority of the voting rights at an ordinary meeting. The subsidiaries whose main business is not banking or other financial activities, are accounted for under the equity method

Table 3.1 (*continued*)

US GAAP	Italian GAAP
Elimination of Intercompany Transactions	
For banks, gains and losses resulting from intercompany trading activity are eliminated from the consolidated financial statement	To the contrary, banks are not required to eliminate gains or losses resulting from intercompany trading activity because these transactions are settled at normal market prices and their elimination would involve disproportionate costs
Translation of Financial Statements Expressed in Foreign Currencies	
Such translation would be performed by using the current rate on the balance sheet, and for income statement items exchange rates in effect when the transactions occurred; an appropriate average rate for translating income statement items may be used as an approximation over a limited period; shareholders' equity accounts are translated at historical exchange rates	The translation is performed by applying year-end exchange rates to the balance sheet asset and liabilities and income statement items, on a line-by-line basis; differences arising by translating shareholders' equity of consolidated companies using the closing exchange rates are included in other reserves in shareholders' equity
Amortization of Goodwill	
Goodwill arising from business acquisitions is capitalized and amortized on straight-line basis over the period of its estimated useful life, generally 10–25 years, up to a maximum of 40 years for companies not in banking	Goodwill arising on acquisition of investments in subsidiaries and equity investments is capitalized and amortized on a straight-line basis, generally over 10–20 years

Table 3.1 (continued)

US GAAP	Italian GAAP
Accounting for Negative Goodwill	
Negative goodwill is allocated on a pro-rata basis against the fair value of non-current assets acquired, other than marketable equity securities; any remaining negative goodwill is amortized on a straight-line basis to income over a period estimated to represent the life of accruing benefits but not less than 10 years	Negative goodwill may be recorded as a component of shareholders' equity, or, when it represents expected future losses, it may be classified as a liability and reduced by a credit to income at the time such losses incurred
Investment and Trading Securities	
Marketable equity and all debt securities must be classified, according to management's intent, into one of three categories: trading, available-for-sale, held-to-maturity	Marketable equity and debt securities must be classified, according to management intent, into either trading or investment
Trading securities are reported at fair value with unrealized gain or loss recognized currently in the income statement; debt and equity securities not classified as either trading or held-to-maturity are also reported at fair value	Treasury stock is reported in the balance sheet as an asset carried at cost; gains and losses on the sale of owned shares or exchange of such shares for other assets, are recognized in the statement of income.
The cost of owned shares acquired is presented in the balance sheet as a reduction of shareholders' equity	Investment securities held for the long term are valued at cost, as adjusted by accrued issue discounts or premiums – but they are written down to reflect any lasting deterioration

Table 3.1 (*continued*)

US GAAP	Italian GAAP
Impairment of Loans and Allowances for Loan Losses	
Gains realized upon disposition of owned shares would be recorded as an addition to paid-in capital; losses realized could be charged to paid-in capital to the extent of previous net gains from sale or retirement; otherwise to retained earnings	in the solvency of the issuers except when suitable guarantees are available
Held-to-maturity debt securities are carried at amortized cost	Market value is based on the average price during the last month of the year for quoted securities listed on regulated markets, cost-adjusted to reflect any significant decrease in value for unquoted shares or estimated realizable value for unquoted bonds
Transfers among categories of investments are accounted for at fair value	Transfers among categories of investments are recorded at their book value at the time of transfer
Impairments in value which are other than temporary are accounted for as realized losses	
Transactions are recorded at trade date	*Transactions* in securities and similar instruments, including forex contracts, are *recorded based on their settlement date*
Impairment of Loans and Allowances for Loan Losses	
Impaired loans are written down to the extent that principal is judged to be uncollectible and the related loan balance, net of charge-offs, is the new cost basis for the loan	Loans are written down to their estimated realizable value by reducing outstanding principal balance; the original value of loans is reinstated through write-backs when the reasons for any write-downs are no longer applicable; write-downs and

Table 3.1 (*continued*)

US GAAP	Italian GAAP
Provision for loans are charged to expenses sufficient to maintain the allowance for loan losses at an adequate level to cover probable loan losses related to specifically identified loans or inherent in the remainder of the loan portfolio that have been incurred as of the balance sheet date	write-backs are recorded in the income statement, in the 'Net adjustments to loans and other provisions for credit risks'
	Default interest is fully recognized as income and a provision received to the extent that collection is not considered likely; a tax-deductible provision can be recorded for the entire amount of default interests
Impairment of larger-balance, non-homogenous loans is measured by comparing the net carrying amount of the loan to present value of the expected future cash flows, discounted at the loan's effective interest rate; or the loan's observable market price; or the fair value of collateral if the loan is collateral-dependent	Capital and interest elements of loans are stated at their estimated realizable value, taking into consideration the solvency of individual debtors and any problems in serving external debt in countries where the borrowers reside; the assessment of performance also accounts for any guarantees received, market prices and difficulties experienced by the different categories of borrowers
	Estimated realizable value is determined based on a detailed review of loans outstanding at the balance sheet date, considering the nature of collection problems The present value of expected future cash flows is considered only in the estimation of realizable value of restructured debts, with expected future cash flows discounted at average cost of customer deposits

Table 3.1 *(continued)*

US GAAP	Italian GAAP
Loan Fees and Costs	
Loan origination fees and direct loan origination costs are deferred and the net amount is recognized as an adjustment of yield over the contractual life of the loan	Non-refundable loan origination fees are recognized as revenue when they are received and direct costs are expensed when incurred
Fixed Assets Revaluations	
Revaluations are not permitted and depreciation is based on original cost.	Fixed assets can be revalued in the application of specific revaluation laws crediting the revaluation surplus to capital reserves as a component of shareholders' equity
Derivative Financial Instruments	
Off-balance-sheet instruments are reported at fair value, with unrealized gains and losses included in the statement of income if: they are entered into for trading purposes; or they hedge items which are or will be carried at fair value; or the criteria for hedge accounting are not met.	Options, futures and contracts indexed to interest rates, interest rate swaps, future rate agreements, held for trading purposes are generally carried at *the lower of* cost or market for quoted securities, or at 'reliable' estimate for unquoted securities
When there is management intent to hold to maturity and hedging criteria are met, gains or losses are deferred for	The results from valuing derivative contracts held for trading purposes are included in profits and losses

Table 3.1 (*continued*)

US GAAP	Italian GAAP
both the hedging instruments and the hedged item and recognized in the income statement at the same time	Derivative contracts related to hedging operations are stated on a consistent basis with the asset/liability they hedge; arising differential are recognised on accrual basis
Premiums received/paid for options are generally market to market, except for purchased options meeting hedging criteria; the time value of the premium paid is amortized over the life of the option, while intrinsic price is considered part of the basis of hedged exposure	The premiums paid/collected on options contracts are recorded as other assets/liabilities until they expire or are exercised; when option contracts expire, premiums paid or collected are debited or credited to income statements
Statutory Pension Plans	
A specific accounting standard governs expenses related to defined benefit pension plans; yearly expenses are based on actuarial computations using only one actuarial method; earnings of fund assets within a pension plan are not reflected in the income statement; expensing cash contributions instead of the actuarially determined amount for financial reporting purposes is not allowed	There is no specific guideline dealing with retirement benefits costs and related disclosure; banks pay monthly social security contributions to the Italian National Insurance Body for all employees, the amount is based on percentages dictated by Italian Law; banks can accrue pension fund liabilities based on actuarial computations

Table 3.1 (*continued*)

US GAAP	Italian GAAP
Taxation	
A tax expense recognized in the reporting period is comprised of: current tax payable or refundable, and deferred tax expense or benefit recognized for the expected future tax consequences of events that have been recognized in the financial statements or tax return	Income taxes for the reporting period are provided on the basis of estimated taxable income of individual companies included in the consolidation; deferred income tax assets arising from differences between the tax basis and the reporting basis of assets and liabilities are not recognized
Deferred tax assets and liabilities are recognized for all future tax consequences attributable to temporary differences between financial statements carrying an amount of existing assets and liabilities and their respective tax bases, and operating losses and tax credits' carryforward using existing enacted tax rates	

External auditors are another party which can identify deficiencies in internal control, particularly now that regulatory authorities are starting to require that certified public accountants (CPAs) also audit internal controls and the quality of the system supporting them. No doubt the Audit Committee itself or any other board member can put a finger on internal control deficiencies because:

- An inordinate amount of assumed risk has shown up
- Some operational errors have been allowed to persist or
- Personal interviews with managers and professionals leave much to be desired.

Once deficiencies are identified, the CEO and senior management should see to it they are corrected in a timely manner. To assure that this is done, the internal auditors should conduct follow-up reviews and alert the Audit Committee and the board of directors about any persistence of weak spots in the bank's internal control armoury.

For instance, the existence of *creative accounting* practices is an indication that the bank's internal control defences are weak or not in place. *If* the board and CEO are unaware of its existence, *then* creative accounting is thriving on the lack of rigorous management control practice. This gap in senior management's authority permits staff to massage the balance sheet and make it look pretty in spite of lots of red ink, inordinate exposure to counterparties and instruments, and other disasters. But it may as well be that the CEO authorizes the massaging of accounting information, and a rubber-stamp board approves such practices:

- Sometimes management condones liberal interpretations of accounting because it shows a rapidly rising profit as the company expands its business or makes a new acquisition
- Yet, the company may be financing its deals by selling stock at ever-higher prices to parties willing to collaborate in non-fair pricing in exchange for other gains.

An example is the Guinness scandal which hit the City shortly after the 'Big Bang', the market deregulation of October 1986. As Guinness' shares spiralled upwards, buoyed by co-ordinated buying from parties not only in the City but also in the United States and in Switzerland, the firm subject to the leveraged buyout complained to the British Take-over Panel about share gearing. The Panel failed to act. Analysts consider this to be the ugliest take-over of the 1980s and they characterize the final 'win' as a dubious glory.

Share manipulation, it was reported, apparently added up to a staggering £200 million ($330 million). Not only take-overs but also many profit reports reflect a clever but unethical use of accounting rules and/or are based on imaginary operations. The result is unreliable financial reporting. Therefore, top management should always be on alert regarding the use of accounting in 'creative' ways (see also a further discussion on creative accounting in Chapter 6). The inflated accounts may concern earnings from:

- Trading
- Loans

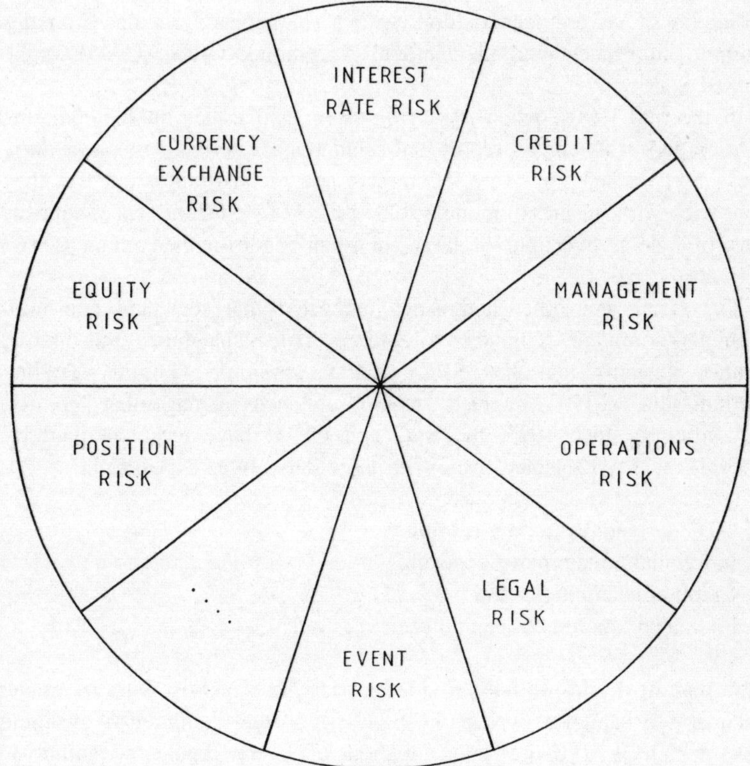

Figure 3.3 The internal control framework of COSO implementation, as seen by the Federal Reserve Bank of Boston

- Acquisitions or
- Any other business.

Internal control has a significant role to play in keeping creative accounting out of *our* company's system. An example on a well rounded reporting structure is given in Figure 3.3. It reflects an internal control framework based on the implementation of COSO (see Chapter 2), the way the Federal Reserve Bank of Boston sees it. I wish I had found many more examples like this in my research.

Internal and external auditors should under no condition pass over the existence of creative accounting practices. Whenever and wherever found, these must be reported both to top management and the regulators – or any other party responsible for redressing false accounts. Sometimes it is the state auditors who find out what has gone wrong, and ring the alarm bell. Examples of government auditors with a sharp pencil are the Cour des Compte, in France, and the General Accounting Office (GAO) in the United States.

In the mid-1990s, when risks from leveraged trades hit the roof, the GAO noted in its annual report that standards for derivatives, particularly those used in hedging, were incomplete and inconsistent – nor had they kept pace with business practices. One of GAO's concerns was about the lack of federal oversight of large, non-banking over-the-counter (OTC) derivatives trades.

The GAO and other authorities requested that regulated and non-regulated companies volunteer to abide by risk management and internal control systems that the SEC, and Commodities Futures Trading Commission (CFTC) agreed would enhance management control. Accordingly, since 1995, the SEC and CFTC have received quarterly information from selected firms with large derivatives exposure in:

- OTC derivatives trading revenues
- Individual counterparty exposures
- Credit concentrations and
- Estimated amounts of capital at risk.

This type of disclosure has provided a basis for supervisors to assess the adequacy of capital as well as keep an eye on the likelihood of systemic risk, which is a major preoccupation of every regulatory authority. Globalization or no globalization, there is no business in the world which can hope to move forward by lowering its defences and exposing itself to all sorts of uncontrolled risks.

Leveraging through derivatives and creative accounting practices are often correlated. From Barings to the Sumitomo Corporation, whether or not they end by using creative accounting methods (Chorafas, 2001a), many organizations that have suffered major losses did so because their internal control was weak and they neglected to continually assess the risks connected to their business activities:

- Critically rethinking the ability of their internal control to spot unwarranted exposures and
- Steadily updating their internal control system, to keep all sorts of risks at an affordable level.

One of the consistent themes of bad management is the reluctance of responsible executives to mind their own business in a consistent and timely manner. Because of this trait, which is universal, the board quite frequently fails to appreciate that even if an internal control system functions well for some traditional-type operating conditions it is unable to handle:

- Leveraged products
- Ingenious deviations from standard accounting practices and
- Complex market environments.

Yet, these are the situations which are full of perils and might turn *our* company belly up. As we all know from practice, market behaviour becomes complex for a number of reasons. The sophistication of clients and products is one of them. The absence of appropriate legislation and regulation – and, therefore, legal risk – is another. After the financial meltdown of 1997 in East Asia, analysts found the hard way that the balance sheets of even relatively healthy local banks were suspect.

Credit institutions which were thought to be solid were highly leveraged and/or featured huge unwarranted and unsecured loans in their books. These banks could no longer recover money owed by recalcitrant local companies because of the absence of effective bankruptcy legislation. At a national level, gaps and defects in local legislation make it almost impossible to attach any sort of value to non-performing loans – which is a frequent happening with globalization. Think about this when you make investment plans about the so-called 'emerging markets' – another creative accounting artefact.

A THREAT CURVE WHICH ADDRESSES OUR PROBLEMS AND THEIR LIKELIHOOD

Globalization and the emphasis being placed on emerging markets sees to it that events like those discussed in the previous section are on the increase. During the last 10 years there has been a growing number of cases where information about inappropriate activities that should have been reported upward through formal organizational channels was not communicated to senior management or the board of directors until the trickle became a torrent.

In other cases, information in management reports was plain inaccurate, creating the impression of a business situation that was in control while losses accumulated and it became necessary to file under Chapter 11 for protection from creditors. In product pricing, too, *volatility smiles* have proved to be an awfully inaccurate information feed to senior management. Volatility smiles often remain unchallenged till pretty sizeable losses hit the bank and create a crisis.

Financial, political, military, or any other crises have some common characteristics from their anticipation to their culmination and their handling. Events can be ordered through a *threat curve*, which expresses their likelihood on a scale of increasing probability, with (usually) the most dangerous threat being the least likely.

Threat-curve graphics are a good analytical tool. Historically, they began to appear in NATO's intelligence offices in the mid-1980s. Their aim was to demonstrate the likelihood of certain dangers, through an ordering permitting intelligence officers to channel a good share of resources to *probable risks*, not only the *worst case* which may be quite unlikely.

Presently, I am not aware of credit institutions using the threat curve for ordering the likelihood of their problems, yet this is an exercise which has merits – particularly within a globalized environment where internal control may spread thin, and confronting *our* institution's operations. Figure 3.4 shows a financial example where the threat ranges:

- From a minor drop in stock price (least threat, most likely)
- To a major loss of market share (most danger, least likely).

The two events are related. A major drop in market share will lead to a major drop in stock price, and the company may find it difficult to raise capital. As Figure 3.4 demonstrates, eight other dangers exist between those described by the two bullets. (For pipeline risk, see Chapter 11.)

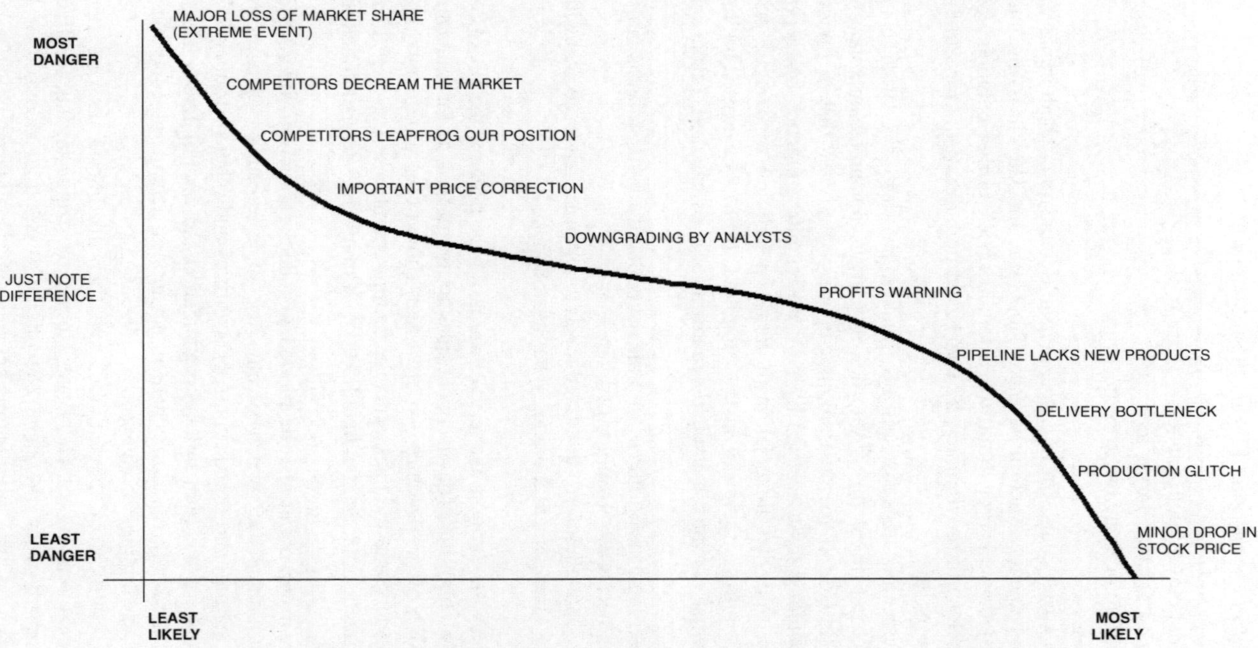

Figure 3.4 By ordering the probability associated with different risks, a threat curve can assist in appreciating their likelihood

Other examples where the implementation of a threat curve may be revealing in connection to business problems are:

- Internal control deficiencies
- Unexpected loan losses and
- Mounting derivatives exposure.

A threat curve could, for instance, help to demonstrate whether and where senior management action has been 'too little, too late' in fixing internal control deficiencies; or if and when this has been further compounded by ineffective audit programmes, by half-baked monitoring and reporting, and by other events.

Globalization does not always weaken an entity's internal controls structure, but this is the way to bet, as existing resources are spread thin. The Basle Committee on Banking Supervision advises that in reviewing major banking losses caused by poor management practices, supervisors typically find that financial institutions have failed to observe critical internal control principles (Basle Committee, 1998). Quite often a pillar or two of what constitutes a sound organization is overlooked. For instance:

- The segregation of duties, with the result that the bank suffers significant losses because of conflicts of interest or
- Limits, and therefore authorized levels of exposure, are exceeded without senior management knowing what has happened.

Sometimes the auditors themselves are at a loss, because the board or the executive committee (unwisely) decides to assign to a senior manager the supervision of two areas of activity which should control one another like the front desk and the back office of trading operations. This is a threat to proper functioning, and the likelihood of 'Barings risk' can be plotted in the appropriate threat curve, for everyone to see.

A threat curve can also be plotted to reflect conflicts of interest in an organizational sense, which permits the same executive to control the buying, selling, and bookkeeping of securities and other instruments. This can happen anywhere in a global organization and when it does it interferes with the bank's feedback mechanism, swamping accounting functions and blurring the findings of auditors.

Other conflicts of interest, too, and their likelihood may be studied through a threat curve. The Basle Committee suggests that conflicts of interest result when the same executive assesses the adequacy of loan documentation, then monitors the borrower after loan origination. Or, when

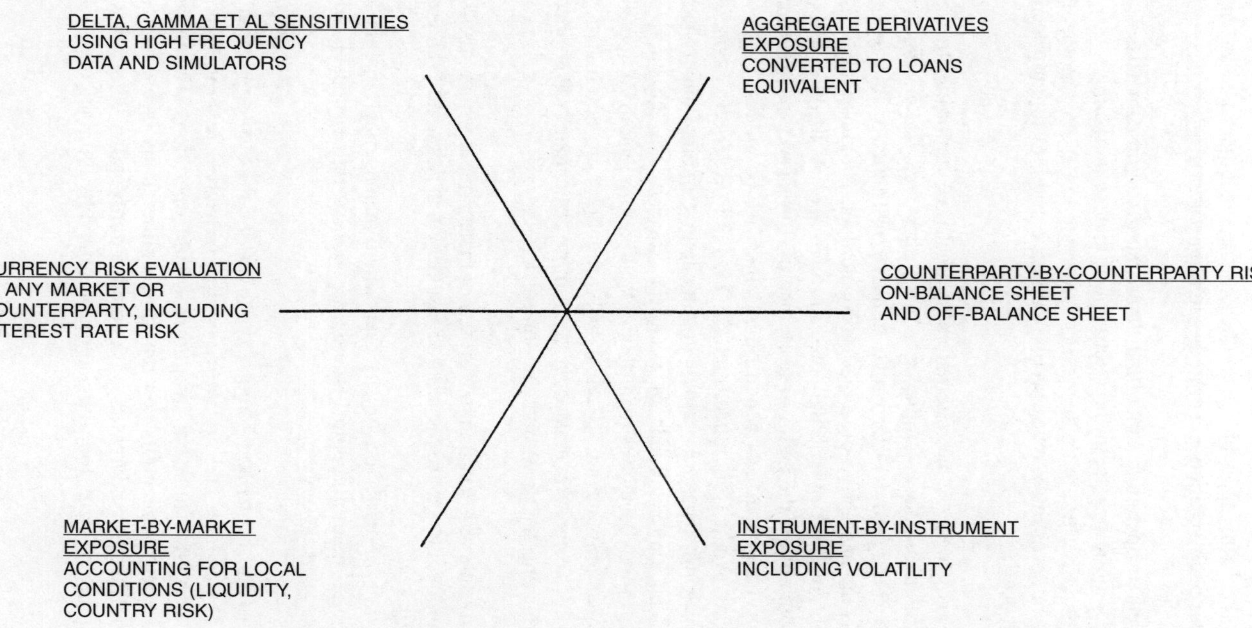

Figure 3.5 Radar chart for off-balance-sheet risk control to keep top management alert

he or she provides information to customers about their positions while screening the loans applications of these same customers and extending credit lines. Such conflicts generate a common pattern:

- The bank's operating units that later report significant losses first announce good profits, in the aftermath of intense marketing.
- Often, these profits are far in excess of expectations for the reported level of risk, but real life catches up and cutting corners eventually leads to major losses.

In my book, there is no alternative to real-time reporting to senior management along the example of a radar chart like the one shown in Figure 3.5. Designed for derivative financial instruments, this reporting structure is an interactive presentation by product, customer relationship, market section, and other vital axes of reference. A flexible reporting system should allow the end-user to change the dimensions of presentation in order to visualize effects which might otherwise be hidden.

The board, Audit Committee, and CEO should be seriously concerned with *out-of-control* patterns which document that internal supervision is wanting. Yet, on a number of occasions, because in the short term deviations from expectations regarding risk and return tend to be in positive territory, questions are not asked and investigations are not started until serious problems make mandatory a much more critical analysis to identify wrongdoings and try to do damage control:

- Sometimes there is a collision with senior management which pushes the rank and file into a course leading to fast growth in sales and even greater profit figures.
- But plenty of cases document that when management intentionally lowers the internal control standards, sooner rather than later the company pays a heavy price.

Members of the board and senior executives should also appreciate that high ethical standards and *preventive control* measures are an integral and important part of a financial institution's daily operations. Examples of preventive control are limits and real-time online audits (see Chapter 1), which can effectively address the risks the institution takes before they get out of proportion. Here, too, the pattern presented by a threat curve can be revealing.

4 New Standards for Auditing Internal Control and the Use of Risk-Based Audits

INTRODUCTION

Accounting and auditing have come a long way since the end of the Second World War. They now feature revamped, stricter, and enforceable codes of ethics as well as new and revised standards, more efficient professional bodies, and much better structured technical examinations which are getting increasingly more sophisticated. Because of these developments, auditing has evolved into a significant aid to implementation and maintenance of an internal control system. The 1990s have seen new audit, accounting, and management control concepts, such as:

- Internal control's expanding horizon
- Integrated auditing approaches
- Database mining for auditing reasons
- Risk-based examinations
- Self-assessment in corporate governance and
- A tougher stance by regulators.

Management control responsibilities have been analyzed and documented with suggestions for improvement by specialized committees, particularly in the United States and the United Kingdom. These new internal control dimensions are expected to strengthen the auditors' hand, and augment the risk managers newly found self-confidence – but they also demand greater skills and better technological support than ever before. What is, however, unlikely, in spite of better-focused auditing and a more efficient internal control system, is the possibility to eliminate the chances of financial scandals:

- From spectacular frauds like that of BCCI
- To mismanaged risks like Barings and Long-Term Capital Management (LTCM).

This may sound like a contradiction, but it is not so if we appreciate that both the possibility of fraud and the likelihood of mismanagement have increased, while an effective control system cannot be implemented without intelligent networks, real-time processing, database mining, and agents – which are mastered only by top-tier banks. It is not enough to have an instrument. We must also use it. We now know it is unlikely that a classical-type audit would uncover the scams of the 1980s and 1990s, because if it could they would not have happened in the first place.

Where many auditors failed their own profession as well as their clients: company management, shareholders, investors, regulatory bodies, and other interested parties, is by not spotting basic control weaknesses or red-flagging them at the very moment they became aware of them. One of the reasons for such failure is that auditing is still largely manual, and to a very large extend depends on tips.

Cognizant people to whom I talked during my research suggested there is between a 15 per cent and a 20 per cent chance that an auditor will find different types of scandals because of a tip, lead, or accidental discovery – and only a 35 per cent chance via an audit done the classical way. The other 50 per cent or so is conditioned by high technology. Therefore, to improve internal control performance, as well as to make a major leap forward in auditing results, we need to:

- Re-evaluate our methods
- Sharpen our skills and
- Use high technology to the fullest extent (see Chapter 13).

Auditors must ask themselves: How dependable is the bank's database? How accurate are the market data streams? How authoritative are management's information sources? Are the bank's professionals competent enough to provide reliable references? Can the audit be based on data made available by the firm, or does this data need thorough verification and screening? Are internal controls rigorous enough to withstand attempts to bend them?

Other critical queries are also calling for dependable answers: How well can the auditors themselves challenge the obvious and dig deeper? Can they live up to their findings regarding internal control dimensions? Is senior management receptive to a better methodology such as risk-based auditing? (See below.) If not, who is mounting the resistance? For what reasons? How far one has to go up the organizational pyramid to take care of the bottleneck?

AUDITING RESPONSIBILITIES PRESCRIBED BY SECURITIES LAWS

As the Introduction to this chapter stated, there have been many reasons that made internal control and auditing more sophisticated over time. Rules and regulations is one of them. Let me take as an example the US Federal Securities Laws, most specifically Regulation §240.17 Ad-13 which focuses on internal accounting responsibilities. It states that every registered transfer agent shall file annually with the Securities and Exchange Commission (SEC), and its own appropriate regulatory agency, a report prepared by an independent accountant concerning the transfer agent's system of internal control and related procedures for:

- The transfer of record ownership and
- Safeguarding of related securities and funds.

The accountant's report shall state whether the study and evaluation was made in accordance with generally accepted auditing standards; describe any material inadequacies found to exist as of the date of the evaluation; outline any corrective action taken; and comment on the current status of any material inadequacy described in the auditing report immediately preceding the current investigation.

The regulators also instruct that the study and evaluation of the transfer agent's system of internal control, for the transfer of record ownership and the safeguarding of related securities and funds, shall cover a well-defined set of requirements. Regulation §240.17 Ad-13 further specifies that the safeguard and transfer of securities and funds should be guarded against loss from unauthorized use or disposition, and that transfer agent activities must be performed promptly and accurately.

All material inadequacies must be identified and reported by the auditors. A 'material inadequacy' is defined as a condition for which the certified public accountant (CPA) believes that the prescribed procedures, or degree of compliance with them, do not reduce to a relatively low level the risk that errors or irregularities would have a significant adverse effect on the transfer agent's ability to exercise due diligence, in the way described in the preceding paragraphs.

Occurrence of errors or irregularities more frequently than in rare isolated instances is evidence that the internal control system has a material inadequacy, or is confronted with conflicts of interest. A significant adverse effect on a transfer agent's ability to transfer record ownership promptly and accurately, and safeguard related securities and funds, could inhibit this transfer agent from discharging its responsibilities in a dependable manner under its contractual agreement with the issuer. The result is material financial loss.

In the United States, if the independent (external) auditor's report describes any material inadequacy, the transfer agent is given 60 calendar days after receipt of the report by the regulators to notify the SEC and its appropriate regulatory agency, in writing, regarding the corrective action taken or proposed to be taken. For all practical purposes, the SEC looks to the pattern rather than to isolated events – a process well served by its ability to exploit its large databases in an effective manner.

This significant strengthening of regulatory control evidently has an effect on both the auditing profession and the attention senior management now pays, or should pay, to internal control. It is quite interesting that while in the early- to mid-1990s the auditing profession resisted the inclusion of internal control and organizational relationships into its responsibilities for study and evaluation, by the late 1990s it had begun to accept this professional need.

In this respect, *Internal Auditor* (February 1998) presented an interesting case study which documents that the audit of internal control should be done from many angles. A CPA was evaluating the accounting books and operations of a given firm. Some elements suggested a lapse of integrity in the accounting system, but there was no hard core evidence. However, toward the end of his work the external auditor examined one of the company's main facilities, particularly focusing on some key internal and external relationships which were not very clear. The elements he was after included relationships between:

- The facility director and the internal controller
- The facility director and the vice-president to whom he reported and
- This vice-president and the administrative vice-president.

As revealed by this part of the audit, organizational and personal relationships between the different people were strained, and troubled relationships threatened the overall performance of the facility's operations. On the basis of his perceptions, the auditor was led to evidentiary documents. Through them he was able to diagnose the source of the difficulties as the poor relationship skills of the administrative vice-president. His actions were said to include:

- Threatening comments
- Unwillingness to help with problems

- Unsympathetic responses to inquiries
- Failure to keep others informed of changed expectations and
- Manipulation of the values to which he held others accountable.

This is an excellent example how the lack of internal control can lead to unwanted results. It is also a good example of duties other than accounting reconciliation by external auditors. The audit report stated that although the evidence from the accounting audit was that in the overall internal control seemed rather satisfactory, some of the concerns over relationships pointed to potential problems in operations. These led to a breakdown in the line of command, and the results of this breakdown filtered all the way into financial reporting.

AGENCY COSTS AND THE IMPAIRMENT OF ASSETS

Matters concerning organizational relationships and how effectively these work were not until recently a concern to internal and external auditors. But once their existence has been established, they should be looked at very seriously. Apart from their impact on financial reports, strained relationships affect what has become known as *agency costs*.

Agency theory has been developed by economists to help the way in which businesses are organized and managers behave, including their organizational relationships and personal interaction. The theory says that companies successfully competing in a given industry are those whose ownership structure allows them to minimize costs. Simplifying the model, these costs fall into two classes:

- Production costs and
- Agency costs.

'Production cost' is the cost of goods sold in the narrower sense: labour, materials and so on. To these should be added marketing costs and administrative costs – as well as costs of staying in business, like research and development (R&D) (see Chapter 12). 'Agency costs' are a metalayer of expenses arising from incentive conflicts and relationship clashes within the firm. Larger companies have several groups of *stakeholders* (don't confuse them with shareholders) whose interests conflict: Owners, managers, employees, business partners – for instance bankers or supply chain associates – with a stake in the assets:

- Agency costs are specifically the costs of reducing these conflicts
- Part of agency costs is the value of output lost because of such conflicts
- Another part is organizational friction, along the lines of the example above.

One of the results of agency costs is *impairment of assets*. There are of course a number of other reasons, physical as well as market-induced, leading to the same result. The Statement of Financial Accounting Standard (SFAS) 121 addresses the impairment of assets. Though the focal point of attention is long-lived assets such as plant and equipment, some of the embedded notions could be carried into financial assets, complementing the notion of their intrinsic value.

According to traditional accounting practice, long-lived assets are generally recorded at cost minus depreciation – that is, *book value* based on the accruals method. The cost is seen as fair value at time of acquisition, but over the years it is subject to changes which may be much more significant than the depreciation permitted by law. Depreciation of original cost is allocated to the period(s) in which the asset is used, for instance through a linear rule. This practice has been somewhat modified with dynamic depreciation. Another modification permits us to reflect the case when an asset is impaired. In that case:

- A loss is implicitly recognized because of impairment and
- The asset is written down to a new and lower carrying amount.

Until recently, accounting standards did not address the issue of when impairment losses should be recognized, or how impairment losses should be measured and reported. This gap has seen to it that the resulting practices were quite diverse – a fault by the Financial Accounting Standards Board (FASB) rectified in SFAS 121.

The concepts advanced by SFAS 121 can apply is all financial assets. The procedure outlined specifies that an impairment loss must be measured as the amount by which the carrying investment in the asset exceeds the fair value of that asset – at the time when the loss is recognized. *Fair value* is market value between a willing buyer and a willing seller in a case other than a fire sale. Quoted market prices (where they exist) provide evidence of fair value. As an alternative, we may use a valuation technique based on the present value of expected future cash flows, which is one of the definitions of *intrinsic value*.

In the general case, not only inventoried physical assets but also logical (virtual) assets can be impaired because of changes in market values and conditions – for example, derivatives contracts in the institution's trading book, or in the portfolio of any other company. Regulators want to know of such impairment, just as they want to know about derivatives exposure and *management intent* in derivatives contracts – whether they are for trading or for longer-term hedging.

In other countries, too, the regulators have come to grips with the need to be informed about derivative exposure. Effective since 1996, Swiss law sees to it that there is a virtual integration of the bank's balance sheet and off-balance-sheet items. Gains and losses with derivatives are respectively presented in the bank's balance sheet as:

- *Other Assets*; and
- *Other Liabilities*.

Such practice essentially amounts in accounting in the balance sheet for all off-balance-sheet items. Prior to this change in Swiss reporting structure, only the replacement values of options were reported gross. In the case of other products, positive and negative replacement values were set off against one another (netting). Now derivatives gains and losses have to be shown separately in assets and liabilities, as shown in Figure 4.1 and Figure 4.2.

In the United States, the FASB has also advanced successive guidelines which amount to a virtual integration of assets and liabilities on-balance sheet and off-balance sheet. SFAS 133 (see Chapter 6) has superseded the previous SFAS 105, 107, and 119, and includes more far-reaching regulatory reporting guidelines than its predecessors. In Britain, the Accounting Standards Board (ASB) also called for integration of on-balance-sheet and off-balance-sheet items in the bank's reporting practice:

- The Income Statement (profit and loss statement, P&L) shows profits and losses which are recognized and realized.
- While the Statement of Total Recognized Gains and Losses (STRGL) shows profits and losses recognized but not realized, including impaired assets.

Though the regulators don't say so, at least not explicitly, losses with derivatives are a major impairment of assets – particularly because derivative financial instruments are leveraged. In principle, the more the exposure, the greater the risk that a temporary panic could cause a run on the bank; and a panic in one market could quickly spread to another.

We should always be ready to learn from historical precedent and the lessons which come with it. The globalization of financial markets is not a

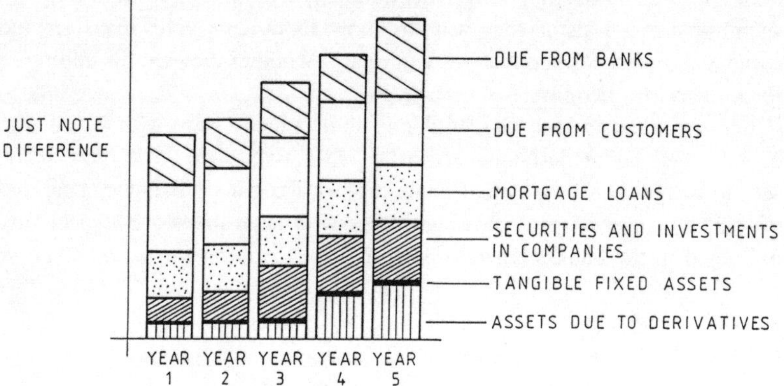

Figure 4.1 Assets in the balance sheet and off-balance sheet of a major financial institution (up to $300 billion)

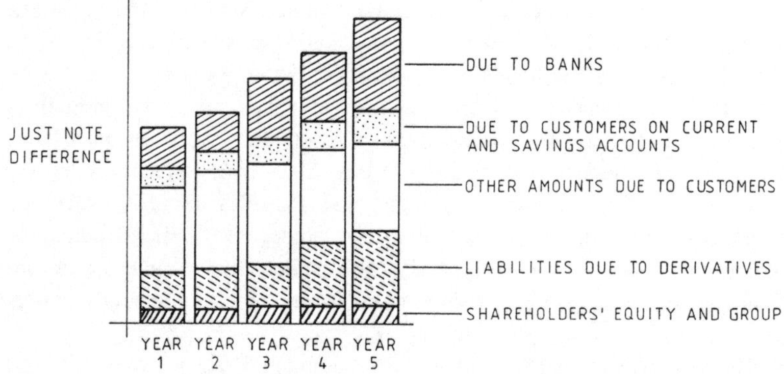

Figure 4.2 Liabilities in the balance sheet and off-balance sheet of a major financial institution (up to $300 billion)

phenomenon just of the 1980s and 1990s. As early as 1875 Carl Mayer von Rothschild described how the 'whole world has become a city' as he watched stock markets falling everywhere.

In a way not dissimilar to what happens today with gearing through derivatives, in the late nineteenth century the dangers of collapse had become greater with the spread of joint-stock banks and the growing scope of speculation. The crash of the respected London firm of Overend Gurney reverberated throughout the world's financial markets and compelled the Bank of England to develop into virtually a 'lender of last resort' – a role today played by practically all central banks, and the International Monetary Fund (IMF) on a global scale.

The difference between 'then' and 'now' is that today with world-wide networks news move much faster. Networks see to it that the world now has an integrated international financial and information marketplace capable of moving instruments, money, and panics to any place on this planet in a matter of seconds. Success in banking depends more than ever on understanding the world, but this is not feasible if we do not first understand ourselves, our strengths, and our weaknesses. This is what internal control is all about.

USING A COMPANY'S CASH FLOW FOR AUDITING REASONS

Increasingly, financial analysts tend to employ estimated, expected future cash flows as a means for determining whether an asset is integral or impaired. For these cases, SFAS 121 specifies that assets shall be grouped at the lowest level for which there are identifiable cash flows. The latter should be largely independent of cash flows of other groups of assets. Estimates of expected future cash flows must be based on reasonable and supportable assumptions and projections. This is a directive which goes beyond classical responsibilities in auditing books and accounts because it brings into the picture an element of prognostication.

This US regulation did not come out of the blue but after elaboration largely based on responses by cognizant people to a Discussion Memorandum. This is practically the way all FASB regulations are developed. The retained criterion is *loss recognition*, which is done *de facto* when the carrying amount of an asset exceeds that asset's fair value. Events or changes in circumstances that indicate that the recoverability of carrying price of an asset should be reassessed by the auditors in their study and evaluation include:

- A significant decrease in the market value of an asset
- Adverse change in legal factors or in the business climate and
- Change in the extent or manner in which an asset is used.

The careful reader will appreciate that these examples have embedded in them an indirect reference to internal controls and the way they function. A significant decrease in market value of an asset would hit treasury positions and cash flow in a big way, if the company kept a large inventory of that asset which the market downgrades. Being overweight of certain treasury positions is in itself an indicator of failure in internal control.

A similar statement is valid regarding any other inventoried item – for instance, parts and machines used internally in the assembly line. In 1999, while the stock market was booming, Compaq lost about 50 per cent of its capitalization because of large inventories of personal computers which were getting obsolete very fast. According to opinions I heard on Wall Street, Compaq's top management was too preoccupied by digesting the acquisition of Digital Equipment Corporation, to follow accumulated inventories closely, and internal control did not flush out danger signals in time.

Other events leading to impairment are also of interest in judging how the internal control system works. An example is the accumulation of costs significantly in excess of the amount originally projected, because of runaway overhead or direct labour factors. Also, a current period operating loss which follows up a trend, and essentially amounts to a history of operating losses. Still another indicator of defective internal control is steady discrepancies between forecasted and current market demand.

There may also be other events or changes in circumstances pointing to internal control deficiencies. For instance, persistent discrepancies between cash flow estimates reported to shareholders and actual cash flows. Such failures may be due to the use of the wrong model as prognosticator, or may be intentional in order to manipulate the stock price. To flush out background reasons auditors need to examine the whole line of management controls and at the same time estimate future cash flows through eigenmodels:

- *Future cash flows* are future cash *inflows* expected to be generated by an asset, less the future cash *outflows* expected to be necessary to obtain those inflows.
- If the sum of expected future undiscounted cash flows is less than the carrying amount of the asset, there is grounds to recognize an impairment loss in accordance with SFAS 121.

Let me give some hindsight on how subjective such evaluations might become. When SFAS 121 was still a Discussion Memorandum, some respondents indicated that a loss must be permanent rather than temporary before recognition should occur. In their view, a high hurdle for recognition of an impairment loss is necessary to prevent premature write-offs of productive assets. Views were by no means universal:

- Some respondents stated that requiring the impairment loss to be permanent would make the criterion too restrictive, therefore impossible to apply with reliability.

- Other respondents noted that anything other than a criterion of permanence was not practical to implement in business activity, because it would lead to ambiguities.

Confronted with these conflicting responses, the FASB opted for what has become known as the *probability criterion*. This calls for loss recognition based on the approach originally taken in SFAS 5, which is a *likelihood method* (see Chapter 3). However, the implementation of probabilities needs skills beyond classical statistics, both by accountants as by internal and external auditors.

An impairment loss would be recognized when it is deemed probable that the carrying amount of an asset could not be fully recovered. A practical implementation of the probability criterion uses the sum of the expected future cash flows, undiscounted and without interest charges, to determine whether an asset is impaired. I personally advise the use of *confidence intervals*, as a value-added notion, the way it has been used in connection with the 1996 Market Risk Amendment by the Basle Committee (Chorafas, 1998b).

Confidence intervals is a powerful concept which has been used in several occasions in finance. One of them is the estimation of money supply. An example from the early 1990s is given in Figure 4.3. The careful reader will appreciate that, more or less, M-3 (the current metric of money supply in Germany), has kept within the 95 per cent confidence intervals. This is true of the extreme event of 1990 which followed German reunification: a 16.5 standard deviations happened.

Confidence intervals are today as much a basic concept in risk management as they are an integral part of *value-at-risk* (VAR) and other models used for monitoring and mapping exposure. A valid method is also necessary for aggregating individual risks into an overall risk measure – and a similar statement is valid about impairments.

As these references document, cash flow estimates are a part of a much larger universe of necessary calculations and projections. For instance, prognosticating and testing the stability of correlations and volatility predictions is vital to a large number of practical problems. Once we are able to establish a basis for predictability, there is the job of fine tuning. In the case of cash flow estimates the rule is that:

- *If* that sum of cash flows exceeds the carrying amount of an asset, the asset is not impaired.
- *If* the carrying amount of the asset exceeds that sum of cash flows, the asset is impaired.

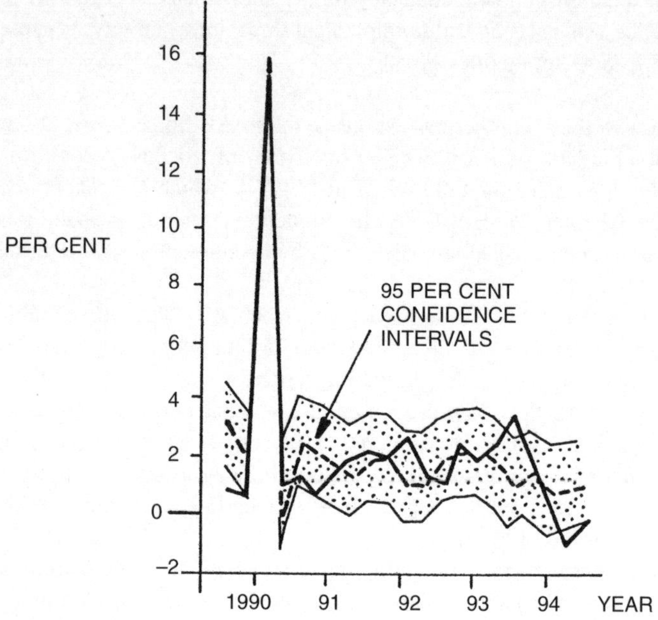

— ACTUAL

– – PROJECTED

Figure 4.3 Seasonally adjusted German M-3 money supply, fluctuation in the 1990 to 1994 timeframe

This turns our discussion back to impaired assets. If the asset is impaired, then it is wise to search for the reasons – all the way to personal accountability. A key element in this search is the role played by internal control as a warning system, and the way in which senior management responded to such warning (if there was a response). Would the impairment have been nil or minimal *if* immediate corrective action had been taken?

Finally, the auditors must pay attention to the notion of *net cash flows* used to describe the expected future cash flows and/or to test the recoverability of an asset. In SFAS 121 reference to net cash flows has been eliminated in order to be consistent with descriptions of cash flows used to determine the fair value of an asset in other pronouncements. It has, however, been retained that the intended meaning of net future cash *inflows* expected to be generated by an asset should be reduced by net future cash *outflows* necessary to obtain those inflows. The inclusion of confidence intervals will enhance the dependability of a cash flow report established along these guidelines.

THE CONCEPT UNDERPINNING RISK-BASED AUDITING

Risk-based auditing is a new method developed by the US Office of the Comptroller of the Currency (OCC). Its fundamental concept is that of merging several aspects of risk management with the characteristics of auditing. This is achieved in an efficient manner by capitalizing on the fact that, at least in principle, internal auditors act as independent agents when they can carry out their study uninhibited by senior management influences:

- Independence permits internal auditors to render impartial and unbiased judgements essential to the proper conduct of audits.
- Well documented risk-based results are achieved through the auditing department's organizational status and objectivity, to which are added analytical control characteristics.

The OCC has established certain requirements for the reliable execution of risk-based auditing. At the top of the line is that for every job they are doing, internal and external auditors should have the support of the board and of senior management. This allows them to perform their work free from interference from different elements in the organization, and it is exactly what an efficient risk control methodology requires. Other requirements include:

- A risk-based audit should benefit from broad coverage
- Adequate consideration must be given to risk management reports and
- Recommendations for corrective action are incorporated into the feedback.

Executives at the OCC made the point, during our meeting, that while risk-based auditing might be seen as overlapping with the work done by line risk management, in reality the goal is different. Risk-based audits are a metalayer of the exercise of line control over the bank's exposure (see a similar reference to internal auditing made by Bank Leu in Chapter 6).

To plan a risk-based audit, the OCC suggests, the auditor should obtain a sufficient understanding of each of the elements of the internal control structure. This understanding should include knowledge about trading policies, and the way they are executed; the nature and extent of supervisory procedures; and the interactive use of databased information. In planning the risk-based audit, knowledge should be used to:

- Identify sources and types of potential misstatements
- Consider factors that affect the risk being investigated and
- Design substantive tests concerning hypotheses which guide the auditor's hand.

The leader of a risk-based audit project should be in direct communication with senior management, because this type of support provides effective means to do a neat job and also permits keeping the board and senior executives informed on matters of exposure. As with all management control projects, independence is enhanced when the board concurs in the appointment or removal of the director of auditing.

To these conditions which have been advanced by the OCC I would add, based on my own experience, that a risk-based auditing effort will be enhanced if the board and CEO carefully define the company's risk tolerance. This should be done by class of instruments: equities, bonds, derivatives – and subdivisions thereof. Metrics used for expressing risk tolerance and for monitoring reasons should be chosen and tested. For instance, a growing volume and/or value of trades in derivatives is an evidence of increased tolerance of risk.

In the background of any tolerance-based approach is the aim of providing the auditors with some quantitative standards for the evaluation of internal control. 'Tolerances' is an engineering design concept which can be effectively used in finance – particularly for setting limits and for risk control purposes. Let me briefly describe what it means.

Let us take as an example a nuts and bolts assembly. To assemble mass-produced nuts and bolts we must observe their tolerance. Quality assurance should see to it that this happens; it does in the upper half of Figure 4.4, but not in the lower. Nuts and bolts coming from low-quality production would not assemble when their dimensions fall in area I, and would hold together in a lousy way when their dimension falls in areas II and III. Think in these terms when evaluating *limits*, whether these are associated with credit risk, market risk (Chorafas, 1999), or other risks.

Quality assurance in a production line, from manufacturing to loans authorization and trading, should be seen not as a one-off event but as a

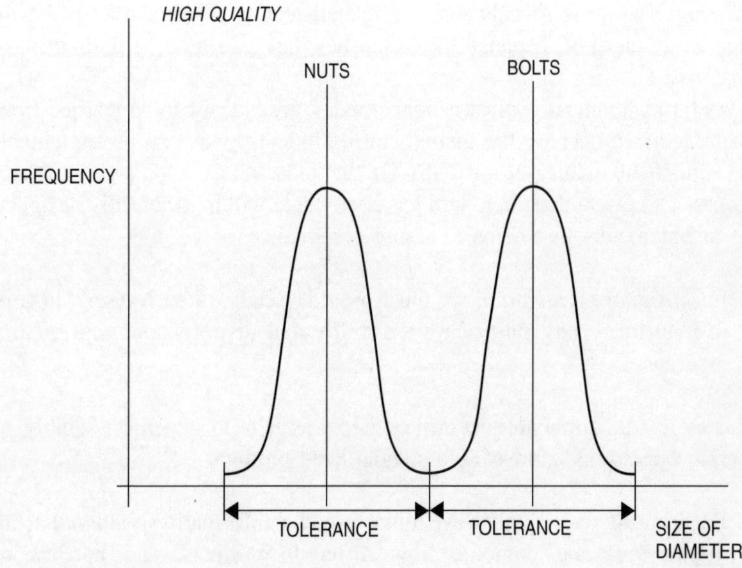

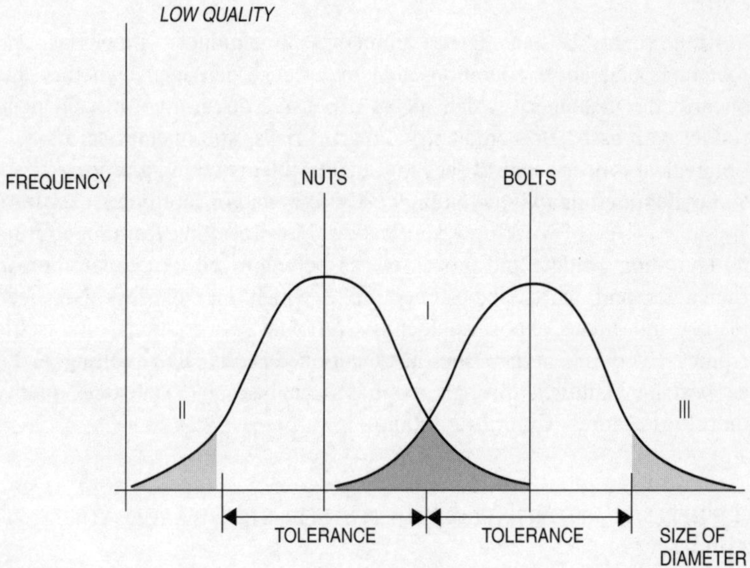

Figure 4.4 High quality means that tolerances are observed at all times; low quality fails to observe tolerances

trend. This is very important for a successful implementation of risk-based auditing: The trend reveals auditing-related secrets which cannot be easily seen in a snapshot, because in a snapshot they can hide behind 'this' or 'that' issue.

As far as financial control is concerned, a great deal can be learned from manufacturing because the manufacturing industry was first in implementing statistical quality control (SQC) methods. Close monitoring of any process can prove that each item has been made within a carefully designed set of parameters that helps to assure compliance:

- For *product certification* we must provide details of each item's history to help trace the chain of responsibility and give 100 per cent quality assurance.

This is just as applicable to critical items as it is to general assembly or service operations addressing a standardized product:

- For control over quality we must use the information gathered from monitoring, and compare how different products, and batches of products, perform.

Real-time analysis can detect anomalies in products, processes and procedures and abort operations that may cause damage – whether this concerns the machinery which incurs expensive down-time or a financial product with associated credit risks, market risks, and operational risks.

Statistical process control sees to it that problems within a process chain can be identified quickly, avoiding costly fixes and/or inordinate exposure. The same is true of workforce verification. Plots resulting from monitoring and recording product and processes can be employed to compare human efficiencies and inefficiencies, determine which line or desk has been creating inordinate exposure, identify problem workstations, and settle disputes. Every one of the issues just mentioned is crucial to auditing, and it can best be identified through risk-based analysts and statistical quality control procedures (Chorafas, 2000a).

AUTHORITY AND RESPONSIBILITY FOR RISK-BASED AUDITING SOLUTIONS

For everything we do, if we wish to succeed, we must develop a sound methodology able to estimate the value, sensitivity, and accuracy of the product or system we are after. This is absolutely true with internal controls, but it is not enough all by itself. Another requirement is to establish the level of authority and responsibility of a risk-based auditing process. These should be defined in a charter, and the chief auditor must seek approval of the charter by the board. This charter should:

- Outline the goal(s) of risk-based audits within the organization,
- Authorize access to records, personnel, and other resources such as databases and
- Define the scope of risk-based internal auditing activities further out in time.

To better appreciate this reference to 'further-out' scope we should recall the comment made by General George Marshall to the nuclear scientists when they presented to the chief of staff of the US military their plans for factories designed for the production of materials for nuclear weapons. Marshall asked one simple question: How many bombs per day were these factories supposed to produce? The bunch of renowned scientists answered that this was not taken yet into consideration, to which Marshall responded that:

- If it is only one shot, it does not really matter how powerful a weapon is.
- The power of the military rests on its ability to continue to deliver.

The same is true of any auditing process, evidently including risk-based auditing and any other type of auditing that matters. The plans for risk-based auditing should definitely reflect the ability to continue to deliver. They should also be consistent with the internal auditing department's charter and with the goals of the organization. This planning process involves audit work schedules, staffing plans, level of technology to be used, and financial budgets. Goals should be:

- Accomplished within specified operating plans and budgets and
- Measurable in terms of deliverables – that is, end-results.

Risk-based audit work schedules detail the activities which are to be audited, when they will be audited, and the exact nature and extent of the audit work to be performed. For instance:

- The precise nature of risk being audited
- Department(s) and people included in the audit
- The amount of financial exposure and potential loss.

Specific requests by senior management may well impact on necessary processes and associated skills on behalf of the audit staff. Staffing plans should make explicit the number of auditors to be employed, their know-how, disciplines required to perform a risk-oriented examination, and tools at their service – including technology tools. Also, the nature and frequency of the activity reports to be submitted to the board and to senior management.

As with all audits, objectivity in risk-based investigations is a mental attitude which should be maintained at all times, in performing the work in question. Reports to the board and senior management should explain the background of basic findings, such as major variances in exposure being taken, and the meaning of these findings. In this connection, SQC charts can be of great service (see below).

Objectivity requires us to perform risk-based audits in such a manner that no quality compromises are made. The general rule is that internal auditors are not to be placed in situations in which they feel unable to make objective professional judgements because there are pressures on them. For instance, it may be that certain managers or professionals may hide information and can get by with procrastination without being sanctioned.

For reasons of professional proficiency risk-based auditing requires a very good appreciation of credit risk, market risk, payments risk, legal risk, technology risk, execution risk, and other risks. Attention should also be paid to the extent of agency costs characterizing the organization (see above). The internal auditing department should assign to each project those persons who collectively possess the necessary:

- Knowledge
- Skills, and
- Disciplines.

Internal auditing should also provide assurance that the technical proficiency and educational background of internal auditors are appropriate for the risk-based audits to be performed. The director of internal auditing should establish suitable criteria of education and experience, giving due consideration to the scope of work and level of responsibility.

The OCC suggests that as risk-based audits spread, the internal auditing staff should collectively possess the knowledge and skills essential to this practice, making, if need be, use of consultants who are qualified in such disciplines as finance, the evaluation of risk and reward, exposure control, statistical quality control, experimental design, engineering, and law.

After a risk-based audit policy is instituted, the chief internal auditor becomes responsible for providing appropriate supervision, including suitable instructions to subordinates. Such instructions should be given at the outset of the audit. He or she must also assure that risk-based audit working papers are maintained and that they adequately support findings and conclusions. Working papers should always be available for control reasons (see Chapter 1).

As a matter of principle, great attention should be paid to audit trails. Since in many computer-based environments audit trails, such as risk-based analyzes and investigations, exist for only a short period of time, the director for audit should give instructions that they are databased. Also, the audit process must move closer to the transactional environment at its entry point into the system . Another requirement is that people involved in risk-based auditing have a say in software development and in system design, to ensure that:

- Knowledge artefacts are on hand to assist in examinations and in datamining
- Fully accurate and complete databases are in place, updated in real-time and
- It is possible to integrate fraud prevention and detection measures into the system.

Because sophisticated solutions create a need for increased reliance on internal controls, internal and external auditors should both periodically and by exception perform comprehensive reviews of internal controls that extend beyond those normally done during the course of a classical audit. An integral part of the methodology advanced by the OCC is to include reviews of internal controls in connection with their ability to monitor the dependability of computer-based solutions – which leads us to the theme of the next section.

PAYING ATTENTION TO INFORMATION REQUIREMENTS FOR RISK-BASED AUDITING

Risk-based auditing has much to do with the premise that the board, the CEO, and senior management are responsible for assuring that systems designed for compliance, risk management, and other critical internal control functions are reliable and are regularly reviewed as well as maintained. Because auditing requirements address not only transactions but also policies, plans, procedures, laws, and regulations, risk-oriented auditing reports should include:

- A brief explanation of why current internal controls track these crucial issues in a dependable manner
- A description of weaknesses found in component parts of the internal control structure
- Any surprises experienced or detected in management's reaction to risk-based findings and
- A track record of immediate corrective action based on previous recommendations.

Risk-based audits should also review the means used to safeguard assets from various types of losses in trading, investing, loans, and other activities; verifying the existence of assets; assuring such assets are allocated where they should be; and evaluating their type, quality and value. Under no condition should a risk-based audit be characterized by lack of attention, time and care – or lack of backbone.

The observance of professional standards is evidently important. This, however, is an issue which should characterize all types of procedures followed by internal auditors and independent public accountants, as well as what they should perform to evaluate transactions positions and records. Therefore, it is not surprising that technology becomes a focal point of interest.

Risk-based audits place a great deal of stress on the information technology used by the institution: networks, databases, workstations, servers, and, most evidently, the accuracy and sophistication of the software being used – including expert systems. They do so in regard to both the state of the art and the connection resources need to focus on the examination of exposure. For this reason, risk-oriented auditors should be computer literate, just as they should understand the overall business environment and how the various accounting systems used in the four corners of the entity relate to one another (see also Chapter 3).

Given that competitive information systems today are based more and more on sophisticated technology, the bank's senior management, internal auditors, and independent public accountants face an urgent need to become well acquainted with computers and models. The better they master interactive computational finance, the better able they will be to make and evaluate decisions about the risks being taken, and the appropriate level of security against fraud and other events.

Because risk-based auditing needs a significant amount of computers and communications technology, there is a likelihood that a risk of computer fraud might be created. Furthermore, since risk-based audit is a new discipline the chief auditor should personally make sure, at least for a reasonable period of time, that reports are accurate, objective, clear, concise, constructive, and timely. Also that there is appropriate evidence to satisfy eventual requests by supervisors that findings are documented.

The OCC suggests that an audit department entrusted with risk-based analyzes and investigations should provide assurance that the work conforms with high standards and that such professional standards are spelled out in the internal auditing department's charter. A quality assurance (QA) programme should include:

- Supervision
- Internal reviews and
- External reviews

Supervision of the work of risk-based auditing should be carried out continually to guarantee there is conformance with standards, policies, and programmes. Performance reviews of processes supported by technology should take place in the same manner, and with the same diligence, as any other internal audit.

External reviews of risk-based auditing should be done to help appraise the quality of the department's operations, executed by qualified persons who are independent of the line organization and who do not have either a real or an apparent conflict of interest. Such reviews should encompass not only skills, but also:

- The reliability and integrity of information being used in auditing and
- The entity's past record of compliance with policies, plans, and regulations.

Among other objectives to be targeted, risk-based audits should ascertain that financial and operating records and reports of the credit institution contain accurate, reliable, timely, complete, and useful information. Also that controls over record-keeping, databasing, datamining, and reporting are adequate and effective:

- Information should be collected on all matters related to the audit objectives and scope of work
- This information should be sufficient, competent, relevant, timely, and accurate.

By 'sufficient information' is meant factual, adequate, and convincing elements so that a prudent, informed person would reach the same conclusions as the auditor preparing a risk-based audit report. Competent information is reliable and typically attainable through the use of appropriate technology, and by means of observing rigorous auditing techniques. Relevant information supports the findings and recommendations of the risk-based audit and is consistent with its objectives. Audit procedures, including sampling and testing techniques employed, should be selected in advance. The same is true about models to be used, including:

- The assumptions sustaining them
- The method of their employment
- The tests of hypotheses being made and
- The milestones to the conclusion and report to the board.

Working papers that document the risk-based audit should be prepared and reviewed by the director of the internal auditing department. These papers should record the information obtained, the analyses made, and the test being used – not only the results. In a factual and documented manner they should support the basis for the audit's findings and recommendations.

A written, signed report should be delivered after the risk-based audit examination is completed. Interim reports may also be needed, issued and transmitted formally or informally. The OCC strongly recommends that the findings of a risk-based audit are discussed at appropriate levels of management in an objective, clear, concise and constructive manner – and followed by corrective action where it is needed. I would add to this conclusion that use of the threat curve discussed in Chapter 3 can be instrumental in visualizing the results of a risk-based audit.

5 A Methodology for Auditing the Internal Control System

INTRODUCTION

The message Chapter 4 has conveyed is that, as a matter of policy, banks should have their internal control system regularly reviewed both by their own auditors and by independent outside parties. This statement is valid for all three major internal control functions: compliance, accounting reconciliation, and risk management (see Chapter 2), as well as many other functions coming under the internal control headline.

While the examiners of the company's internal controls should start at the level of board decisions, it is evident that as auditing proceeds down the organization many functions being analyzed will have their own requirements in terms of special attention to be paid by auditors and other examiners. The reviews of risk management, for example, should focus on:

- The adequacy of risk measurement and monitoring
- Assumptions made and their assessment
- Models and parameter values and
- The methodology being used.

Along with recommendations for improvement, the results of every internal control audit should be reported to senior management and the board, and acted upon in a timely manner. This is a regular process. Companies should review their system of internal control at least annually, and when this is done a number of critical queries must be asked:

- How many incidents have taken place since the last audit regarding compliance?
- Which accounts failed to reconcile? How often? What is special about these accounts?
- Have the limits set by the board been always observed? How many deviations took place? Where did they happen?
- Are risk exposures maintained at prudent levels? Are they being visualized when reported to management?

Queries should particularly centre on how well the methodology which is employed is performing: Are risk measures being taken appropriate to the nature of the exposure? The type of transactions? The contents of the portfolio? Is the security of private information guaranteed? Are board members, the CEO, and senior executives actively involved in the risk management process and in the control of compliance? Among other critical queries the following four are applicable in the majority of cases:

- Are policies and procedures well documented? Are they followed?
- Are the assumptions regarding exposure well documented? Have they been validated?
- Is the auditing staff adequate? Is the risk management staff adequate?
- Is data captured and processed in real-time? Is reporting done online? Is it interactive? Is it comprehensive?

Any change which took place since the last audit should be noted. Have there been any significant changes to the institution's system of internal control during the last two, six, 12 months? Have the most recent recommendations made by auditors and other examiners been enacted? Is there evidence that internal controls are adequate in their current status? Which have been the weaknesses which have shown up since the last review?

Many cognizant executives participating in this research commented that the assessments of internal controls, as required by auditing standards, is a complex job while internal control testing may vary significantly from one company to another – not only between institutions but also from one financial statement assertion to another, even for the same account balance. The betting is that differences stand a good chance of being significant among different account balances.

Because the audit of internal control requires lots of skill but also imagination, as we will see in the next section, a good first step is *discovery* based on diligent research. This is no routine matter. The auditing of accounts should follow principles well defined in Statements of Financial Accounting Standards (SFAS); that is a structured process. By contrast, discovery is *heuristic*. Speaking from experience, both in auditing and in discovery it is likely that the conclusion being reached is only a hypothesis – and we need a first-class methodology to prove it.

DISCOVERY IS THE FIRST MAJOR STEP OF A VALID AUDITING METHODOLOGY

Even when the risks and weaknesses associated with internal control are considered by the auditor as likely to require management action, the auditor may need to perform substantive tests for efficiency reasons and for documentation. An example is an assertion concerning account balances. Verification provides a degree of confidence and it is also a good way of limiting the tests performed *post mortem* when the author's findings are contested by interested parties. Verification also permits concentrating full attention on the weak links in the chain. Verification means testing:

- Through testing, the auditor obtains additional knowledge about the effectiveness of internal controls, or their lack of focus.
- Substantive testing is quite important even if its details might be confusing to third parties.

Some of the senior executives who participated in this research suggested that communicating to third parties the complexity found in the examination of an internal control system might lead to certain issues being misunderstood. But others said that, on the contrary, this process demonstrates how sophisticated the auditing of an internal control system needs to be – and provides evidence that the job has been well done.

Many of the experts whom I met said that in their opinion the best methodology in getting ready for auditing internal controls is similar to that followed by lawyers in their pre-trial preparation. F. Lee Bailey, an American criminal lawyer, puts in this way the benefits derived from doing one's homework:

> My experience has taught me the importance of – in fact, the absolute necessity of – thorough pre-trial preparation … Cases are seldom if ever won in court. They are won by the side that comes into court fully prepared because it has slaved to find the facts of the case before the trial begins. (F. Lee Bailey, 1975)

Quite similarly defects and weaknesses in the internal control system of a financial institution and any other organization, are seldom found while its formal auditing is in process. They are flushed out during *discovery*, the nearest thing to pre-trial preparation, which permits us to identify weak spots, dubious records, conflicts of interest, and other problems – and focus on them when the auditing takes place.

Discovery should not be confused with the *conclusions*. Indeed, there is a significant difference between the two. As shown in Figure 5.1, discovery is analytical, and, up to a point, more rigorous than conclusions. Discovery is an unrelenting research into historical evidence. Turning over stones invariably lets sunlight onto some creatures of the shadows. Borrowing a

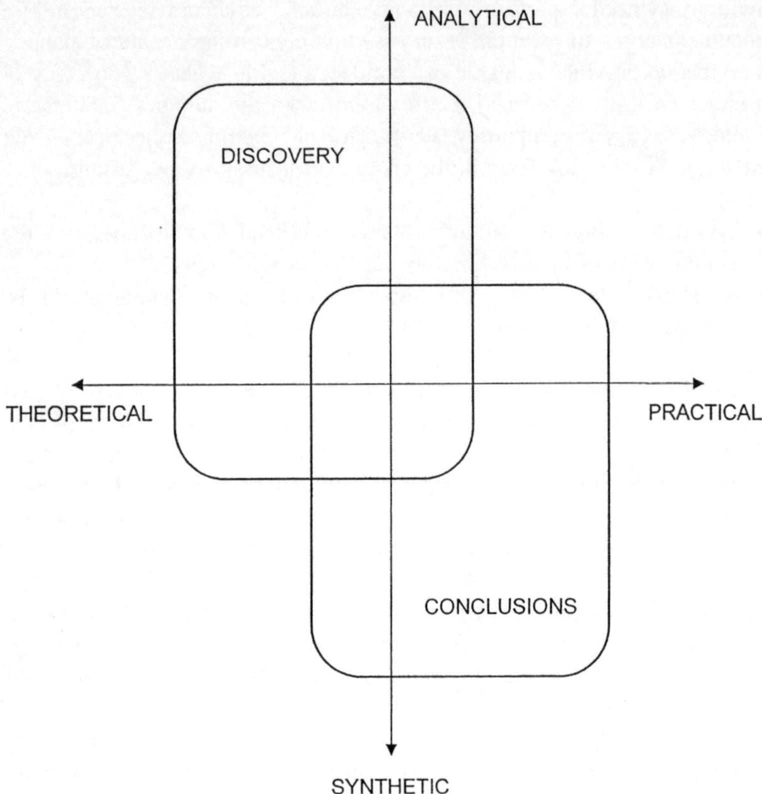

Figure 5.1 Discovery is an analytical process, while legal conclusions are synthetic and practical

lead from the book of criminal lawyers, discovery provides the ability to unearth every element which helps, or even might help, to prove that the counterparty in a litigation:

- Is of bad faith
- Has given false references or
- Has tried to hide its weaknesses through lies.

By contrast, the core matter of conclusions is practical and constructive. The contents of conclusions should be synthetic, building upon the results of discovery. The goal is not only to bring into perspective in a comprehensive way the weaknesses of the counterparty and the soft underbelly of its defences but also to document these weaknesses in a convincing way. It follows, logically, from this explanation that discovery should take place well before entering into conclusions.

Discovery makes it feasible to travel back in time and find out the origin of a decision, of a transaction, or of any other activity. When did that activity take place? Who authorized it? Who made it? And for what reasons? The answer to these questions must be precise, whether the 'who' is a single person or a committee, they are crucial queries which should receive factual answers. A good example on a methodology is provided by Cicero's six evidentiary questions (Marcus Tullius Cicero, Roman senator and orator, 106–43 BC):

- *Who*, apart the person who signed, contributed, or was witness to this action?
- *How* did the person(s) involved, alone or by committee, come to this action?
- *Where* was the evidence which led to the commitment being made?
- *When* was this decision, transaction, or action originally made, and under *which* conditions?
- *What* exactly did the action in question involve? Was the original decision subsequently changed or manipulated?
- *Why* was the decision made, at *which* precise goal was it targeted or intended to avoid? Was there a conflict of interest?

I am indeed surprised how often companies I work with or meet in my research have not thought about asking these queries in relation to important matters, let alone providing factual and documented answers. Not long ago, a major British bank asked its lawyers to comment about legal issues associated with the following critical query: 'Is our risk exposure managed by 50 per cent or 90 per cent?' The lawyers said, 'We don't know' – and this is the most consistent response one gets, in three short words, from every financial institution in connection with this particular query. 'We don't know' is not an acceptable answer by legal counsels:

- Top management has the *right* to know and to be presented with *evidence*, not just words.
- The institution's legal department must respond in a factual and documented manner to the demands being posed.

A similar statement is valid about the auditing department and the results of its examination of the company's internal control system. In a credit institution, for example, much can be learned through focused queries such as the following: Are our credits diversified or concentrated in a few names? How are our credits distributed by our counterparty – By interest rate? By currency? By maturity? What is the pattern of our credits – By credit officer? By branch? By foreign subsidiary?

Other critical queries following the lines of Cicero's seminal work are: Is there any abnormal number of 'weak' credits? Is the same credit officer always dealing with the same counterparty? Is the same derivatives dealer following a repetitive pattern with the same instrument? With the same counterparty? Why is *this* counterparty dealing in billions of dollars in swaps? Is the counterparty a steady user of over-the-counter (OTC) trades or balances with exchange-traded products? What is the net and gross exposure with this counterparty? Is the account executive aware of such exposure? What has he done about it?

When factual and documented answers are obtained to these and similar queries, the auditors can effectively document if there are weaknesses in the company's internal control system and the way it works. Historical evidence is of prime importance in this type of analysis, because there is often the excuse that a certain misadventure is a one-off affair which 'never occurred in the past' and 'is not going to happen again'.

Discovery does away with these silly arguments, because it helps to unearth a pattern of backpedalling and evasion – if there is one. Another value of discovery is that it brings to the fore elements of which we might not have thought earlier in support of our position. It also speaks volumes about weakness in the arguments presented by the opposite party, which eventually lead to the identification of conflicts of interest of which senior management might not have been aware.

AUDITING STRENGTHS AND WEAKNESSES OF AN INTERNAL CONTROL SYSTEM: AN EXAMPLE FROM A MONEY CENTRE BANK

This is a case study based on a real-life audit, made by independent auditors in one of the better-known money centre banks. Let's call this institution: UNIVERSAL. At headquarters, its board was concerned about the likelihood of potential negative changes in the bank's financial position position as a consequence of unexpected or uncontrollable events.

Therefore, the board asked for a new risk management concept to be developed by central operations, in collaboration with senior executives in charge of key divisions, and required this new system is thoroughly audited. The board's directive has been that:

- should be integrated into the new risk management concept Existing internal control principles and systems and
- Prior to its implementation the new solution should be audited by an external independent agent.

The board's wish has also been that from the start and during the development of the new control concept, the independent auditor must be involved in periodically reviewing specifications and tolerances, in order to input additional experience and expertise. Another goal of involving an independent auditor was to provide a third-party assessment of the coherence and practicability of the new management control system under study, step by step.

The project started smoothly but, before too long, it hit resistance because of conflicts of interest. Several divisions of UNIVERSAL wanted to derive concrete benefits from the new system but without giving up information they had traditionally kept close to their chest. Because of this, each new feature became the subject of a trade-off. The independent auditor therefore commented that it was not feasible to try and assess the new risk control concept in absolute terms but, rather, in relative terms – particularly in regard to its effectiveness in supporting:

- The business objectives of UNIVERSAL division by division and
- Its global financial operations as a system, provided this proved feasible.

Centralization and decentralization of internal control activities has been one of the early points of contention. Centralization won and, in terms of an overall architecture, the internal control system under study was more centralized than the one it intended to replace. Responsibility for overall control and monitoring of risk rested with the centre, but at the same time a new notion of 'distributed responsibility' was advanced aimed at maximizing flexibility in controlling risk. This was delegated to the business units.

Even if the concept of centralization prevailed, some of the senior executives at UNIVERSAL objected to this definition, which they interpreted as a dilution of internal control. They were also unhappy about soft-pedalling on internal control information by other divisions than their own. In a curious twist of modern principles, the new concept projected that internal control reports would be submitted in the future monthly rather than weekly, as per current practice.

In fact, the first weaknesses the independent auditor identified concerned the proposed monthly frequency of reporting which, for any practical purpose, limited the scope and extent of internal control information provided by the periphery to the centre. The bank's executives who promoted the slowdown in reporting said that there were major benefits in this approach, but their arguments were not convincing. These arguments were that:

- It observes the decentralized management style of the bank
- It is relatively simple to implement in terms of information technology requirements and
- It poses no need for investment in real-time systems.

This reference to a 'real-time system' has been a curious argument contested by the independent auditor. The fact, however, was that information technology at UNIVERSAL was still (in the mid-1990s) mainframe-based with some 30 million lines of code in COBOL programs. Some of this in-house software was maintained by young programmers who were born after the application programs in reference were written, but the managers of data processing resisted change. To them, even the word 'real-time' was anathema.

The independent auditor was most critical of the fact that the technology necessary for real-time control has been put on the back burner. He demonstrated that UNIVERSAL's information systems were still, to a very large extent, characterized by Palaeolithic concepts from batch processing to personal computers used as non-intelligent terminals. The bank's current systems 'solution' was way behind the state of the art, and incompatible with what the board wished to obtain in terms of a well functioning internal control system.

The independent auditor pointed out that all three premises in the above bullets points were wrong. The reason why the board wanted a new internal control solution was to tighten the reins on risk-taking by the subsidiaries at home and abroad, by means of exercising more timely control. No internal control system which worth its salt is 'simple', and while simplicity is welcome the level of simplicity or complexity of the solution to be chosen must be commensurate with the level of risk being taken.

As a result of these considerations, the independent auditor advised that the proposed approach will neither allow a first-class internal control structure, nor will it permit the short-term dynamic utilization of capital at risk, as some of the divisional executives wanted. Particularly ineffectual would be any attempt to have a frequent and close monitoring of risk positions. When done on a monthly basis this monitoring is an aberration similar to the allocation of risk capital on an annual basis. Yearly allocation of capital at risk and monthly internal control reports are incompatible with the concepts of:

- Dynamic assignment of capital at risk, according to the pulse of the market and
- Tick-by-tick risk control so that top management is ahead of the curve in identification of exposure and corrective action.

The independent auditor particularly underlined the need for a methodology which could truly serve the board's objectives, rather than one which bent over backwards to please those people with invested interest in the status quo. The auditor also suggested that it should be possible to overcome current weaknesses within acceptable time and investment limits, by implementing a solution which allowed the flexible use of new technology rather than depending on old connections.

High technology aside, the audit paid attention to the requirements imposed by a concept of dynamic capital allocation, in line with the board's wishes. The challenge has been one of experimentally defining an amount of risk capital by country, division, and desk as a subset of total available capital at risk at Group level, then allocating such funds to risk types. This approach, the independent auditor suggested, was consistent with the trend currently prevailing at leading institutions.

As a part of the audit of the project's basic concept, the independent auditor proposed that the institution tooled itself up with what it took to do real-time simulation and experimentation, in an effort to provide an adaptable and flexible decision-making process. The audit also underlined that the solution to be chosen should neither encourage overleveraging nor create a risk-averse approach.

Most importantly, the independent auditor said, such solution should be consistent with the culture of the bank and its risk-taking policies. In terms of methodology for risk assessment the auditor brought to the board's attention that the currently prevailing practices limited the level of accuracy in risk assessment. But the way it was projected, the new method would not improve upon this situation. By keeping to batch processing it was heralding 'simplicity of implementation', the benefits to be derived were practically nil.

Between the lines of this case study the careful reader will appreciate the existence of a methodology for auditing strengths and weaknesses of an internal control system, whether this is already in place or constitutes a new development. The first and foremost factor in getting results is top management support. This was practically the only requirement being fulfilled given that the board asked for the audit. The board was, however, misled in regard to the methodology and the mechanics of the implementation as explained in the next section.

THE METHODS OF INTERNAL CONTROL RESEMBLE THOSE OF MILITARY INTELLIGENCE

The point has been made in earlier chapters that different organizations have different ways of looking at internal control. Some see it as a web of responsibilities, others, as a department charged with compliance as its major duty, still others as a system which, while abiding by a conceptual definition of accountability, is largely computer-based. This system uses the services of different other departments with accounting at their core. The outer envelope is high technology, with ample facilities for simulation and datamining. Figure 5.2 integrates these definitions while preserving the high-tech role for all of them.

Take as an example the real-time input which is the lifeblood of any management planning and control system. The data feed for *internal control intelligence* can be effected in two ways which complement one another: A *data collection plan* which reaches every operation, transaction, or position, and leads to the next step: *data collation*. The data collection process can, and should be, supplemented by:

- Datamining of the company's transactional database and of decisions stored in the corporate memory facility and
- Personal interviews which are the only way of reporting on *intentions*, a critical element in intelligence.

Data feeds, datamining, and the results of interviews must be combined into a coherent pattern. 'Collation' is the process of putting together information from different sources which might be far away from one another as well as heterogeneous. For instance, the best bet is that the databases to be mined will be incompatible, and the results of interviews will be primarily qualitative, yet internal control intelligence must benefit from a homogeneous format in its presentation and from quantification of results.

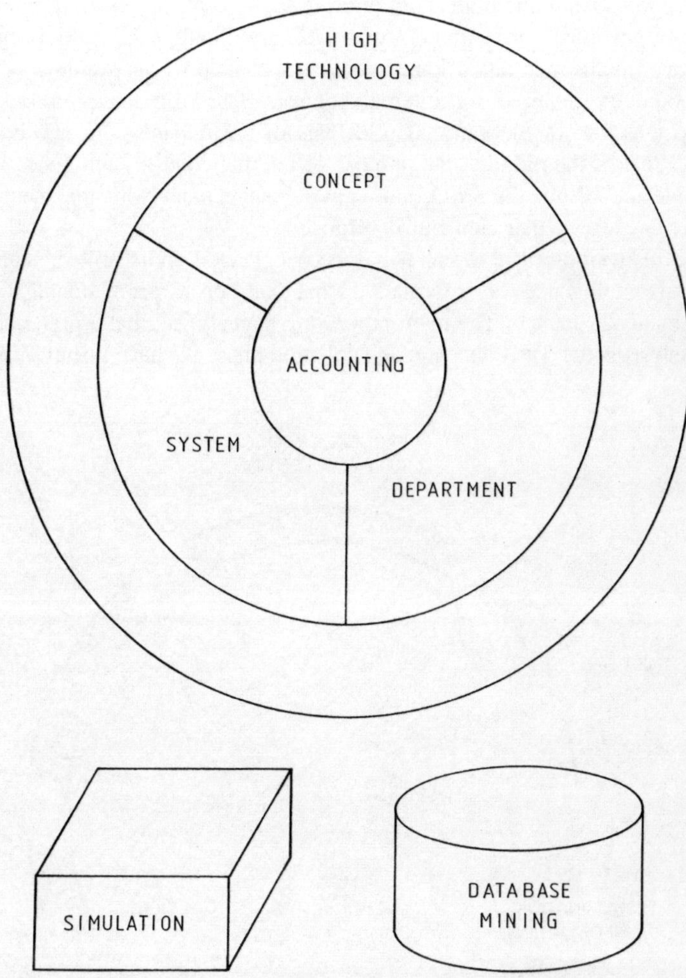

Figure 5.2 There are three ways of looking at internal control, with accounting at the kernel and high technology the outer layer

A crucial aspect of the process of collation is *filtering*. In today's practice any information system is overloaded, with the result the forest may hide the trees. *Data analysis* seeks trends and patterns and these can be developed when there is rapid retrieval and response benefiting from many sources characterized by timely and accurate information elements.

It follows from this brief description that a systems approach to internal control has much in common with military intelligence, and because military intelligence has a long history it can help as an example of the methodology required for internal control. Based on the premise that surprise is one of the cardinal principles of any business, in a way not unlike that of the military, the purpose of internal control intelligence is to provide the board, the CEO, and senior management with the means it needs to exercise that element of surprise.

No matter how and where it has been collected and distilled, internal control intelligence is information that has been professionally and systematically treated. The main processing is analytical, but a prerequisite to analysis is the data collection and collation phase we have just discussed.

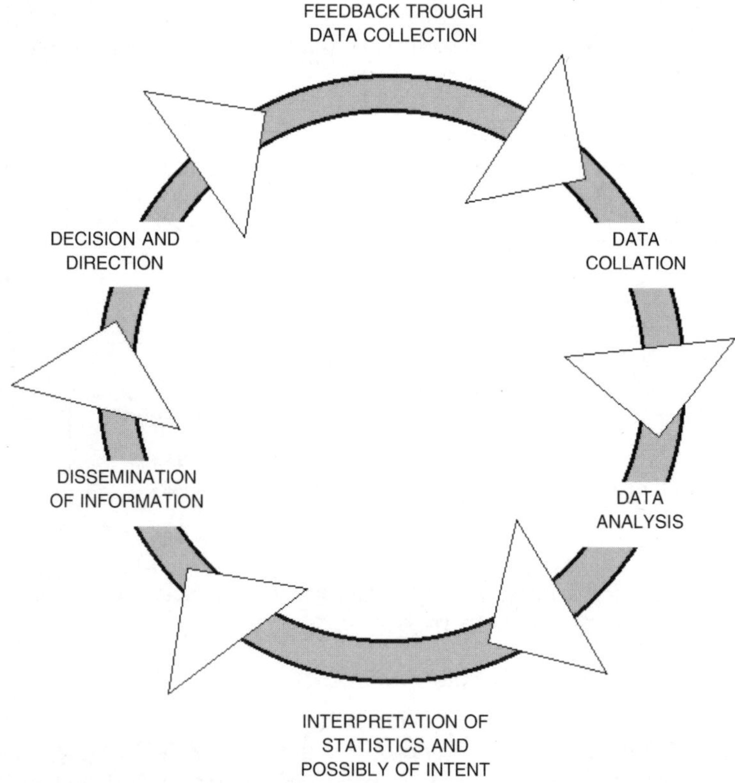

Figure 5.3 The internal control intelligence cycle consists of six major steps

Any solution worth its salt must be enriched with means for interactive presentation, such as those we know from interactive computational finance. Figure 5.3 presents in a nutshell the six major steps constituting this process.

The ability to see through a pattern, and most particularly a dynamic pattern, is most valuable to internal control intelligence because it shows the organization's pulse and leads to estimates of trends (we will see an example with risk analysis later). However, patterns and trends need interpretation of intent. Some clues might have been provided by the auditors and through personal interviews, but several questions typically remain.

Some of these questions have to do with the interpretation of intent; others with *decision and direction*. Between them comes the task of *dissemination* to whomever has the right to know. In the early 1990s as derivatives risk boomed, the board of J.P. Morgan wanted to get a shot at 4.15 p.m. on assumed exposure. From this largely visual presentation came the value-at-risk (VAR) calculation, which was later been prescribed for wider use by the 1996 Market Risk Amendment by the Basle Committee (Chorafas, 1998b). In a nutshell, banks which adopted a strategy of informing daily their top management on exposure aimed to:

- Ensure a comprehensive consideration of risks in conducting business activities
- Achieve a good fit between a current policy of decentralized responsibilities and centralized control
- Provide an information stream able to answer internal control requirements.

A *real-enough-time* (say daily) reporting to the board will be more effective if proper attention is paid to the sophistication of risk management, compliance, and accounting reconciliation activities. Characteristics of companies considered to be at the leading edge is that concepts and systems being developed are driven by a strong need to maximize return on scarce risk capital (see the next section). Accordingly, major investments have been made in areas such as:

- Dynamic limits and group-wide real-time systems and
- Implementation and auditing of a strategic internal control intelligence.

All financial institutions face this challenge of timely dissemination of intelligence. Able approaches to the dissemination challenge are a key target of internal control. In the containment of exposure, for example, what senior management is after is intelligence on *toxic* waste – the further-out aftermath of leveraged derivatives transactions as well as pitfalls existing with other instruments like investments, loans, and guarantees.

A huge amount of exposure is usually assumed to maximize returns without properly counting the risks which come with gearing. In the mid-1990s, for instance, this led to the forced liquidation of a $600 million US fund specializing in toxic waste, specifically the residue of Collateralized Mortgage Obligations (CMOs). The amount of these leveraged deals generated a selling climax in the US bond market and the fund came down in flames as highly geared bond trades got unstuck when the Federal Reserve successively raised interest rates in 1994:

- The gamble on low interest rates was a short-term game for short-term profits in a market which turned sour and got the gamblers unaware of changed winds.
- The markets went into a tailspin because too many players thought they had a lock on the way interest rates were going, and bet their shirt to make fast bucks.

Another example of toxic waste is that absorbed by GE Capital when General Electric sold the remains of Kidder Peabody to PaineWebber. In December 1994, deals which did not enter into the Kidder Peabody portfolio taken over by PaineWebber created for GE Capital, General Electric's finance unit, a rumoured loss of $800 million.

The message to retain from these examples is that internal control intelligence should give itself the mission to take hold of mounting exposure before the red ink becomes a torrent. Typically huge losses are not created overnight. They accumulate over a period of time because of unwise commitments. Limits are broken and nobody in top management knows about them until it is too late. But data analysis and timely dissemination need as a counterparty the ability of the firm's leadership to keep a steady watch, comprehend what is reported, and take immediate action.

INTERNAL CONTROL INTELLIGENCE AND THE CALCULATION OF ASSUMED EXPOSURE

One of the particularities with off-balance-sheet financial instruments is that they are priced through models, and because many of these models, like Black–Scholes, are generally available their usage does not provide pricing headroom for issuers. This means that they have to deduct the monetization of assumed risk out of their projected profit, rather than by putting a premium at issuance at the expense of the counterparty.

This shrinking profit margin weights negatively on the trillions of dollars' worth of derivatives held by banks, insurance companies, mutual funds, pension funds, and other institutions. Until the 1996 Market Risk Amendment, a great deal of exposure assumed with inventoried positions also went undetected, since recognized but not yet realized losses were not recorded in the books the way accounting practice wants it since the fifteenth-century seminal work by Luca Paciolo, the Italian monk and mathematician who in 1494 established the rules followed until today by double entry accounting. See also Chorafas (1995a).

Most often because of the complexity of the derivatives business, the board, CEO, and senior management have no way of knowing what pressures are building up in the market and where a major weakness might be in the positions inventoried by their institution. They don't have this information unless internal control intelligence brings it to their desk through interactive online reporting observant of transparency requirements. A properly tuned framework is necessary to break down *our* institution's exposure by:

- Desk and trader
- Type of instrument
- Counterparty
- Industry and
- Country or geographic region.

Interactive computational finance should make this information available intraday, trader-by-trader, bank-wide, and along any other dimension chosen ad hoc by the end-user. Both tolerance limits and control limits must be shown in the graph. The careful reader will observe that in the upper half of Figure 5.4 the tolerance limit is above the control limit, as should always be the case. The lower half of Figure 5.4 presents the pattern of three traders A, B, C, quite distinct one from the other.

An infrastructure designed to support internal control intelligence will see to it that trading lines and operating units be given responsibility for data collection and collation of local input – a process to be periodically audited. Risk calculation must be done centrally following data analysis which uses:

- Worst-case scenarios and
- The threat curve.

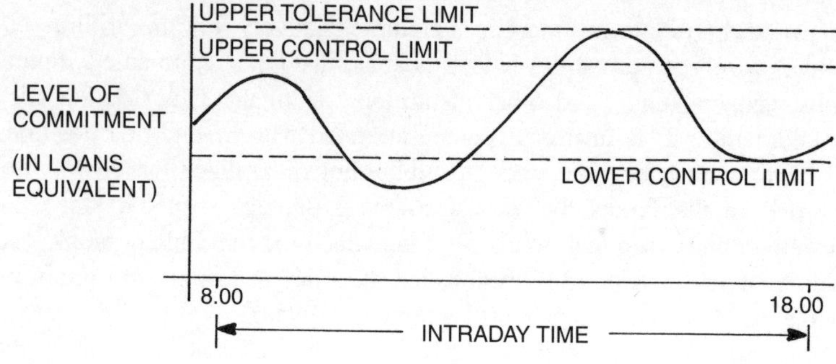

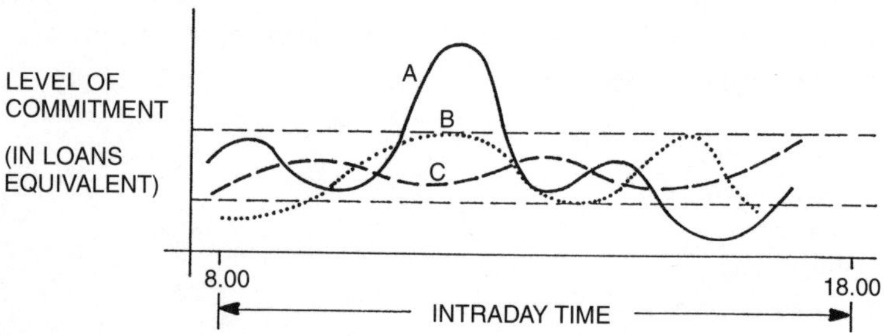

Figure 5.4 Intraday follow-up on exposure, bank-wide and trader-by-trader

The former is based on use of worst-case probability of loss, keeping with generally established practice. As we saw in Chapter 3, the latter follows maximum likelihood. Let me add that the practice of worst-case analysis is subject to lots of exceptions as well as cutting of corners. One of them is *exclusion of risk correlations*. What this means is that correlations between risks are to be ignored in the first phase of defining and implementing risk management because of difficulties in:

- Accurately calculating risk correlations and
- Understanding total risks by inclusion of correlations.

In my book, these are improper excuses. While they are supposed to lead to 'realistic simplifications' (see above), they reduce the accuracy of the method. As such, they are counterproductive and have the drawback of misrepresenting the amount of risk. Therefore, they are underestimating the need for risk capital. Such 'simplifications' become meaningless, if not outright misleading, when *our* company has to face the realities of the marketplace.

Oversimplifications are likely to radically reduce the monetization of risk to be included in transaction pricing. Yet, a significant cost to the institution may result in toxic waste. On the contrary, I look favourably at *net present value* (NPV) accounting (Chorafas, 2000b), for all instruments, which is a leading-edge market practice. The benefits are:

- More accurate management control information and
- Consistency across different business types.

An important element of the discovery phase is the unearthing of what is wanting in transaction pricing – from hypotheses to models, including volatility assumptions. Transaction pricing should be characterized by a comprehensive and flexible system including both the cost of risk and asset costs in the pre-pricing of transactions. Care is needed to ensure that in the calculation of costs:

- There are no assumptions mispricing risk because of wrong hypotheses about volatility, or other reasons.
- But our models do not place our institution at an unjustified competitive disadvantage when pricing low-risk transactions.

This dual objective places upper and lower bounds to the monetization of risk and it can be attained through tolerances. Tolerances, or limits, are based on the loss potential of positions, hence the use of risk capital. The regular reassessment of limits is a 'must' and position reporting to the centre must be steady – done both regularly and ad hoc, as the situation warrants.

The careful reader will recall that I have insisted on the need for real-time data collection and collation, as well as for interactive online reporting. Some of the banks I have worked with as a consultant had the policy of setting limits yearly, then forgetting about them. This is *absolutely wrong* and I never failed to say so. Another practice which should be condemned is that of reporting positions on a monthly basis (see also the case study above). This is nonsense:

- Positions should be reported at least daily; even better, intraday, particularly so when the market is nervous.

- The positions database should be updated in real-time for any instrument and any counterparty anywhere in the world.

In my professional experience I found online real-time handling of information to be most effective in supporting internal control intelligence, and in allowing the dynamic management of tolerances. This makes it possible to maximize usage of capital at risk, while top management can react rapidly to changing circumstances in full knowledge of exposure.

Several senior executives I met during my research underline the benefits to be derived from calculating return on capital at risk. Such a ratio should be computed for *risk units*; for instance, counterparty credit risk. Also for trading lines. On the assumption that trading lines deal with only one clearly dominant risk type, some banks believe that allocating the trading line involves only one risk category. This is not the way to bet.

Simplifications like these turn back our discussion to the issue of risk correlation. Leaving out correlations existing between risks embedded in different instruments might produce what at first sight looks like 'an acceptable solution', but even then the absence of risk correlation must be thoroughly tested.

Other 'simplifications', too, can prove to be unwarranted. Low-technology banks which have lowered their internal control sights compute the ratios they use on the theoretical total risk capital allocated to each business unit. While this approach is relatively simple to implement it definitely:

- Limits the level of information for assessing consolidated return per risk type and
- Makes impossible short-term optimization of consolidated return on capital at risk.

Few companies truly comprehend the weaknesses in the solution they have chosen for risk management purposes, if they have a solution in the first place. They underestimate what it takes in terms of methodology and effort to obtain internal control intelligence, and just hope that through some miracle they will get what they need – but usually are mistaken. Here is a short list of weaknesses I have found in my practice, during the last 15 years, in internal control approaches:

- The system is too slow in data collection and collation
- Adopted analytical approaches leave much to be desired

- Management does not support close day-to-day monitoring of individual and consolidated risks
- There is no way to dynamically allocate capital at risk, to optimize short-term consolidated returns
- The method depends too much on the beaten path and old technology to be efficient.

My recommendation to reduce the impact of such weakness is to concentrate first and foremost on the most crucial, widespread, and significant risk types. The first priority is that of rigorous analytics. The second, a cost/benefit study of investing in a real-time system. The combination of the two would allow a flexible use of counterparty limits and tolerances for instrument exposure in all business units and regions. Being penny-wise makes no sense when institutions bet their future with new financial instruments.

INTERNAL CONTROL INTELLIGENCE AND DYNAMIC COMPUTING OF CAPITAL REQUIREMENTS

Internal control intelligence, the dynamic computation of minimum capital requirements, and auditing of assumed risk correlate. Classically, minimum capital requirements constitute an instrument of banking supervision used to ensure that proper reserves are in place in each credit institution with regard to its business operations. This is primarily done in connection with:

- *Credit risk*, which has been the traditional reference frame
- *Market risk*, implied by the 1996 Market Risk Amendment
- *Operational risk*, whose capital requirements will most likely follow the 1999 New Capital Adequacy Framework (Chorafas, 2000d).

A comprehensive view of major risks will involve correlation between any two of these bullets points, and all three of them. This is shown in Figure 5.5 in connection with credit risk, market risk, and operational risk (see also Chapter 2). My bet is that in the coming years operational risk will cover the whole operational environment in which management of other risks takes place, because it infiltrates into these other risks even if for no other reasons than that:

- The skill of managers and professionals, or lack of it
- The ever more present impact of technology and
- Execution risk which enters into any transaction (Chorafas, 2001b).

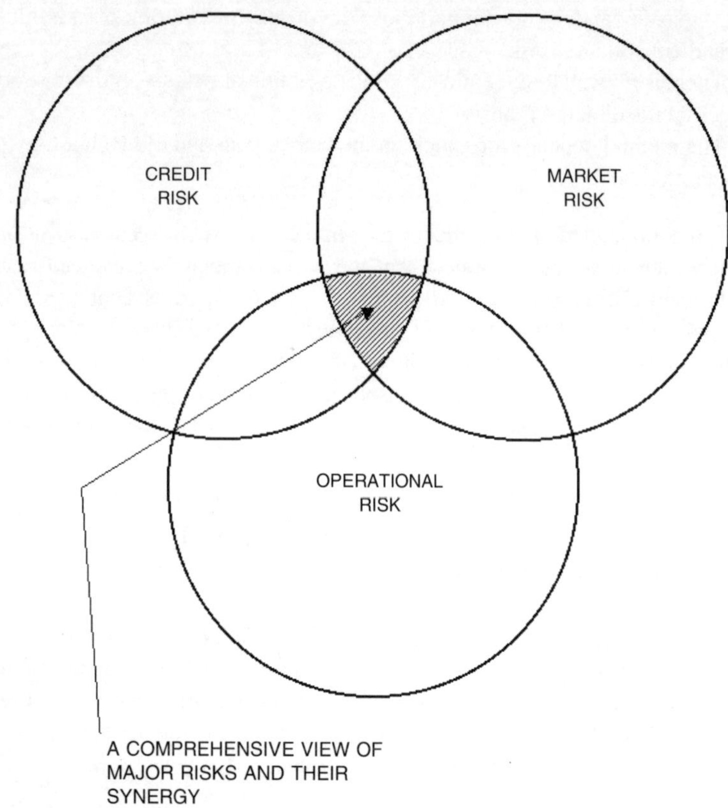

Figure 5.5 There are common elements in different types of risk: with new instruments, these should be addressed on the drawing board

Barings crashed owing to failure of market risk management within a failure of operational risk management. It is easy to project a similar interaction of operational risk with credit risk. This leads to the concept that even the best credit risk and market risk control systems exist by necessity within an environment of operational risk control. Regulators are justified in wanting capital requirements for operational risk; the problem is there are not yet clear ideas about the method.

Minimum capital requirements for each major category of exposure are of interest not only to the regulators but also to the board and the CEO. They are, therefore, a legitimate issue to be included in internal control intelligence. The previous two sections pressed this point; they also presented to the reader a methodology for implementing the notions which I describe here.

A special concern connected with minimum requirements is regulation of the responsibilities on the bank's management at all levels. The emphasis placed on senior management responsibility by reserve banks and other supervisory authorities makes it clear that even those executives who are not directly responsible for risk management must be accountable for:

- Assuring the proper organization and monitoring of trading, investing, lending, and other activities throughout the operations of *our* institution and
- Establishing appropriate organizational measures and analytical tools, necessary to keep compliance always actual and business risks under close supervisory control.

The internal control aspect of this area is further enhanced by the fact that banking regulators increasingly require that they are informed of manipulations by disloyal staff. Fraudulent massaging of information by individual staff members, at any level in the organization, are an indication of internal control flaws which can threaten the institution's viability both in the short and in the longer term.

Timely and accurate notification enables the supervisory authorities to take appropriate measures in time. Senior management, however, has the greatest interest in taking a comprehensive view of risks through fast feedback by means of internal control intelligence, followed immediately by corrective action. This must be done well before the regulators need to be informed.

The methodology the previous section advised, together with real-time system support, will assist these requirements in a very significant manner. The same methodology will be instrumental in seeing to it that transactions are concluded only on terms that are in line with internal limits and risk tolerances, the latter being dynamically adjusted to reflect constraints in capital at risk and external market conditions,

Transactions at prices or rates out of line with limits and market conditions invariably play a major a role in spectacular cases in which banks run into difficulties. This statement remains valid even if creative accounting is used to arbitrarily shift losses (or profits) to other accounting periods or falsify financial statements. As a Chinese proverb says 'lies have short legs'.

Reliable financial reporting is a hallmark of well managed companies (Chorafas, 2000a). It is also valid regarding the observance of sound organizational principles. Many banks are well aware of the significance of a clear functional and organizational separation of trading activities from the other operations such as back office processing, accounting, and monitoring. Somehow, however, management fails to effectively implement the necessary separation of duties and responsibilities.

Whether we talk of compliance, accounting reconciliation, reliable financial statements, or observance of sound organizational principles, solutions cannot come by means of lip service. For instance, the principle of a separation of functions has to be ensured by top management decisions, appropriate procedures, and safeguards – plus the feedback provided by internal control intelligence.

This reference to procedures, safeguards, and internal intelligence is valid not only in the bank's country of origin but also abroad, wherever *our* institution operates. It is also crucial in connection with both local information technology and cross-border teleprocessing, including computer-based trading systems and their software. Attention must also be paid to the fact that the distinction between processing and accounting is not so clear-cut, and in a number of cases this has led to fraud.

Based on personal experience and the results of intensive research, the examples which I give will help in documenting that it is part of top management's responsibility to assure there is in place a rigorous process for measuring, analyzing and, monitoring. Monitoring chores should address both what happens and what *does not* happen but *should have* taken place:

- Executives who are worth their salt appreciate that both *events* and *non-events* are important for good management reasons
- A meaningful pattern leading to the interpretation of intent can be developed only when we know the outliers and missing points.

The concepts presented by these two bullet points further substantiate my advice that all critical information must be reported daily – and, even better, intraday. Also that while necessary it is not sufficient to ascertain that management believes in performance control. Performance evaluation must be sustained through internal control intelligence. Senior management should:

- See to it that it receives the results of a steady review process and is involved in further development of the internal control system and

- Gets involved in the test phase of new internal control solutions, at least for high-risk transactions, new products, and new markets.

This places heavy demands on the management of credit institutions. The reader should, however, appreciate that these demands are in line with the Basle Committee's risk management guidelines, including their emphasis on internal control, the setting of limits, use of models, and observance of risk tolerance criteria.

Personal accountability of board members, the CEO, and senior management is increased by the fact that management control requirements are never static. While some companies do have in place effective risk measurement and limits systems, there is documented evidence that the majority of banks are not yet in a position to implement and operate a real-time uniform integrated solution for the entire institution – the way it has been explained in the previous section and this section.

SYNERGY NECESSARY BETWEEN BUSINESS UNITS TO MAKE INTERNAL CONTROL A REALITY

Because this chapter has seriously questioned the skill and determination of senior management in implementing an effective internal control system, Part II will start with a focused view on requirements and responsibilities connected with internal control at policy-making level. Designed as a bridge between Part I and Part II, the present section is a preview of what will be discussed, with particular emphasis on the synergy which should characterize the functions and responsibilities of *our* company's divisions, departments, and independent business units among themselves.

Policies established by the board in connection with internal control and technological infrastructure should act as catalyst in providing this synergy. As a matter of principle, the task of real-time capturing, collating, analysis, interpretation, and reporting of risk for all and every type of *transaction* must be entrusted to a member of senior management who has no direct responsibility for day-to-day trading activities. In my book (Chorafas, 2001), this is the role of the Chief Risk Management Officer (CRMO).

The CRMO should work together with the Chief Credit Officer to assure that not only there is accurate, timely, and detailed reporting to board members, but also that all senior managers are informed at least daily of risks and performance trends in individual business areas. Therefore, as I never tire repeating, a system must be in place to immediately draw everybody's attention to:

- Overshooting of limits
- Unusual events or deals and
- Events which should happen but do not.

It is absolutely wrong to believe that when the CEO, or any other member of senior management, has given an order this order will be executed. Harry Truman used to say that the greatest of all the frustrations of the executive office was to see that nothing happened after he gave an order. Napoleon had a policy of personally controlling whether his orders were put into effect by those people responsible to act on them.

This feedback on timely and proper execution of orders is in my judgement, a key element in the internal control armoury, and it is inseparable from the responsibilities of the board (see also Chapter 7 below). The purpose of strengthening it through financial technology is to keep management informed of all risky transactions in order to prevent lax attitudes to order execution as well as abuses or cover-ups. And in order to ensure that both expected and unexpected risks are followed up steadily.

For instance, the manager responsible for a certain product or trading activity is totally accountable for controlling this activity on the basis of comprehensive and detailed operational feedback. This must be done on a regular basis. On one side is the fact that new products, new markets, and other new developments should undergo a *test phase* on a readily manageable scale. On the other, prudential supervision does not end with tests; it is an ongoing process at execution level.

Front desks, back offices, risk controlling units, auditing, information technology, and other functions should always work in synergy well beyond the test phase. Regular involvement in internal control should lead to thorough and accurate computer-based documentation, which can be periodically audited. This helps to attest:

- The existence of qualified staff
- Appropriate observance of guidelines and procedures
- Properey established feedback channels and auditing practices.

Furthermore, as I have already underlined several times, the information technology solution to be adopted must be commensurate with the financial products in which *our* bank trades or invests, market conditions, risks being taken, the determination of limits, and positions and results and changes in the operating environment. In addition, there are auditing needs, which tend to get more complex.

The reader's attention has also been drawn to the fact that a significant part of auditing should be done online through database mining. Audit reports must be interactively available to all authorized members of management. Defects must not only be remedied systematically and promptly, but also weighted and re-allocated through an internal system of *demerits*. For a number of companies, this is a cultural change because in most cases shortcomings identified by internal auditors are not remedied speedily, nor are they reflected in the record of those responsible for the failure(s). Therefore, internal control requirements must prescribe what should happen concerning:

- Defects not immediately remedied and
- Recommendations not yet implemented.

Delays are punitive to the company and to the majority of its people. 'Delays' mean anything beyond a prescribed short timeframe for corrective action. It is also wise that the tasks of internal auditors should be specified in the company's rules and bylaws. Since Chapter 1 the point has been made that effective internal auditing is one of the key instruments for detecting and remedying undesirable developments, whether in internal control or in any other function. We will look further into this issue in Part II.

Part II
Management Appraisal of and Accountability for the Internal Control System

6 Senior Management Responsibilities for Internal Control

INTRODUCTION

The best way to value differentiate a business enterprise is to consider if the company, its products, and its services solve a problem, or make someone else's life easier. A product or service helps in solving a problem if not only other companies and people need it but are also ready to pay for it. At the same time, because many products and services involve risk, the company must be able to take hold of its exposure(s), including the risk of non-compliance to rules and regulations.

This paragraph encapsulates to a considerable extent the sense of 'wealth management', as distinct from an accumulation of wealth not constrained by prudential guidelines. In a memo to himself, Andrew Carnegie once said that the amassing of wealth is one of the worst species of idolatry. He then added that to continue much longer overwhelmed by business cares and with most of his thoughts wholly upon the way to make more money in the shortest time, must destroy his self-esteem beyond hope of permanent recovery.

According to Carnegie, wealth management is not a race but an orderly procedure which abides by self-imposed tolerances, as Part I has documented. In the broadest possible sense, senior management responsibilities in an enterprise are practically synonymous with the administration of wealth, and fulfilling such responsibilities requires plenty of attention, including:

- The policy of deciding only after one thinks about the likely aftermath of his contemplated decision(s) and
- The self-assurance to stand firm in spite of complaints or adversity, as a well studied plan is executed.

Internal control is to a company what self-control is to a person. Prior to globalization and deregulation, internal control (as discussed in the preceding five chapters) used to be a rather minor field in credit institutions, and it was often unheard of in other companies even if they had a certain awareness of the desirability of management control. But with globalization, deregulation, innovation, and technology the market became dynamic and management found out the hard way that:

- Practically every enterprise involves risks which must be controlled in a systematic manner through policies, tools and personal accountability and
- These risks are partly similar and partly different from those of other companies, even in the same sector of the economy, because they reflect both internal and external conditions.

Risks must be controlled for the survival of *our* company, and this should be done in a way which is both regular and efficient. The board must set internal control standards; define and develop detailed policies; establish risk tolerance levels; and ensure the company has in place a system for identifying, measuring, monitoring, and reporting all kinds or types of exposure.

Companies which lack internal control culture and the appropriate system for internal control intelligence, experience difficulties in finding anybody – even in the higher reaches – who has the necessary sense of personal accountability. Invariably these are the companies which drive themselves to extinction. Audits done at the 12th hour or as a post mortem reach conclusions about the top management's ethics and behaviour which are interesting to read but useless in terms of damage control.

Eventually the *stakeholders*: shareholders, employees, customers, suppliers, and other business partners, will be the losers. They will find to their dismay, and that of others looking for firm business leadership, that the company is dead in the water because both ineptness and conflicts of interest interfered with its day-to-day activities and its longer-term plans. Accountability is always taking leave when internal control is wanting.

LEGAL REASONS WHY INTERNAL CONTROL MUST BE MANAGED

The principle on which this book is built is that internal control does not come as a matter of course: it must be *managed*. This is a responsibility of the board of directors which must be exercised not through a raw demonstration of power but as an energizing theme and sign of good conduct. A well oiled internal control system is a sign that management responsibilities have found a fifth gear.

Take top management responsibility for reliable financial reporting as an example. In the United States, management accountability for the accuracy of the bank's financial statement is established under both federal statute and common law; it both a personal and a collective responsibility. An interesting precedence was the *Atherton* v. *Anderson* case (1938), when the Sixth Circuit Court of Appeals held a bank's directors liable because the CEO had falsified the institution's financial reports.

Since then, the directors' accountability has been institutionalized. During the late 1980s, the Federal Deposit Insurance Corporation (FDIC) has brought to court a number of suits against bank directors, because of negligence in supervising the conditions and statements of banks that had failed. Though not all court suits were successful, the original 1938 jurisprudence has been reinforced.

The US Congress has also passed legislation which strengthened the control of illegal practices by bank management. Examples from the 1990s are the Federal Deposit Insurance Corporation Improvement Act (FDICIA); the Foreign Corrupt Practices Act (FCPA); the Financial Institutions Reform, Recovery, and Enforcement Act (FIRREA); and the dreaded Racketeer Influenced and Corrupt Practices Act (RICO).

Each one of these Acts impacts in an important way on what can be perceived as malpractice. With FDICIA, for instance, external auditors have been directed to attest to management's assertions regarding the effectiveness of internal control, as well as the compliance with safety and soundness laws. External auditors are responsible for reporting:

- Instances of non-compliance and
- Weaknesses in internal control.

Though external auditors have no specific duty to regulators at the commissioning end, the external auditors' opinion on financial statements is heard by supervisors in all countries. In the case of the United States, United Kingdom, Germany, and Switzerland the external auditors' opinion on internal controls is not only welcome but requested by the regulators. The legal infrastructure compels external auditors to be most inquisitive while studying the bank's financial reports.

Because sooner rather than later weaknesses will come to the fore, prudent management of the institution's internal control policies and practices is in the board members' best interest, not just as directors but also as individual citizens accountable for their actions. New laws and regulations see to it that directors can no longer hide from operating management's malpractice or outright bankruptcy:

- Supervisory authorities – and, to a significant extent the courts – tend to think that bankruptcy *was* the plan and
- Directors must appreciate that it is better to amputate a leg, if it is unavoidable to do so, than to sit on a financial corpse.

I would go further than that by stating that it is better to amputate a leg in one single operation than to lengthen the process by cutting off four inches at a time. For this reason, it is a sound policy for both internal and external auditors to dig diligently into the differences between reported values and fair values, including underlying facts and circumstances which might account for such differences – bringing to top management's attention all the discrepancies they find.

The target must be to establish in a factual and documented manner if internal control intelligence and an audit's findings constitute a material difference in financial statements. In consequence, irregularities involving senior management and material differences established at any level in the organization should be reported directly and in a timely fashion to the board's Audit Committee which has the responsibility to act (see Chapter 1).

Some executives commented, during my research, that the fact internal auditors are employed by the company and external auditors are remunerated directly also by the company they advise, can raise questions about the independence of their judgement. True enough, there seem to be some cases of that type. This is an argument particularly pressed by liquidators of bankrupt enterprises who brought certified public accountants to court for damages because of failure to disclose weak financial conditions; but it is not proper to generalize.

Furthermore, in connection with American financial institutions the Federal Reserve, FDIC, Office of the Comptroller of the Currency (OCC), Office of Thrift Supervision (OTS) and Securities and Exchange Commission (SEC) use their own examiners. In contrast to external auditors, bank examiners working for supervisory agencies tend to take a deeper and more sceptical view of assets, liabilities, financial reports, and management quality. They are also more inquisitive when they feel that they confront a bank of:

- Questionable financial condition, or with
- Unreliable financial statements.

Central bankers and regulators are concerned about system risk not only by looking at exposure figures post mortem. They are also very helpful in providing the institutions they supervise with appropriate tools for proactive measurement of exposure. One of the best examples I found in my research is the method the OTS uses to keep control of the thrifts' exposure owing to interest rates. This method is based on minimum net portfolio value (NPVR) and it has has given excellent results in terms of thrift survivability, as Figure 6.1 documents.

The careful reader will remember that Part I made reference to the OTS method by stating that it requires different scenarios represented by immediate parallel movements in the term structure of interest rates of plus and minus 100, 200, and 300 basis points – *as if* these were permanent. In reality, they are deviations from actual term structure. Table 6.1 presents an illustration of limits and minimum permissible NPVR:

- For each interest rate change listed in column (1), the institution's NPVR should fall to no less than the level shown in column (2).
- For evident reasons, NPVR limits in Table 6.1 are more demanding in falling interest rates than in rising interest rates.

Like the examples we have seen in preceding chapters, the limits shown in Table 6.1 represent a useful reference frame. They can provide a greater degree of comparability across institutions (or independent business units of the same bank) than achieved through previous measures. They also mesh better with guidelines established by OTS for sensitivity to market risk component rating.

A bank's NPVR for a given interest rate scenario is calculated by dividing the net portfolio value that would result in that scenario by the present value of the institution's assets in that same scenario. The NPVR is expressed in percentages and it is analogous to the capital-to-assets ratio used to measure regulatory capital. NPVR, however, is measured in terms of economic values (present values) on a particular interest rate scenario.

NPVR limits are chosen so as to reflect the board's expectation that the bank should perform better with falling interest rates. The set of limits will typically require frequent review and adjustment by the board. This summarizes the underlying methodology. It also outlines the kind of internal control intelligence required, so that the institution's overall control over exposure continues to operate in a dependable way.

This example on prudential supervision of interest rate volatility is one among many which document that even if there were no other reason for

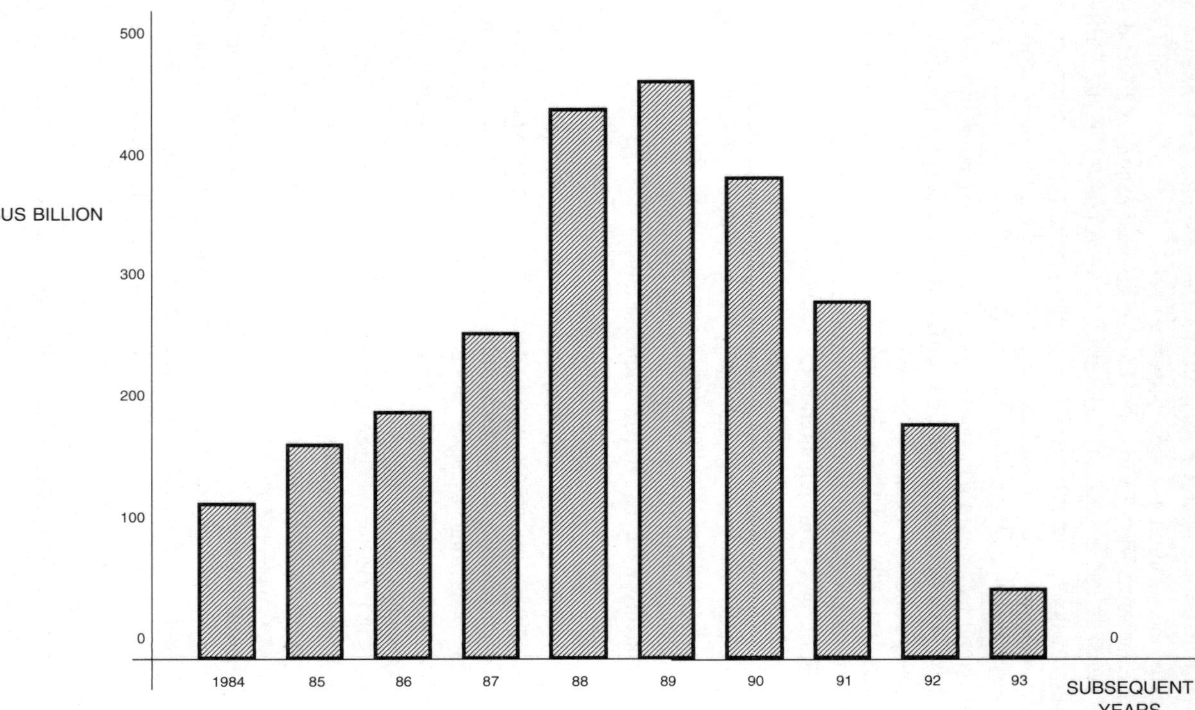

Figure 6.1 The policy of the OTS has borne fruit: no thrift failures since 1993

Table 6.1 NPVR limits in connection with changes in interest rates

Changes in market Interest rates (basis points) (1)	**Minimum permissible NPVR (per cent) (2)**
+300	10
+200	11
+100	12
0	13
−100	14
−200	15
300	16

managing internal control with an iron hand, and there are plenty, the fact that in the 1990s regulators made the quality of internal control a focal issue of their examination should make directors and CEOs think twice before adopting a lax attitude. They should also appreciate that while it is essential it is not enough to state that responsibility for internal control starts at board level. The whole system of management control must be thought out – and it must make sense.

Let me give an example of what I consider to be weak practice. 'The executive board and the risk council are in charge,' said the senior executive of a major institution. Then he added 'the risk council meets every fortnight' which pulls the rug from under the previous statement that the board and the risk council are in charge. A fortnight is an aeon in a dynamic market. The bank can go belly up in a couple of weeks: look at Barings.

As if this leisurely pace was not enough of a negative, the senior executive in question rushed to add that the risk council's mission is to address market risk and operational risk, but not credit risk which is the domain of a different unit. In other terms, there is split responsibility leading straight into the law of unintended consequences so well expressed by Murphy: 'Anything that can go wrong, it will!'

EFFECTIVE INTERNAL CONTROL REQUIRES TRUSTWORTHY PEOPLE

Because organizations are made of people, it is to people that we have to look for trustworthiness. Siegmund G. Warburg (1902–82) used to give a good example of how trustworthy people are brought up since childhood through a reference to the family of his mother. When she was young her father told her: '[If] you need to choose between two courses, ask yourself first of all which is the most difficult – because that's the one which will prove to be the better one of the two' (Attali, 1985).

The character of individuals really shows up when they are confronted by difficult times and adverse conditions. 'Most of the triumphs of people faced with adverse conditions are won by the person's character rather than his intelligence', Warburg advised his friends, customers, associates and assistants, adding that: 'High quality people find it more easy to pardon others than to pardon themselves.' The careful reader will remember the reference made in the Introduction, that internal control is to a company what self-control is to a person.

Correctly, the great banker had perceived that the worst that can happen to any organization is 'auto-satisfaction', because it leads to negligence and to lack of interest in what one does. That's exactly when internal control is at its lowest – and with it each individual executive's self-control. One of the ironies of human nature is that people are either overdemanding of themselves or oversatisfied with themselves. The first are those who contribute to progress. 'Who faces great challenges is the real winner in life', as Siegmund Warburg was to suggest.

Can this brief description of business ethics help in evaluating the personality traits which should characterize board members and CEOs? The answer is: 'Yes!' In my book, the most common qualifications necessary for membership of the board of directors are the ability to preserve and protect the company's assets, augmented by professional expertise in both perceiving opportunities and controlling risks. The problem is that in many cases the requirement of professional expertise is not clearly spelled out. Generally, however, this is interpreted as the ability by board members to bring to fruition in their organization a variety of skills and experiences, including:

- Ethical values promoted by means of repeated personal examples
- Awareness, understanding, and observance of laws and regulations and
- Consultancy skills in business opportunity analysis in specific fields, not only at large.

Typically, board members head organizations which are active in similar or complementary walks of industrial and financial life. Though some people maintain that expertise in a given industry is not critical to the director's job or even at CEO level, my statistics and experience demonstrate that it is indeed quite crucial. It is therefore regrettable that most organizations do not take care to describe, much less define, what makes a good director in *their* environment; inor is it easy to find somewhere the answer to the questions:

- What are the most important personality traits which make a good director?
- What should *our* organization expect from people qualified for board membership?

In a world characterized by steady and often profound changes general traits can be misleading, but there is at least one common denominator which might be worth considering. This is the board member's ability to examine the critical factors that affect organizational survival, including the capability to forecast, introduce, and manage *change*. Like internal control, change has to be managed.

I would be pushing at an open door to say that ours is an age characterized by technological progress which outpaces anything we have known ever before. But technological progress is only one side of the coin. Globalization, innovation, and market dynamics are the other sides; with market dynamics leading to non-linearities many people find difficult to comprehend. Every company, from the simplest to the most sophisticated, lives and operates in an environment in steady evolution. No board can successfully manage its company's business if its members:

- Permit themselves to get obsolete or
- Distance themselves from steady innovation.

Innovation takes place in the market in quick succession to what happens in the laboratory. Shrinking the time-to-market is most important to survival. Therefore, the personalities of members of the board must be tuned to the management of change. After all, their knowledge, information, drives, decision styles, and, on the bottom line, the strategies and tactics they choose and follow, make the corporate culture. They also affect the life cycle of their organization.

Beyond the ability to manage change, board members must have background and experience enabling them to guess accurately the direction of coming events. The effectiveness of implementing change depends on qualifications for which no theoretical models can be developed or current instruments for measurement and monitoring effectively used. While the quality of management is most critical to every company, it is not easily quantifiable, if it is quantifiable at all.

Together with analytically qualifiable personality traits and decision-making styles, a critical characteristic of board members is their ability to live with their time and be somewhat ahead of the curve. Computer literacy is a good example from the 1980s and 1990s, but today it is not the only one. Equally crucial is the willingness to keep ourselves and our own level of knowledge in steady evolution. This requires *lifelong learning*, but also presupposes the will:

- To remain active
- To be involved and
- To look after detail.

None of these three bullet points has a unique interpretation. Its meaning and significance is influenced by the state of development in which a company finds itself: start-up, growth, maturity, or decline, along the ogive curve shown in Figure 6.2. General Motors in the 1920s was a growth firm, today it is one in decline. The maturity/decline curve is never the same for all organizations; each has its own characteristics like the *A* and *B* trends shown in Figure 6.2.

In their early stages organizations are often animated by thinkers with a lot of imagination. In the Standard Oil empire, John D. Rockefeller, its originator and animator, was a thinker. He conceived the idea of commercializing oil moving from wholesale to retail – and invented the means for making this possible. By doing so, he created a market which had never before existed.

During the growth phase of Standard Oil, however – and most particularly the consolidation which followed as the oil industry approached maturity – organizational skills became more important than new ideas. Without organization skills, the company would have fallen apart. Such skills were provided by John Rockefeller, Jr, the son of the founder who led the company into its maturity phase and established it as a global corporation which ran like clockwork.

The work ethics, efficiency, and training policy followed by John Rockefeller, Jr, can be best appreciated through an example. In the mid-1960s I met Dr David Rockefeller in the course of a project on the brain drain I was doing at that time (Chorafas, 1968). Dr Rockefeller was saying

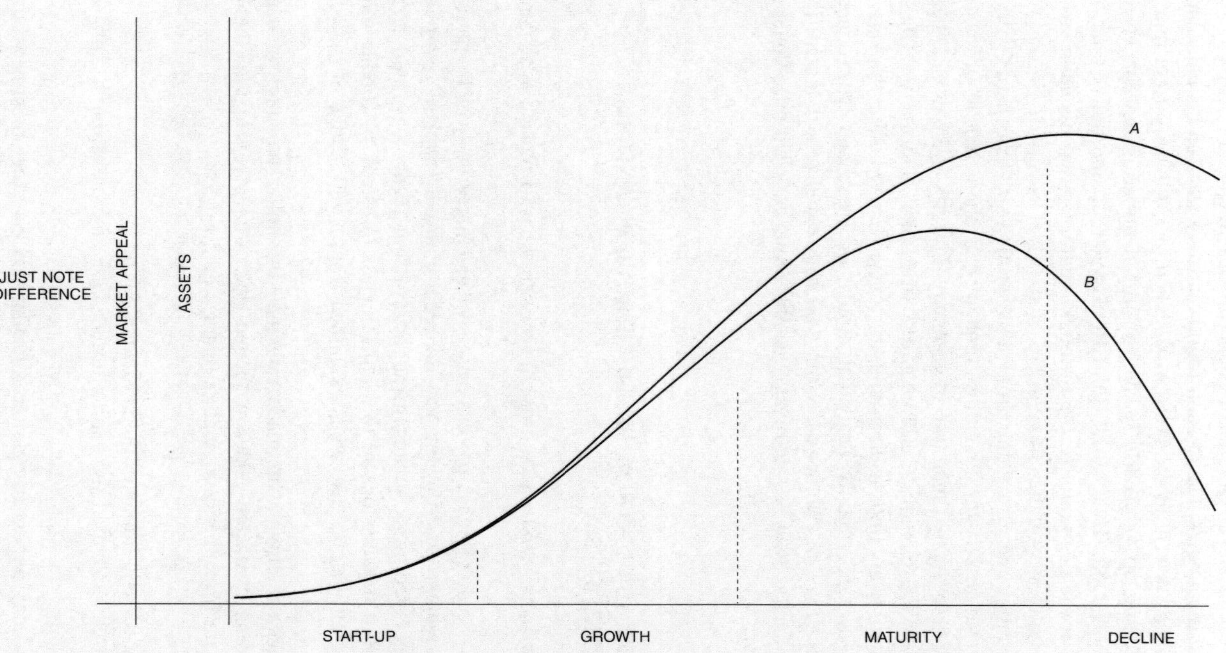

Figure 6.2 The life-cycle of a business passes through successive phases, each requiring specific skills

that his father wanted all of his children to learn the value of money. Therefore he never gave them pocket money; they had to earn it.

As the youngest, David soon found that his sister and his elder brothers had taken care of all the housework. Therefore, for his pocket money he was getting up very early in the morning distributing newspapers in the neighbourhood. That's how, John Rockefeller, Jr, the richest man in the world at the beginning of the twentieth century raised his children – and that's how every father should.

The message to retain from this section is that hard work and trustworthiness is the first most fundamental characteristic of successful people at large, and therefore of company directors and CEOs. Other add-on characteristics are to a large extent situational, and many relate to the time a company finds itself in in its life cycle. It may be that thinkers are in prime demand, mainly analytical minds; or organizers with conceptual qualifications; or company doctors who can revitalize a dying institution. But it may as well be that other specialist skills are what one should really be after.

INTERNAL CONTROL, PRODUCT REVIEW, AND RISK ASSUMPTIONS

'In our bank,' said a senior executive with whom I met on Wall Street,

> we hold regular product review meetings in which participate representatives from finance, the legal counsel, [market] risk management, credit risk management, information technology, and taxation. One of the missions of these meetings is to establish whether the new product makes sense when examined from a wide range of viewpoints.

Another executive who made reference to similar meetings of a cross-functional character, added a second goal: that of evaluating the likely exposure from this new product under a dual aspect:

- Normal conditions of market behaviour and
- Extreme events if the market turns against the prevailing hypotheses.

Subsequent to these discussions a broker said that since most new products are personalized, as a matter of policy in his firm any new product is accompanied by the analysis of the client's (or clients') risk profile. Attention to risk profiling proves to be invaluable when financial products are designed, and even more so when they are costed and priced.

Another financial institution has established a review process which tackles both broker profitability (and hence commissions) and client profitability in the sense of market value derived from proposed trades. Every desk is treated as profit centre, with full account taken of projected earnings, costs and risks. Figure 6.3 presents in a block diagram the methodology being used, including thc mining of databased information in which is stored internal control intelligence and auditing results.

Much of this broker's review process is steady. The steady part is done by computer-based models which inform the account manager on the result of an evaluation, and if there exist any compliance risks. A rule built into the expert systems being used sees to it that if commissions on the same client run high and the leverage high, something is likely to go wrong; this leads to an alert.

Is this control activity a 100 per cent safeguard against snags? The answer is: 'No!', but it can be of significant help – if for no other reason than that it provides ad hoc documentation, and therefore food for thought. 'What is really difficult in risk control in financial institutions,' said a risk management officer, 'is that this is a reactive job. Even if we see that an inordinate [amount of] risk is taken, it is hard to prohibit certain trades.'

It is quite different if the necessary controls are established at product design level and steady evaluations which happen thereafter are databased. Then, they become part of the institution's decision methodology and will be there for anyone to see in product and sales reviews. By embedding into the specification's design characteristics and the response to them, this methodology highlights some subtle criteria which subsequently influence product evolution without being seen as breaks in the sales effort connected to a specific instrument.

A couple of senior risk management officers expressed the opinion that a major contribution which can be made through modelling is an improvement in *transparency*. They also added that unless senior management appreciates information regarding the quantitative level of exposure taken by the institution, and decides to act, much of what is computed in terms of risk is of only academic value.

Understanding by the board and senior executives can be promoted through training in analytics, which explains both the mechanism of calculating each type of risk and the meaning of levels of confidence. It is particularly important is to recognize that the weakest part in an algorithmic representation of real-life market situations lies in the *assumptions* being

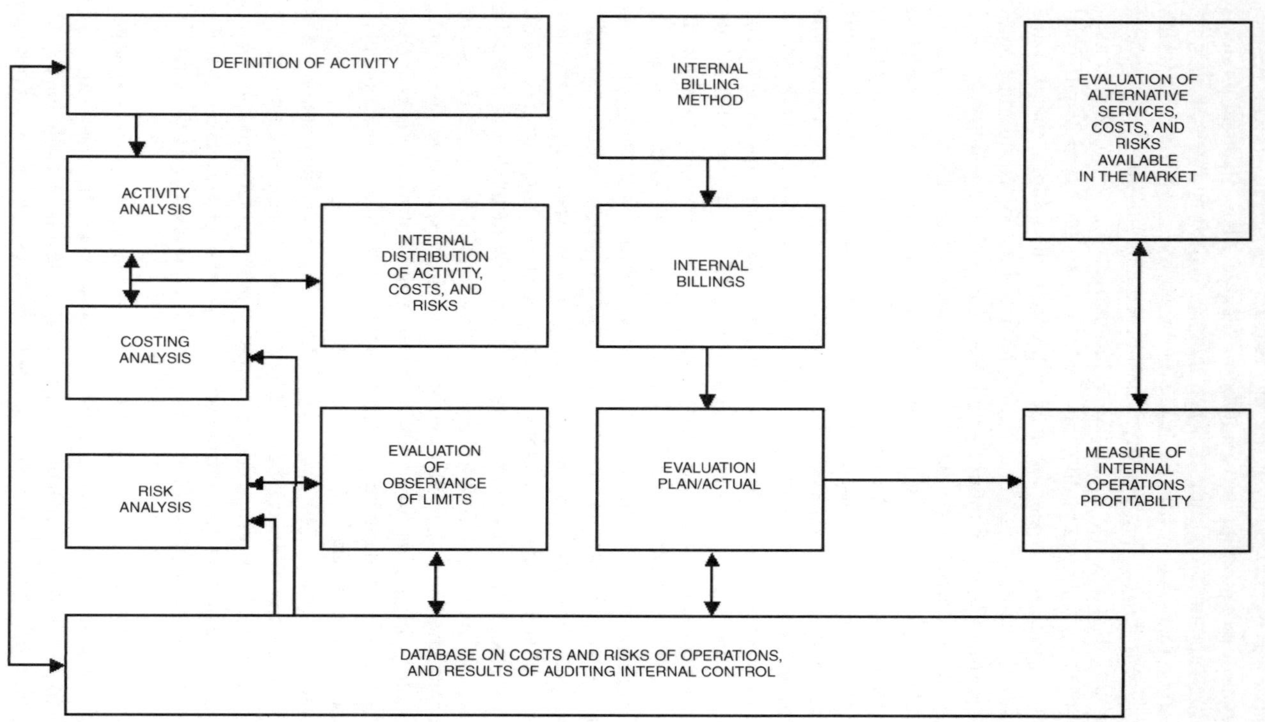

Figure 6.3 Block diagram of profit and loss (P&L) analysis of a profit centre

made. Therefore, examining the assumptions which have been used in developing models for financial instruments, as well as the instruments themselves, provides a lot of background in comparing:

- Design characteristics
- Pricing skills and
- The internal control culture.

While many financial products are personalized, and therefore unique, others are designed to appeal to the mass market. But are they really doing so? Are they flexible enough to adapt to a changing mass market? Are they helping *our* company to adapt itself as the market changes?

Taking an example from aeronautical engineering, Concorde was an inflexible product which managed to shoot itself in the foot because it got boxed into one single market sector in the air transport industry. By contrast, the Boeing line of 7×7 aircraft has been able to adapt itself to customer requirements, and made a fortune for Boeing. (See also Chapter 11 on product development and engineering design reviews.)

Concorde never recovered its R&D costs, because its design was based on the wrong assumptions. Who says 'assumptions' says 'estimates made about future market wishes, conditions and trends, whether these concern volatility, prices, market potential, or other key variables'. For instance, in finance these 'other variables' may be gearing and exposure to high volatility, as well as hypotheses on risk and return.

Let me take a couple of examples. One of them concerns junk bonds whose defaults grew during 1999. As many as 5.3 per cent of US companies with outstanding junk bonds defaulted on interest payments in the 12 months September 1998–August 1999, up from 2.1 per cent in a similar 1997–8 timeframe – and the fastest pace since 1992. This was seen by many analysts as a countes-indication in an economic boom, which defied some carefully crafted hypotheses.

The other example is a statistic which gives plenty of food for thought. As the bulls roared at Wall Street, in the 1995–9 timeframe, gearing became a major concern, particularly in the loans-for-shares business. In just five months (end 1997 to 31 May 1998), outstanding margin credit, which essentially represents loans to finance investments in shares expanded from $127 billion to $143 billion, according to Federal Reserve figures.

This relatively steep increase was made on the assumption that the market would continue expanding as the aftermath of the East Asia crisis faded and there were no other visible clouds in the horizon. However, the

Russian meltdown of August 1998 was not far away and the result of lower share prices which dominated mid- to late August and early September 1998 was to force margin investors either:

- To deposit more cash with their brokers or
- To unload some of their shareholding, further depressing prices.

Less than two years later, in the March–April 2000 timeframe, this same phenomenon of stock price deflation repeated itself with a vengeance, particularly in the domain of technology stocks. 'The Internet stocks are our Indonesia,' a New York broker told me. In a fortnight, as the NASDAQ lost 35 per cent of its value, some of its stocks dropped by more than 50 per cent, repeating a negative performance which had taken old economy stocks the whole of 1999 to establish.

Since these rapid inflationary/deflationary developments are negative for the stockmarket, regulators are concerned that the loans-for-shares bubble might explode, particularly if the normal signs of bear markets – which are declining profits and volatile interest rates – persist. Assumptions entering into trading decisions by bankers, treasurers and investors which do not consider the aftermath of a downturn are short-signted – and so are the models, no matter how sophisticated the algorithms which have been used.

SENIOR MANAGEMENT CANNOT DELEGATE ITS ACCOUNTABILITY FOR INTERNAL CONTROL

It is a basic principle of management that responsibility is never delegated. Only *authority* is delegated. The responsibility – and, therefore, accountability – remains with the senior managers and at the same time it is also assumed by the persons in the middle and lower echelons of supervision who accept the authority they have been delegated. Yet,

- Most often senior management delegates its responsibilities for internal control to executives in charge of a particular unit's day-to-day activities and
- Fails to ensure that the people to whom internal control authority has been delegated develop and enforce appropriate policies and procedures.

Another fundamental failure connected with personal accountability is the lack of a well documented organizational structure that clearly shows lines of reporting back to senior management on all internal control findings. As a result, there are *gaps in reporting lines* which weaken overall management control and see to it that it is not extended to all levels of the organization and the business activities performed at each level.

Through these gaps in an institution's reporting structure filter many internal and external events that could adversely affect the achievement of objectives, or significantly increase exposure. Because of these 'organizational crevasses' some critical events are not recorded, evaluated, and controlled. As a result, risk assessment is not properly conducted at the level of individual business units across the wider spectrum of an expanding market horizon. The A, B, C of senior management responsibility is that:

- There should be in place a proper *risk assessment process* able to evaluate all events, qualitative and quantitative, to determine current and potential exposure.
- For risks that are *directly controllable*, senior management must assess whether to accept them or mitigate them, through appropriate procedures including hedging.
- For risks that *cannot be directly controlled*, senior management must decide whether to accept them and lick its wounds, sharply reduce the level of business activity which generates them, or get out of that line of business altogether.

For instance, after its huge losses with in its derivatives deals with Bankers Trust, Procter and Gamble decided to sell its portfolio of derivative instruments. The input for the decisions to be taken in respect to current and potential exposure comes from internal control. Such decisions bring into perspective the issue of senior management accountability in regard to practical aspects of day-to-day operations.

It is the duty of top management to assure an organizational plan of action characterized by clear definition of delegation of authority and, with this, of duties between operational, administrative, and control tasks. This plan must clearly underline each manager's and subordinate's accountability. It is also the responsibility of senior management to set up measures to safeguard the bank's property and assets:

- Establishing and maintaining adequate risk identification and monitoring systems and

- Paying a great deal of attention to less dependable elements and causes of fraud.

Even in connection with complex and specialized business products and services, such duties can be handled in an able manner if the preoccupation with internal control intelligence is felt both at the top and at the bottom of the organizational pyramid. Another requirement is that everybody in a position of authority welcomes the internal control practice.

A pattern of statistics from daily operations can be of significant service to internal control intelligence, because it shows a trend. Statistics on profit and loss are an example. Figure 6.4 shows the distributions of daily trading revenue at Crédit Suisse First Boston for the years 1997 and 1998, based on the bank's 1998 *Annual Report*.

The mean of both distributions in Figure 6.4 is roughly Swiss Francs 30 million ($19 million), but their shape is quite different. The P&L of 1998 presents a wider spread and has some outliers on the negative side. It is up to management to estimate if these differences have been induced by market forces, a change in trading pattern, or other reasons. Similar distributions exist in regard to any other crucial variable which decision-makers must consider. For instance,

- Discounted cash flow (Chorafas, 1995a) and
- Gains and losses recognized but not yet realized.

Statistical distributions can easily be plotted by area of operations, desk, and trader, revealing a pattern of dealing habits. Statistics for this type of analysis do not need to be collected ad hoc at extra cost. They are part of data captured in connection with transactions and their execution. What is important is that the system of internal control serves as the collator (see Chapter 5) and does so at all levels in the organization – while remaining independent of day-to-day transactions associated with the execution of trading, investments, loans, and other duties.

Statistical inference, however, requires a pragmatic interpretation. In this connection, independence of opinion is most crucial. I had a professor at the University of California who taught his students that the chief auditor should be a person by the end of his career, not for reasons of greater experience (for some people 30 years of business practice represent 1 year's experience repeated 30 times), but because he would have an independence of means and of opinion. He would not be subject to career-type pressures. At least, that's the best bet.

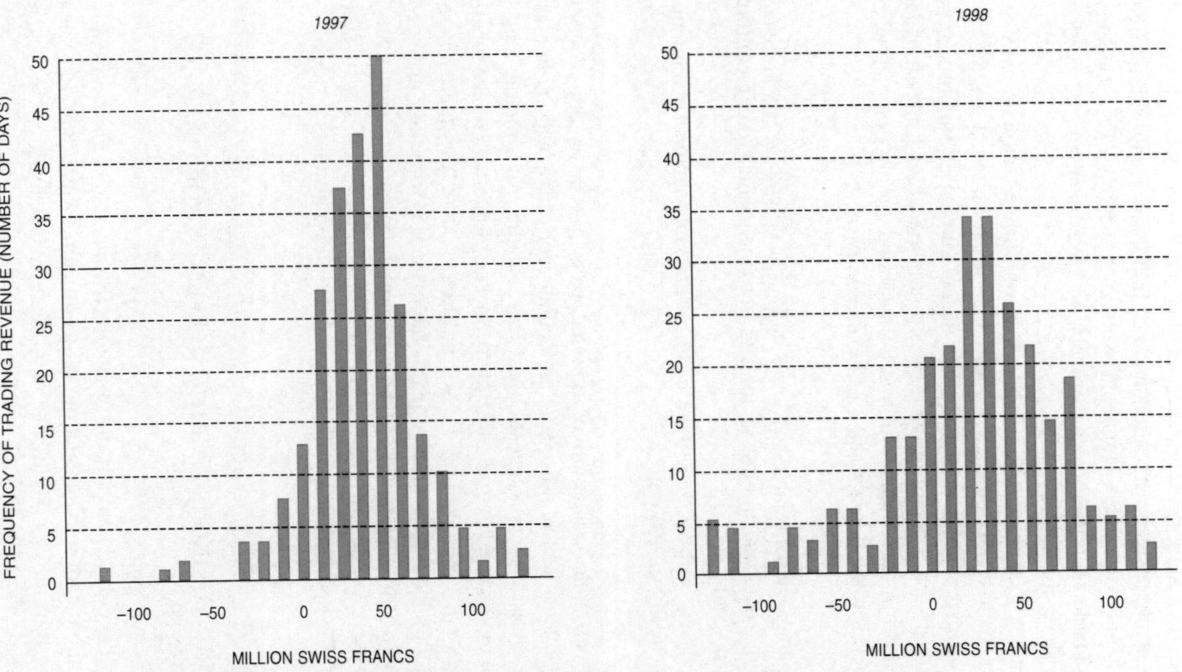

Figure 6.4 Distribution of daily trading revenue (P&L) at Crédit Suisse First Boston, 1997 and 1998

This characterization of independence of means and of opinion fits all persons with a direct responsibility on the feedback lines of internal control, and the interpretation of intelligence it provides. This should also bring to the reader's attention another important organizational requirement. Internal control functions should be entrusted to persons not accountable to traders, loans officers, or investment managers (there is more about this below).

Among themselves, the duties I have outlined explain why senior management cannot delegate its accountability for internal control, or walk away from it in good conscience. The deeper internal control mission is that of analysis and it is part of the feedback function which brings intelligence embedded in data streams from any transaction, at any time, anywhere in the world to the board's and CEO's attention:

- Testing against established limits and other criteria, for exceptions
- Doing database mining to unearth activities which don't conform to norms and
- Bringing critical information to senior management's attention – practically in real-time.

The finer-grade evaluation of reported facts has to be done by senior management, which must take immediate corrective action, but as the above bullet points suggest, both independence of opinion and high technology play a key role in the performance of internal control functions. As I never tire repeating in my lectures, one of the prerequisites in performing the duties outlined in an able manner is for senior management to establish and maintain *real-time information systems* covering every line of business: putting in place a network of administrative expert systems able to track compliance with laws, regulations, and internal rules.

RESTRUCTURING IS A CRITICAL ELEMENT OF FINANCIAL INNOVATION

One of the critical components of an effective internal control system is the elaboration and implementation of a structure which not only makes feasible, but also *promotes*, the immediate remedial actions which must follow internal control findings. Only then can the risks encountered in the execution of a company's strategies and objectives remain under control. Furthermore, the institution's internal control system needs to be frequently revisited to appropriately address any new or previously uncontrolled risk and/or sources of fraud.

Previously unknown sources of fraud come up all the time, particularly connected with new products and services. For instance, fraud with cards is not new, but in January 2000 in France developed a new species as the main three wireless companies offered the possibility to download credits from one's bank account to pay for telephone services – doing so without PIN protection. Because when one pays with a credit card the merchant's slip shows the card number and such slips are usually throw-away items, the fraud consisted in recovering these sales slips and using the credit card number for downloading. Such charges were evidently unknown to the card's legal owner. Some 50 000 card holders were taken to the cleaners with charges worth beyond Fr. 30 million ($5 million). For some people, the surprise bill run up to Fr. 13,000 ($2,150).

It is part of senior management's responsibility to see to it that the internal control system is regularly revamped to keep it up to date, reflecting product and process changes. Such a steady process of revaluation and restructuring has been made necessary because of *financial innovation*. Every dynamic organization has to reinvent itself in order to survive. Therefore, it needs to rethink its products, its markets, its structure, its systems, and its procedures as new business opportunities come onstream. Control processes are inseparable from the exploitation of market opportunities.

- A dynamic market does not present only opportunities but also a range of possible problems, from misunderstandings by customers to unwarranted exposure and operational failures.
- New risks can often best be comprehend when considering how various scenarios affect cash flow, earnings and different types of exposure, in the short and in the longer term.

The so-called 'Asian Tigers' (Thailand, Malaysia, Indonesia, South Korea, among others) offer a good example of unwarranted exposure. To a very substantial measure, the 1997–98 crisis in East Asia was caused by inadequate internal control at both company and government level – and by substandard risk management tools and methods in the massive short-term bank-to-bank international capital movements. Because of their failure to match financial innovation with sharper internal control, many parties lost lots of money:

- Red ink flowed. The Japanese, European, and American banks which had unwisely lent huge sums to the 'Tigers' banks and companies, had to face hefty losses.
- The East Asian economies themselves were penalized by a gross devaluation of their currencies, a mountain of foreign debt, and sharp drop in their stock markets.

The magnitude of the downturn in Asia caught everyone by surprise because most people did not realize that today's global economy is more integrated than ever before. The freedom of capital and currency movement causes a great deal of volatility in the markets, and the main players have been exposed without appropriate internal controls which are established at the centre but must be present at every corner of operations.

One of the lessons to be learned from the Asian meltdown is that while each company must have first-class internal controls, the globalization of financial business creates a need for individual controls to work together as a system. Cross-border exposure increases not only because of deregulation but also because the products and services offered by banks are becoming:

- More complex
- More exotic and
- More universal.

Since supervisory authorities tacitly or explicitly approve dealing in high-risk financial instruments, it is part of everybody's duty to assure that internal controls are in place and that they have the sophistication necessary to immediately report exposure embedded in each and every financial transaction. If this calls for a thorough restructuring, so be it.

Organizational restructuring and a radical revamping of information technology should move in tandem. Intelligent networks, for example, magnify a bank's reach and make its business much more rewarding in terms of business opportunities. But technology should also be used as the mind's eye in risk management. It is unrealistic to expect that every single executive and every single professional will keep tags on every single trade. Even if this were feasible, the global pattern would be missing. Therefore, internal control must:

- Highlight every exception and provide documentation on every variance.
- Compute trends and patterns permitting us to judge individual and cumulative exposure.
- Make it possible for every manager to focus on detail, in order to evaluate outstanding risk or likelihood of fraud.

To improve accuracy in prognostication, we must focus internal control not only on foreground but also on background reasons; visualize results in a way that they become more comprehensible; and audit the way the system works to ascertain that it functions satisfactorily. A great deal of attention should also be paid to the synergy between internal and external controls – the former are exercised by top management, the latter by supervisors (see Chapter 14).

This emphasis on both foreground and background reasons for exposure is commensurate with the fact that the surge in interest for internal control in the late 1990s was a direct result of very important losses incurred by several companies during that decade. Many of these losses could probably have been avoided if senior management had established and maintained an effective system of internal controls enabling early detection of the problems being faced – and hence limiting the amount of damage.

In conclusion, thoroughly studied and properly established internal controls are the best guarantee that *our* company will sustain its profitability in the longer term, controlling risk by maintaining a rapid, reliable reporting system. A solution permitting interactive presentation of internal control intelligence also helps to assure that *our* organization complies with laws and regulations and that the risk of unexpected losses or reputational damages is minimized.

BEWARE OF CREATIVE ACCOUNTING: IT IS POISON TO INTERNAL CONTROL

Part 1 brought to the reader's attention the fact that even the most perfect internal control system is vulnerable two problems: obsolescence of the tools, procedures and systems on which it rests; and tinkering by insiders and outsiders, which creates temporary or permanent damage. The accounting system should be seen by everybody as a most critical element because in prudential management:

- It serves for both measurement and monitoring of exposure and
- It constitutes the basis of reliable financial reporting (Chorafas, 2000a).

But there is a catch. Not only accounting rules and regulations vary from one jurisdiction to another, as we saw in Chapter 3, but also sometimes these rules allow certain freedoms some companies are only too happy to exploit. There are also, so to speak, trends in business which create conditions inducing the board to lose control over what is going on.

'Years of rising land and commodity prices had distilled the idea that debt was a blessing,' says James Grant (1992), who cites the case of 37 primary banks of the Farm Credit System and their hundreds of outlets run by local boards elected by farmers. The farmers saw the riches inflation brought to their door but not the risks, and they borrowed in a big way. As part of this dreamland, 'Corners were cut, rules bent, and exemptions admitted ... the system in 1986 was permitted to employ accounting techniques to postpone the recognition of loss.'

But the day of reckoning did come, as invariably always happens, and business failures hit the roof. The process James Grant describes is the so-called *creative accounting*, which specializes in money of the mind and has many tricks in its bag. Italy's Fininvest, for instance, concedes that from firms in which it has a 20–50 per cent share, it consolidates profits according to its proportion of the equity. But it does not consolidate their debts.

One of the areas where creative accounting biases facts and figures is in how the value of assets is computed. When in the late 1980s Crédit Lyonnais went in a global buying spree and granted big loans left, right, and centre, its main shareholder (the French government) bloated the bank's balance sheet by transferring the equity of other nationalized companies valued at unrealistic prices. In Fininvest's case, too, analysts said that values of assets, particularly its television rights, were way too high. Although Fininvest reported that shareholders' funds were 1.5 trillion lire ($810 million), other information suggested that *if* this were adjusted for Fininvest's:

- higher true debt and
- lower true book value for its assets,

then the true figure for shareholders' funds was not very positive. This is, of course, of concern not only to shareholders but also to other stakeholders like Fininvest's creditor banks, which included Banca di Roma, Banca Commerciale Italiana, and Cariplo. (The first two are closely connected with Mediobanca, Italy's major merchant bank.) Because Fininvest's debt was mostly in form of short-term loans with an average maturity of 26 months, the banks could exert continuous pressure on the company if they wanted to read what lay behind creative accounting practices:

- Creative accounting filters through the cracks of laws and regulations.
- In many cases, it is not illegal in the strict sense of the term, and it is rather widely practised.

Here is another example. On Wall Street, maintaining a high stock price is the key to corporate success. Aggressive accounting practices reduce the impact of a buying binge on earnings. For instance, in an act of creative accounting Softbank decided to write off \$2.7 billion in goodwill from its Ziff-Davis and Comdex buyouts over 30 years rather than the more conventional 10–15 years. 'If they wrote off the goodwill over 10 years, they would barely be profitable,' Jonathan Dobson, a fund manager with Jardine Fleming Investment Management's OTC Fund, who in July 1996 dumped his \$30 million stake, about 5 per cent of his total Japan holdings, figures (*Business Week*, 12 August 1996). It is therefore not surprising that many serious analysts and investors look at creative accounting as a source of unreliability in financial reporting.

These examples should ring a bell for the careful reader who will appreciate that there is a dual danger connected with internal control. The one comes from breathtaking complacency of boards of directors, CEOs and senior managers who operate through highly leveraged instruments without appreciating that exposure can bring the company to its knees – the LTCM-type risk. The other is putting creative accounting into the picture, which makes a mockery of internal control.

In conclusion, in terms of senior management responsibilities there is no substitute for internal control intelligence which is factual and documented. A few of the executives I met in the course of my research said that they can move through phone calls a better supervision than any accounting figures would provide. This is not a serious argument, particularly for a big company. As the Romans proved over 500 years ago, the only way to defend a far-flung empire is to have a strong mobile force able to deploy rapidly, using internal lines to any threatened point on the perimeter:

- The mobile force is the internal auditors (see Chapter 1) and
- The internal lines are those provided by internal controls.

Fragmentation of effort and some phone calls now and then; interruption of the internal lines through creative accounting; patchy auditing; and a lack of real internal control intelligence lead to unmitigated disaster. Doing away with internal controls, or bypassing them where they exist, is dangerous nonsense. Sooner rather than later the company will pay dearly for this state of affairs and for mismanagement – which speaks volumes for the board's responsibilities, as Chapter 7 documents.

7 Internal Control Implementation Must Focus on Core Functions

INTRODUCTION

Chapter 1 explained that auditing is a core function for any company, no matter the business it is in. Chapter 2 made the point that internal control, too, is core to any enterprise. It was also stated that fraud has been one of the first reasons why a company needed a reliable internal control system, but today a more important background reason is exposure to credit risk, market risk, operations risk, and other risks.

Chapter 1 insisted that internal control must be audited, and presented the requirements to be satisfied by a dependable auditing function. One of these requirements is internal discipline and self-appraisal. Whatever activities they undertake, companies run the risk of losses arising from failure to apply adequate internal control. In its more classical form its implementation includes the principles of:

- A dual control basis
- Separation of functions
- Establishment of exposure limits
- Internal auditing and
- Rigorous risk management.

The absence of self-discipline imposed by the board gives rise to the risk that the different layers of bank management do not exercise sufficient control over daily operations, and the auditors may not pay enough attention to whether the activities taking place comply with rules of governance and regulatory directives.

Chapter 2 made reference to the steps involved in internal control implementation. It also made the point that failure to apply an effective internal control system means that the board, CEO, and senior management have no sound basis for planning, monitoring, and controlling the different exposures to which the market subjects the bank. Nor are they informed about fraud in a timely manner, whether this originates from inside or outside the entity.

Chapter 3 brought to the reader's attention the fact that dependable accounting systems must be in place to enable independent checking, reconciliation, and compliance procedures to be carried out with regard to the detection of potential losses. Without a system of checks and balances thoroughly studied and implemented, the risk of fraud and of inordinate exposure will increase as a function of time.

Bank boards and senior managers need both formal policies and timely controls to govern all trading, lending, and investment activities, particularly when the market demands quick decisions. For the same reasons, companies need to re-examine the structure of their internal control and accounting systems, as well as their information technology supports. The infrastructure must be evaluated to ensure that all information is in place for a decision to be taken, after due appreciation of risks.

These statements are valid for every company and every function, but it is no less true that one should not spread the human resources and technological supports too thin. Therefore, this chapter emphasizes the need to account first and foremost for *core functions*. The best bet is that core functions will be the first to suffer important damage from inadequate control.

The damage to a company's core business is bound to grow as the market becomes increasingly more demanding and complex. Therefore, appropriate internal controls and sophisticated information technology must be in place to ensure that the entity's core activities, whatever their nature, are properly kept within limits established at senior level, and that all actual and potential exposures can be measured and verified in real-time, and corrective action taken.

WHICH ARE THE CORE FUNCTIONS OF A FINANCIAL INSTITUTION?

A discussion on core functions can be much more rewarding if it is centred on a specific branch of industry, for instance, banking. In a nutshell, the core functions of a credit institution are those essential to engaging in the provision of financial services. They include the development, management, marketing delivery, and after-sales service of financial products – as well as the control of exposure involved in financial transactions of all sorts.

The after-sales service of financial instruments is a provocative concept. Easy recognizable in the manufacturing industry – for instance the maintenance of computers and servicing of autos – it is more difficult to visualize in finance and banking. Yet, it is there. Asset management is an example of after-sales service of investment products.

The concept brought to the reader's attention in the opening paragraph of this section is a general statement, which can be further detailed by paying more attention at specific characteristics of an entity's business. While some features of core functions are the same from one institution to the other, others vary according to the particular market a bank is in, as well as the organization's history and culture. Typically, common core functions in commercial banking include 15 channels:

1. Accepting customer deposits
2. Making loans to customers
3. Making credit and actuarial assessments
4. Managing own investments to meet deposit and other liabilities
5. Underwriting financial issues and (maybe) insurance
6. Developing and managing new products
7. Trading in securities for own and for customer accounts
8. Providing custodian services for securities
9. Assuring trustee services for clients
10. Developing and sustaining fee services
11. Engaging in derivative financial instruments for hedging
12. Capitalizing on the globalization of financial markets
13. Swapping costs and increasing stockholder value
14. Managing risk in the most effective manner
15. Equipping itself with the best information technology the market can provide.

The asset management function, which I took as an example of after-sales service in banking, uses three of the aforementioned channels: custodian, trustee, and fee services. It may even use four if the customer has given *our* bank full powers to trade on his behalf and debit/credit his account.

Some of these issues, like capitalizing on the globalization of financial markets, are core for money centre banks, but not necessarily for local retail institutions even if some participate in foreign loans by big banks. Others, like effective risk management and top-notch information technology, are core for *all* financial institutions – whether or not they appreciate it.

The reason I make this statement is that many banks and insurance companies consider information technology as *not* being one of their core functions. As a result, they leave it at a Palaeolithic state of development, or they outsource it. That is wrong. A bank which does not take the best possible care of its information technology is like a ship that won't float or a dog that won't hunt. It keeps on pouring money into the bottomless pit of old IT, and budgets no return out of it (Chorafas and Steinmann, 1992).

Some of the core functions correlate. For instance, technology leadership and managing risk in the most effective manner. In fact I could have added one more dimension in the core business reference – that of mathematical modelling, which has entered the into banking in a big way with the 1996 Market Risk Amendment (Chorafas, 1998b) and now, with the 1999 *New Capital Adequacy Framework*, has expanded into internal rating models for credit risk.

There is a different way of judging core functions which eventually converges with the one we just went through. This is to look at the evolving prudential rules of regulation. What was essentially said by the 1999 New Capital Adequacy Framework of the Basle Committee on Banking Supervision? Here are in a nutshell its top three rules:

- Minimum capital requirements under 'standard' and 'advanced' solutions
- Steady review of capital adequacy by national supervisory authorities
- Market discipline to encourage reliable financial disclosure. (Chorafas, 2000d)

Each one of these rules makes reference to one of the bank's core functions. *Capital adequacy* as originally established in connection with lending and therefore credit risk. Its objective as to improve the banks' financial staying power, when hit by adversity. Capital adequacy, however, expanded to cover market risk, and before too long it will also address operational risk.

Fulfilling the requirements of the third bullet point, *market disciplines*, requires transparency, and I expect that the evolution of global regulations will sooner rather than later make transparency a core function, not only in banking but in any industry. Let me add that the 1999 New Capital Adequacy Framework contains four other guidelines which identify underlying core functions:

- Use of external ratings by reputable independent agencies: Standard and Poor's (S&P), Moody's, IBCA
- Need to analyze operational risk and provide capital to face its aftermath
- Recognition of credit derivatives as means of managing credit risk volatility
- Internal ratings by technologically advanced institutions, probably leading to precommitment.

External credit ratings are essentially the outsourcing of part of the bank's internal ratings, which has classically been part of the core functions. The analysis of the many aspects of operational risk (see Chapter 3) has also become a core activity. Because, among other reasons, credit derivatives are adopted by the banking industry as a means to improve their liquidity, they add to the core function of lending and expand the core function of securitization.

A POLYVALENT APPROACH TO THE IMPLEMENTATION OF INTERNAL CONTROL: THE COMMISSION BANCAIRE DIRECTIVES

The Commission Bancaire of the Banque de France said during our meeting that to be effective internal control functions must be polyvalent. The Commission Bancaire advises the financial institutions under its regulatory authority that to increase the efficiency of management control they must have the following systems solution in place which responds to at least five requirements:

- Properly functioning accounting and information technology
- Steady monitoring of operations and internal procedures
- Timely and factual documentation on all transactions and positions
- Detailed measurement of risks and
- Steady surveillance of exposure.

Ways and means put in place to implement and sustain such systems must be dimensioned in a way which corresponds to size of the institution and the complexity of its business. Each risk poses its own conditions for effective control. For instance, credit risk must be approached on both an individual and a consolidated basis. Auditing must be regularly done and, the Commission Bancaire underlined, it is preferable that the auditing function reports to a board-level Auditing Committee (see also Chapter 1).

The Commission Bancaire advises the banks under its authority that senior management must pay personal attention to market risks, including interest rates and exchange rates – as well as liquidity, payments and settlement, and operational risks. Also, to what the Commission Bancaire calls *risk of maximum exposure*, which is in essence a worst-case scenario. Senior executives are responsible assuring that:

- The activities of the institution are in line with those described in its charter and

- Each person responsible for a desk or department is in charge of the exposure assumed by his or her unit.

A polyvalent approach to internal control should see to it that accounting and other financial information functions operate in a 100 per cent reliable way, and that the system for evaluation, databasing, and reporting on risk-connected decisions and events functions properly. The Commission Bancaire places particular emphasis on organizational matters such as the separation of authority and duties for front desk and back office – not only at headquarters but also in any division or branch.

Correctly, emphasis is placed on skills: the background and experience to be possessed by the human capital of a credit institution. A special focus is qualification of risk controllers and means put at their disposition – particularly those connected with analysis of all types of risks. One of the prerogatives for good management outlined by the regulators is that skills and tools must be commensurate to the problems posed by:

- The instruments the bank promotes
- The risks which it takes and
- The degree of its geographical dispersion.

Another basic requirement expressed by these regulations in France is that financial institutions must do a regular review of the system of measurements addressing the risks they are taking, including the establishment and follow-up of limits, analysis of extraordinary events in the market, and ways and means used to realize timely analyzes of assumed exposure.

Accurate journalizing is still another prerequisite, since the rules of Commission Bancaire call for the ability to reconstitute transactions and other operations in their chronological order, in full respect of established general accounting principles. The top management of financial institutions is asked to make sure that there is necessary detail, depth, quality, and reliability of:

- Accounting and risk control information and
- Methods for evaluation of market data streams.

Fulfilling these prerequisites calls for the exercise of great care by the institution's accountants and auditors in certifying the accuracy of accounting schemata. Beyond analytical skills and know-how, requirements include the expertise to correct deviations if and when they arise.

Auditing of accounting books must be done at least monthly. Similar controls on information technology must ensure that:

- The level of security is acceptable from the viewpoint of rigorous management and
- There is enough backup of information services to pick up the backlog created by a system failure.

The Commission Bancaire also pressed the point that uninterrupted information technology services constitute a necessary infrastructure to the steady evaluation of on-balance sheet and off-balance sheet exposure – from counterparty risk to market risk, operational risk, and other risks. It also underlined that factual and documented evaluations of exposure must be based on both:

- Qualitative and
- Quantitative information.

The point was further made that credit risk analysis should not only account for the financial condition of the debtor, trading partner, or other counterparty, but also consider the profitability of loans and other transactions. In turn, profitability analyzes and return on investment studies require an established standard costs structure which permits us to evaluate direct and indirect expenses connected to products and services offered to clients. These are *a priori* studies into which we look in greater detail below.

Let me conclude the discussion on internal controls and auditing policies advised by Commission Bancaire with the following thought. To glide smoothly across the cracks between its public image and its internal reality, a credit institution must increase the depth of its core functions. It is unhealthy in a business sense to require uniformity from all managers and professionals, but the board and CEO must insist on conformity – which needs strong internal controls.

WHY BOTH *A PRIORI* AND *A POSTERIORI* STUDIES IMPROVE INTERNAL CONTROL

An *a priori* evaluation is done before a commitment is made; an *a posteriori* evaluation takes place after the fact. An *a priori* evaluation might be made by the seat of the pants (which is the approach I encounter most frequently, but do not advise); might be based on long experience and expert judgement; or might be assisted through *simulation*, (Chorafas, 1995a), which augments the personal experience quotient and permits experimentation.

Simulation is a working analogy. When analogous systems are found to exist, we may use one of them as a platform in studying the behaviour of the other. Typically, the *model* we use for our *a priori* study is a simplification of the real world. Simplification is done by means of abstraction which, as Figure 7.1 suggests, permits us to simplify the representation of complex entities like a financial market, an information network, or an airframe.

Models are not supposed to be fool-proof, but when they are realistically made, they constitute a valuable assistance to analytical tasks and experimental approaches. Models are a second nature to physics and engineering. Few people, however, appreciate that what we consider today as the *accounting system* was a model of record-keeping for business transactions by Luca Paciolo, and dates back to 1495.

There is a variety of reasons for which we develop models, experiment, and simulate. One of them is prognostication. An accurate prediction of the future does not really occur through extrapolation of known phenomena. Rather it is made by means of analogical reasoning. A deep professional experience is instrumental in judging by analogy.

Hypotheses are crucial to analogical thinking. A *hypothesis* is a tentative statement made to prove a theory or lead to the investigation of one another. The art of modelling rests on two principles:

- The assumptions we make must be factual and
- The algorithms we use should realistically reflect the real world under study.

Well made models have provided significant assistance to the *a priori* evaluation of a loan, a trade, an investment, or some other activity for which they have been *specifically* designed. Models don't have the last word. When the user deems it advisable, he or she may override the model's signals. This happens under certain market conditions to which, the user believes, the model is not as sensitive as it should be. A frequent reason for discrepancy are the assumptions behind the model:

- One model may assume that positions change relatively quickly, and uses an intraday market data feed to update its values.

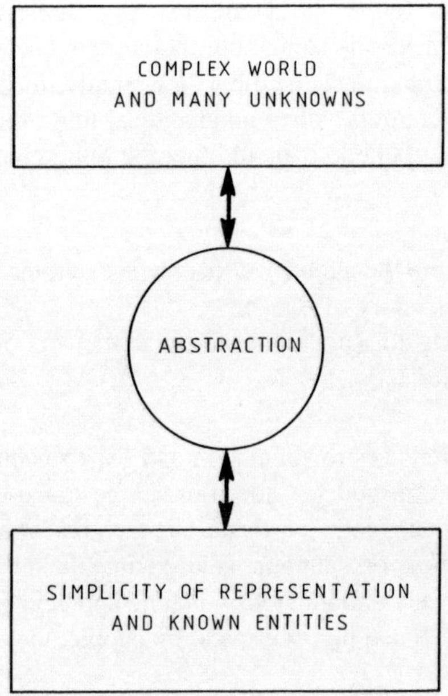

Figure 7.1 Abstraction is the two-way interface between complexity and simplicity

- While another model has been designed to be rather static for a market whose values change slowly, though it may be used for situations to which it is not designed to respond.

Not all models are computer-based. In the pre-Second World War years, the study of waterdams and airframes was made, respectively, through artificial basins and wind tunnels. Some simulators are built for training. Just prior to the Second World War, the UK secret service discovered that Germans brought tons and tons of sand to Ulm and nobody understood why. Post-war it was found that German tanks for projected operations in North Africa were being tested in Ulm.

One of the domains where the use of models and advanced statistical analysis is instrumental is the study of outliers and other extreme events. Thinking in terms of a normal distribution, where 99.73 per cent of the area under the curve lies within ± 3 standard deviations from the mean, any point at, say, $10s$ is taken to be an *anomaly*. But is it really so?

'I have always found the word *anomaly* interesting,' says Warren Buffett. 'What it means is something the academicians can't explain, and rather than re-examine their theories, they simply discard any evidence of that sort.' To the contrary, when an analytical mind finds information that contradicts existing beliefs, it should feel the obligation to look at it much more rigorously:

- The problem with the majority of people is that their mind is conditioned to reject contradictory evidence.
- When something does not fit the narrow framework of their theories, they express disbelief.

As these rapid references to simulation and experimentation suggest, there is a polyvalent use of models. Indeed, it can be stated that each model has its application domain, and vice versa. The fact that when a model made for one product, market or situation is used in another it may lead to an irrelevance – or even contradictions – is little appreciated. Nor is it true that models never fail. Since they are made by people, they quite often behave like them.

- One may be signalling that a long position in a futures contract should be held
- While another is signalling that funds should no longer be invested in that trade.

Or, one of the models may trigger a long position signal in one delivery month while another recommends a short position in another delivery month of the same futures contract. On occasion, investment models might even suggest the opposite positions in the same delivery month of the same commodity or financial instrument!

It should come as no surprise that some traders and investment managers like these contradictions. They believe that utilizing more than one trading system on the same or similar types of trades offers a diversification of viewpoints, and could be beneficial when numerous contracts of each commodity are traded under more or less uncertain conditions.

How much more flexible – and, as an end result rewarding – the adherence to a models-and-human-judgement strategy is, can be seen in Table 7.1. Based on a real-life experience with a financial institution, it gives the results of 12 months of trading on a given instrument starting with

Table 7.1 Net asset value on year-to-year basis through two different trading strategies

Month	**Use of both models and human judgement**	**Blind trading through modelling**
January	100	100
February	114	99
March	110	98
April	120	100
May	123	95
June	116	93
July	121	87
August	117	90
September	113	86
October	118	85
November	122	87
December	120	85

net asset value equal to 100 and ending with a totally different outcome in terms of managed wealth.

A priori evaluations are done prior to commitment. But there is also the need for a steady revaluation of the inventory of contracts, since these represent commitments which may have a long life. Figure 7.2 dramatizes the fact that a month may make a great difference with regard to the value of inventoried bond position – though in some countries the change in yield curve may be more important than in others.

Supervisory authorities are well aware that the worth of inventoried positions in institutions under their control can vary significantly with time. Therefore, the new regulations regarding P&L evaluation by the Commission Bancaire of Banque de France prescribe *a posteriori* analysis of credit operations. As in the case of the Office of Thrift Supervision (OTS), we saw in Chapter 6, senior management is asked to make such a *posteriori* studies at least once per month – which is an excellent idea in terms of:

- Feedback (see below) and
- Internal control.

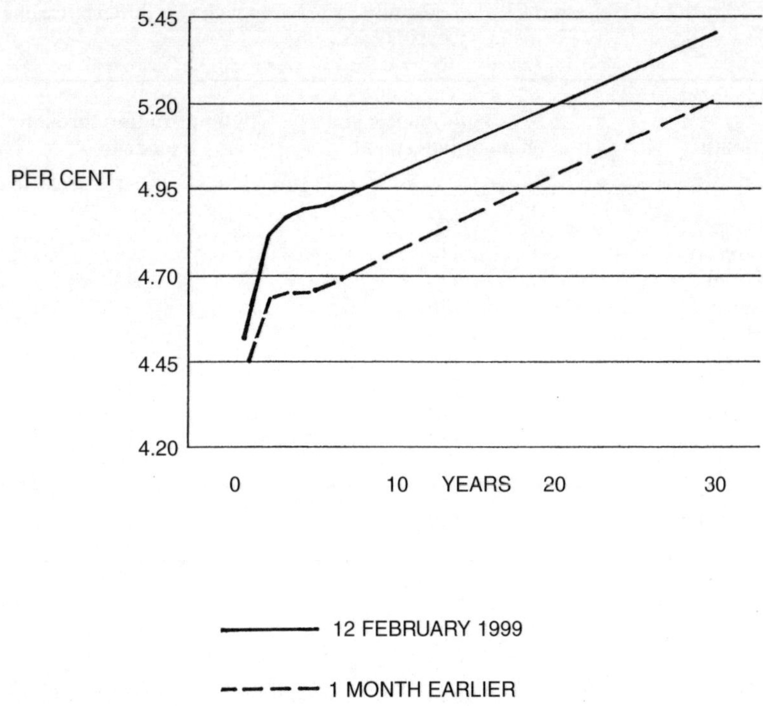

Figure 7.2 The difference 1 month makes: benchmark yield curves with 30-year bonds in three G-10 countries: United States

Another good case of *a posteriori* evaluation for feedback reasons is the requirement that credit institutions must do at least quarterly a thorough analysis of the evolution of credit risk in their books, *by counterparty*. This and all other systematic controls must consider the validity and coherence of hypotheses and parameters used in credit decisions, including modelling. A similar requirement is valid in connection to estimated market risks.

Finally the same directive by Commission Bancaire brings the attention of credit institutions' top management to the need to consider operational risks and legal risks in the same detailed manner. The need for close supervision by the board of the way internal control operate, is also underlined. It is also interesting to notice that there is a bifurcation

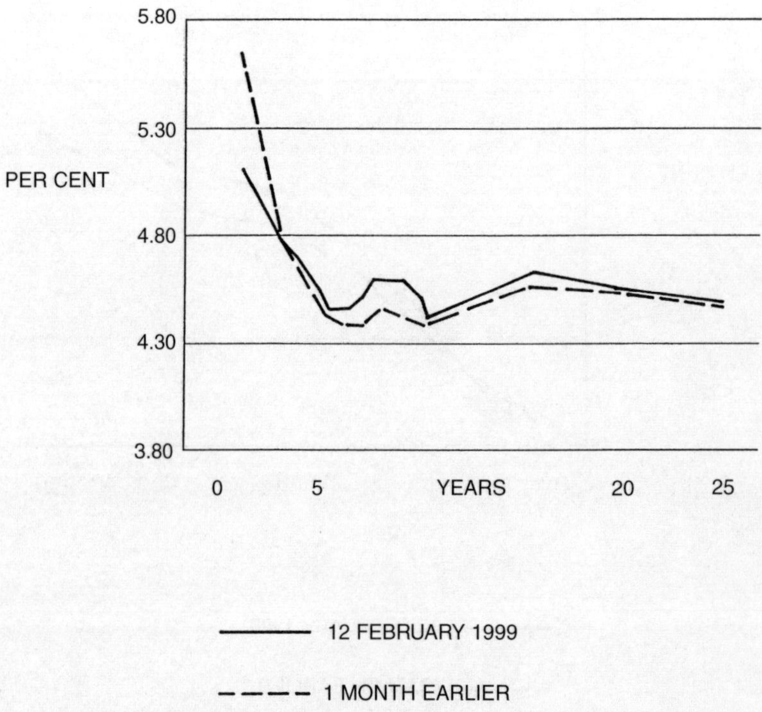

Figure 7.3 The difference 1 month makes: benchmark yield curves with 30-year bonds in three G-10 countries: United Kingdom

regarding the frequency with which a rigorous review should be done. If there is an Audit Committee, this review can take place once per year. If not, the frequency of an *a posteriori* examination should be twice per year or more.

In conclusion, both *a priori* and *a posteriori* analytics are important to a credit institution's operations, assisting managers and professionals in making commitments with better insight, and providing a valuable input to internal control. Today regulators look quite favourably on experimental approaches through modelling, and shape financial reporting requirements to accommodate them. But models are *not* infallible, like organizations, models are made by people.

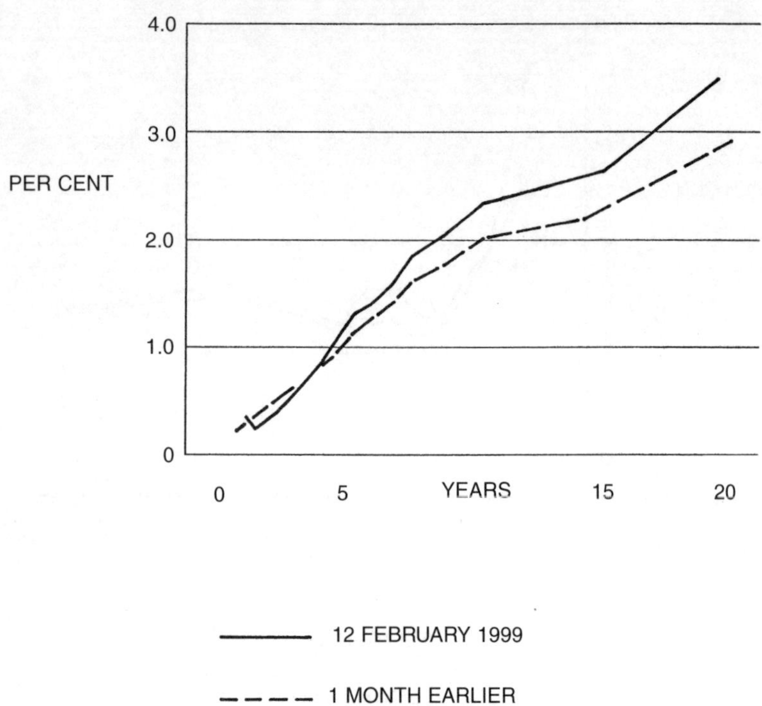

Figure 7.4 The difference 1 month makes: benchmark yield curves with 30-year bonds in three G-10 countries: Japan

DO WE NEED A SEPARATE DEPARTMENT TO LOOK AFTER COMPLIANCE? THE CASE OF TWO SWISS BANKS

In my book *compliance* is a core function for any company and most particularly for a financial institution. It is a back office function (some say a middle office function) contrasting with other operations like book-keeping (also done in the back office), as well as with deposits and loans which are front desk functions. Two different banks do not attach the same meaning to compliance.

For instance, in Switzerland Bank Leu uses the term 'compliance' in a way which is much more extensive than the sense it usually has in the United Kingdom, because it takes a broader view. Compliance at Bank Leu acts as the kernel where all management controls are defined, including an answer to queries such as:

- Which control?
- What does it cover?
- Who is responsible?
- How often it must be exercised?

At Bank Leu, the compliance operation also produces documentation necessary for control action. Senior management considers this to be most important for effective risk management, because damage containment cannot be exercised without knowing what the different professionals do, or without timely data streams which are uninhibited, complete, correct, and accurate.

Compliance is not the only management duty whose exercise requires data streams of the quality described in the preceding paragraph. Another of the company's core functions is *pricing* of product and services. Pricing is an opportunity, but it can also be a curse. Having argued themselves into a corner because of wrong pricing policies, many institutions seem to be too embarrassed to get out of it:

- Pricing and business strategy correlate both between themselves and with the broader perspective of risk management.
- Pricing and compliance also have much in common because some of the worst violation of rules and regulations start with overestimating or underestimating prices.

Though the pricing of physical products or financial instruments is a core function at any company, the case of a separate department to set prices is indeed rare. The more common approach is that at a tactical level this is done by marketing. At a strategic level, the board and senior management must not only establish pricing strategy but also approve major pricing changes.

The risks assumed with a new instrument, product or services, should enter into pricing decisions. The same is true of all considerations associated with compliance. This is a policy followed only by the best organized banks, in other institutions, pricing policies and procedures fall out of control from time to time, and the same is true about the observance of rules and regulations.

I will be pushing at an open door if I say that effective risk management requires knowledge on how the bank is organized and supervised. But few banks appreciate that the roots of an inordinate exposure can be found in pricing. This happens because few learn from events which have happened

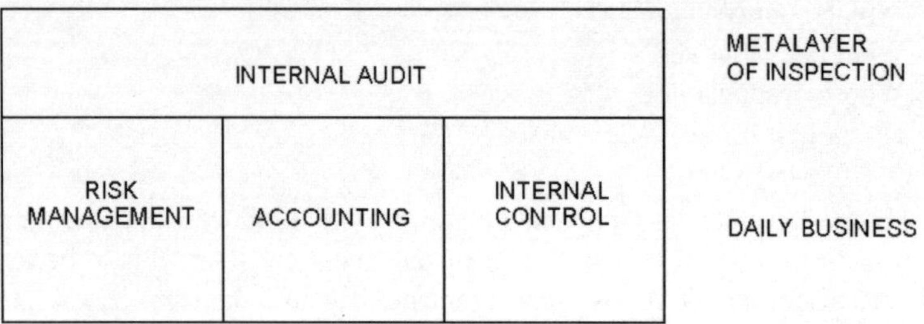

Figure 7.5 Auditing is a metalayer whose business is rigorous inspection, not the day-to-day control of operations

in the past, lessons which are costly and should not be repeated. On the basis of an *a priori* examination, senior management must decide on:

- The right price tag for a product
- What the prudential limits should be
- Which control process fits best the bank's profile and
- How and how often special audits have to be made.

Bank Leu did not speak about the first two bullet points; this was not the point of our meeting. But, like the Vontobel Bank, it did emphasize the latter two – associating the solution with the role of auditing as a supercontrol activity, indispensable to the firm and endowed with independence from day-to-day business.

As shown in Figure 7.5, according to this definition auditing is a *metalayer* – a supervisory body operating at a higher level. The mission of internal audit is to inspect not to operate in the sense of current business. Therefore, for day-to-day compliance activities Bank Leu has instituted an internal control function:

- On a day-to-day basis, internal control concentrates on spotting facts particularly relating to compliance, and putting them into perspective.
- The mission of auditing is to look for presence or absence of the *normal*, including what is normal in the work internal control does.

At Vontobel, internal auditing performs analytical tests including value-at-risk (VAR) (Chorafas, 1998b) and stress analysis. A quantitative example is given in Table 7.2. As the careful reader will appreciate, if VAR for derivatives is 100 then VAR for loans is 30. This is more or less the ratio

Table 7.2 A bank's exposure to loans and derivatives risks, standard VAR v. stress analysis (Just note difference)

	Loans	**Derivatives**	**Total**
Standard VAR	30	100	130
Stress analysis	70	1400	1470

VAR reflects normal conditions; what is important is exposure under stress.

prevailing in most institutions. Very interesting, however, is the fact that *stress analysis* alters this ratio:

- Under stress, loans exposure increases by 233 per cent.
- But derivatives exposure zooms up by 1400 per cent.

That's where the inordinate risks lie. While Vontobel watches its loans and derivatives exposure carefully, the lion's share of attention is evidently on the derivatives side. Other banks don't follow this wise policy. That's what brought down in flames the formerly prosperous Bank of New England (BNE). Whichever way one considers the BNE case, it was an unmitigated disaster.

As a case study on the rise and fall of a credit institution, the débâcle of the BNE makes interesting reading. At the end of 1989, when the Massachusetts real estate bubble burst, BNE became insolvent and bankruptcy was a foregone conclusion. At the time, this institution had:

- $32 billion in assets and
- $36 billion in derivatives exposure (notional principal amount).

To keep systemic risk under lock and key, the Federal Reserve Bank of Boston took hold of the BNE, replaced the chairman and pumped in billions in public money. Financial analysts said this was necessary because the risk was too great that a BNE collapse might lead to a panic in the market of derivative financial instruments:

- On *$36 billion* in notional principal
- BNE had *$6 billion* in hard core derivatives losses.

This would make the demodulator of notional principal equal to 6 rather than 25 which I have often used (Chorafas, 2000c), even if this factor of 25 is criticized by some bankers as 'too conservative'. The Bank of New England was closed by regulators in January 1991 – at a cost of $2.3 billion to the taxpayer. At that time, its derivatives portfolio was down to $6.7 billion in notional amount – or roughly $1 billion in toxic waste which represented pure risk for its counterparties.

Mismanagement at BNE saw to it that this has been the second most costly bank failure to FDIC in US history, after the 1988 failure of First Republic Bank of Dallas. Both incidents were largely connected with overexposure to the *real estate bubble*, and to *derivatives*. As such, they help to demonstrate where the lack of internal control may lead.

What can we learn from these case studies: Bank Leu's and Vontobel's carefully crafted layer/metalayer structure of compliance, analytics, and auditing, on one side – and a highly leveraged system which runs out of control, on the other. In the case of the two Swiss banks top management has been in charge. It made the right decisions and through auditing it carefully watches over the shoulder of operations.

On the contrary, in BNE's case management control was mediocre, and auditing support entirely insufficient to permit doing a proper job in the oversight of the bank's core business. This I have found in my practice to be the hallmark of poor management; BNE is neither the first nor the last species of its kind.

MANAGEMENT INTENT: ITS IMPACT ON INTERNAL DISCIPLINE AND FINANCIAL REPORTING

Boards and CEOs who intend to keep personal responsibility for overseeing all corners of the organization are keen to assure that internal auditing flows directly from themselves. For instance, Wilhelm F. Duisenberg, the president of the European Central Bank (ECB) is responsible for External Relations, Protocol *and* Internal Audit. And as we saw in other cases auditing often reports directly to the board's Audit Committee.

In more than one way, internal control and rigorous auditing are synonymous with internal discipline, and internal discipline starts at board level. Also at the level of the board, CEO, and executive committee is to be found a process known as *management intent*. This should not be confused with strategy, though it overlaps with strategic planning, as shown in Figure 7.6.

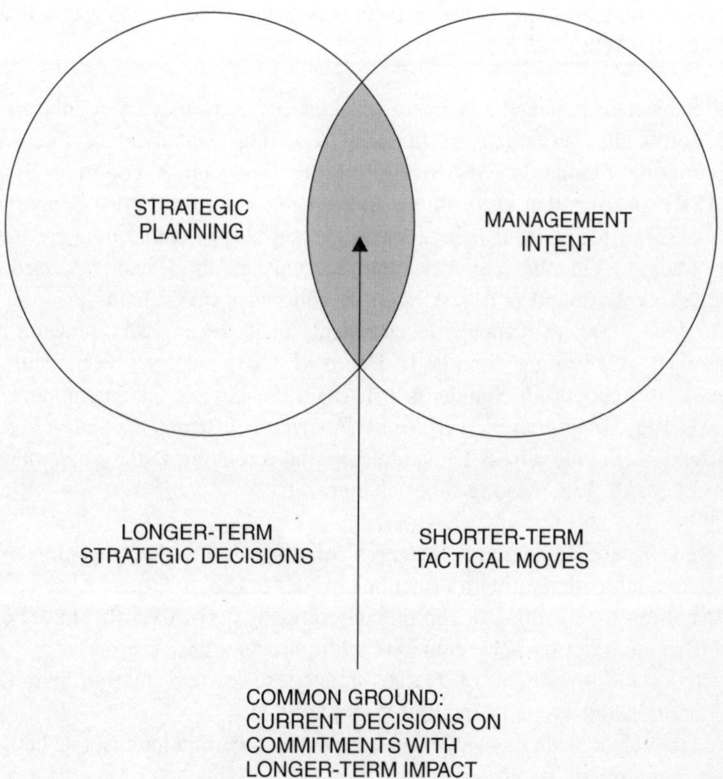

Figure 7.6 Management intent and strategic planning overlap, but basically they are different concepts

Management intent identifies the real purpose of a certain commitment, be it a trading transaction, derivatives deal, investment decision, or loan made to a 'valued client' for handholding reasons. To a substantial extent, internal control is a matter of management intent which often reflects *profit motives* but also *vigilance* and *virtue*. These issues are of a practical nature because they make the difference between the chemists and alchemists of financial systems. As Michael White says in the biography of Sir Isaac Newton:

> The intellectual as opposed to the motivational foundations of chemistry and alchemy overlapped ... Chemists and alchemists dealt with the same compounds, even used the same apparatus and shared inherited

> knowledge; what lay between them was *approach* and *intent*. (emphasis added). (White, 1997)

The subject of management intent is taken very seriously by regulators in the norms they establish for financial reporting. Statement of Financial Accounting Standards (SFAS) 133 of the Financial Accounting Board (FASB) specifies that all positions in the bank's portfolio must be marked to market or to model if management's intent has been that they are there for trading. On the contrary, the accruals method can be used if management's intent is to hold them as long-term investments.

In June 2000, in response to comments made by industry players, the Financial Accounting Standards Board (FASB) released Statement of Financial Accounting Standards (SFAS) 138. This is an amendment of SFAS 133, *Accounting for Certain Derivative Instruments and Certain Hedging Activities*. SFAS 138 addresses issues relating to the implementation of SFAS 133. Among other changes, it:

- Reduces the number of categories of transactions that are subject to treatment as derivative transactions in SFAS 133.
- Modifies the handling of certain intercompany derivatives that have been offset on a net basis by contracts with unrelated third parties.
- Alters the treatment of hedges related to certain foreign currency denominated assets or liabilities; and
- Makes changes in the way the effectiveness of certain interest rate hedges is determined; therefore impacting on their pricing.

Pricing and financial reporting aside, the aftermath of management intent takes also other forms – for instance, generalized personal accountability. In its fundamentals, the reason for minutes and signatures is that they serve as documentation of accountability. Managers can delegate tasks and the authority to do them – but not the responsibility for their execution – and they continue carrying on the responsibility for the decisions they have made.

This issue of assigning individual responsibilities as part of management intent can be brought a step further to include the policy that after accounts have been independently verified, and all exposures to individual counterparties considered in detail and regularly reviewed, responsibilities are reassigned: in other words, they are kept dynamic. This makes more meaningful the policy that all instruments with significant risk exposure be centrally monitored in real-time.

Under the overall concept of 'management intent' one may also place the policy that technology is used by the company in a way commensurate to the business opportunities it exploits and the risks it takes. Since many of the innovative financial products are critically dependent on computers, databases, networks, and models management needs, as I have underlined so often, to have access to state-of-the-art technology – a tough task because technology continuously evolves:

- Both internal and external audits should encompass the monitoring of systems adequacy, including technical competence of personnel.
- This is part of *internal control auditing*, something that goes beyond the actual risk exposure figures, the preservation of assets, and general fitness.

To appreciate the reason behind these two bullet points, we must talk of *feedback*. In engineering, the feedback loop is the crucial element of a controlled system. Its function is to continuously measure the deviation of the key controlled variable and translate this deviation into a correction of system input. This is the concept underpinning automatic control.

The concept of feedback adds in a way both to the complexity of a system and to its cybernetics. This concept is present in internal control and auditing, where we are essentially talking of a two-level feedback, as shown in the block diagram of Figure 7.7. Under the perspective of Bank Leu's definition, $F(A)$ is a feedforward function with internal control intelligence, while $F(B1)$ provides feedback on the audit of internal control and $F(B2)$ feedback on every other function.

Let me repeat the notion underpinning this schema. The $F(B1)$ loop targets the issues connected with internal control. Qualification criteria, quantification models, and standards are necessary to keep this feedback channel in good functioning order. Statistical quality control (SQC) (Chorafas, 2000a) provides an example on what be achieved through available, dependable tools which can help immensely in visualizing the finding of management control – therefore of organizational feedback.

Chapter 4 introduced the concepts of 'quality' and 'tolerances'. SQC charts permit us to map tolerances in such a way that deviations are measured against them tick-by-tick. The visualization is user-friendly and easily comprehensible. Therefore, it can lead to immediate corrective action. (SQC charts are discussed in Chapter 9).

Textbooks usually do not say so but SQC charts are a *graphical feedback*. They also help in the implementation of a process of management discipline characterized by reduced, normal, and tightened

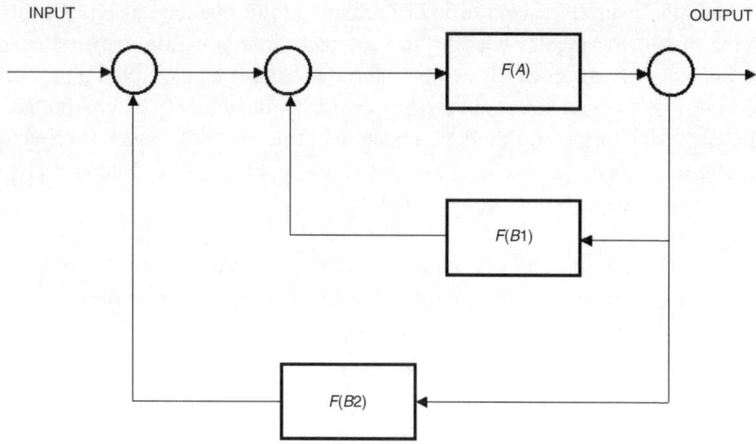

Figure 7.7 A feedback mechanism characterizing both engineering constructs and financial markets, but many bankers lack this sensitivity

inspection. An interesting implementation domain is provided by the 1999 New Capital Adequacy Framework. With this revised capital accord, the Basle Committee is committed to making capital requirements more sensitive to the volatility of credit risk (Chorafas, 2000b) than ever before. Therefore, it is proposing to reduce risk weights of certain high-quality assets based on favourable:

- Default history, and
- Price fluctuations.

This corresponds to *reduced inspection*. By contrast, the Committee intends to weight more heavily the risk of other types of assets. Weights greater than 100 per cent are examples of *tightened inspection*. A 150 per cent risk weighting category is tightened inspection, which would include instruments by sovereigns, banks, and corporates rated below B–, as well as securitizations that are rated between BB+ and BB–. Table 7.3 presents in a nutshell the inspection guidelines by the 1999 New Capital Adequacy Framework.

The point the reader needs to retain from this discussion is that the more sophisticated becomes the way we look at exposure, the more necessary is management discipline and the clearer should be management's intent. Internal control needs tools, metrics, and unambiguous descriptions, it cannot be done by word of mouth. Taking a leaf from engineering, it is

Table 7.3 Reserve requirements for loans to sovereigns, banks, corporate clients, and securitized instruments based on ratings by independent agencies[1]

Rated by

	High quality	**Average quality**		**Low quality**		**Unrated**
Standard & Poor's and Fitch IBCA	AAA to AA–	A+ to A–	BBB+ to BBB–	BB+ to B–	Below B–	
Moody's Investors Service	Aaa to Aa3	A1 to A3	Baa1 to Baa3	Ba1 to B3	Below B3	–
Export insurance agencies	1				7	–

Claims on (per cent)

Sovereigns		**0**	**20**	**50**	**100**	**150**	**100**
Banks[2]	Option 1	20%	50%	100%	100%	150%	100%
	Option 2	20%	50%[3]	50%[3]	100%[3]	150%	50%[3]
Corporates		20%	100%	100%	100%	150%	100%‘
Securitized instruments		20%	50%	100%	150%	Deducted from capital	

Notes:
[1] For other claims, 100 per cent weighting would remain the standard risk accounting approach.
[2] With Option 1, risk-weight is based on risk-weight of the sovereign in which the bank is incorporated. With Option 2 risk-weight is based on assessment of the individual credit institution.
[3] Claims on banks of original maturity less than six months would receive one category more favorable risk-weight than is usual on bank's claims.

possible to plot management intent as tolerances, then use SQC charts to ascertain whether the process is in control.

NEW RULES OF COMPETITION AND THE NEED FOR MARKET DISCIPLINE

The new rules of competition require senior managers to start by asking what is important not only to their bank but also to their customers, and where their company can find new sources of income. Armed with this information, they need to reinvent their business to create the next profit zones, because otherwise the institution will not be able to survive.

To be competitive and to sustain its competitiveness, a company must steadily evaluate itself, its organization, its products and services. On the bottom line, this should be one of the key objectives of internal control intelligence. The board and the CEO must know their strengths and weaknesses to position the company against both market forces and its challengers. Flexibility, innovation, and value differentiation require a lot of intelligence on how well product and services perform; also in regard to production facilities, delivery channels, profitability, cash flow, and ways and means in place to assure accountability for results.

The concept that part of top management accountability is transparency which a company owes to its regulators, shareholders, business partners, and (in a growing sense) the general public, is not new to the reader. This concept is now strengthened by rules of the New Capital Adequacy Framework which state that transparency plays a major role in *market discipline*. Transparency and market discipline correlate. Both are seen as the means to encourage high disclosure standards, inducing credit institutions to hold adequate capital, commensurate with the risks they take.

Market discipline is management intent in connection with the core function of financial reporting. The Basle Committee plans to issue further guidance on public disclosure, because it looks at market discipline as having the potential to reinforce capital regulation and other supervisory procedures. The goal is to put in place strong incentives on institutions to conduct their business in a safe and efficient manner, including the establishment of an appropriate cushion against potential future losses arising from trading, investments, loans and other exposures.

Both the board of directors and the supervisors of a company have a strong interest in facilitating effective market discipline as a lever to strengthening the banking system and its safety nets. The Basle Committee's *Enhancing Bank Transparency*, issued in September 1998, explains how a bank that is perceived as safe and well managed in the marketplace is likely to obtain more favourable terms and conditions in its relations with depositors, creditors, investors, correspondent banks, and other counterparties.

Major players today pay a great deal of attention to creditworthiness. They require higher risk premiums, and additional collateral or other safety measures if the institution with which they deal presents more risk. The same is true of whole markets. An example is the *Japan premium* instituted by the financial market in the late 1990s as soon as analysts perceived that the shaky nature of Japanese credit institutions, largely owing to gearing and overexpansion, led to much higher risks than previously anticipated.

Companies with a high degree of transparency, which are generally perceived as abiding by the rules of market discipline will, in all likelihood, be the first to be allowed by regulators to experiment with *precommitment* – if precommitment comes of age. As Alan Brown, of Barclays Bank, aptly suggested, precommitment assumes that the management of banks worries about position exposure and that it will be risk prudent every day. This involves self-discipline and management intent at the same time.

Dr Neil Jacoby, my professor of business strategy at UCLA, taught his students that one should not expect to see the strategy of a company printed in black and white in a neatly bound book. Instead, to find out the strategy one has to read policies, directives, and accounts – both the lines themselves and between the lines. We must also examine the way in which a company's top executives behave:

- Some people are a little cavalier at the end of the day and these are typically the people who lack self-discipline.
- Since organizations are made of people, they too may lack self-discipline, and by extension market discipline as well.

People and companies without self-discipline expose themselves to *reputational risk*. An example is unwillingness to face up to one's own commitments. Some organizations would rather dent their reputation than pay the losses resulting from the contracts they have signed. One of the more glaring cases following the East Asia meltdown was the refusal of SK Securities of South Korea to pay the $480 million it owed J.P. Morgan from losses in derivatives trades.

There is no such thing as 'a somewhat dented' reputation, as there is no way of being only somewhat pregnant: either a company has a reputation for integrity, or it has not. Similarly, there is no such thing in banking as just a little warning. The slightest signal that a credit institution or any other company is regarded as a liability has to be taken seriously and be fully accounted for for risk management reasons.

The lessons to be learned from the huge September 1998 losses with derivatives by Long-Term Capital Management (Chorafas, 2000c) is that the banking system needs new standards of responsibility, of self-discipline, of financial reporting, and of transparency. For their part, the regulators – the men entrusted with policing the banking system – need to be assisted through rigorous analytical techniques and high-technology solutions in order to stay ahead of the curve.

An interesting document along this line of reasoning is *Framework for Supervisory Information About the Derivatives Activities of Banks and Securities Firms*, issued in May 1995 by the Basle Committee on Banking Supervision and the Technical Committee of the International Organization for Securities Commissions (IOSCO). The Basle Committee and IOSCO addressed through this Framework the requirements for supervisory information on derivatives' activities of banks and securities firms. The document consisted of a catalogue of data on derivatives activities, broken down into the areas of:

- Credit risk
- Liquidity risk
- Market risk and
- Earnings.

When these frameworks and references are put on a global footing, supervisors can draw us more advanced guidelines which permit them to expand the analytics and improve upon the details of their financial reporting systems. The May 1995 Framework by the Basle Committee and IOSCO also included recommendations on what supervisors must have available to themselves to execute their prudential functions in an adequate manner.

Other organizations, too, can learn a great deal from this Basle Committee/IOSCO supervisory framework. While getting exposure to an asset for a significantly low financing cost is the target of most leveraged deals, counterparties entering into such transactions must be aware that they might have to liquidate assets under very unfavourable conditions if the market turns against them. Maximizing profits by using geared instruments like derivatives is no one-way street to higher returns; it can also lead to credit defaults and market meltdowns.

8 Establishing an Efficient Internal Control Structure

INTRODUCTION

Whether the bank's operations are centralized, decentralized, or organized along the principle of federated independent business units, a number of basic organizational prerequisites must always be present to ensure the observance of necessary functions and the fulfilment of basic requirements in the development and execution of internal control policies. The board and senior management need an internal control system able to support six basic issues characterizing a sound business practice:

- Goals of compliance, accounting reconciliation and preservation of assets
- Internal intelligence objectives for exposure control regarding trades, inventoried portfolio positions and other operations
- A mechanism for tracking fraud and other misdemeanours anywhere in the world, at any time
- Feedback risk control and other management controls everywhere the bank operates, at all organizational levels
- Feedback for corrective action, actuating the brakes to regulate or stop the risk-taking machine
- Feedback to assure that managers, professionals, and other employees operate in a manner commensurate with personal accountability.

The flexibility, adaptability and accuracy with which the internal control system operates is crucial in connection with each one of these references. The system must be structured in a way which makes it possible to obtain dependable results. Here is how Securum – the Swedish financial institution which in the 1992–7 timeframe became the most successful rescue operation – characterized the role of its internal control system.

Securum was set up by the Swedish government to take over the non-performing loans, real estate holdings and industry holdings of Nordbanken, which was at the time the second largest Swedish institution, largely under government control. Securum's credit-oriented restructuring had to be dependent on careful internal monitoring. This was achieved through a three-layered organisation shown in Figure 8.1.

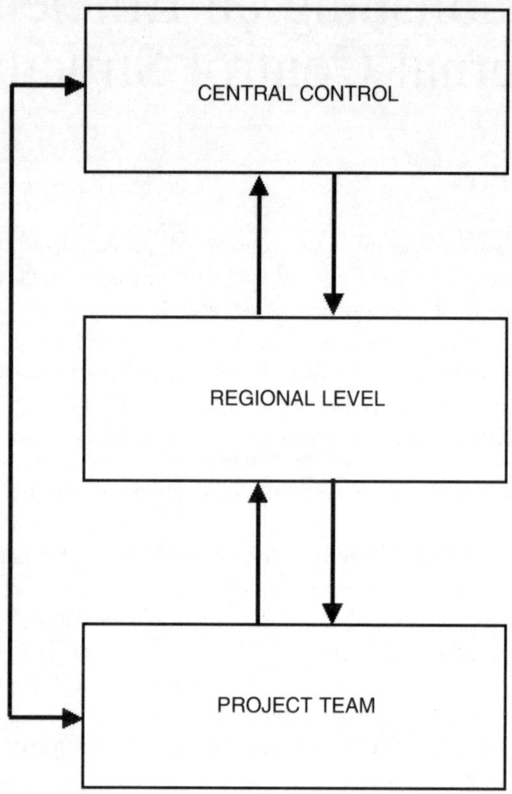

Figure 8.1 Securum's three-layered internal control organization for credit exposure

Each credit restructuring and/or liquidation case was first handled by a project team within the framework of general directives. The action plan was reviewed by Securum's regional credit authority. After receiving approval, the project moved on to the central credit committee, which included members of Securum's board of directors. At the same time, the financial company's top management ensured that:

- Decision-making channels remained short and
- The credentials of each case were not altered as it went up the hierarchy.

Presentations to the central committee were usually made by the leader of the project team, or in his the presence. While it was ensured that the cases were handled quickly at each level of decision making, the CEO watched that discovery-type (see Chapter 5) and analytical requirements were fully observed. Transparency was a keyword in this successful salvage operation; internal control was the watchdog.

One of the facts that impressed me in the case of Securum was the speed at which a newly constituted management team was able to put in place an *efficient* internal control structure. This is the best evidence ever in my database of being able to develop from scratch a whole internal control system in less than 3 months; 3 months was also the time necessary to put in place, and have up and running the core of a real-time information technology system (on client-servers) v. the 5 years that an outsourced mainframer had asked. This speaks volumes about the speed of deliverables when timetables are stringent and top management *wants* to see concrete results. The two projects were done in parallel.

ORGANIZATIONAL SOLUTIONS FOR INTERNAL CONTROL AT EDWARD JONES

Edward Jones is a well known broker in the United States. Its practice of auditing internal controls provides one of the best case studies I came across in my research. A sound policy starts with objectives and expectations. Ann Ficken, director of internal audit at Edward Jones, stated that

> a process of internal control can typically only provide reasonable assurance to top management that objectives, such as safeguarding assets and preventing fraud, are met. An acceptable process of internal control need not provide absolute assurance to management that those objectives are met.

Other companies, too, made the point that because a system of internal controls has to deal not only with planned events but also with those which are unexpected as well as with the law of unexpected consequences, there might be cases internal control does not detect the first time they show up. Therefore, it is a reasonable assumption that absolute assurance cannot be given, though the better is the organization and structure of internal control, the greater the likelihood it will function as intended.

Based on her experience as director of auditing, Ann Ficken identified the following issues she would focus on in auditing internal controls:

ensuring that transactions are authorized by the appropriate people; that transactions are completed in a timely manner; that transactions are completed accurately; that transactions are executed completely. She also noted that the next most important topics are:

- Whether the control process in place is working as efficiently as possible to maximize the results while minimising the cost and
- Whether the objective of the area being audited is consistent with the overall objectives of the firm.

At Edward Jones top management is directly responsible for the system of internal controls. The Internal Audit department has been charged with the responsibility of auditing this system. There have also been specific requests to the firm's *external auditors* for specific reviews of its internal controls. The Internal Audit department, Ficken said, is subject to Institute of Internal Auditors (IIA) standards, which state that an examination of the adequacy of an organization's system of internal control must be included in an internal audit function's responsibilities:

- Technology, Edward Jones suggested, has contributed to enhancing its system of internal control.
- The firm is proactively identifying risks and developing technology to mitigate these risks.

Is internal control at Edward Jones a concept, a process, or a department? The answer has been that internal control is viewed as a process composed of several components across the firm, some interrelated, but all considered to be management's responsibility. The company's system of internal control covers:

- The effectiveness and efficiency of processes.
- Reliability of financial reporting.
- Compliance with applicable rules and regulations.
- Security and accuracy of the firm's information.

It also provides reasonable means to prevent fraud. Edward Jones does not have a separate risk management function. Top management is accountable for managing the risks within the processes and systems, where they are embedded logically and globally. There is one executive responsible for global expansion, but he is supported by an other member of senior management in controlling the risks associated with globalization. The necessary intelligence is provided by internal control.

One of the issues discussed with Edward Jones was organizational prerequisites for internal control connected to globalization. The answer has been that globalization has not yet had a significant impact on the company's system of internal controls, but continued international expansion beyond Canada and the United Kingdom will have an impact in the future.

Management expects that the firm's international organization, and each regional and local operation, will have internal control procedures very similar to those currently in the United States. Initial processes are being established accordingly. Said Ann Ficken: 'We will monitor their systems of internal control in a similar manner as we do in our US operations.' She also added: 'We feel there will be some changes to our system of internal control because of globalization as there will be new laws and regulations that our firm must comply with.'

This is a reference made by most companies with transborder operations participating in this research project. Regulatory differences between the countries where they have a presence requires tuning up the internal control environment and adapting it to local conditions. Typically this leads to an organization more restrictive rather than less restrictive than the one already in place in the institution's home environment.

Ann Ficken also added that over and above market risk and credit risk operational risk exits in many areas, primarily in her company's operations division. (For the definition of operational risk see Chapter 2.) The management of the individual operational processes and systems is responsible for taking care of this risk; there are, however, some processes and systems where operations risk is integrated with credit risk and market risk – for example, all three of these risks exist in executing a customer trade.

The point was further made that one aspect of operational risk is that procedures and systems are not established, and that the processing of a trade will be subject to human error or fraud, or inappropriately recorded. Also, there could be a lack of segregation of duties between the trading areas and the operational and settlement processes.

To the query: 'How many people are currently involved in internal control activities', Edward Jones' answer has been that there are several members of top management across the firm who are responsible for the internal control system. These members of management report to the managing principal who, along with the management committee, sets the firm direction and objectives. In Edward Jones' opinion, senior management is responsible for establishing, revising, and upkeeping the internal control system.

By contrast, the Internal Audit department is responsible for auditing the internal control system, to determine whether controls are effective in achieving defined business objectives. At Edward Jones, Internal Audit submits to senior management reports of audits of components of the company's internal control system. These reports are mainly qualitative and are given to the firm's managing principal and the responsible management of the component:

- The report to the managing principal does not exceed a couple of pages in length.
- The report to management varies from 5 to 12 pages in length, depending on the audit.

Some operating units also prepare monthly measurement reports on the achievement of the firm's objectives. These are mainly quantitative. As an example of the audit of qualitative characteristics of internal control, Edward Jones emphasized learning about how management of associated business areas communicate with one another, and with the basic organizational structure of the area.

For greater efficiency in communications, for example, trading desk management in its trading area is located directly on the desks working side by side with the traders. That close proximity can't be quantified, but experience has taught the company that it adds to the internal control environment in the area as management can see and hear on a daily and intraday basis what is happening.

This reference brings up another example on the effects of proximity. In its lecture to the Third International Symposium on Risk Management (Geneva, March 1999), Britain's Financial Services Authority (FSA) spoke about two London-based investment banks. The one had a risk management group of 30 people located some 30 miles from London; the other had 5 people in risk management, but on the trading floor. Of the two, FSA suggested, the second was more effective.

THE PROCESS OF INTERNAL CONTROL AND THE PREREQUISITES FOR RISK MANAGEMENT

The careful reader would have noted the attention paid by Edward Jones to internal control as a concept, process and organizational solution. All three aspects are important. One of the conclusions cognizant people reached after Barings is that if the derivatives market poses a particularly dangerous threat to the well-being of a company and of the financial system at large, this primarily happens:

- Because of the way the product is used and misused – and therefore it is the *process*.
- Rather that the *product* – derivatives – which generates the risk.

Not everybody appreciates the fine print of the distinction between these two bullet points. Yet, the difference is significant. When asked about his opinion regarding a plan, President Eisenhower is said to have answered: 'The plan is nothing. Planning is everything.' It is planning, the process, which is most important – just as it is *controlling*, the process, to which should plenty of attention be paid. That's one of the reasons why I liked Ann Ficken's response.

Look at the failure and near-failure of Nordic banks in the late 1980s and early 1990s, and their subsequent salvage. In the case of Nordbanken the process of internal control was said to be practically non-existent while its mainframe technology remained that of Palaeolithic times. Securum was a *process* of liquidation of wounded Nordbanken assets which managed to salvage 75 cents to the dollar v. 35 per cent in a fire sale. Salvaging by Securum was a well run process which:

- Pulled wounded product out of the abyss and
- Redressed a dismal financial condition.

There are plenty of examples from the same frame of reference. One of those which should become a textbook of events never to be repeated again is the bottomless pit of Crédit Lyonnais which cost the French taxpayer a rumoured $35 billion by pouring good money after bad, rather than instituting a process of the salvaging Securum type.

The roads followed by Nordbanken and Crédit Lyonnais, two credit institutions salvaged by taxpayers' money at the 12th hour, have many similarities. In both cases there have been years of bad loans, substandard investments, and poor management. Both banks racked up losses in billions of dollars. By and large these came from the old banking businesses, such as loans, rather than from the new derivative financial instruments. This does not mean that derivatives are not dangerous, but they are not the only game in town where a bank can go broke:

- The *process* was rotten because internal controls were not in place to put a lid on exposure.

- This is what happens to banks which lack even elementary internal controls, a fact exacerbated by the ineffectiveness of norms set by the board.

Combined with superleveraging, which has become a trend these days, this failure of internal control processes raises serious questions about the stability of financial institutions. Precisely for this reason, as we saw in Chapter 7, one of the most demanding jobs confronting the board is to keep in touch with internal control realities, always remembering that authority may be delegated but responsibility stays with he (or she) who delegates.

To keep pace with market developments, the board and the CEO should continually draw up supplementary sources of new knowledge, making sure that the information channels function properly at all times. New policies must ensure a steady interaction between all divisions and departments whose tasks are directly or indirectly affected by risks: credit risk, market risk, operational risks and other risks. By means of simulation and *steady experimentation*, policies must encourage a search for improvements in products and processes to meet new needs:

- The notion of improvements should be inherent in the design of an internal control system.
- The opposite is also true – efficiency in internal control is integral part of 'improvement'.

As Edward Jones suggested internal control plans and goals must be widely communicated. A plan that is held close to the chest of a manager or his assistants will have little or no effect on the operations of the bank. Adequate communication is required to provide officials at all levels with an understanding of policies and processes regarding compliance, preservation of assets, and control of exposure, particularly as they affect their own areas of authority.

Let me immediately add that keeping a lid on exposure does not mean zero exposure; zero exposure is not attainable, even if it were desired. I had a professor of banking at UCLA who taught his students that a loans officer who has no bad loans is as counterproductive as one who has many bad loans, because in the process he has thrown away a lot of good business. In a similar manner, while the use of derivatives sees to it that the bank assumes lots of risk quickly, as an instrument they have some advantages – for instance, the possibility of hedging (within limits) and of providing the sort of liquidity the market needs. There is also the effect of innovation, of which we spoke in Chapter 2.

The downside with derivatives is that the risk may increase exponentially because *leveraging* is overdone owing to lust and greed. This is particularly the case when the internal controls are coarse-grained or have been allowed to rust. Hence the attention the board and senior management should play in ensuring a first-class system of checks and balances, at all levels of the organization – while never forgetting that process design and implementation is specific to the needs of *our* institution. Every bank has its own organization and management style which should be reflected in internal controls. As a matter of principle:

- The internal controls solution must be rigorous but custom-made.
- Even a first-class system for one bank may be overshooting or underserving the needs of another.

The process established for internal control must not only be robust and fine-grained, but also *time-sensitive*. Time is a vital resource, while appropriate timing is a cornerstone in management control. Everything done in the bank or by the bank requires adequate timing. Scheduling key events is critical to an orderly and efficient accomplishment of end results. Keeping exposure at reasonable levels calls for an appropriate scheduling algorithm which is understood and followed by all concerned:

- The timing must permit adequate consideration and co-ordination of the various steps involved in control action.
- It should be neither too strict nor too lazy, and should provide for performance to be evaluated through feedback.

Such a policy strengthens the validity and continuity of the internal control process. It also leads to a shake-up of the complacency characterizing many banking activities. This is the sense of dynamic management discussed in the next section. Along with time-sensitive considerations, an efficient custom-made system of internal controls should be culture-sensitive. As we saw in Chapter 7, every bank has its own culture which must be fully taken into account, otherwise chances are that the checks and balances put in place for internal control will underperform or overshoot.

COMMERCIAL RISK, FINANCIAL RISK AND THE TUNING OF INTERNAL CONTROL

Banks often deprive themselves of alternatives in risk management. They either bet on rocket scientists who are good in mathematics but know nothing of trading, or hire ex-traders who grasp what makes sense in risk control but have neither background in mathematical analysis nor experience in the experimental approach. Contrary to this one-way street, *our* institution should be keen to merge trading and analytical skills.

It takes teamwork to understand where the most troublesome exposure occurs, along the line of the threat curve discussed in Chapter 3. Nobody can say 'what has happened to others couldn't happen to us,' but everybody in a position of responsibility in *our* bank should be able to answer critical questions, including some pertaining to the belief structure (or culture) of the organization:

- The best, most efficient, internal control policies and processes are based on shrewd judgements.
- The worstreflect mediocre planning, too rigid timetables, and an entirely inadequate top management support.

One way to look at the checks and balances needed for internal control is to distinguish between *commercial* and *financial* exposure. Commercial risk comes from the choice of counterparties. Financial risk is the result of adverse changes in market conditions and/or mispricing (see also Chapter 8). Mispricing happens quite often, frequently as a result of misjudging volatility. As a consequence, the asked price may not cover the risk being taken, or even the cost.

Mispricing is often related to commercial risk. Pure commercial exposure represents adverse changes in credit risk and trading conditions, but the price of the product might be the real problem. When it is too high, it prices the financial instrument out of the market. When it is too low, it fails to cover risks and costs. 'Too high' and 'too low' are relative to what the market considers to be a 'fair price'; they are not absolute values.

Another characteristic of problems connected with an instrument's or commodity's price is exposure to loss from the exchange value of the commodity. For instance an adverse movement in exchange rate may reduce cash income and credits or, alternatively, increase cash expenditure. The aftermath would:

- Negatively affect the value of foreign assets
- Increase the value of foreign liabilities and
- Generally damage *our* company's competitive position.

Commercial risk has also much to do with commissions paid to traders, as the March 1997 loss of £90 million ($153 million) by NatWest Markets documents. Financial risk may be leading to reputational risk. Commercial and financial risks combine to make legends in mismanagement: Long-Term Capital Management (LTCM) is an example.

It is indeed fascinating when one stops to think about it, that a whole bunch of people with an IQ of 160 and a couple of Nobel Prize winners at LTCM could lead their company, to such a débâcle. However, that is what has happened and that's why truly intelligent people:

- Stick with simple things in finance and
- Put ethical values above everything else.

The Morgan Grenfell scandal is another example which raised many questions about the safety and suitability of the unit trust (mutual fund) as an investment vehicle for millions of customers. It all started on 2 September 1996, when Morgan Grenfell issued a statement which said that dealings in three of its investment funds had been suspended following the discovery of some potential irregularities in the valuation of unquoted securities:

- Morgan Grenfell European Growth Trust, with 70 000 investors
- Morgan Grenfell Europa, with 20 000 investors and
- Morgan Grenfell European Capital Growth Fund, a Dublin-based fund with 1800 investors.

One of the executives in charge of the valuation of the funds appears to have used a large slice of the $1.75 billion (£1.13 billion) invested in them to circumvent rules governing how mutual funds are managed. This steered investors' money into investments of exceptionally high risk, using a complex web of shell companies set up by himself with the help of Wiler & Wolf, a Swiss law firm. As much as 37 per cent of the funds' cash was invested in unquoted companies, and though this was later reduced to 23 per cent it still broke the rules without being detected in time by the company's system of internal controls. This failure is a good example on how weak internal controls can get bypassed, because Morgan Grenfell had established rules for mutual funds management which seem to have been bent. These rules forbid trusts from:

- Holding more than 10 per cent of any one company and
- Investing more than 10 per cent of their portfolios in unquoted securities.

As in the case of Barings, Morgan Grenfell had failed to implement a rigorous system of internal controls. As a result, it was revealed post mortem that a big chunk of the investment was in obscure unquoted companies. This amount seems to have been so large that it became impossible to value the portfolios properly and therefore publish an accurate price for buying and selling units in the funds. The bank went on selling the funds even though the prices given might not have been accurate, thus misleading investors.

To save the day Deutsche Bank, Morgan Grenfell's parent, had to put DM 240 million (£85 million, $130 million) into the trusts to make good any misvalued holdings in unquoted stocks. Thereafter, it was possible to pay compensation to those who lost out because of buying units in the funds at artificially high prices. An auditing firm, Arthur Andersen, was appointed to calculate compensation. To do so, it had to track back to the point where the portfolios began to deviate from the rules. Arthur Andersen:

- Valued the portfolios on each subsequent day, recalculating unit prices and
- Compared these prices with the unit prices published at the time.

The lesson the reader should retain from this case is that every bank will be well advised to have in place a system of internal controls which is regularly audited, as well as to have available the technology able to do in real-time what Arthur Andersen had to do post mortem. Since Chapter 1 I have pointed our that agents and expert systems can do a first-class job. Any financial product can be mispriced, and any account can be massaged. There is no better way to get to know about it than through comparative scenarios and analytics.

As an advice, this has to be done case-by-case for important clients, in a way which provides the added benefit of calculating, also, the exposure our bank takes with each counterparty and the money it makes from that account. By contrast, for smaller accounts, statistical inference should be used. This, too, is an important element in establishing the quantitative infrastructure of rigorous internal controls.

SHOULD WE ANALYZE THE BEHAVIOURAL PATTERN OF OUR TRADERS?

The careful reader will recall the reference I made about my professor of business strategy at UCLA who taught his students that one should never expect to find the strategy of an institution or any other company to be written in black and white in a manifesto. But it is possible to make *inferences*, which prove to be quite accurate, based on patterns. The pattern in Figure 8.2 is that of the evolution of longer-term financial assets v. the trading portfolio in one of the better known money centre banks:

- From Year 1 to Year 4 this bank's behavioural pattern reflects a rapid growth in trading revenues – evidently, a top management decision.
- As this strategy has gained momentum, in Year 4 the board decided to focus on financial assets without soft-pedalling on trading.

This dual strategy based on one theme at a time worked well. From Year 1 to Year 5 the financial institution in question more than tripled its business connected to these two channels. It also took some added risks. If we wish to understand the risks *our* bank takes, we should establish behaviour

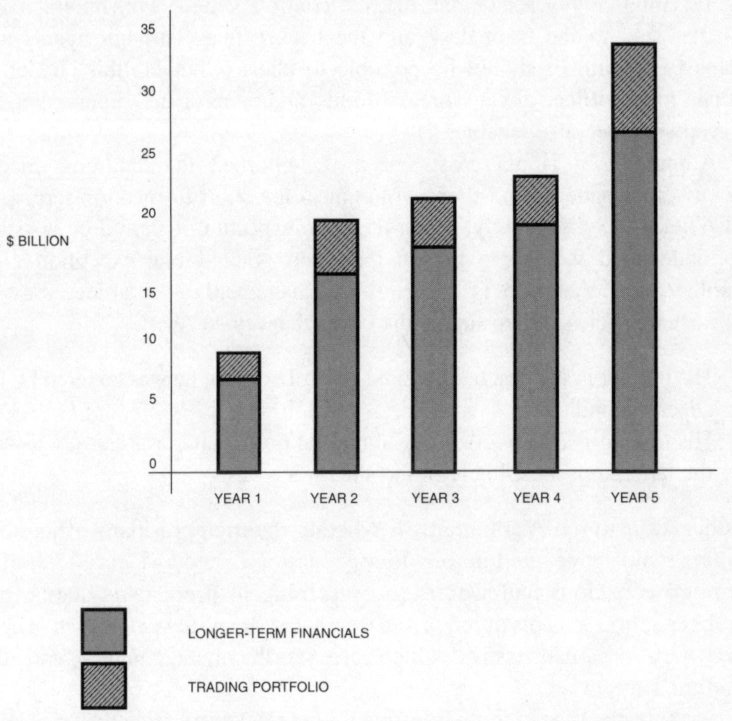

Figure 8.2 Evolution of longer-term financial assets v. the trading portfolio at a money centre bank

patterns not only of the institution as a whole but also of our professionals: loans officers, investment experts, and traders.

Behaviour patterns also assist in detecting possible fraud, and they can serve as prognosticators of coming trouble. For any practical purpose, patterns of the type I am discussing are a qualitative expression of *sensitivities*, and internal controls can make good use of them. For this purpose, some banks have developed a battery of tests which assist in establishing behaviour patterns, particularly looking for traders who:

- Refuse to talk to auditors, no matter what the reason
- Never take a holiday and even come to work on weekends
- Put firewalls in their databases and remove floppies 'for security reasons'
- Arrange their system so that nobody understands the maze of passwords they are using.

The fact that the last two bullet points have to do with networked workstations is not accidental. Internal controls should work interactively all the way to the front desk and the back office. Through agents and database mining it should be possible to check whether 'this' trader or 'that' loans officer always breaks limits and/or asks his supervisors for exceptions (see also Chapter 9).

Admittedly it is not easy, but it is important that auditing checks behavioural patterns and their evolution in the short to medium term (see also below). Subsequently, by on-the-spot inspection it should be possible to understand whether a person has been granted one exception after another, and therefore is treated by management as a golden boy, a protected species. When this is the case, chances are that:

- His trading in the past has escaped control because he was covered by his superiors and
- His trading is characterized by abnormal profits and/or abnormal losses, the latter kept most likely in the shadows.

Other ways to look for patterns is whether the trader or loans officer has a large mortgage, and/or big house, and/or expensive car; is status-symbol conscious and would do everything to protect his status; has trouble at home: is divorced or separated and the wife is after him. These are very practical issues which are worth management's and the auditor's attention.

Some banks now tune their informal internal controls in a way that they are able to detect whether some of their traders and officers are anti-social introverts, and in a bad mood even when making money. Or, are heavy drinkers or even on drugs. Or, shout at the back office and are always in friction bad relations with the risk management personnel.

'As a matter of principle,' said a senior risk management officer in London, 'the louder a man shouts the more he has to hide.' The same is true about being unavailable, too busy to look into control results, or unable to explain the mechanism which led to abnormal profits and commissions. Because of these cases, only a steady and careful:

- Measuring
- Monitoring and
- Analysis

can help to find out what happens to *our* bank's exposure. The notions underpinning a systematic process of measuring, monitoring, and analyzing can be traced back to the early twentieth century when Frederick Winslow Taylor studied the time it takes to handle ingots. In the mid-1920s Dr F.B. Gilbreth examined the statistics from time studies and found that:

- The plotting of performance time tended to approximate the normal distribution; this greatly assists in matters of control.
- In about 95 per cent of cases the ratio of higher to lower productivity was about 2.2 – the other 5 per cent was exceptions.

Even exceptions, however, have limits. If a factory worker is superfast and always ends up with a very high ratio, he has a gimmick. A similar principle applies with traders who always fabricate high profits (and commissions for themselves) – but invariably the institution they work for ends up with toxic waste – and therefore with losses.

Though there are exceptions with outliers in profit figures (as in productivity), if these 'exceptions' multiply then the system has loopholes. But it may also be a spike is legitimate. Therefore the chief risk management officer should think before he shouts, by having his assistants dig deeper into each case, and by asking the auditors to do their part of the job. Statistics are a valuable indicator not *the* evidence that something is right or wrong.

Digging deeper means examining the pattern (and the books) to find factual and documented evidence. Is the trader's record characterized by large trades in notional principal amount? Is he always betting on the same instrument? Does he have a significant number of forward transactions? Or a hoarding of:

- Long-term forward rate agreements?
- Currency-based swaps?

- Illiquid positions?
- Very long maturities?

An internal control system should include models able to help in looking into behaviour patterns by default. Is there a diversification in regard to counterparties? In a steady observance of management policies and regulations? In a considerable measure, these are questions the auditors should be after. But qualitative answers can go only so far. A better method is quantification and the use of statistical quality control (SQC) charts. An example is shown in Figure 8.3 (Chorafas, 2000a).

This text has on repeated occasions brought the reader's attention to statistical distributions and tolerances. One of the key services offered by SQC charts is that they help in the exploitation of *intraday* statistics. Even if *our* bank's reporting system works interday, because of low technology, the trades which we do and the commitments we make are done intraday. Are we able to:

- Check for intraday trading?
- Look for intraday patterns?
- Analyze how each dealer is trading?
- Find out with whom he is frequently in contact?

In other words, are the internal controls able to assist senior management in drilling down the layers of responsibility? Can the internal control system flush out who hedges and who speculates? Designing, implementing, and testing our institution's system of internal controls is a job-oriented proposition. Hence, the custom-made characteristics of the solution, to which I so often make reference.

The underlying control principles, however, are much more general and they get increasingly enriched with mathematical and statistical tools. An example is General Electric's Six Sigma methodology for quality control implemented not only by GE's manufacturing divisions but also by GE Capital. In a way very similar to the solution I have suggested, this methodology involves:

- Statistical quality control methods
- Chi-square testing to evaluate variance between two populations[1]
- Experimental design to permit a methodological test of hypothesis
- Graphical tools for process mapping
- A rigorous defect measurement method
- A dashboard to map progress towards customer satisfaction (very important in banking)

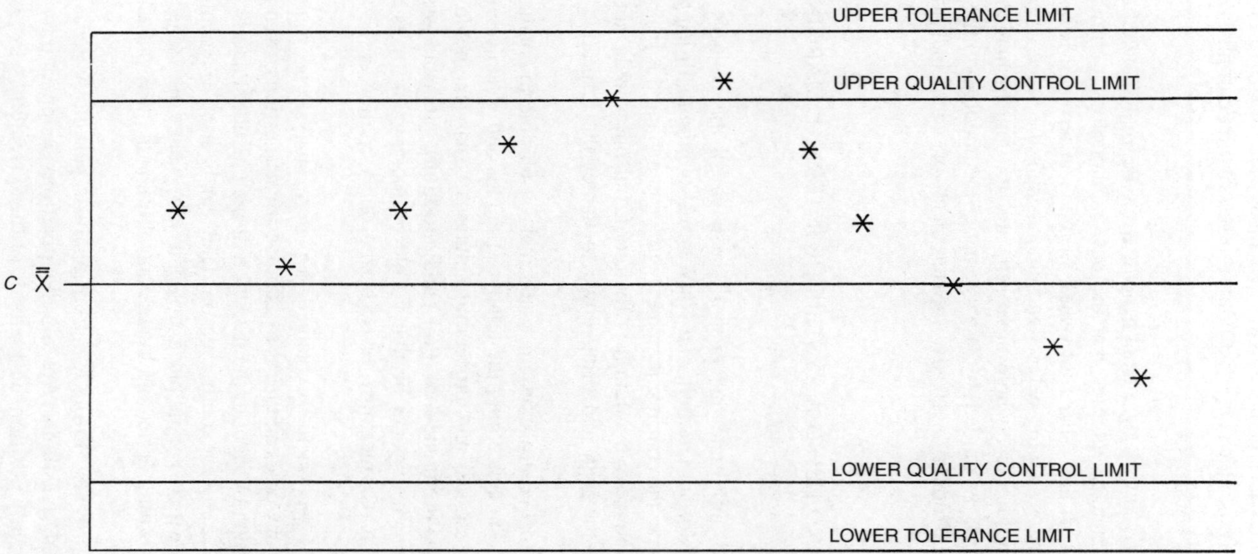

Figure 8.3 An SQC chart with tolerance limits and control limits

- A Pareto diagram which exhibits relative frequency and/or size of events
- Root-cause analysis which targets original reasons for non-compliance or non-conformance

GE Capital has derived very significant benefits from the implementation of Six Sigma. GE management says that the new methodology permits to focus on quality, cost and other root issues. In practical terms, it helps in reducing cycle time, swapping defects and emphasising the value of each individual contribution. The whole approach, and its implementation in financial operations, is guided by a systematic methodology utilising training tools and doing a steady measurement of each individual performance.

DEVELOPING AND USING A SYSTEM OF INTERNAL MARGIN CALLS

The reader would appreciate that even if we have all the controls the Barings, LTCM, Morgan Grenfell, and NatWest cases might still happen. But if we do not have the controls, then they *will* happen – and this makes a great deal of difference. No solution is foolproof, but one should not let every fool run in the wild and bring down in flames the institution for which he works.

A rigorous internal controls system would make it feasible to conduct a practical investigation concerning the relative strengths and weaknesses of the current organizational and procedural solutions. Analysis should go beyond the classical profit and loss (P&L) and into future gains and losses, including items which may not be that visible by looking into facts and figures presented in risk meetings, or by basing one's opinion on how is risk spoken about.

As the previous section has explained, a pattern analysis is valuable because it gives many clues and leads to asking critical questions, even if it might not be pointing outright to the detection of malpractice. Patterns are also an instrumental tool for another reason. They can be used to reconfirm that the controls which are in place do their job. That's the sense of keeping a process within upper and lower control limits the way presented in Figure 8.3.

The visibility provided through pattern analysis permits us to ask a number of crucial questions: Are all the positions mapped into the system? Are there any positions left outside of the system? If 'yes', why is it so? Have the internal auditors highlighted these exclusions as shortcomings? Are these shortcomings taken seriously and acted upon? A good investigative policy is to ask everyone individually where the greatest risk lies in the trading book, then compare the answers to queries like the following:

- Is the independent risk management function really independent?
- Are there provisions for bad risks? If 'yes', at which level of confidence? Who decides about them?

Simulation can complement such findings, as well as help to answer other queries: How much can *our* bank lose in an event like the 1987 stockmarket crash? In a débâcle of bonds similar to that of 1994? In a meltdown like the East Asian in 1997 and Russian in 1998? Where is the biggest risk in our portfolio? How big could be the loss? Is this possible loss within the risk appetite of *our* bank? Within the time horizon which reflects the policy of the board?

But simulation needs not only models. It is also very hungry for input. Typically, mathematics is the 20 per cent of the problem; the other 80 per cent is data. Therefore internal controls should be worked in a way which promotes complete, timely, and accurate data collection by pinpointing individual responsibilities. We have spoken on several occasions of this requirement.

An example on what is feasible in terms of processes and responsibilities in a risk control sense is a system of *internal margin calls*. Such procedures have been established by some institutions. Let me start with a query by way of introduction to this subject. Is capital a substitute for risk management? Fundamentally, the answer to this query is 'No!' Because:

- *If* we cannot quantify the possible size of our losses
- *Then* we will run out of capital very fast.

There is a joke at Wall Street that the way to make a small fortune is to start with a big one. Using a comfortable amount of capital for trading, or as insurance, is no comprehensive approach to risk control and, quite definitely, it is no good measure for setting internal control alerts. But used in an ingenious way, capital at risk could be an instrumental input (Chorafas, 2000b). That's why a system of internal margin calls can be a good way of checking on exposure:

- Based on the standard deviation of the risk distribution
- Using the concept of a central reinsurance policy and
- Leading to dynamic analysis of recognized gains and losses.

For instance, any individual member of the operation at the front desk, from loans to derivatives and other channels, should be reinsured by a central fund to which it contributes part of its profit margin when it is contracting business. Also, when realizing profits. This sort of insurance system is an interesting concept which has characterized the Federal Deposit Insurance Corporation (FDIC), since its inception in the 1930s (Chorafas, 2000d).

One of the advantages presented by a steady internal reinsurance solution is that it puts the breaks on extravagant profit claims and commissions. Another is that capital is put aside for the rainy day when the situation is manageable. Internal margin calls or reinsurance contribution should be calculated not just on actual amounts, but also on the basis of risks being taken some time in the future – because of the commitments being made.

This approach revamps and restructures the concept of capital at risk. It makes risk positions a function of business opportunity in the face of uncertainty involved in assumed position(s). Banks which in their internal controls have followed a strategy of internal margin calls found that, over time, risk becomes more limited because it is more visible. Internal margin calls confine it to a level where capital loss does not jeopardize:

- The substance of the bank's activities
- Its assumed risk profile(s) and
- The profit expectations by operational unit.

Banks do calculate a risk profile, but in the majority of cases they keep at a summary level which is not enough. The statistics in Figure 8.4 come from a money centre bank and identify average market risks assumed in five major channels of activity in two consecutive years at the end of the 1990s. These market risk statistics are classified in five major channels. It is evident that, for internal control purposes, there should be at least two further layers of detail.

Notice that in Year 2 the institution in question reduced its *cross-risk* by half, and also slightly its interest rate exposure. To the contrary, currency exchange risk has increased by about 15 per cent, essentially absorbing the reduction in business in the other channels. Figure 8.4 provides a good estimate of this bank's strategic approach to exposure to its main five trading channels, but internal control should offer much more than that. It should feed detailed data into real-time simulators which upkeep the

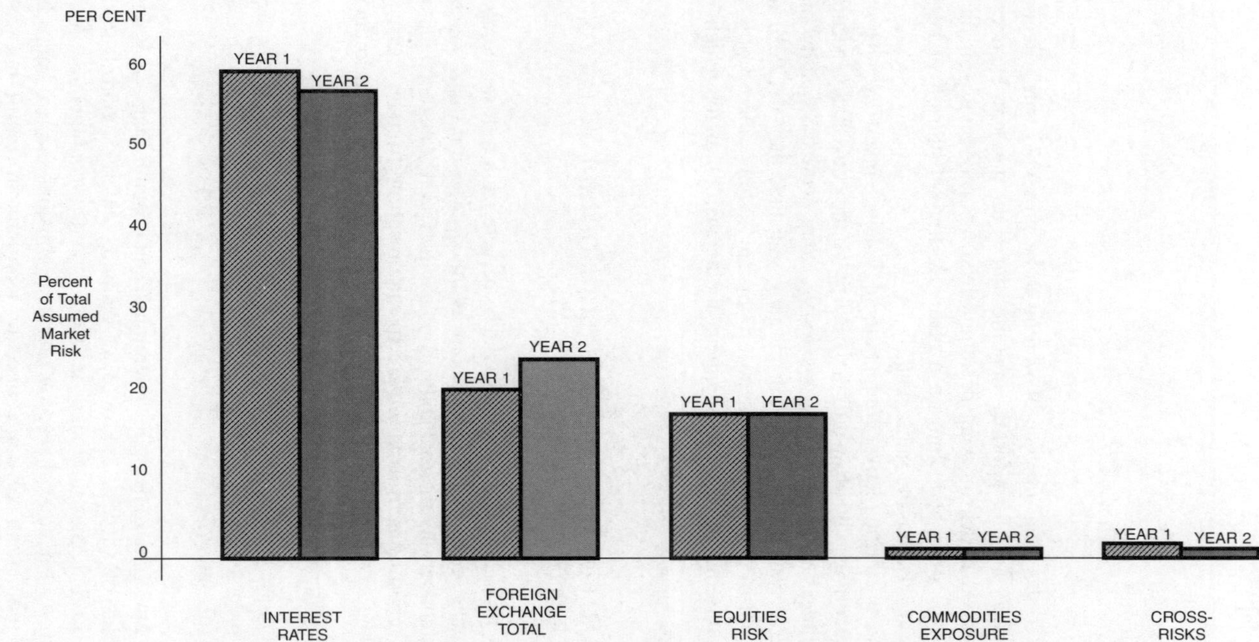

Figure 8.4 Average market risks of a money centre bank, over a period of 2 years

management information system, enabling authorized executives to reach exposure figures by:

- Instrument
- Counterparty
- Branch and
- Trader.

Contrary to the usual practice of waiting to be presented with a report, a good manager asks for information at the spur of the moment. He does not give advanced notice on what he might need, and does not wait for the answer to be brought to him on a plate. He finds it himself or herself, through database mining and agents.

By means of interactive computational finance, board members and senior executives who are worth their salt judge the consistency, accuracy, and timeliness of their bank's position – along with the quality of its information system. By following intraday statistics, they decide if their people control the assumed exposure or are simply after profits and commissions, no matter what happens to the institution for which they work.

INTERNAL CONTROLS SHOULD HIGHLIGHT INFORMATION TECHNOLOGY FAILURES

Let's talk first about the principles which characterize a well run company. *If* top management really cares about assumed exposure, then structural decisions concerning internal controls reflect the fact that a crucial factor in financial reporting is *transparency*. Exposure resulting from any activity is tracked, and to do so in an adequate manner the missions given to internal control:

- Are very clear
- Well understood and
- Self-explanatory.

An order always risks being misinterpreted, and misunderstanding is one of the enemies of success. Like project planning, internal control needs a framework and the first step is correct and unambiguous problem definition. As I have explained on repeated occasions, no two banks have the same problem to solve in connection with internal control, but we can always learn from those that have effective solutions. What practically all have to face, however, are problems connected with their information technology which are very similar.

Information technology problems are so similar from one company to the next because they have common roots. These are first of all an 'EDP' mentality. In the 1950s the anagram used to mean 'electronic data processing'. 50 years down the line, say tier-1 banks in New York, EDP means 'emotionally disturbed people'. That says much about the culture. But there are also other reasons for backwater conditions in information technology.

Company politics is one of them. To eat up a huge budget every year, with so little return on investment, the way EDP does, it must be that somebody is covering the unable, the unwilling, and the unnecessary. Usually, this is the board when its members are not computer literate. This is of course to the detriment of the company and its interests, as divisions, departments, and branches are left with obsolete mainframes, substandard 20-year or 30-year old software, and other frills.

It is in no way a coincidence that companies which are interested in establishing and maintaining a system of internal controls pay a great deal of attention to streamlining their information technology, and to developing solutions which are state of the art. In a meeting in Boston, State Street Bank mentioned a manufacturing company specializing in building materials whose chief risk management officer is a senior executive in the treasury unit. His mission is to:

- Look at commodity prices globally, projecting on price evolution and auditing procurement practices and
- Evaluate the company's dependency on information technology and the risks it is taking when there are IT failures.

Few companies appreciate the importance of this second bullet point, and usually banks are not among them. Yet, the effectiveness of all the internal controls we put in place depends on information technology. If communications, computers, and software don't use knowledge engineering artefacts and don't work with 99.99 per cent reliability, the company will be hurt. It may even be paralyzed in its risk management functions.

This statement is true for any company but, other things being equal, multinational enterprises are more vulnerable to IT hangup and failures than local ones. In the example of the manufacturing company used by the State Street Bank, about 50 per cent of the business is in the United States, the other 50 per cent international. For many years, the management of this company has been decentralized and P&L has been good. Then, a rigorous audit found that:

- There was no effective global control over the many and different types of risk the company was taking, because both the range and magnitude of risks continued to grow.
- This led to the institution of a chief risk management officer position, a custom-made organizational development to fit the company's unique profile.

Is there a similar example from the banking industry where rigorous audits have found that there is much to be desired in terms of IT services and return on investment in Information technology? To say the answer is: 'Yes!' is to state the obvious. One of the most recent issues which attracts attention in connection with Information technology is that most institutions have substandard services, in spite of huge outlays.

Not that information technology should be considered as being the only persistent weak spot. The other eye-catcher is the irrationalities built into the bonus system. The current practice of inflated bonuses:

- Promotes risk-taking rather than risk control and
- Leaves the institution with lots of toxic waste.

Among regulators, the Bank of England is worried that some incentive schemes, including big lump-sum payments for hitting specific profit targets, may tempt traders to take excessive risks. Other central banks, too, have come to believe that huge bonuses might be creating a system of stars who feel compelled to justify their status by taking greater risks in hope of making much higher profits:

- The good news is that the current cultural climate makes trading flourish, creating innovative banking and a global economy.
- The bad news is that it also promotes financial products with many unknowns, which are not controlled as they should be.

Financial analysts in the City think that behind the Bank of England warnings are fears that overpaying and high-rolling risk-taking could damage the financial industry. They may as well aggravate the cycle of booms and busts. One of the options currently being discussed in connection with operational risk is that the G-10 central banks might set higher capital ratio requirements for financial institutions with risky pay arrangements.

In my book, I would like to see higher capital requirements applied also to commercial banks who do not provide hard core evidence they are beefing up their IT support to be ahead of the curve. IT is an operational risk *par excellence*. In recent research on operational risk the majority of participating institutions identified lacklustre information technology, and the slow pace of its deliverables as their No. 1 headache (see also Chapter 12).

Part III
Case Studies on the Implementation of Internal Control

9 Applying Internal Control to Our Institution's Limits System

INTRODUCTION

In my postgraduate studies at UCLA I had a professor of banking who taught his students that 'no matter how good a new deal is, if the counterparty limit has been reached no further deals are possible'. This is not the message the majority of credit institutions give to their traders and credit managers, and even those who want to see limits set by the board fully observed at all time are unable to hit that goal so because:

- The prevailing level of detail is not appropriate and
- There is no real-time reporting on internal controls, including limits.

Excuses why 'limits should be observed but can't be always observed to the letter' wear thin. We must always be ready to learn from great bankers. Beyond the broad scope of his vision, Dr Pierpont Morgan was extremely attentive to detail – and the observance of limits means detail. He took pride in the knowledge he could sit down at any clerk's desk, take up his work and go on with it. 'I don't like being in any man's mercy', he used to say. Throughout his career:

- He never renounced the founder's right to know the most minute details of the business
- He examined the cash balance daily, and boasted he could pay off debts on 2 hours' notice
- He had an eagle's eye for fake figures and massaged accounting data in scanning a ledger and
- He *personally* audited the books of his bank every New Year's Day.

In these times, J.P. Morgan had tough lending limits. 'We used to think of Morgan as a nice small bank,' remarked Guido Verbeck, then a Guarantee Trust officer, 'Because of their lending limits, when they participated in large loans they could only take a small share and they were very worried about it' (Chernow, 1990).

Whether limits are set for credit risk or market risk, the concept underpinning them is to assure that traders, loans officers and other front desk professionals don't bet the bank when they are transacting business. For this reason the board, the CEO, and senior management need a system which reports on detailed limits and their usage in regard to:

- Counterparty risk
- Interest rate risk
- Currency exchange risk
- Equity derivatives risk and
- Other business risks the bank is taking.

Most financial institutions have a summary system in place with relatively large reporting intervals. That's absolutely nonsense. Only tier-1 banks have gone a big step further to study and established dynamic limits with tick-by-tick updates and intraday reports – which can tell when trading is prudent and when it is exposed to overruns which exceed the risk threshold implicitly or explicitly set through board policies. The theme of the present chapter is why and how risk thresholds should always be observed and what internal control can contribute to this process.

LIMITS, MARKING-TO-MARKET, AND THE CONTRIBUTION OF INTERNAL CONTROL

The establishment of prudent limits on risk exposures is a characteristic of sound management. Compliance with limits for borrowers and trading counterparties reduces within acceptable levels the bank's concentration of credit risk. Limits associated with interest rates, currency exchange, equity indices, and other commodities help in keeping market risk under control. They also assist in diversifying the institution's risk profile.

Experience with the management of exposure by leading financial institutions demonstrates that an important aspect of internal control is the periodic review of compliance with prudential limits. To be effective, limits must be kept dynamic and be regularly monitored in terms of their observance, including approvals and authorizations associated with exceptions:

- All transactions over established limits must be authorized by higher level management, with authorizations databased.
- A person, helped by expert systems not a bureaucratic department, should ensure the responsibility associated with limits.

'The way we manage risk is not the same with a consolidated balance sheet,' said a senior executive. 'We must break risk down to each post and to its basic elements, and pay due attention to *risk tolerance*, not only at bank level but also all the way down to the trader.' At Merrill Lynch, risk tolerance at trader level is allocated by the desk head. Assignments at desk level are done after study of the level of corporate risk tolerance. Hence, they are part of a co-ordinated system.

This approach to detail makes sense. It also helps to establish personal accountability. As the reference changes from corporate to desk level it makes it feasible to analyze risk management along a multidimensional frame, the way shown in Figure 9.1. The crucial issue, however, is that steady observance of limits must be a subject of verification of transaction details.

- Both for credit risk and for market risk this must be assisted through simulation models used by the bank as part of its planning and control activities.

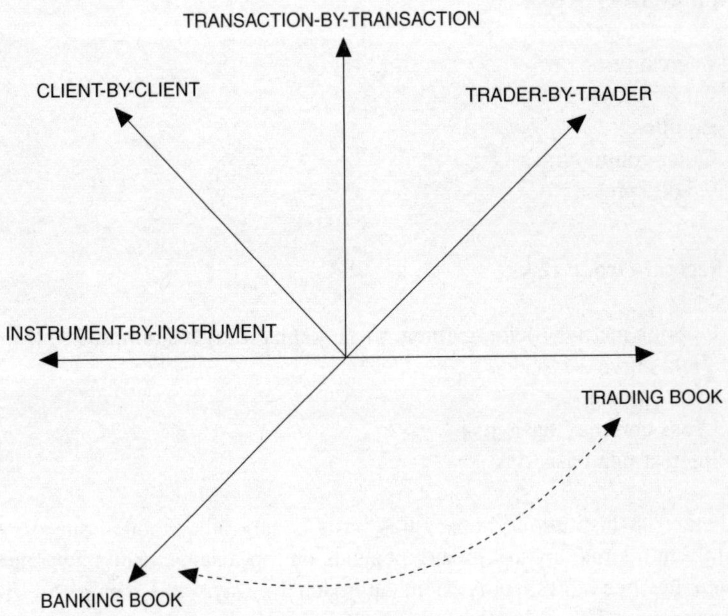

Figure 9.1 Risk management should be studied in a multidimensional space, in a manner similar to process control

- The real-time data streams making possible both the setting and the control of benchmarks should be assimilated and reported by internal control.

All of the computational chores must, of course, be automated. Reconciliations comparing cash flows to account records and other statements can identify activities and records that need correction. When real-time controls are applied to day-to-day operations, they permit quick responses to changing conditions, helping to avoid unnecessary risks.

The question then becomes: Which are the risk metrics better suited for internal control of limits other than the more classical benchmarks (see below). There is no unique answer to this query as each bank follows its own method and chooses its own tools. Some institutions, however, have better methods and sharper tools than others. One of the best I found in my research comes from Crédit Suisse and since it has been published in the 1997 Annual Report it does not constitute a trade secret. Crédit Suisse distinguishes between *First-Order Risks* and *Second-Order Risks.*

1 First-Order Risks

- Interest rates
- Currency rates
- Equities
- Other commodities
- Credit spread.

2 Second-Order risks

- Options metrics (delta, gamma, theta, kappa, rho) (Chorafas, 1994b)
- Yield curve
- Swap spread
- Cross-currency basis risk
- Interest rate basis risk.

Whether an institution chooses this basis or any other model, success or failure in internal control greatly depends on top management's awareness about the need for a polyvalent approach to ways and means for risk management. This polyvalence is integral aspect of business activity and, in principle, it is a safeguard of the values in the trading book and in the banking book.

Top-tier banks supplement their system of market risk and credit risk limits, which ensure adherence by the operating units to ceilings set by management, by a more sophisticated approach. The policy behind this approach and its tools revolves around the ability able to measure market risk and credit risk exposure of each and every position using analytical techniques:

- Gains and losses are determined by marking positions to market on a daily basis or, even better, intraday – a job done through expert systems using market data feeds (Chorafas and Steinmann, 1991).
- A *virtual balance sheet* statement of total recognized gains or losses, as well as an income statement, is constructed interactively as required, with real-life data updated as of the last 30 minutes.

Rigorous risk management models are available to permit online experimentation on exposure, with the results handled and visualized through internal control. Whether the trading book portfolio consisting of instruments traded in the exchanges is marked daily or intraday, depends on the level of volatility. Over-the-counter (OTC) transactions, for which no official market prices are available, are valued using sophisticated eigenmodels established and tested for risk management reasons.

Many banks see to it that mismatch exposure in the loans book is weeded out of it and into the trading book through internal interest rate swaps. Typically this is done for internal management accounting reasons, not for reporting to supervisors. Both market volatility and liquidity are regularly monitored to assure that the bank does not find itself confronted with serious unpleasant surprises:

- Volatility and liquidity *per se*, are not part of internal control but their aftermath on exposure is a vital element in risk management.
- Nor is liquidity a monolith, limited issue is one of the most pervasive elements in finance and banking.

As Figure 9.2 suggests, liquidity has at least four main dimensions and these have to be controlled intraday for reasons of sound management. The most visible dimension is that of regulatory capital requirements and special reserves needed by *our* institution. Each transaction, however, has its own liquidity characteristics – whether medium term bought money, overnight deposits and money coming from derivatives trades or due to counterparties. *Our* bank's liquidity pattern varies *intraday*, and it should be controlled on that basis.

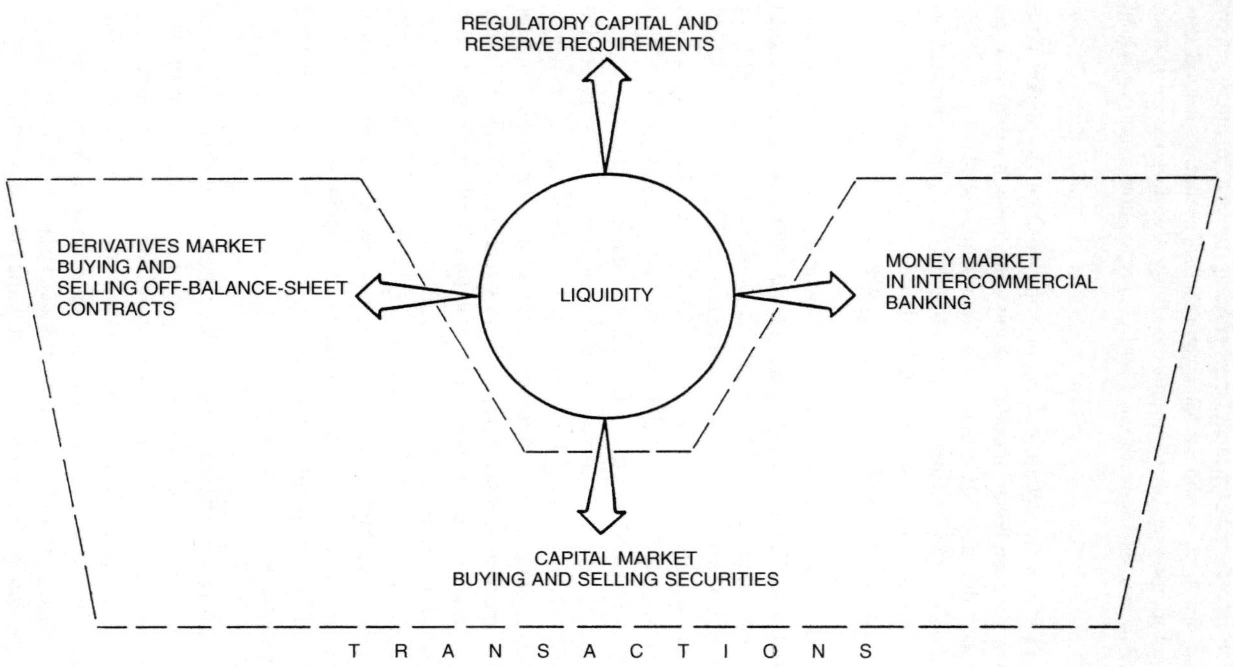

Figure 9.2 Four different dimensions of liquidity to be controlled intraday

INTERNAL CONTROL AND THE ROLE OF BENCHMARKS

The message this section aims to convey to the reader is that, as experience demonstrates, it is rewarding to effectively compare results against some norm or standard. This is the sense of plan v. actual evaluations which we do with budgeting, production goals, and marketing plans. In banking, plan v. actual comparisons are done by setting limits, establishing benchmarks, and regularly monitoring credit risks and market risks arising from trading, lending, investments, and other activities.

This approach is the cornerstone of *management by exception*. The rationale for comparisons lies in the fact that the risks a company takes cannot be fully appreciated in an abstract sense. They must be seen relative to a *benchmark*. This is one of the roles of first- and second-order risks of which we spoke earlier. Benchmarks must be pragmatic and they should be accurate. A good way for establishing them is to identify *our* institution's:

- Objectives
- Activities
- Practices and
- Risk appetite.

Take as an example fixed internet rate instruments, a very common investment vehicle for banks. Few credit institutions really appreciate that even with a basic product such as bonds they must set clear investment objectives and limits on:

- Duration risk (Chorafas, 1995a)
- Currency risk and
- Composition risk.

Here is, in a nutshell, the meaning of these references. *Duration risk* reflects the impact of interest rate volatility on the instrument's maturity. *Currency risk* is always expressed in connection with one base currency (or a basket of currencies) *our* company uses for management reasons and financial reporting practices. *Composition risk* distinguishes among financial products in the bank's portfolio.

Let me also stress the importance of the method being used in measuring exposure in connection with the aforementioned dimensions. The old way was to consider volume and maturity. The new and much better method is *duration*. It reflects sensitivity of prices, but says nothing on the risk-weighted effect of these changes. This can be done by thorough value-at-risk (VAR) measures (Chorafas, 1998b). The weakness of this method lies in the assumption that history repeats itself.

One of the senior executives participating in this research suggested that while necessary a limit set at an absolute level as a threshold is not enough. Part and parcel of the objectives senior management sets should be the return for the risks being taken. This, too, is a benchmark. Capital preservation and cash flow are other examples:

- How much money can we expect on a given date?
- How much can we make if currencies move the way we project?
- How much can we make from projected changes in interest rates?

Indivisible from a risk and return computation is the development and use of (1) worst-possible loss scenarios, (2) higher-likelihood events. Such prognostications should lead to quantitative benchmarks.

Because markets are dynamic, the most critical scenarios have to be tested *every day*, if the need arises – not every week or every month. Scenario analysis is a good complement to duration and VAR. Here are two queries reflective of the aftermath of changes in market conditions:

- *What if* the Federal Reserve does 'this'?
- *What if* the Treasury does 'that'?

It is always a valuable experience to take into account the likelihood of major events as well as the aftermath of changes, but it is also a difficult practice because of large numbers of '*What ifs*' which may characterize market conditions. Internal control is not concerned with the practice of '*What ifs*', but it is interested in communicating the results of the analysis.

Beyond scenario analysis, stress testing is a way to apply rigorous computational algorithms on a homogeneous basis for comparison reasons. A good example is the demodulation of notional principal amounts to obtain risks comparable to those of the lending practice (Chorafas, 2000c). This demodulation should definitely be an input to the internal control system, particularly so because it speaks a language practical all board members understand.

Duration, UAR, scenario analysis, stress testing, and demodulation are valuable methods which work best when there are benchmarks – hence the limits system. Dynamic limits established by senior management tell the bank's traders, loans officers, investment executives, and other professionals how to go from 'here' to 'there' without crossing over wires which can burn down part of the business, or even turn the whole company belly-up.

A thoroughly studied system of limits, and the operational rules underpinning it, should aim to serve the bank's business strategy and the individual products in which it deals, the markets in which it trades, the lending business which it makes, as well as the legal and supervisory framework within which it works. The internal control framework associated with these activities should be designed to:

- Maximize the efficiency of the company's executives, and their reach
- Minimize the costs incurred in connection to data collection, processing and reporting.

The functions and responsibilities of individual members of management and of work units must be clearly seen through this internal control framework, and the reporting system must be served by means of both reliable internal accounting procedures and the interactive visualization of internal control intelligence. Internal auditing should exercise due diligence in evaluating the monitoring system – as well as in judging whether interactive reporting requirements are satisfied, and corrective action taken without delays.

ANSWERS BY LEADING INSTITUTIONS TO AN INTERNAL CONTROLS AND LIMITS QUESTIONNAIRE

At the Skandinaviska Enskilda Banken, limits are set by the board, with accountability for their observance going all the way to the head of the business unit. There is a steady re-evaluation of limits and the existing limits system is enriched by the VAR algorithm. At ABN–AMRO, limits are generally set annually and re-evaluated annually; however, as the committees that set these limits meet frequently, changes and revisions are quite normal.

- Credit limits are set by the institution's credit committee.
- Trading limits are set by the asset and liability committee at Group level.

Trading limits are being translated throughout the investment bank of ABN–AMRO into VAR equivalents as fast as systems development in the different countries the bank operates permits. Following up on limits is delegated downwards to lower-level committees and to the risk control area which monitors usage of limits and positions – the whole being part of internal control structure.

At Commerzbank, the risks embedded in assets and liabilities management are continuously monitored through a system which adds VAR limits to the more classical system of limits established by the board. The whole framework of limits-related exposure is tracked through a system of computation which focuses on:

- Daily risk and
- Daily assessment.

Commerzbank said during the meeting that it has developed an information technology infrastructure which targeted credit risk and possible market risk crisis scenarios, also their impact on the institution's financial results. This is used for management information purposes; the executive I was talking to said his bank considers this approach as a solution parallel to the more classical internal control structure. Management finds such information very useful:

- When setting lower pricing limits for loans and
- In the calculation of customer profitability.

What senior management gets in VAR values is presented in a nutshell in Table 9.1 and Table 9.2. Both are based on statistics from Commerzbank's 1997 *Annual Report*. The VAR in Table 9.1 pertains to 1997, at the 95 per cent, 97.5 per cent, and 99 per cent level of confidence. The stress scenario is computed at 5 standard deviations. Table 9.2 shows the growth in VAR in 1996 over similar figures in 1996, also at three levels of significance.

Commerzbank stated that in connection to risk profiles and for the purpose of setting and monitoring trading limits, market price risks are now quantified on the VAR basis of. Risk variables are determined for the Group's individual units, with portfolio effects included. For internal purposes, a historical simulation model draws upon an observation period based on the past 250 trading days, a one-day exposure, equal weighting for observed data, and a confidence level of 97.5 per cent.

Since April 1998 this method has been applied on a daily basis. Commerzbank also works on historical simulation for capital adequacy purposes linked to the 6th amendment of the Principle I German Banking Act (KWG). The institution manages the market risks related to trading by setting for all its operative units risk limits, primarily for VAR and stress scenarios, but also as stop-loss limits.

Other credit institutions follow a different policy. At the Austrian Creditanstalt, the solution regarding the setting of limits is top-down. As

Table 9.1 VAR in Commerzbank's trading portfolio, 1997, Holding period equals 10 days (DM million)

	VAR at confidence interval as of 31 December 1997			**Average 1997 value at 99 per cent**	**Stress scenario (5 standard deviations)**
	95 per cent	**97.5 per cent**	**99 per cent**		
• Total portfolio	253	294	310	324	768
• Interest rate instruments (IRI)	99	130	162	215	319
• Currency instruments (CI)	199	229	240	240	610
• Equity instruments (EI)	25	27	27	33	106
• IRI/Total (per cent)				66.3	41.5
• CI/Total (per cent)				63.3	79.4
• EI/Total (per cent)				33.3	13.8

Source: As stated in 1997 *Annual Report*.

Table 9.2 VAR in Commerzbank's trading portfolio, 1996, and 1997–1996 comparison, holding period equals 10 days (DM million)

	VAR at confidence interval as of 31 December 1996						Average change in value at 99 per cent		Stress scenario (5 standard deviations)	
	95 per cent		97.5 per cent		99 per cent					
Year	**1996**	**1997–1996**	**1996**	**1997–1996**	**1996**	**1997–1996**	**1996**	**1997–1996**	**1996**	**1997–1996**
• Total portfolio	177	+43	215	+37	241	+29	280	+16	349	+120
• Interest rate instruments	176	–44	225	–42	267	–40	350	–39	293	+9
• Currency instruments	85	+134	94	+144	120	+100	89	+130	204	+199
• Equity instruments	81	–70	92	–71	98	-65	92	+17	198	–46

Source: As stated in 1997 *Annual Report*.

my research has documents, this approach is gaining increasing acceptance in the banking industry and is promoted by regulators. According to the management of Creditanstalt:

- Limits are set *monthly* by the board and the market risk committee.
- VAR limits are used together with other types of limits.
- There are special limits for highly volatile markets and for markets of low liquidity.

Creditanstalt policy sees to it that there are limits for: counterparty risk, market risk, liquidity risk, and settlement risk. Operational risks are covered by special procedures on which the credit institution did not elaborate.

My discussions with regulators tell me that they are not very happy about using VAR as a substitute for classical prudential limits. The Swiss Federal Banking Commission stated during our meeting that such substitution is not correct. Banks need both prudential limits *and* VAR. The position of other regulators, too, is that the head of trading can use VAR if the board decides to fix VAR limits on a daily basis. This is not usually done. Therefore both limits and VAR are needed. Besides this, the lower levels of supervision require:

- Liquidity and
- Concentration limits.

Attention should also be paid to the fact that some limits might be manipulated. For instance, limits on equities and on indices might slide into other trading channels like interest rates and commodities. Safeguards must therefore be provided by senior management to avoid such slides at lower levels of supervision, and such safeguards must be supported (as well as deviations reported) by the internal control system.

SETTING LIMITS IS A BUSINESS REQUIRING KNOW-HOW AND IMAGINATION

Because limits must be realistic and their study should account for both risk and return, one of the first questions senior management should ask itself is 'Do we have an instrument which permits us to reach a consensus in counterparty risk? In market risk by channel?' The answer to each of these questions is never a pure 'Yes' or an unambiguous 'No'. The complexity of an answer is often influenced by the bank's own culture.

Maynard Keynes once said that the majority of economists are most economical about ideas: they make the ones they learned in school last a lifetime. This fits well the practice of using average level limits. Few people really appreciate that an average level of reference would not do, because limits established in the average are nearly useless. For major counterparties and key market risks they have to be set counterparty by counterparty.

Counterparty-by-counterparty

By and large the lion's share of credit risk is embedded in transactions done with *our* bigger and more demanding clients and correspondent banks. Based on a study I did with a major financial institution, Figure 9.3 shows how a population of 2 million business clients has been stratified through criteria based on a combination of:

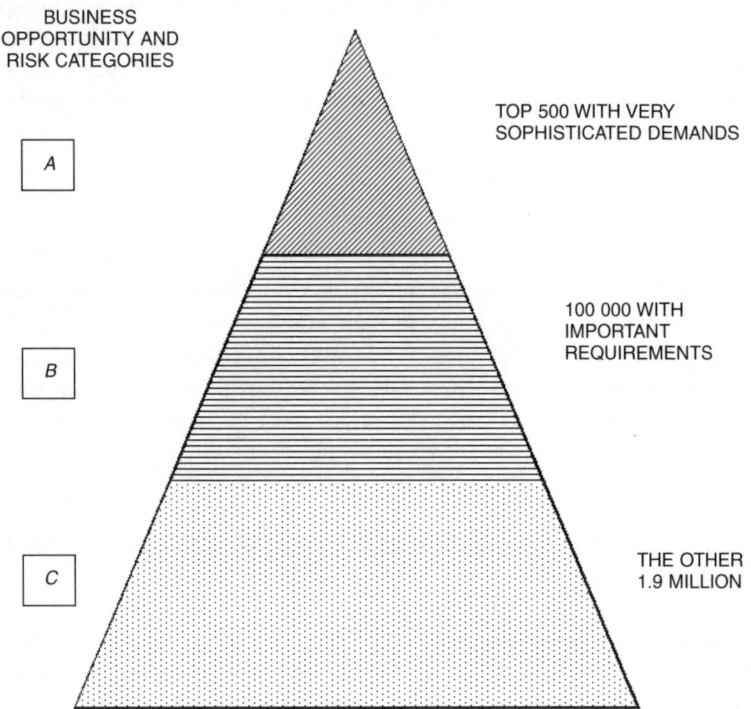

Figure 9.3 A classification of business partners based on sophistication of client demands and potential risk exposure

- Sophistication of client demands and
- Potential exposure to counterparty risk.

These two criteria correlate. As shown in Figure 9.3, 500 business clients fell into category *A* (the numbers are not those of the study in question, but the ratios are exact). Category *A* is high business opportunity and potentially top risk. These are the clients to be watched individually and case-by-case in big transactions.

The clients and correspondent banks in category *B* have important requirements for products and services; however, both their sophistication and potential exposure are lower than in category *A*. Still, individual follow-up is advisable. By contrast, clients in category *C* are typically served through existing products and services. The risk is relatively low, and so are the profit margins.

The careful reader will observe that this distribution obeys Pareto's Law. Individual limits are very important for categories *A* and *B*. For category *A* they should be definitely updated intraday in real-time. The internal control system should reflect individual intraday counterparty risk at least for *A* business clients and correspondent banks; eventually it should do the same also for all *B* clients.

Let me add another thought to this connection. While we often make reference to *the market*, we should never lose sight that the market is not a monolith. It is stratified. As with the example we just saw, typically a small group of clients represents a big group of our bank's gains and losses. As I mentioned, this is consistent with Pareto's law. Here is an example. Day-in and day-out, at 2.00 p.m. Manufacturers Hanover Trust had, in its time, an exposure of about $2.5 billion with just one client: General Motors.

Because a big amount of risk is taken with relatively a few clients, Dai-Ichi Kangyo Bank follows very carefully in a special database the 1 per cent of its business clients: 200 000 out of 20 000 000. The system we establish should also be in a position to inform senior management in real-time on market risk, including interest rates, foreign exchange, rquity indices and so on.

Market risk-by-market risk limits must be consistent. We should also account for the fact that a well managed bank acts in a market-oriented way which makes system sense, because it is the market that presents the business opportunities – but also creates volatility and impacts on liquidity, therefore establishing the level of risk for each position.

For the same reasons explained in the preceding paragraph internal control should pay attention to the effective management of limits through a dependable evaluation based on hard numbers and on market assessment. Skilled bankers also appreciate the sense of confidence intervals when the input they get concerns VAR. We have seen an example on p. 000 with Commerzbank.

The careful reader will also recall from Tables 9.1 and 9.2 that Commerzbank uses 5 standard deviations for stress testing. My policy is to use 5*s*, 10*s* and 15*s*, 15 standard deviation events are extreme. Some risks can be devastating when positions are hit by an extreme value. The problem with the so popular normal distribution is that it says nothing of extremes, yet:

- The October 1987 major market correction which at the New York Stock Exchange was a 14*s* event and
- In Chapter 4 we have seen an example on money supply with an extreme event of 16.5*s*.

These and plenty of other references raise the issue of competence in judging outliers, and in prognosticating them. Let me add that the job of managing risk based on VAR is for general management and for risk controllers not for traders. Usually, the traders don't wish to understand the message delivered by VAR, though they may care for delta and gamma hedging:

- The best tools for the trader are those he or she can work with because he or she can appreciate them and see their impact.
- Limits are understood both by the trader and by senior management. Hence, it is possible to work with them.

This does not mean that VAR and other models have no role to play in business transactions. They do. What it means is that managers and professionals should not use VAR as substitute for limits and good sense which comes from experience and from understanding the business. Qualitative values and models are aids to thinking, not a substitute for it.

THE STUDY OF INTERNAL CONTROLS BY THE EUROPEAN MONETARY INSTITUTE

In connection with trading and follow-up on inventoried positions, apart from following up on limits and highlighting exceptions, internal control must ascertain the level of confidentiality in business activities: loans, investments, trades, and guarantees. Issues relating to confidentiality, should be periodically reviewed and, when necessary, revised by senior management. Confidentiality has many aspects, from revealing information without authorization to database access and the handling of records by staff members.

A study on internal controls by the European Monetary Institute (EMI, now European Central Bank, ECB) suggests that it is the responsibility of senior management to ensure that all professionals and other staff involved in front desk operations, back office processing, accounting, monitoring, auditing, risk control as well as the organization of trading and controlling, have a comprehensive knowledge of

- The bank's policies
- The products traded and
- Risk management rules (EMI, 1997).

To avoid incentives for excessive risk-taking, EMI's advice is that salaries should not overly depend on trading performance. Furthermore, the heads of trading desks must keep a close eye on their employees' relations with business associates, brokers, and clients, as well as on the acceptance of favours and gifts. They should also ensure that information on business relationships and the closing of deals is treated as confidential.

I emphasize these issues because they constitute the alter ego of a system of limits and of VAR. The job we expect internal control to do is both qualitative and quantitative. When we talk about the internal controls' contribution to the observance of limits we should not consider only the quantitative aspects. That's why too much dependence on VAR might be counterproductive, apart from the inherent limitation of the method.

Transactions on terms not in line with the bank's policies, prevailing regulatory guidelines, and market conditions should be captured by internal control and sanctioned by senior management. For this purpose, each transaction must have a proper audit trail. As I never tire of repeating, a fundamental principle of the control framework for operational procedures is the design and maintenance of independent responsibilities and clear functional separation between front desk and back office.

EMI suggested that violations of limits tend to become more transparent if trading is organizationally separated from record-keeping functions. This structural and functional division of duties must be ensured by senior management – whose level it must reach. Quite often, functional separation is said not to be possible owing to certain organizational prerogatives or the size of the bank. In the large majority of cases, such a statement is nothing more than smoke and mirrors.

Over and above the structural separation to be guaranteed by appropriate procedures and safeguards, the control framework must specify the required IT supports. Some of these supports are elementary – for instance, the journal in which transactions are registered showing time of execution, trader, counterparty, type of instrument, currency, volume, terms, maturity, and so on. Other controls are more sophisticated, like cross-validation, indexing, and automatic search to uncover validation errors.

I would add to these EMI guidelines that registration and analysis must be made online in real-time, while online *agents* working for the back office scan the documents to find faults (Chorafas 1998a). There exists plenty of opportunity for real-time analysis through knowledge artefacts because trade documentation is not monolithic. Expert systems can be instrumental in investigating specific domains of risk such as the concentration of exposure by:

- Counterparty
- Instrument or
- Market.

Data mining helps a great deal in the process of compliance because limits aim at spreading the concentration of exposure. Feedback by agents can be an important criterion in prognosticating looming trouble. Many bank failures have been caused by too much exposure to too few areas of business or counterparties which was not found in time to steer away from risk.

This concentration may have taken place, for example, with a small group of clients, over too long a time, creating an uncontrolled business environment. Or, the concentration might have happened because of overdependence on a few instruments. In either case, a vital test of financial health is the ability of internal control to document such concentration and bring the facts to the board's attention.

There are always reasons for 'this' or 'that' type of failure. Quite frequently, the reason is that there have been poor management decisions which senior executives subsequently try to cover up. When this happens, it defeats one of the basic goals of internal control which is monitoring the performance of critical functions and bringing deviations to the attention of the board and the CEO.

Rules and regulations established by the board should promote this polyvalence in internal control activities. They should forbid such practices, but they should also press home the point that senior management is responsible for assessing concentrations of risk and the way this impacts on the institution's assets and liabilities, as well as on commitments which have been made. A system should be set up for measuring and monitoring future risk and for analyzing the loss potential, as the next section suggests.

ADVANCE NOTICE CAN HELP IN LIMITING FUTURE LOSS THROUGH REPOSITIONING

Peter Drucker used to say that prognosticating the future is not so much about future business, as it is about the future aftermath of current decisions and commitments. This explains nicely the role of internal control in conveying to the board and senior management prognostications made on exposure. Because it is always easier to accumulate exposure, internal control should steadily track the risk involved in *our* bank's portfolio, including:

- Repayment history of counterparties
- Analysis of gains and losses by loans officer
- Poor loans mix and/or overconcentration
- Gains and losses from trading by customer and by instrument and
- A large concentration of over-the-counter (OTC) trades, as compared to those done in exchanges

Typically, concentrations are the way some professionals use for bending the board's guideline for granting loans and making trades. A crucial job of internal control is rapid identification of such deviations, with accuracy and dependability in reporting. Senior management should take all proper measures in implementing a system able to respond to such requirements, evidently supported through high technology.

Reporting on the violation of credit limits should show not just independent events but also trends and accumulations. The evaluation algorithm used for reporting should account for the fact that limits to concentration are easily breached when a given transaction looks really attractive, or it has evident advantages over other transactions possible at a given point in time.

Quite often, diversification v. concentration lines become blurred because of imprecise definitions. In other cases they become hidden due to human factors. As I have already underlined elsewhere (Chorafas,

2000d), it is a natural tendency for loans officers to follow names that are highly correlated with one another, either because of ownership or for some other reason like an industry targeted by *our* bank.

Concentrations result when an institution or an investor has a level of exposure to a single name, be it a company, or a sovereign, or some other variable which makes risks of similar nature cluster together. Adverse developments amplify this exposure; they not only hit the bottom line but also hamper the institution's ability to function properly, hence they constitute a legitimate area for internal control action. For instance:

- Concentrations of credit risk may be generally characterized by inordinately high levels either in absolute numbers or relative to capital.

Regulators are very careful on how the institutions under their authority fare on this particular account. For instance, the Bank of England wants to know if a bank under its authority has 10 per cent of its capital put at the same name. Other central banks set a 5 per cent threshold.

- Not only loans but also securities with common characteristics or other common exposures which affected entities or groups of entities constitute a concentration.

Because of these factors, the amount of credit risk diversification achievable in a portfolio – be it loans, securities or some other asset – depends on the correlation between default risks within this portfolio. It follows logically that internal control must provide management with information on concentrations of any type at any time, and it must do so as a concentration takes place so that there is time to take corrective action.

Corrective action can be taken, for example, through a financial instrument which permits us to unload some or all of the concentration of exposure. The securitization of loans has made it possible for banks to shed unwanted credit risk concentrations (Chorafas, 2000d) but this does not mean that those weeded out are not replaced by others equally unwanted. In fact, asset concentration refers to both:

- An unacceptably high exposure or
- An unprofitable exposure to the bank

Other internal control information which can strengthen the board's hand concerns the results of investigations and analysis made for assets and liabilities management (ALM) reasons. The term describes a process for evaluation of net worth as well as for control of liquidity and of equity capital. Information on ALM serves both strategic and tactical decisions.

One of the reasons for exercising direct management control on the way assets and liabilities are handled is that these assets and liabilities must be structured dynamically to reflect the institution's sensitivity to market conditions. A good example in damage control by real-time response to adversity is the reaction by Bankers Trust in the wake of the Iraqi invasion of Kuwait in August 1990.

The Iraqis invaded in the early morning local time. It was night in New York but midday in Hong Kong, where Bankers Trust's director for Asian operations was located. He caught the news and immediately called the institution's CEO in the United States. Capitalizing on the high technology already in place, which enabled the bank to have available real-time information on every commitment, the executive committee met in the early hours of the morning and found that, in the aftermath of this event, much of its assets and liabilities were in the wrong side of the balance sheet:

- By 8.00 a.m. New York time, using its operations in London, Bankers Trust had fully repositioned itself and its assets.
- By contrast, one of its competitors took 2 days to do so; another need a whole week, still another nearly a month.

Repositioning is a major exercise to be conducted at board level when adversity hits. To be done in an adequate manner, it requires the most actual and detailed information as well as ample means for online experimentation on all assets of our bank: interest rate instruments, currency exchange contracts, equities, and other commodities which can turn into liabilities if we have been betting the wrong way or if the market has significantly changed:

- The risks to both capital and earnings from adverse movements must be monitored and controlled at the level of each individual business unit.
- This ALM monitoring and control should be separate from any treatment of risk associated with trading positions, though both may share the same input information.

The role of internal control in the Bankers Trust case and other similar events is demonstrated by the fact that in most cases damage control must be instantaneous, or there will be no damage control at all. In normal times, with no extreme events around, risk positioning is typically managed by controlling:

- Money market exposure
- The bank's own debt portfolio
- Exposure due to derivatives trades
- Securities investments and other factors.

A similar reference is valid regarding interventions in customer assets under management. But repositioning is a different ball game. It involves a variety of balance sheet positions, including damage suffered in capital markets and money markets (or risk of it); detailed off-balance sheet accounting; prognostication of trends related to OTC and exchange traded instruments. Top management must closely watch future cash flows arising from all interest-bearing transactions on both the assets and liabilities sides of the balance sheet, including cash flow discounting.

This proactive strategy calls for a whole range of standards and scenarios, able to indicate changes in cash value that would result from movements in market interest rates, currency exchange rates, equities, options, swaps, futures, and forwards. Such changes must be compared with limits and VAR estimates; they must be analyzed in a way that top management has a consistent and meaningful pattern of assets and liabilities.

Let me conclude the present chapter with this thought. Who ever runs a business today must understand that the risk that increases is a risk that will have to be borne. Therefore it is important that internal control information is proactive and helps in prognostication. 'Data after the fact', might have been good for the old static economy, not for the new one.

10 Auditing Counterparty Limits and Trading Limits

INTRODUCTION

Chapter 9 has explained that limits to the line of credit of a counterparty, particularly in connection with loans, are nothing new. Indeed, they constitute one of the earlier and better examples of internal control. What is new is the cross-functional and transborder dimension of credit limits which should characterize their setting and their follow-up. Similarly market limits today have a dynamic structure, leading to the conclusion that both the limits themselves and the way in which they are set and they are observed must be audited.

In a globalized, deregulated economy, limits to counterparty credit and those established for trading purposes have to be continuously evaluated and reset as the market changes, because of credit risk crises, liquidity, volatility, extreme events, and other reasons. This runs contrary to current culture, as traditionally banks calculate these limits in a static way. They may be revised from time to time, but this happens:

- In a slow fashion, for instance once per year, per semester, or trimester and
- Without full evidence of the changes taking place in every corner of the global market.

These two bullet points, plus the fact that a number of traders and loans officers take a cavalier attitude towards limits, document that there is plenty of scope in auditing the practice of limits. This is further promoted by the 1999 New Capital Adequacy Framework by the Basle Committee. The rating of counterparties by independent agencies greatly impacts on credit risk, while volatility and liquidity can affect market risk in a big way – but there is still plenty of scope for internal auditing.

Chapter 1 described auditing the way it is generally considered in textbooks and perceived in daily practice. It also brought to the reader's attention the fact that the results of auditing help in making supervisors and the institutions themselves control conscious. The supervisors must be satisfied that the institutions they oversee have adequate control environments. To do this, they must have the appropriate mechanisms:

- Statutory authority
- Financial means and
- Human resources.

The board, CEO and senior managers of credit institutions will use auditing reports prepared by internal auditors and by certified public accountants (CPAs). Of the two, internal auditing findings are better positioned to control the existence of and adherence to limits because they can access confidential information to which CPAs may not be privy.

When investigating the observance of limits, auditors should not craft a 'one-size-fits-all' sort of investigative framework, as each instrument has unique aspects and characteristics impacting on the way the organization conducts its business. Nor should auditors let their work fall below acceptable levels of standards regarding the analysis and interpretation of facts and figures.

Auditors should appreciate that not only in regard to limits but as a general principle, static solutions are the wrong way of looking at internal controls; they are not an acceptable practice for well managed companies. Management controls at large are much more effective when they are dynamically readjusted to the pulse of the market as well as to *capital-at-risk* (CAR) in all lines of *our* bank's business. Because limits are characterizing exposure, tier-1 financial institutions now follow the policy of *worst-case factor* defined as the ratio of:

- The traditionally required counterparty risk premium in the worst case to
- The required counterparty risk premium according to current assessment.

In this sense, the worst-case factor reflects a possible deterioration of the counterparty's external credit rating because of its total exposure. This contrasts to the static credit limits which have been classically calculated on the basis of internal customer ratings and the rather vague notion of the 'customer relationship'. The new approach rests on two pillars: the regular watch of exogenous factors such as counterparty risk and market risk, and a real-time follow-up of endogenous factors connected to the bank's own CAR and other crucial issues defined by the board.

INTERNAL CONTROLS AND DYNAMIC LIMITS MANAGEMENT

Banks which have properly studied ways and means for a thorough system of internal controls suggest that the best approach is that of establishing an *interactive limit management procedure*. They use risk premium and default probabilities as a means of converting the default risk of their portfolios into a common metric. With derivatives, for instance, this may be equivalent to default risk of a AAA, AA, A, BBB or BB rated security.

In Chapter 7 the reader's attention was brought to the fact that with the 1999 New Capital Adequacy Framework the work of independent rating agencies in evaluating creditworthiness came to centre stage. Ratings are incorporate into reserve requirements for loans; that is exactly where their impact on the bottom line is mostly felt. Chapter 8 also gave in a snapshot the impact of ratings regarding claims on:

- Sovereigns
- Banks
- Corporates and
- Securitized instruments.

As personal advice, the board and senior management should require that internal control intelligence also focuses on *confidence intervals* regarding counterparty risk. These confidence intervals must be audited regularly to assure what is has been decided *a priori* is dependable. By using analytical techniques and confidence intervals to guide its hand in decisions, the board can be ascertain whether there is a similarity between:

- The default risk connected to loans
- The default risk in its derivatives book and
- The default risk inherent in an investment-grade security.

This approach conforms to developing policy among a growing number of banks which maintain that a sound way of establishing credit limits is based on a combination of marking-to-market exposures plus a margin for volatility. What the above three bullet points add to this concept is a correlation between default risk associated with loans, unwillingness to perform with derivatives, and shareholdings losses – all concerning the same entity with which *our* bank deals.

Board members should return to fundamentals to appreciate how this system works. First, the overall counterparty risk premium limits must be allocated irrespective of instruments. Risks associated with leveraged financial instruments are accounted for through an iteration, for instance, by taking into account the algorithm which provides the credit risk equivalent of a derivatives transaction (Chorafas, 2000c):

- Credit limits become more pragmatic if they are market-weighted, facilitating the integration of credit risk and market risk and
- Credit limits complement rather than substitute minimum acceptable ratings even in cases of pure counterparty risk.

Other things being equal, market-weighted approaches increase the reported level of exposure as the maturity of the transaction increases. As a matter of policy, the most competitively managed banks see to it that the counterparty risk premium limit is observed by the beneficiary as an overall limit. At a higher level of detail, individual loan and trading limits are approved in accordance with the board's guidelines. The role of auditing fits well within this framework of objectives quantified by means of:

- Individually allocated limits according to board guidelines
- A risk premium which is computed to observe market conditions and
- Correlation between counterparty risks connected to different instruments.

My advice is not to try to provide this sort of a complex solution manually; except for sampling reasons in a superaudit. Normal auditing chores, which should be regularly done, must be done online through models and knowledge artefacts, which work day and night in real-time, and interactively report their findings.

Studying and auditing through knowledge artefacts, as well as sampling by human experts, should target all business channels and their transactions. For instance, whether or not traders, loans officers, and credit approval officers follow the outlined compound approach; and whether executives responsible for setting limits base their decisions on dynamic risk management. This is particularly important in connection with counterparty risks.

What I am suggesting is by no means a revolution. It is only an improvement over current practices where banks see to it that the overall risk premium limit for counterparty risk is proposed annually and in a summary manner rather than individually and on the basis of changing market conditions as well as in the function of the requirements of operating units. Indeed, among top-tier banks limits are subject to dynamic appraisal and factors taken into account include:

- Risk-grade profile and distribution of credits by level of risk grade
- Prevailing portfolio mix and leverage of the client company
- Changes in amounts and instruments by the customer from one period to another
- Longer term trends of weighted risk rating, percentage mix, ratios, and amounts outstanding in trading, loans and investing.

Not everything described by these four bullet points needs to be information obtained ad hoc at extra cost. In fact the majority of necessary information elements should come from other work done by the five layers in Figure 10.1. Trading and portfolio management, and therefore

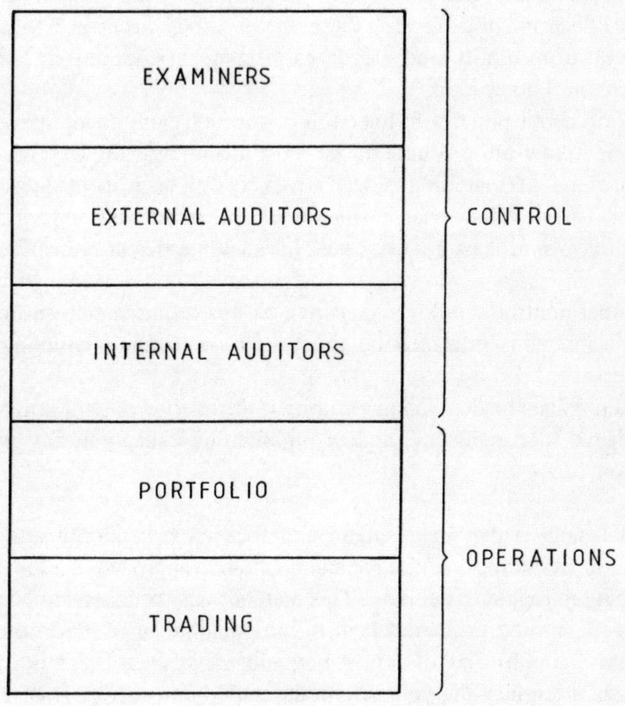

Figure 10.1 A thorough evaluation of VAR requires that three metalayers work in synergy

operations, would provide the bulk of needed data. Input from internal auditors, external auditors, and examiners of regulatory authorities should be used for validation.

What I am writing is consistent with the fact that the process of internal control resembles intelligence assessment of raw material: Is 'this' true? Is it credible? Is it confirmed by other sources? Operations provide an input resembling raw data. This data is treated to extract useful information. Auditing does the confirming, or points out wrong hypotheses and other fallacies.

Some assessments are more involved than others. The job of auditing individual limits gets complex when the computation of weighted-risk rating and of percentage mix becomes sophisticated because of reasons of greater detail, individual attention to each customer, and the proliferation of financial instruments. Besides these factors, it is necessary to calculate variances from limits and target exposures experienced in the short, medium and longer term.

Talking about policies followed in connection with counterparty limits, and their follow-up, a couple of the most technologically advanced banks suggested that OTC trading in derivatives, as well as deals made in markets without margin calls, must be measured and monitored against counterparty limits on at least a daily basis. Intraday metrics are much better:

- Internal control should be sensitive to this requirement, ensuring that management is informed on timely basis if a rapid sampling rule is observed.
- Auditing has the dual job of ensuring if the internal control infrastructure is fit for such reporting, and of highlighting exceptions for corrective action.

In conclusion, better management and focused risk control are the real goals of the dynamic quantitative and qualitative approach like the one I am describing in regard to auditing. This method must be extended beyond the control of limits to included the computation of *replacement value* (Chorafas, 2000b) and of *future potential exposure*. These are add-ons which should reflect the volatility of the underlying currency, interest rate, and other critical factors.

- Replacement value cover the potential credit exposure of a transaction during its remaining life.
- This market risk factor works in synergy with credit risk, a reason why tier-1 banks control client-by-client, for all important clients.

While it is necessary, it is not enough that the system of internal controls put in place sees to it that counterparty risk and market risk are followed up, monitored, and evaluated using a fully integrated global exposure system. This system and its add-ons like replacement values and future potential exposure must be regularly and thoroughly audited. Auditing reports must say if such system is in place, if it works in a satisfactory manner, and if improvements need to be made.

THE ROLE OF AUDITING IN CONTROLLING THE CALCULATION OF PRICES AND RISK PREMIUMS

I had a professor of banking at the University of California who taught his students that practically every bank had its own algorithm for the calculation of risk premium – and most of them were obsolete. There exist, however, some common rules on how to go about risk premiums which are worth bringing into perspective. One of them is that we must consider the synergy between instruments, transactions, and counterparty risk – rather than looking at each of them independently.

People and departments who should study the synergy of risks are those who set the limits. Typically, guidelines are established at headquarters within the context of board decisions and legal/regulatory constraints, but nobody says that finer definition of thresholds is not done down the line, or that guidelines are applied uniformly. Auditing must watch for compliance with guidelines, ideally within acceptable limits characterizing:

- Trading lines
- Inventoried positions
- Underwriting
- Loans and other service business.

Nothing moves in a straight line, no matter how tough the controls and audits may be. We have spoken about upper and lower tolerances, upper and lower control limits, as well as confidence intervals. In a normal distribution, the spread of values around the mean reflects the fact that measurements have variance, but as long as these values fall within prescribed limits, the process is in control.

What was said in the preceding paragraph is valid all the way, including for the demanding jobs of setting prices and of computing risk premiums. But there are also other principles of which to take notice. A sound practice sees to it that counterparty risk premium is separated from product-related risk and income:

- Risk premiums connected with counterparty exposure must cover the default probability of the debtor.
- Product-related premiums should account for a possible increase in market uncertainty and the likelihood of extreme events.

To explain this point, Figure 10.2 shows a chi-square distribution of credit exposure, differentiating between expected risks, unexpected risks and rare events (Chorafas, 2000e). Similar graphs on likelihood can be done for trading lines which maintain positions in securities, as well as in connection with underwriting positions. The probability of default enters into many financial products. This probability is usually an estimate which should be monetized – and its likelihood must be audited.

There is nothing unusual about this subject. The price of bonds is determined by the rating of the issuer, and for AAA or AA issuers most banks charge no risk premiums for such positions. Attention should nevertheless be paid to the tact that even triple A issuers are subject to operational risk. As I have explained, even the best credit risk and market risk management systems exist within an environment of operational risk control:

- Operational risk covers the whole environment in which management of other risks takes place.
- Since operational risk pervades all other risk areas, it is evident that it also impacts upon prices and risk premiums.

What sort of algorithm should we use to calculate the risk premium in accordance with board guidelines? A theoretically correct answer to this query is that the equation should be non-linear, because that is the nature of counterparty risk we are facing; particularly so as it is amplified by operational risk. Most banks, however, choose a simple linear algorithm of the form:

Risk premium = *F* (Customer rating, Risk premium rate per annum, Remaining time to maturity)

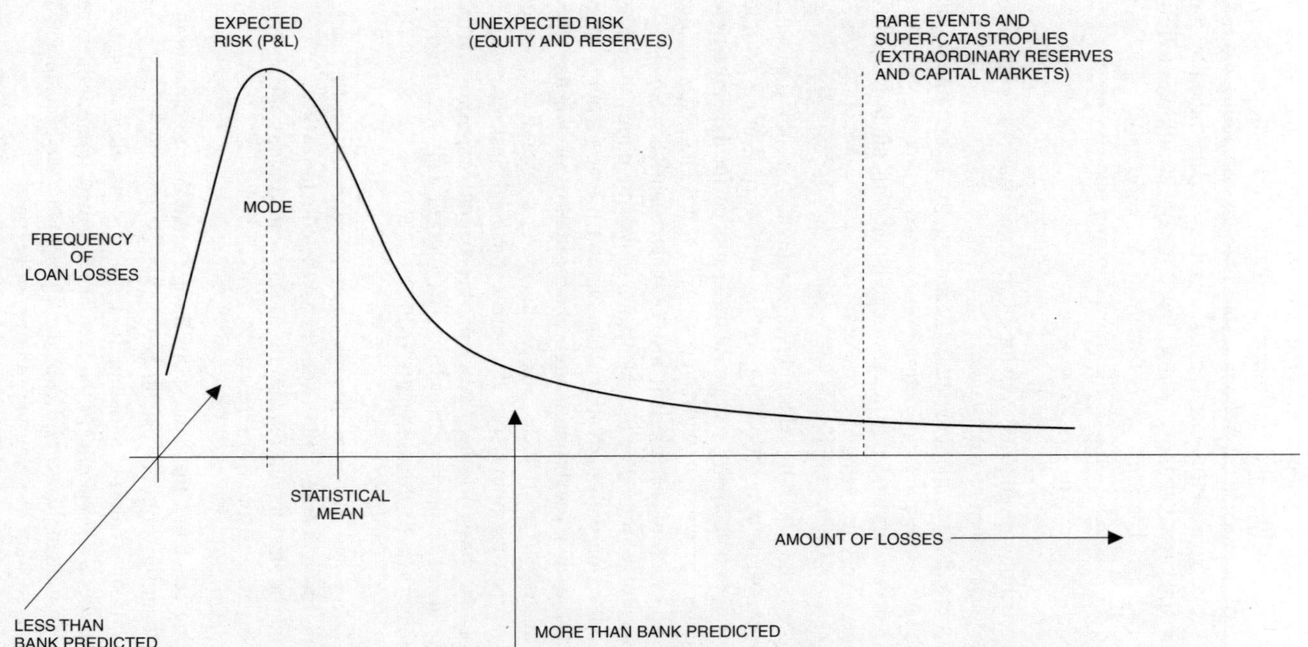

Figure 10.2 The statistical distribution of loans losses classified into three major categories

But implementation policies diverge and auditing should show if prevailing policies within the institution are being observed. Similarly, differences exist in procedures. Who is responsible for computing the risk premium? A valid approach is that the risk premium is determined by the person responsible for counterparty risk, but different institutions follow different procedures. The principle is that this calculation should give the same answer for the entire time of the transaction no matter who does it. However:

- When negotiations are engaged with the client, some banks prefer to have an *a priori* calculation of risk premium.
- Others see to it that the amount of counterparty risk premium is determined at the time the transaction is concluded.
- In either case several subjective factors see to it that computational results are not necessarily the same.

Different approaches end by charging a premium, but not the same premium for the same transaction. Algorithms vary even if in connection with trading lines counterparty risk premium is applied for the entire time of the transaction. By contrast, with interest business it is charged when the interest is due, which is characteristic also of other business channels.

Differences also exist on how the calculation of risk premiums should be applied in connection with derivatives. One approach is to compute it on the basis of the individual transaction, independently of whether this transaction increases or reduces the counterparty's overall exposure. Alternatively, risk premiums for derivative financial instruments are calculated on the basis of the change in the overall exposure of the counterparty caused by the new transaction. Connected with this approach is the question of whether counterparty risk:

- Must be borne and managed through a central authority in the bank, responsible for the entire credit exposure of the counterparty,
- Or, should be instrument-related in a way integrating outstanding counterparty risk arising from the new activity.

Far from being academic, these questions have a great deal to do with the way internal controls should be established, how they must work, and what should be scrutinized during auditing to help in controlling exposure. Sound approaches also account for the fact that risk assessment influences both *pricing* and internal *costing*. I consider a pragmatic, well documented internal costing system as being very important because:

- In the last analysis it is the market that determines the price; only highly innovative new products take freedoms in pricing.
- Costs and assumed risks that are not recovered through pricing are negative contributions to the bottom-line.

Internal controls should also see to it that the board, CEO, and senior management are immediately informed about discrepancies between costing (including monetization of risk) and pricing. Internal auditing should check whether *every* department controls its costs and has established and maintains risk-related performance measures. To be effective, this requires a methodology of quantifying performance, and an information technology able to capture and report risk and return.

INTERNAL CONTROLS, LEVERAGING, AND THE EVALUATION OF RISK AND RETURN

Chapter 2 made the point that internal controls should be proactive. A good example on the use of internal control intelligence in prognostication is the way in which it can help in pre-evaluating risk and return from an organizational and an operational viewpoint. Chapter 9 has explained that prognostication is an issue to which few banks have paid the attention which it deserves, yet it is so much more rewarding to be ahead of the curve than behind.

Internal control will function so much better if we assure that *our* institution's accounting and risk management environments are consistent with the general framework of operations, control functions are documented and approved by the governing body, and the bank can demonstrate to supervisors and external third parties that it has policies and procedures in place to ensure that assets and capital are safeguarded from unauthorized use. Also, when *our* institution is in a position to provide:

- Risk-adjusted return analysis done in a proactive way and
- The ability to forecast the aftermath of top management decisions.

A sound organizational practice is that contracted risk premiums are separated from other income and shown as such in internal financial accounting. There should be an effective distinction between default risk-related results within each operative unit, and those factors affecting the bank as a whole because of cross-border exposure relating to other aspects of business contracted with important clients and correspondent banks.

It may as well be necessary to implement a procedure which involves charges related to the counterparty risk component; inter-operating units; an internal billing process similar to the one done in connection to the billing of cost centre services. A credit institution has much to profit from a financially sound separation of:

- Default risk-related results within each operating unit and
- Financial charging between operating units for well documented reasons.

This can be effectively done after many connected issues have been worked out, from client- and instrument-related factors, to marketing, sales, and taxation. At desk level, it is also appropriate to account for *risk appetite* by traders, loans officers, investment advisors; also for *risk tolerance* by the bank itself and its clients. Risk tolerance is a fundamental reference in all risk and return studies, and internal control should monitor whether ongoing business observes its limits.

For instance, investors, with high risk tolerance may use derivatives to leverage their portfolio for higher returns. The assumption of greater risks and the tracking of these risks, however, requires managing investments through models and doing so in real-time. The higher the gearing, the more the pressure to do what I have just said. Some banks leverage bond, equity and currency deals through gearing raised to:

- 300 per cent for currency and equity modules and
- 600 per cent for bond modules and related instruments.

Today a leveraging factor of 3 or 6 is thought to be acceptable. MeesPierson mentioned during our meeting that a gearing of 10 (or 1000 per cent) used to be an outlier for its client institutions. Now it is taken as being nearly normal. But a leveraging of 15 by a client who took a loan against collateral would not allow the chief credit risk management officer to sleep quietly at night.

Yet, several institutions leverage their assets far more than that. When in September 1998 Long Term Capital Management (LTCM) went bankrupt, and was saved at the 12th hour through a salvage operation mounted by the New York Fed, it that was revealed that gearing of its equity stood at 50:1. Rumours had it that when Tiger Management went out of business, at the end of March 2000, its leveraging was not that much less than LTCMs.

Runaway investors and other speculators fail to understand that real life is finally catching up with superleveraging, and this can be disastrous because the risks being taken are no more commensurate with the returns. Able hedge funds managers see that and change strategy – as George Soros did with his Quantum Fund in late April 2000. Soros appreciated that:

- As formerly novel strategies wear out, superleveraging no longer offers high returns.
- But the toxic waste remains, and overexposed institutions can turn belly-up.

It takes a smart operator, like Soros, to understand the meaning of this reversal in the risk and return equation. When by 25 April 2000 his funds had lost 30.9 per cent of their value compared to 3 March of the same year – dropping from $11 billion to $8.2 billion – he decided to change strategy. This was, incidentally, the largest loss Quantum had experienced since 1996.

Loans are in a way controlled by the authorities in the sense that gearing is kept in check through capital requirements imposed by regulators. But the way credit institutions are gearing themselves through derivatives is not so easily controllable. Table 10.1 presents in a nutshell statistics on equity, assets, and derivatives exposure of six big American banks. Official statistics show derivatives exposure in notional principal amount (NPA), this however is an inflated figure when it comes to estimating true risk. Therefore, it has to be *demodulated* to the level of credit equivalent risk (Chorafas, 2000c).

In column (4) of Table 10.1 demodulation is done using a factor of 30. Notice that 30 is very conservative. In volatile markets 20 would have been a more appropriate demodulator, with the result that the derivatives exposure shown in column (4) would increase by a cool 50 per cent. Even with a demodulator of 30:

- Bankers Trust has leveraged its equity by 1820 per cent
- JP Morgan by 1610 per cent and
- Chase Manhattan by 1450 per cent.

The gearing of Chase in regard to its equity and assets is shown in Figure 10.3. Other, more conservative banks use much lower leveraging. For instance, Banc One leverages its equity by 240 per cent. More conservative banks also consider fixed income investments as a market risk area which should be managed through limits. In this connection, limits

Table 10.1 Demodulated derivatives exposure compared to equity and assets of major credit institutions (billion dollars), as of 31 March 1999

	Equity (1)	**Assets** (2)	**NPA in derivatives** (3)	**Demodulated derivatives exposure**[a] (4)	**Ratio to equity** (5)	**Ratio to assets** (6)
JP Morgan	11.3	261	8.861	295.4	×16.1	1.132
Bankers Trust	4.7	133	2.563	85.4	×18.2	0.642
Chase Manhattan	23.8	366	10.353	345.1	×14.5	0.943
Citigroup	42.7	669	7.987	266.2	×6.2	0.398
BankAmerica	45.9	618	4.438	147.9	×3.2	0.239
Banc One	20.6	262	1.472	49.1	×2.4	0.187

Note:

a By a factor of 30.

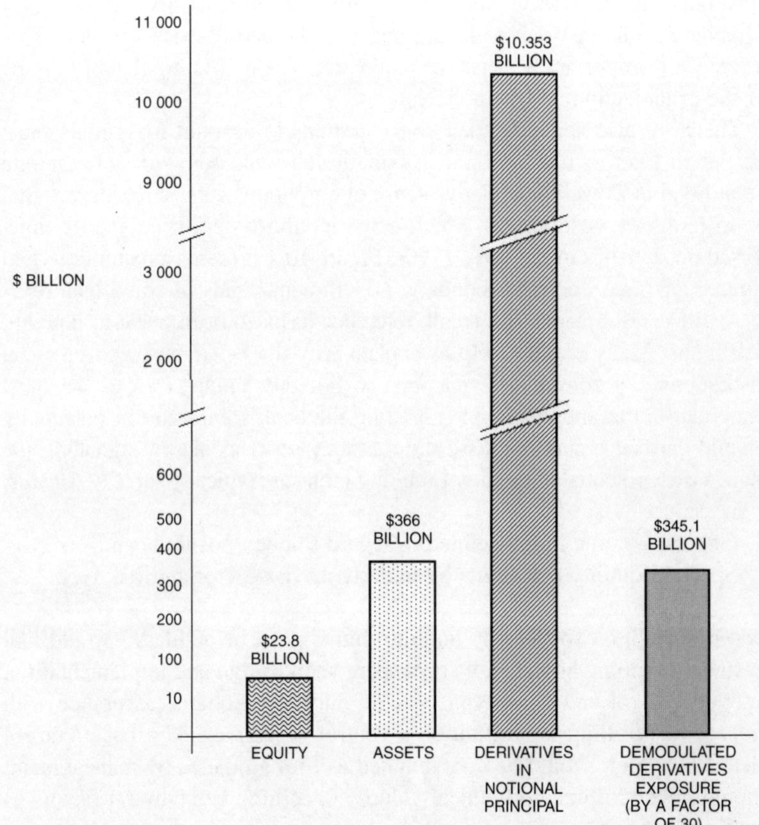

Figure 10.3 Some frightening statistics on equity, assets, and derivatives exposure by Chase Manhattan

assist in establishing capital at risk assigned by top management because of volatility in:

- Interest rates
- Currency exchange
- Equity index and
- Other exposures.

As a matter of good business practice, alert bankers see to it that interest rate and other market risk limits are elaborated in the form of both an absolute reference level and of sensitivity to threat-curve events (see Chapter 3), taking stock of leveraging and the board's risk appetite. This reference is important because the nature and scope of internal control must fit the organization and its policies.

There are also some detailed considerations to account for. Limits must be put to interest rate risk not just in the absolute sense of interest rate volatility, but as well in a relative sense of corporates versus treasuries – that is, in terms of yield spread which can vary most significantly over time. Based on statistics of the early 1990s, Figure 10.4 presents a pattern of yield spreads of AAA corporate bonds v. government bonds of equal maturity.

As the careful reader will recall, reference has also been made to liquidity risk limits. Many reasons help to explain why the better managed financial institutions pay considerable attention to liquidity limits. Two of the most important is that they assist in restricting the bank's exposure in potentially illiquid currencies and markets; and that they serve as alarms signalling the bank's own potential illiquidity. Liquidity limits are typically set at two levels:

- General volume limits defined in regard to open positions and
- Special liquidity risk limits by underlying risk factor and risk type

I do not need to explain why liquidity limits must be audited. I would like to stress the point, however, that irrespective of design and implementation, internal control and audits can provide only a reasonable assurance with respect to fulfilling an institution's control objectives. The basic control elements, which should be disseminated as firm guidance by management, should cover cultural and ethical values concerning behavioural factors as well as the bank's books, records, and reporting practices.

SHOULD INTERNAL CONTROLS REFLECT A PORTFOLIO'S DIVERSIFICATION?

Chapter 6 supported the thesis that the best internal controls are custom-made. Say, as an example, that because the globalization of financial markets tends to create risk correlation which did not exist at earlier times, top management decides to follow a strategy of greater diversification in investments. If so, appropriate internal controls should be put in place to see such strategy through and to assure its longer term soundness.

- With diversification, attention must be paid both to new business opportunities and to how risk correlations change.

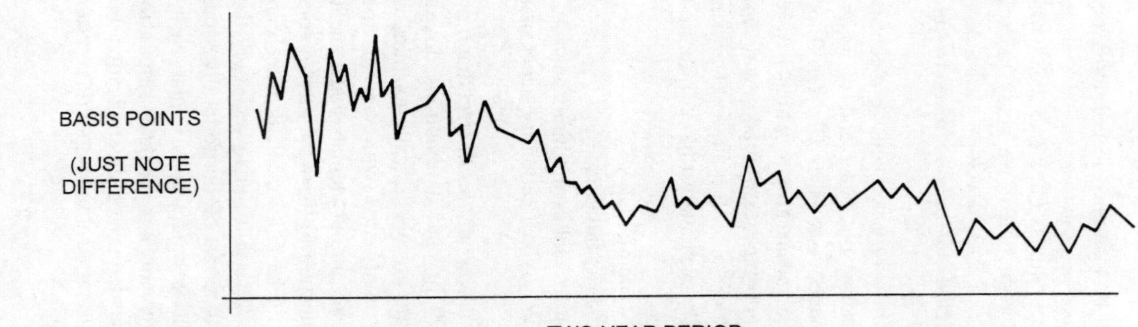

Figure 10.4 Yield spread average of AAA corporate bonds v. equal maturity government bonds

- Diversification must be well rounded, focusing not only on equities but also on loans, through credit derivatives (Chorafas, 2000) and all other instruments.

Risk correlation should be examined in full understanding of the fact that this is a pervasive issue. In principle, global markets correlate with one another even if some economists think that the contrary is true. However, we can still have risk reduction if we study negative correlations most carefully. This means if we develop yardsticks on how to invest internationally with regard not only to markets but also to instruments and industries.

What really matters in a very competitive global economy in regard to diversification is balancing out risks and their likelihood to improve medium term performance (see also Chapter 3 on the threat curve). Ultimately, performance means growth which is a reflection of management's ability to build new businesses, find new revenues to drive earnings up, and create shareholder value. It is however important to add that each institution and practically each analyst has a different approach on how to:

- Make 'this' or 'that' type of analysis
- Study markets and their correlations
- Proceed with hypotheses and assumptions and
- Proceed with portfolio diversification for better management.

A rigorous analysis would account for the fact that financial markets are not efficient (Chorafas, 1995b), and assumptions done to the contrary are bound to fail. We should always critically examine our hypotheses – are they acceptable when confronted with real-life market tests? Always remember that hypotheses are only tentative statements. This brings up an important point in connection to the way internal control must work.

Internal control should be able to tell if every person in a position of authority is able to make rigorous analyses, study their assumptions, and evaluate alternatives in terms of portfolio diversification. This can be assisted through knowledge artefacts that mine each account executive's portfolio. Top management has evident responsibilities not only in connection with the mechanics of diversification but also in regard to what a diversification strategy should target. It is wise to establish whether *our* bank's policy is to:

- Maximize expected return for given risk or
- Minimize risk for a targeted return.

Running after both objectives is like trying to kill two birds with one stone. It is best to target one objective at a time. After this decision has been made comes the challenge of risk evaluation in a realistic diversification framework.

Far from being theoretical, these considerations have much to do with practical, day-to-day issues and their analytics. Often the solution we choose is temporary because it introduces new factors which must be examined. Other things being equal, as the number of different assets grows the correlation among them may also tend to increase. A similar issue exists regarding newly made choices of industries and of markets.

If auditing is given the mission to check hypotheses underpinning decisions on limits and policies on diversification, *then* the control of correlations becomes an integral part of its functions. In Europe today it is very difficult to find markets that are not really correlated. This makes diversification difficult, frustrating efforts to reduce assumed risks significantly.

Nor is diversification at any price a sound policy. Even if the index goes up as the economy grows, some of its constituent elements may not share in the good fortune. A superleveraged firm which made the wrong choices, like Tiger Management in 1999 and 2000, will not be able to survive in the longer term, while one on sound financial footing survives and then stands to prosper once favourable business conditions return:

- Companies that think ahead of their exposure in bad times tend to be the long-haul survivors.
- Survivors are also those companies whose management sets aside sufficient funds to permit their adaptation to new conditions.

It is inevitable that all this is a reflection of management skills and company culture. Successful solutions are not a matter of faith but of painstaking analysis. One of the methodologies which have been used with some success in connection to diversification is to classify historical data in different stockmarkets separately:

- By risk and
- By return.

Such statistics can be revealing. After the 1997 crash, a thorough analysis of financial markets in East Asia showed that some markets had been low return but high risk for a long time, but investors had not done their homework. This big negative, for instance, fits the Indonesian stockmarket. For nearly 10 years Indonesia was an investors' darling because it had low correlation with the United States and Europe. But when Index Indonesia was compared with other indices, such as Index Asia and Index World, some interesting results popped up.

This risk and return approach is known as the *efficient frontier analysis*. Its underlying concept is shown in Figure 10.5. Under certain conditions this type of study helps to develop a methodology able of signalling a path towards optimization – if there is one. In other words, diversification can be studied analytically through risk and return by means of an equally weighted portfolio (which is not necessarily optimized); or an optimized portfolio targeting the absence of strong correlations, if such markets exist.

Where does this leave the issue of auditing? The answer is on two levels. At the lower level, the auditors should check whether the sort of studies this section has outlined have been done – if the talk about diversification is factual and documented or just a 'me too' approach to portfolio management. More complex would be the higher-level study of of involvement, checking assumptions, and models. Today this is not typically done by auditing but with *model risk* on the increase it may well become necessary.

INTERNAL CONTROLS AND LIMITS FOR EQUITY TRADING

Equity investments and equity index trades need to be managed within broader overall limits established by the board and by area of operations. Any valid system of internal controls would try to balance centralization v. decentralization; usually, however, the centre has the power to override local decisions Banks which use high technology go through frequent re-examination of the *limits of equity price risk*. They do so several times in a year, involving a number of crucial variables such as:

- Stock exchange
- Currency and country
- Industry where investments are made and
- Individual equity.

Every institution should have in place a system of checks and balances permitting if to control exposure with equities, along this multiple frame of reference. Auditing should ensure that equity limits are observed, and that corrective action has been timely if and when they have been exceeded. This is part of the policy highly competitive companies follow; that is why they run their business on a sound financial footing.

The study of limits for equity trading and their capital allocation is part of the foundation on which to base decisions regarding the distribution of CAR in connection with equity trades. In most institutions the overall limit

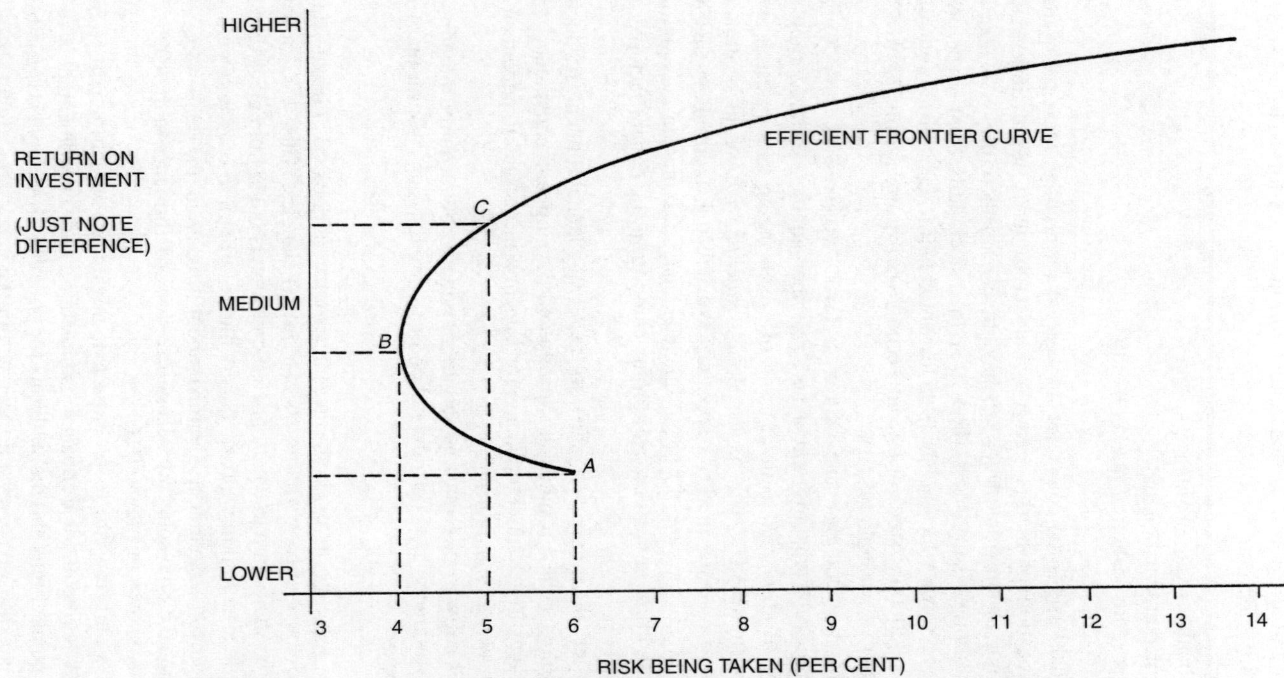

Figure 10.5 An efficient frontier analysis tries to balance risk and return, eventually leading to portfolio optimization

for equity holdings is proposed annually to the board for decision. Such a proposal is based on:

- The bank's requirements
- The market situation and
- The prognostication of market trends.

An annual basis is too coarse for my taste, if for no other reason than that prognostication of market trends is subject to many uncertainties and forecasting an individual stock's behaviour is even more tricky. A couple of bad earnings surprises suffices that this stock falls from grace. An example is Xerox which in late 1999 lost about half its capitalization; while in January 2000 the stock of Lucent Technologies dropped from $72\frac{3}{4}$ to $53\frac{1}{2}$ in a matter of a couple of days.

Lucent Technologies and Xerox as well as Novartis, the Swiss pharmaceutical company, and a host of other equities suffered from a new type of *event risk*, a direct result of mismanaging their research and development (R&D). This is essentially *pipeline risk*, or lack of new products to feed the market's appetite. (We will talk more about this in Chapter 11.) In the case of Lucent, financial analysts expressed the opinion that the shortfall in business and profits came from three main factors:

- A faster than expected shift to new 80-channel optical products technology which resulted in capacity and development constraints.
- Shortages in certain components for Lucent's infrastructure equipment, which was a planning mistake.
- Lower software revenues as service providers now acquired programming products more evenly rather than through large fourth-quarter purchases.

Analysts were positive about the longer-term outlook of Lucent, but penalized the company for its short-term deficiencies. This was shown through the sharp drop in equity price. Some angels fallen from grace come back to life after building a base. Others find it difficult to recover. Cypress Semiconductor shareholders learned about this issue the hard way as demonstrated by the company's lacklustre stock performance in the 1995–7 timeframe, shown in Figure 10.6.

Because surprises are to be expected, institutions which benefit from interactive computational finance, simulation, and experimentation re-examine equity limits and the sublimits for price risk by equity class and by investment. They do so several times within the year, and auditing should ensure that such board policy (if it exists) is observed. Procedures should be in place for controlling equities exposure based on regular:

- Monitoring and controlling the maintenance of limits and
- Pre-auditing the observance of limits by each asset manager.

In my book, statistical quality control (SQC) charts can be instrumental in this sort of supervision. The control of limits must be done interactively, preferably *intraday*, rather than through printed reports of the operative units which are obsolete by the time they reach the control authority. Internal controls should see to it that such interactive presentation:

- Is done according to trading lines and non-trading lines and
- Is detailed to the level of the individual equity, currency, country, or stock exchange.

A general statement with equities is that while the volatility of indices is important, left alone an index helps little if we target risk and return not on the local currency but on a base of a *reference currency*. Some financial analysts challenge this notion, expressing the opinion that:

- With equities, exchange rates are not so important, because equity volatility is greater than currency volatility.

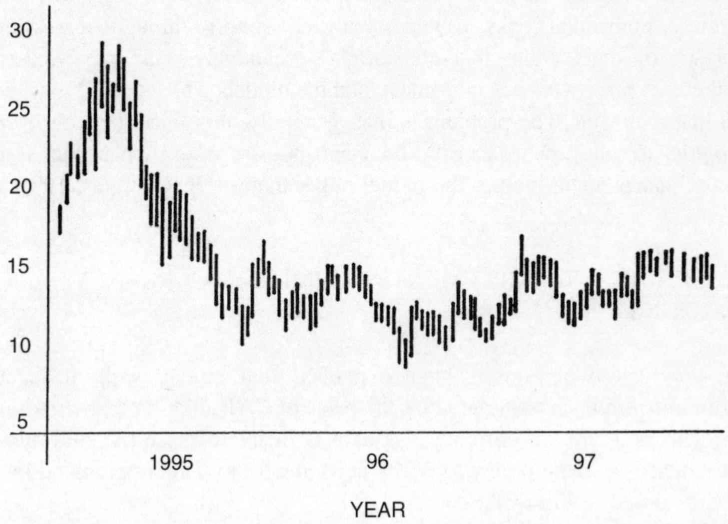

Figure 10.6 In mid-to-late 1995, Cypress Semiconductor lost 60 per cent of its capitalization

- On the contrary, both currency exchange rates and interest rates are very important with bonds.

I don't buy this argument. The fact that volatility of a stock index tends to be greater than currency volatility in no way means that currency volatility does not matter. It does matter a great deal as we will see through a practical example below. Currency volatility and equity or equity index volatility can have compound effects.

By means of modelling procedures, positions in equities must be monitored for both equity price risk and currency risk – compared to maximum exposure in a specific individual equity and industry branch in the home market. This requires effective co-ordination between the different risk limits established for every single line of activity. It also calls for special attention during auditing on whether or not the necessary co-ordination is in place.

Qualitative procedures must be enriched with quantitative benchmarks, which usually require algorithmic solutions for effective computation. It is proper to keep in mind that in connection to market risk the weight of each security in the portfolio is proportional to its value. Because asset rates of return are usually not normally distributed, higher moments in calculating a portfolio's and position's risk and return should be chosen.

In conclusion, auditing should pay attention to the assumptions being made. For instance, the assumption that markets behave in a linear way and therefore embedded risks can be analyzed simply through regression analysis; or that certain markets correlate negatively with one another. Markets are *par excellence* non-linear, and the models which we use must be non-linear as well. The problem is that, generally, non-linearities are *terra incognita* to many players in the financial industry – and when things go wrong, management blames the model rather than itself (Chorafas, 1995c).

EXAMINING AND IMPLEMENTING LIMITS IN CURRENCY POSITIONS

The previous two sections have explained that among well managed institutions limits are computed on the basis of CAR distributed by trading line. This is as true of currency risk as it is of interest rate risk and other instruments. A sound policy typically accounts for maximum potential loss to be assumed in the worst case:

- A worst case in forex represents the largest change in currency exchange rates documented through historical volatility.

Typically among well managed credit institutions the worst case is determined on a two-tier basis: a long historical basis to serve as a guide, and a short-term overnight basis for operational reasons. This is done with reference to a given currency basket and/or a single currency:

- The overnight position limit is computed by dividing the risk capital by the short-term worst-case factor.

A prudent policy, however, will also consider the longer-term worst case, leading to a threat curve, like the one in Chapter 3. A limit should be calculated for each currency. Attention must also be paid to each trading line, including the net present value (NPV) from forex trading and bank note trading. Some institutions add to this calculation precious metals trading, other commodities, and the NPV from their other trading lines.

In the non-trading lines, exposure is computed per currency balance from receivables and payables, taking into account balance sheet value – for example, for interest-bearing investments the current value according to original yield. Each institution has its own procedures, but in the general case, exposure calculations consider:

- Discounted future margins on fixed-interest assets and liabilities in the interest rate business
- Discounted results from open fixed interest rate positions, also in the interest rate business.
- Accrued interest and commissions connected with foreign currency trading and positions.

The specific approach varies by institution. Some do not allocate limits to individual currencies, but treat them in a common pool at the discretion of the trading linc. The rationale is that the position per individual currency is not considered as a risk position *per se*, as risk position is taken as the average from:

- The trading currency and
- The counter-currency.

The position of a pair of currencies is taken as the sum of both currencies, converted into the basic currency and divided by 2. This value is applied to the utilization of the position limit. Banks with lower technology do not apply the limits to the utilization of the risk capital on an intraday basis because of the short response period this makes necessary. On the contrary, banks with high technology increasingly tend to apply the limits intraday.

Auditing departments should appreciate that not only does an intraday approach support much better risk management and personal accountability, but also the overall limits for currency risks are more effective, because they can be regularly examined and dynamically adjusted. The need for a dynamic control of limits and exposure has been explained above. As a matter of principle:

- The fact that market risk and credit risk change with timecalls for permanent watch of market behaviour.
- Internal controls must steadily track interest rate risk and currency risk as well as the analytics needed for their control.

Auditing must examine whether the institution's internal control system can fulfil what is stipulated by the second bullet point above provided this is indeed our bank's policy as should be the case. The reader should appreciate that many of the examples I am giving arc chosen because they are part of the competitive edge in financial business.

Competitive firms run on a sound financial basis understand that in a global market with few negative correlations the tracking of both equity volatility and currency volatility is most important. Let's look at an example from volatility of the $/yen exchange rate in the early 1990s. Evidence indicates that after the crash of the Nikkei the volatility of the yen against the dollar has been much greater than the volatility of the Tokyo stockmarket. As for NYSE and NASDAQ their bull market continued more or less unabated from April 1995 to March 2000, fuelled by:

- Strong economic performance
- A declining budget deficit and
- Wide interest rate differentials

A strong US dollar helped these stockmarkets. Since the birth of the euro on 1 January 1999 the dollar has advanced more than 28 per cent on a trade-weighted basis and more than 26 per cent in absolute terms. The dollar depreciated against the yen, but let's not forget that from its April 1995 lows to July 1997 the dollar had appreciated more than 50 per cent v. the Japanese yen and 25 per cent v. the Deutsche Mark. Analyzing the underlying reasons for these statistics is part of an institution's own homework.

In conclusion, any attempt at risk control by means of prudential limits which do not account for currency exchange rate volatility will hold unpleasant surprises. The same is true of interest rate volatility and market liquidity. Stockmarkets are sensitive to all of these factors: interest rates, currency exchange rates and liquidity. Therefore, it is wise to audit the hypotheses we make, the models we build, and the use we make of these models. Audit must be able to tell its story in regard to their validity.

11 An Internal Control System for Engineering Design, Product Development, and Quality Assurance

INTRODUCTION

Experts believe that in the future sustainable competitive advantages will come from innovative firms that know how to use their store of knowledge in the best way possible. Innovation really goes beyond creativity, because creativity alone might not help in obtaining better business results. Chapter 10 has given an example of companies punished by the market because of pipeline risk. This, so far, has not happened to Intel, Microsoft, and Sun Microsystems because they have sound innovation policies.

The first ten years of the twenty-first century will provide plenty of proof that, while necessary, simply investing in research and development (R&D) is not enough. The creativity coming out of laboratories must be immediately converted into products the market wants because it appreciates that it could benefit from then. The most credible equation of business innovation has three components:

- Advanced technology
- Effective marketing and
- Immediate implementation.

Time and again, the so-called *killer products* typically manage all three aspects well. If we look back in business history since the industrial revolution we will see that, in the majority of cases, most profits do not go to creators of new technology but to *implementers*. This is precisely the domain where an internal control system must apply itself in an engineering company. Internal control intelligence in engineering is vital for many reasons; topmost are:

- Rapid product development
- Steady, rigorous cost control,

- Fast flow replenishment and
- First-class quality assurance.

When new products are in the lab, these goals are served through regular and ad hoc *design reviews* (see below) which must be soul-searching. Design reviews typically take place in a grey zone where success and failure are equally likely. Studies suggest this is the area which produces the most information. By contrast, when we operate in safer zones where the chance of success (or failure) approaches 80 per cent or more, the odds are such that they radically reduce internal control intelligence.

Engineering and manufacturing are not the only domains where the 'grey zone hypothesis' is valid. What have I just said can be applied to any decision process such as finance and commerce. A design that is certain to work removes most learning from process inspection, but nobody can be sure *this* design will work until it is inspected by design reviews and tested through market approval. In engineering, this gives plenty of scope to both internal control and auditing.

A great deal of companies view design failures or uncertainty connected to investments as something bad. They overstress the importance of success and encourage people to adopt risk-free, mediocre design solutions. Almost invariably, whether in engineering or in finance, this proves to be counterproductive. Even in well established manufacturing industries with a record of producing great designs, one must probe near the limits of the design space by:

- Taking significant risks and
- Managing these risks in an able manner.

Knowledgeable engineers appreciate that if they stay too far away from the boundary of innovation, competitors will find the limits before they do so – and take the market away. At the same time, if they consistently overstep the boundary, they will never produce a viable design. Risk-taking is not carefree. A good design, like a good investment, must explore the grey zone of which I spoke above, where success and failure seem almost equally likely. That is where in the longer run the best results can be found.

LONG-TERMISM AND SHORT-TERMISM IN R&D

Short-termism in technology, and most particularly in R&D, is a term coined to identify the drive for rapid deliverables. A market place more competitive than ever sees to it that the time-to-market gap must continue to shrink, with R&D results brought to market at a fast pace. By contrast, *long-termism* means that deliverables can have a long wait. That's not the footing on which well managed companies choose to run their business.

The concept of fast time-to-market has become the hallmark of competitive companies only since about 1985. Prior to that, opinions were divided on whether short-termism or long-termism was better. During the 1960s and 1970s, as consultant to the board of AEG-Telefunken, Olympia, Univac, and General Electric-Bull, I often had to fight against long-termism addicts who had top management's ear. In my book, long-termism in technology is a negative. This sort of spirit can survive only when governments, engineering firms, banks, and other businesses conspire to resist:

- Accountability to shareholders and
- Exposure to international competition.

In its fundamentals, long-termism means locking oneself into a particular R&D project or a particular technology for a long time. But other people's technology does not stand still, and almost by definition a long-term project will be useless on maturation. During the 1980s, for example, the Japanese government poured some $400 million into the Fifth Generation Computer project. That investment in new hardware so frightened other governments that:

- The US government came up with MCC
- The UK government with Alvey and
- The European Union with Esprit.

Having hooked themselves on a fat budget, largely financed with taxpayer's money, none of these projects was in any hurry to produce results. The Fifth Generation Computer failed commercially on its inception, and MCC, Alvey, and Esprit did not prove to be good investments. The real profits during the 1980s and 1990s were made by entrepreneurs who plunged into the business where they perceived opportunity and ran fast to get the market – from Intel and Microsoft to Sun Microsystems.

While the long-termism of Japan's Ministry of International Trade and Industry (MITI) was a disaster in picking technological winners, Microsoft's advances were incremental short-term: that way, each step was both feasible and profitable. That is the way to make money out of technology, and this is the mission which should be given to internal control in an engineering company:

- Provide intelligence on project marketability, cost compliance, and time-to-market.
- Ensure that the feedback channel remains open, and management has the guts to kill a project before it kills the company.

Long-term programmes may sometimes be appropriate for basic science, but for a private firm R&D projects must move rapidly, or they will go nowhere. To achieve rapid deliverables, bigger projects must be broken down into discrete short-term smaller projects, each of which is rapidly brought to the market and is individually profitable.

The message these references aim to convey to the reader is that internal control has become a 'must' in engineering, manufacturing, and marketing – because science and technology advance so rapidly and so unpredictably that members of the board, CEOs, and senior managers must be wizards in exploiting the unexpected, rather than putting their bets on a long-range predetermined course. Just as the board of a credit institution must be informed of assets, exposure, and assumed risks, the board and CEO of an engineering firm must be regularly informed on:

- Deliverables
- Timetables
- Costs
- Quality and
- Financial matters.

This is what a shrewd manager would demand. Individual productivity and cost/effectiveness are also vital issues for internal control action. Take software and hardware for computer-aided design (CAD) as an example. One of the reasons for dissatisfaction with CAD is that people involved in choosing a system (usually middle management) are not familiar with the needs of designers, because the proper analysis of design tasks has not taken place. That's wrong. The thought that CAD will 'automatically' enhance engineering productivity is definitely a misconception which had its origin in the late 1970s. At that time, at the dawn of CAD, only the most simple and boring of tasks were performed by early computer-based tools. That's now past, and it is also appropriate to appreciate that even today's workstations are not capable of replacing skilled designers. A distinction must be made between:

- The use of CAD way down in the engineering design food chain and
- The sophisticated use of CAD which requires a first-class methodology (Chorafas, 1987).

What CAD systems do way down in the food chain is to remove drudgery and frustration, and somewhat improve quality by automating routine tasks, thereby allowing the designer time to be more precise and thorough. A better way would see to it that CAD provides an efficient communications system between designers working on the same project. A still higher level of CAD implementation makes feasible experimentation by collaborating designers, often leading to changes of mind. This is very important because:

- It permits us to make online modification that would otherwise require months to come to fruition and
- It accounts for the fact that globalization makes necessary rapid changes in design parameters, to beat the competition.

The better of *our* competitors never stand still. As Figure 11.1 suggests, able solutions to research and development projects must have globality, benefit from high technology (of which advanced CAD is just one component), observe standards (where they exist), and be subject to revamps if current design fails any of the critical variables established at project definition. In Figure 11.1 I give seven criteria, but there may be more. Whatever their number, internal control should track each one of them – and do so within stringent timetables.

Sam Walton had a policy that *flexibility* is the best pivot point. This can be characterized as the ability to turn on a dime (Walton, 1993). It is difficult to find a dictum which fits better the most basic characteristic of a good R&D project, or explains more vividly what is meant by 'flexibility'. The problem is that few companies have the sense of what it takes to be flexible.

The message the reader should retain from this section is that a truly sophisticated solution uses a methodology which permits significant flexibility. The next section discusses such a methodology and explains the role internal control and auditing must play. We then focus on project management, outlining how timely action can save both money and market position. We next introduce to the reader the contribution of prototyping, while the theme of the following section is how to conduct design reviews and what to expect from them. The final section concludes the chapter by presenting an infrastructure for quality assurance.

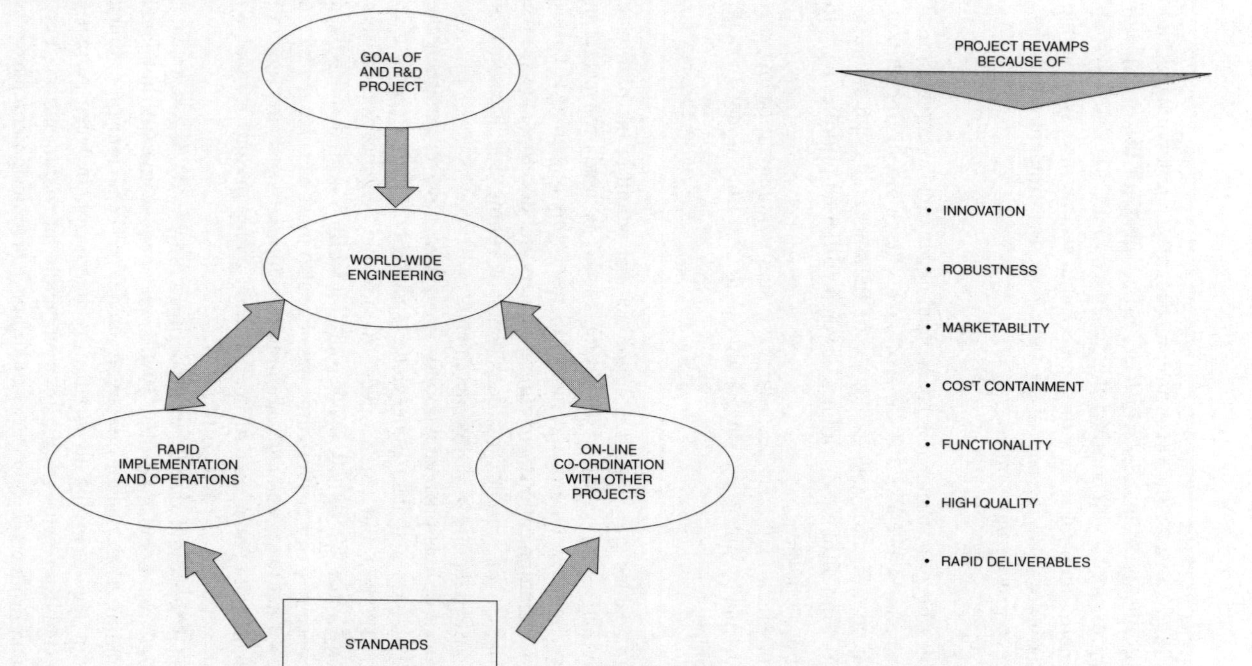

Figure 11.1 Able solutions to R&D must have globality, benefit from technology and standards, and be subject to critical project revamps

A METHODOLOGY FOR INTERNAL CONTROL APPLIED TO ENGINEERING DESIGN

Before tackling the vast issues of project management, prototyping, design reviews, and quality assurance, which are prime areas for the exercise of internal control, we should consider the dynamics of a CAD/CAM system and how internal control relates to them. Central to this discussion is the need for flexibility in design and, at the same time, for stringent timetables. The dynamics rest on three pillars:

- Timetables become faster and faster, leading to rapid compression of design schedules, because that's one of the results of global competition.
- Effective co-ordination and avoidance of frictions is at a premium, as engineers from different disciplines driven by different priorities have to collaborate closely.
- Conflicts which may arise because of the dual requirement of low cost but high quality must be solved almost in real-time – not through documentation.

As far as timetables are concerned, a product that would in the past have taken more than a year or two to design must today be ready for market in less than six months. One of the means to reach this objective is CAD-based online communications, enabling designers and developers to see the whole landscape of complex mathematical algorithms, specifications of parts, and visualizations of design parameters.

Effective co-ordination and flexibility in design have in common the ability to database and data mine at the speed of a click. Agents help (Chorafas, 1998a), but in essence the whole engineering design methodology must be turned inside out. Flexibility is a double-edged knife: it is necessary for cost/effectiveness but also must be achieved with a perspective of hardware and software in full evolution: A growing range of alternatives and the emergence of integrated on-a-chip designs are making obsolescent what has existed so far.

Traditional tools and design methods, including CAD as we knew it in the 1980s and most of the 1990s, are geared toward low-level implementation. They cannot effectively model the behaviour of complex systems, not are they able to handle the interaction between formerly discrete design teams whose skills are now rapidly integrating into systems, packages and products. Using classical approaches to design complex new products:

- Dramatically increases the risk that the resulting solution will not be competitive
- Jeopardizes the goal of bringing product innovation to market ahead of competition and
- Practically assures that the result will be high-cost/low-quality, rather than the other way around.

What is necessary in order to be competitive is a new interdisciplinary process that combines advanced tools, integrative design disciplines, and the results of design reviews; and, hence, of internal control intelligence. This new methodology should allow engineers to share the results they obtain in discrete areas, and achieve a common vision of a product's architecture, performance, and market behaviour.

The development and application of a new methodology should account for the fact that both business products and consumer products are more and more communications-enabled. The convergence of communications and computing creates tough design challenges for hardware designers and embedded software developers. Basic technologies also change. Digital signal processing (DSP) is superseding traditional analogue approaches, but there is still the need to integrate analogue and digital components.

Many of the challenges exiting within the design landscape I am describing are largely created by the integration of hardware and software from analogue and digital solutions. Internal control should take care of the cracks which invariably show up when formerly distinct or outright contradictory technologies merge – and for the same reason internal control should be the subject of auditing procedures. This brings into perspective another issue.

Computers and auditing can be compared to a two-way street. Projects in advanced technology (which invariably involve some sort of computers or microprocessors) and their methodology must be audited regularly for a number of reasons, which range:

- From using state-of-the-art technology
- To how well and how consistently this technology is used.

Internal control intelligence should focus on the first bullet point while, as stated above, the control of a project's progress is done through design reviews. At the same time, auditing can effectively use computers – most specifically knowledge artefacts, networks, and databases – to sharpen its focus. This is precisely what tier-1 companies have accomplished.

Computer-based auditing does not limit itself to financial and accounting matter. It can also be successfully applied in connection with computers, communications, and software. Indeed, since the 1980s auditing has extended its reach into information technology. Now it must do the same with regard to both components and systems design. The challenges, or barriers, are that:

- Quite often, there is no single view of design specs among co-operative professionals
- The risk of error-prone, manual translation of algorithms into designs is always present
- It is difficult to explore component interactions inside a new product to their full extent
- There exist duplications of test benches among different intellectual centres working on the same project
- Some R&D centres are characterized by slow adoption of new technology, with sub-optimal product performance and
- There is a lack of integrative view of system design, leading to misunderstandings and misapplications.

Added to these factors is the fact that because of different backgrounds by team members quite often design specs get misinterpreted, while design verification and therefore corrective action occurs too late. When this happens, the risk of design flaws increases and some of the goals originally enunciated cannot be feasibly implemented.

The challenges I have just enumerated may have different origins, but they all contribute to the same problem: lack of a shared view of the product results in delays, high costs, and inadequate quality. What is necessary therefore is a common view, a system-level or component-level solution that makes it feasible for different members of the design team to contribute in meeting co-ordinated technical requirements.

Based on these premises, internal control must assure that no project is organized as a series of discrete steps or stages, starting with esoteric algorithms and part-by-part specifications, then moving through separate hardware and software designs and prototypes, testing and verifying component after component – without a system view. Auditors must examine if this happens – and, if so, bring the malpractice to the attention of senior management for corrective action. Auditors, too, must be aware that part-by-part approaches introduce errors that may not be detected until a prototype is built and tested (see below). They should therefore examine if all components, and design stages, are worked on within an integrated product information flow, through interoperable tools, and a well coordinated design approach.

In conclusion, achieving first-class results in engineering design requires an internal control system able to provide intelligence on methods, tools, tests, timetables, and the company's design culture – targeting both effectiveness and efficiency. Internal control is very important whether there is a closed or an open approach among co-operating design teams. The latter facilitates interaction between system designers of different disciplines, and makes feasible better results whether the object is quality, performance, timetables, costs, or other factors affecting deliverables.

INTERNAL CONTROL'S CONTRIBUTION TO THE PROJECT MANAGER'S JOB

There used to be a time when internal control was not seen as a legitimate issue in an engineering and manufacturing firm. This time is assuredly over and the pace of development experienced in business and industry has a good deal to do with this situation. As dramatized in Figure 11.2, in the 1990s the keyword was *acceleration* in the rate as well as sophistication of solutions we are after, and in their implementation – so much so that formerly advanced tools and methods often become barriers to further progress.

For instance, they became *discipline barriers* as interlab and interpersonal communications broke down even between teams working within a single project or stage nearby one another. Moreover, important discontinuities took place when design cycles were longer and/or engineers within each discipline continued to pursue their own portion of a larger design independently of their colleagues, leaving integration for later on. By contrast, when design teams cross disciplinary barriers at the beginning of their design process, they:

- Discover opportunities to optimize their work taking advantage of emerging technology and
- Help to eliminate expensive and time-consuming integration errors later in the development cycle.

Tool barriers also must be overcome, whether these are a classically used CAD solution, algorithms, system diagrams, embedded software, or a hardware description language. Not only aged means of design but also a tool's specificity can be a weakness when it comes to sharing results among labs or with colleagues who don't use that same tool(s). Differences between 'new' and 'old' tools are an important element of which auditors must be aware.

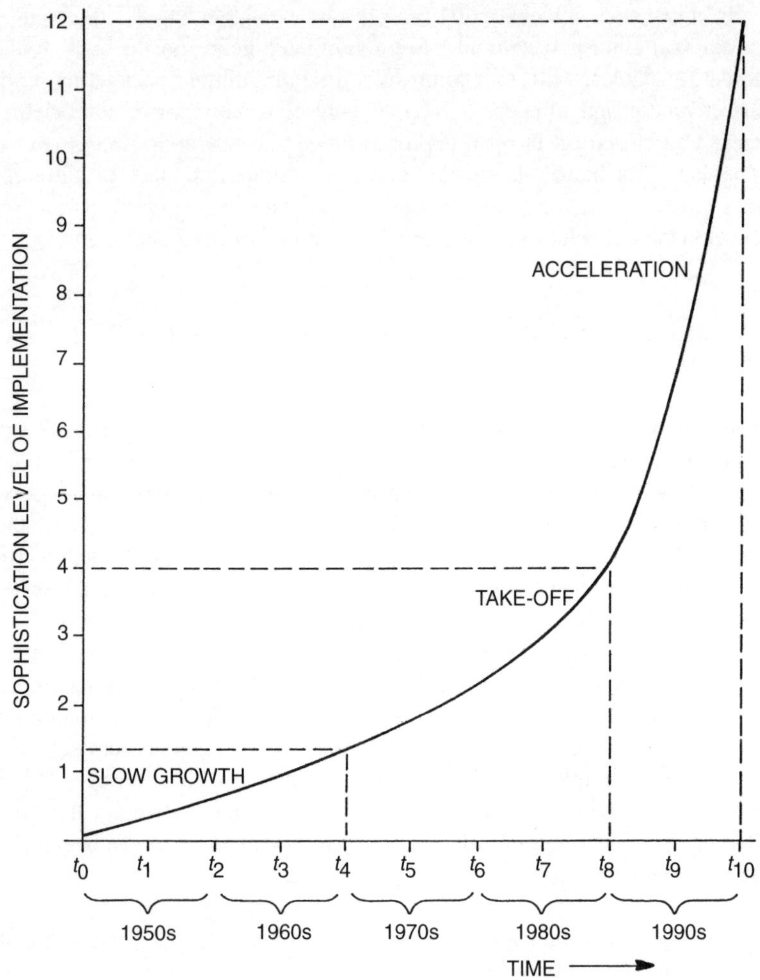

Figure 11.2 The acceleration in technology characterizing the mid-to-late 1990 is expected to continue well into the twenty-first century

If I pay prime attention to this subject, it is because computer-based tools can help both the designer and the project manager. Tools, however, cannot substitute for skill and the will in doing the job one is supposed to be doing in the best possible manner. 'Best possible' means according to tough criteria and a good methodology. Here are some hints about developing and sustaining a personal methodology, which can help in project managers a significant way.

The first and foremost rule is to *plan the project right* by means of milestones which will constitute pivot points of the design reviews to follow. Jean Monnet, the father of the European Union and former international banker, advised that the best way to start the planning process was to focus on the last milestone – the *deliverables*. Figure 11.3 shows Monnet's concept by means of five milestones, moving from deliverables to initial conditions:

- When the plan is made, the process goes from the expected end result backwards to the project's starting point.
- By contrast, execution of the plan will proceed from the start towards deliverables through successive milestones.

Notice that this concept of project planning and execution is equally valid whether we talk of engineering, banking, or any other business. *Risk factors* can be integrated into the planning process shown in Figure 11.3. At the Royal Bank of Canada, for instance, every project has a risk factor associated with it. Demerits accumulate and if the project is late or of low quality, the decision is made to kill it.

The best way to assign merits and demerits is through *design reviews* which are made at regular intervals – for instance, weekly or every two weeks, evaluating the progress of a project, its manager, and its members. To survive, project managers must perform according to plan or better. In my experience, performance will be much more visible if a project manager:

- Sorts out his or her priorities by properly ordering goals and subgoals, which are put in writing.
- Commits to a clear definition of goals, by mapping objectives into the time schedule and budget.
- Schedules a few minutes at the beginning of each day (and of each week) to compute plan/actual and update the programme.

The first step, once the priority list is prepared, is to begin execution. This seems to be self-evident, yet it is not that easy to move from inertia to doing something. Rubinstein once said the hardest part of practising was sitting down at the keyboard; and the next toughest thing was to interrupt his daily exercise to go for lunch.

Regarding the second and third bullet points in our list, the successful project manager regularly reviews and controls objectives, as well as measuring progress against milestones. He or she also appreciates that

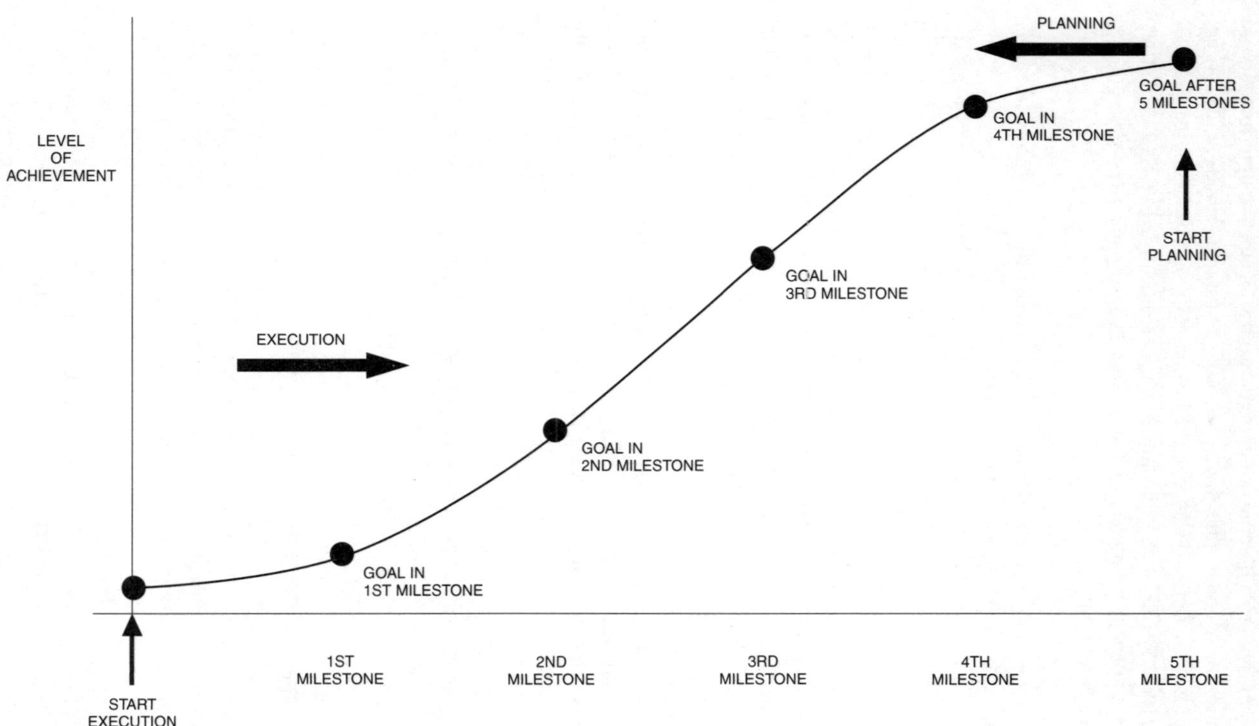

Figure 11.3 According to Jean Monnet, planning for the future should start at end-results level and move toward the beginning

because the environment is dynamic, specific subobjectives and the means that have been put to work to reach them may be changing. There is always a very delicate balance between:

- Providing for continuity and
- Managing the process of change.

The project manager must inform senior management of any problems, and the latter should keep itself informed of this balancing act at project level through feedback provided by internal control. This is a central issue. By assuring project transparency at top-management level, it is possible to remedy deficiencies when it is still time to do so without negative results.

A greater visibility should be everybody's concern. The successful project manager should recognize that the most notorious of all time wasters is undue preoccupation. This includes spreading one's attention too thin by engaging in something other than the salient problem. As Franklin D. Roosevelt once said: 'We have nothing to fear but fear itself' – provided one is appropriately doing one's job.

Furthermore, the successful project manager should be asking the questions, and instead of having subordinates bring problems he will have them bring answers. From these answers, as well as from all other input he receives, a project manager worth his or her salt will filter out the irrelevant and concentrate attention on what is crucial for the project:

- Informed in a timely manner on how each project proceeds, senior management should not change project leaders midstream – unless there is a very good reason for doing so.
- If a project fails in its objective(s), its budget, timetable, quality of deliverable, or some other crucial variable, then the whole project may need to be killed.

There is in business practice also argument on whether project leaders should be switched around. One school of thought says that a product development team should have a single leader from cradle to grave. I espouse this concept because continuity of leadership is vital to the success of any project; it is also a good way to track performance on a measurable basis.

The other school of thought, however, objects to this notion of continuity, asserting that leadership should change to satisfy the technical needs at each particular stage of a project or programme. Since key competencies required of a leader change during the course of a given project, the way this notion goes is that the leader should be changed as well. People with experience in project management appreciate that the argument of this second school of thought does not hold water. The hypothesis that leader competencies change during the project because of change in some of the technical issues, assumes that a project leader's primary contribution is technical expertise. This is rarely true, and it is certainly not what we want during a rapid-development programme.

If the project leader is nothing more than a technical contributor, *then* the technical tasks which he or she must address in detail would steal time away from the managerial content of the job. This is counterproductive because in any major project most time is almost always devoted to managerial work, to keeping the team members continuously busy in a creative way and properly co-ordinated – as well as solving all sorts of problems as and when they arise.

There is a second major flaw in the notion of changing project leadership because of technical specialization. The need for ultimate technical knowledge at project leadership level assumes that this is where detailed technical expertise belongs. By contrast, what we are after in project leadership is rapid development, high quality and short time-to-market. This process rarely puts upon the project leader's shoulders the task of making all key decisions:

- Modern R&D teams are increasingly teams of *equals*, while project leadership retains the right to change direction.
- In terms of purely technical skills we shift decisions to lower levels, and there it is where we must put specific expertise.

The role of the project manager is best exemplified by planning, organizing, staffing, and controlling. These are the tasks which get performance out of a project. Technical skills are very important. The organizing and staffing functions of the project leader must fully account for them. But strictly speaking technical skills will not excel if project planning and control is deficient.

INTERNAL CONTROLS FOR PROTOTYPES AND FOR MEASUREMENTS CONNECTED WITH DIFFERENT PROJECTS

Typically, the product design team should develop a breadboard model, followed by a prototype. When the design file is closed, it will be passed to manufacturing, first for small-series, then for large-scale production.

After that comes marketing and after-sales service. A prototype is no theoretical product: it is a working model which can come in one or more copies, and it can be implemented in the environment for which it has been conceived.

Prototypes are job-specific, not a generality. However, because of increasing personalization of products and processes, the concept behind *prototyping* becomes that of a *user-driven* rather than *technology-driven* design. This poses requirements of its own including the need for flexibility and experimentation to ensure that:

- Product characteristics can be personalized and that
- This can happen with minimal delays and at a reasonable cost.

Every self-respecting company must have a policy of prototyping not only in R&D for hardware but also for software. The development of software prototypes helps to compensate for the fact that end-users do not necessarily define in clear terms what is to be done, and they subsequently change their opinion; while software developers rarely appreciate what is in the end-users' minds in terms of requirements.

Few companies truly understand and emphasize the role of effective two-way communications in the success of their projects. A sound policy sees to it that internal control addresses the communicative aspects of the work done in project groups. Feedback to management must make it feasible to analyze the development process in order to provide help in cases where communications-related problems have occurred.

A sound engineering management practice also poses other prerequisites. To appreciate them, we should recall that most often basic research is done in one lab, while applied research and development takes place in another. All told, there is a transition between:

- Research
- Development
- Manufacturing
- Sales and
- After-sales service.

This transition should be smooth and seamless. In fact, seamless processes should characterize the passage of product files from research all the way to commercialization and field maintenance. The main strength of a seamless approach is that it eliminates the loss in efficiency which results when a project moves from one department to the next. Based on my experience with General Electric-Bull in the 1960s, Figure 11.4 shows what I mean by loss of efficiency:

- Internal control should act as watchdog in this transition, identifying both what moves and what does not move.
- Seamless transition has become most vital to many aspects of engineering; it is a critical *value-added* characteristic of global competition.

Delays owing to loss of efficiency have a negative impact on the successful completion of a project, the observance of its timetable, and the quality of deliverables. Quality can be improved through timely and accurate measurements. A basic element of any science and of any engineering discipline is the use of measurement for planning and controlling processes and products:

- Measurement represents the best means for the observance of tolerances in spite of the variability of production.
- Internal control should be able to track and report on both measurement methods and project evaluation procedures.

Experience from engineering design demonstrates that up to 70 per cent of development time can be spent revising and revamping projects rather than generating new intellectual property. This particularly happens when there is no method able to integrate progressively more realistic representations of measurement and evaluation procedures. A well managed project sees to it that concepts flow seamlessly into a reference design and prototype, which then serves as:

- An executable specification
- Test bench for further refinement and
- Reference model for measurement reasons.

Any measurement process is abstracting, up to a certain level, other factors such as physical characteristics or instrument complexity. However, it is retaining key empirical relationships as well as those properties being measured which are necessary for sound design – from study of variables, to description of surfaces and evaluation of the outcome of tests. This is a concept of wide applicability because it characterizes the expansion of measurements from physics and engineering to domains such as financial analysis and software development.

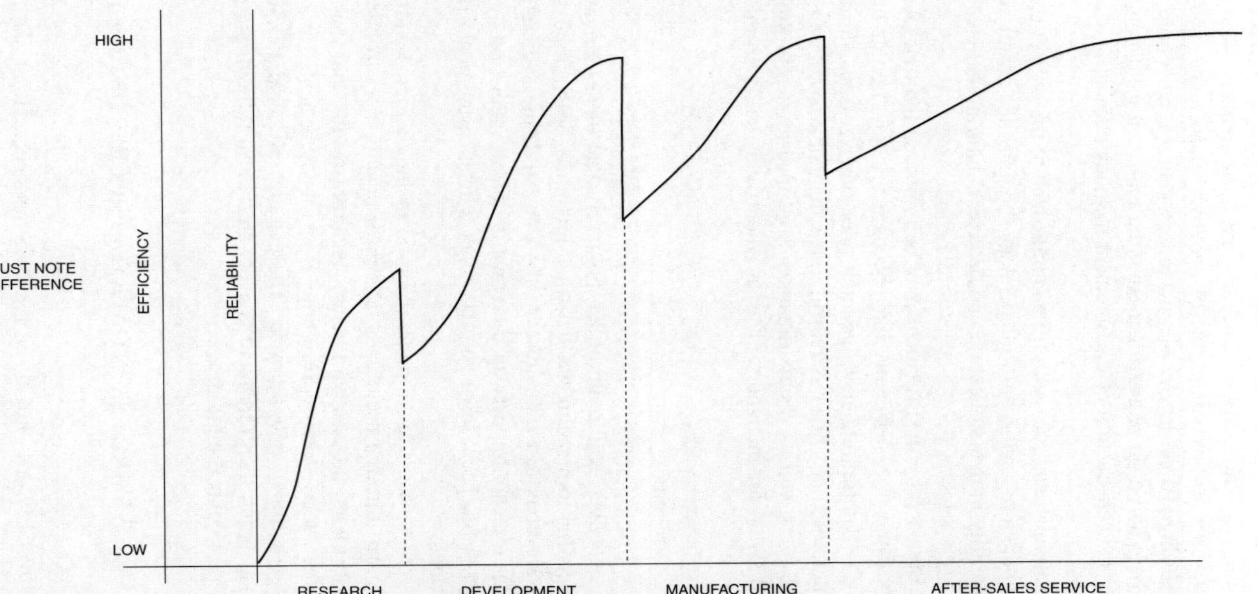

Figure 11.4 Non-seamless interfaces significantly reduce the efficiency and reliability of engineering work during product transition

The careful reader will, however, notice that in any and every application, including the physical sciences, metrics and measurements also reveal deficiencies which are a consequence of employing inadequate methods in design and testing. To be dependable, measurements must have both a solid conceptual base and a procedure for meaningful empirical validation. Errors made during the construction of measurement methods include:

- The use of small samples with little significance to the project on hand
- Misinterpretations connected to dependent variables and correlations
- Poor reliability in data collection and databased information elements.

The results obtained by measurement may be improved through feedback. At the same time, measurements may become invalid through untested procedures for determining new parameters or other reasons, leading to incorrect interpretations. For this reason, measurement concepts, measurement processes as well as results obtained from measurements should be audited, and tested for materiality. Measurements may suffer from:

- Wrong hypotheses and
- Untested correlations.

The result of either and both bullet points is that measurements are misplaced, leading to meaningless statistical inference, or the impossibility of applying rigorous test methods. On the one hand, the availability of reliable measurements impacts on the construction of prediction systems. On the other hand, because of shortcomings with measurements models become unstable.

An improved measurements method would include easier definition of attributes studied through prototypes, allow for development to become a more straightforward process with better visualized results, and make sure that both the data streams resulting from measurements and their exploitation are timely and accurate. These issues are vital to effective project management, therefore there is every interest in following them up through internal control intelligence.

DESIGN REVIEWS ARE ESSENTIALLY A PROCESS OF RIGOROUS AUDITING

The successful CEO does not sit on his or her projects. He or she passes them onto people and gives them authority and responsibility to do them fast and well. The successful project leader not only plans the work but also controls through milestones the time people (depending upon him or her) are spending, as well costs, quality and plan v. actual in deliverables. The leader should handle each project *as if* his or her professional status depended upon it.

The project leader, and sometimes the CEO, or one of his immediate assistants, keeps in contact with the project through *design reviews*. Regular (read *minor*) design reviews should be done weekly and be computer-supported through spreadsheets and modelling. Minor and major reviews have different goals:

- *Minor* design reviews would typically take a couple of hours, may or may not ask the sponsor and users to participate, and the decision will be given as the session's end – typically in the form of an advice.

This information, however, should be carried through to all parties interested in the project, and it should be databased for further use. Also, it should be used to enrich the corporate memory facility and the interactive files of the project:

- *Major* design reviews should be done at 25 per cent, 50 per cent, and 75 per cent of budgetary allocation, and co-involve the sponsor as well.
- According to the policy I learned in the 1960s with General Electric, the executive in charge of the major design review must have the right there and then to kill a project (we shall consider on this more later).

Minor design reviews are the project leader's best tool to ensure that he or she is in control of the project. They consist of well-timed, rigorous evaluations of crucial variables on which the project's success depends. The chosen process must ensure compliance with requirements expressed through goals and specifications. Formal methods are necessary and it is possible to use both quantitative scores and qualitative comments to express the design review's results.

Major design reviews, at the 25 per cent, 50 per cent, and 75 per cent budgetary milestones, are much more elaborate. Beyond the sponsor, they must involve other users as well as marketing and lead to a formal decision which will be of the Go/No go type. 'no go' means killing the project, but 'go' may not be free of trouble either.

The person who chaired the major design review, usually the CEO or a senior executive, may impose conditions to future funding: for instance, the timetable must be accelerated, costing may have to be redone, product quality might need to be beefed up, or design changes could be necessary. Figure 11.5 presents in a nutshell this process of major design reviews from a budgetary viewpoint, and underlines the importance of the four intermediate milestones which are most critical to any project's life. As the careful reader will observe, there is a non-linear relationship between time and cost:

- If the first 25 per cent of the project's time is applied research, the betting is that costs will progress slowly.
- Costs will pick up somewhat in the next 55 per cent of project time which is CAD-based co-operative work.
- Prototyping sees to it that the cost curve is steepening, and the same is true of small-series production.

While all design reviews are a form of auditing, as I mentioned already, major design reviews at the milestones noted in Figure 11.5 should have associated with them the authority to kill the project if it has fallen behind, overrun its budget, produced unwanted quality or presented other major problems. It is better to do away with a project half-way when about 25 per cent of the budget has been spent, than throw double that time and the whole budget away by waiting till its completion.

Minor reviews, too, could contribute to killing an ineffectual project or thoroughly revamping it by informing on its status and performance. Internal control intelligence should keep top management posted with minimal delay so that projects which do not perform to exacting standards are stopped cold in their tracks.

In other words, internal control should be omnipresent with design reviews, both regular and major. For this reason, after each evaluation, the compliance to product specs and timetables must be expressed as a *score*. Some organizations do this using analytical techniques – for instance, evaluating perceived quality, adherence to deadlines, and so on through rating. Others value by attribute on the aforementioned Go/No go basis.

Let me also bring to the reader's attention another crucial issue. Some of the companies I was consultant to the board had 100 or 150 projects running in parallel. That's absurd. It is an example of how to spend time, money, and manpower doing nothing, and therefore I used all my power of conviction to change this inefficient way of during R&D. No CEO can follow 100 projects or more. He might do so for half a dozen or at most a dozen. The others will be loafing.

Limiting the number of projects, but seeing to it that those retained are well equipped and fast-moving is vital for another reason. Today's technology and markets are non-linear. Auditing non-linear processes is a

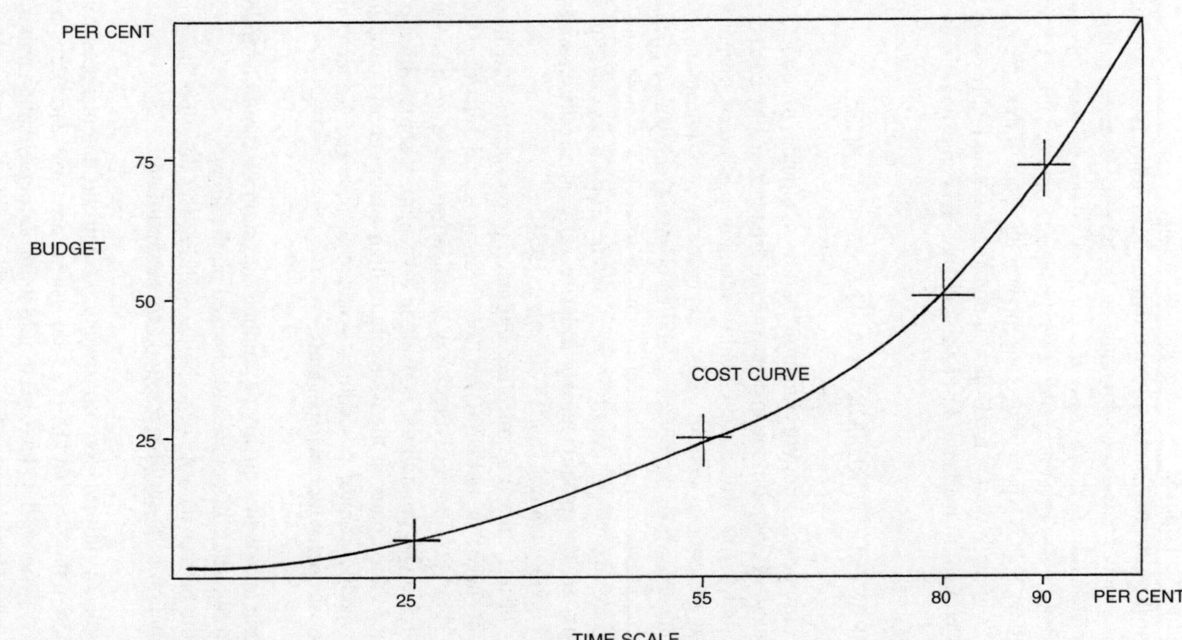

Figure 11.5 The need for design reviews is present in any project

tough job, yet it is necessary if a company wants to exploit its R&D investment, gain dominant market share, and answer in the best possible way requirements posed by a dynamic economy.

One of the advantages offered by a dynamic economy is that by running faster one can overtake those who might at one time have been way ahead but somehow are slowing down. Also, if a company comes up short on one item or more but thinks it can do better it works hard to advance itself where it is really strong. That is what global competition is all about. If there are no major drawbacks in the way, it is likely that an organization with highly competitive products brought to market at fast pace will leave its competitors in the dust.

AN INFRASTRUCTURE FOR QUALITY ASSURANCE

Another important auditing function is the assurance of *total quality management* (TQM). If done in a bureaucratic manner quality control is not a friend but a foe. But a total quality function performed properly and supported by internal control assists everyone in a responsible position, because it serves both the company and its clients. Quality assurance (QA) is very important both in engineering and in finance. Japanese banks, for instance, are masters of *quality control circles* (originally, an American invention). In the manufacturing industry, QA is greatly assisted by statistical quality control charts (Chorafas, 1960).

Going back to the fundamentals, engineering companies and financial institutions need an infrastructure for measuring and reporting quality results. They also require precise goals against which results can be measured. No QA programme is made in a vacuum. It starts with a policy statement by the board on the necessity of high quality at low cost, and of rigorous quality control procedures – and it is followed by an in-depth definition of quality control standards:

- The principle is that quality of products and services should be followed up through their life-cycle and checked all the time.
- This dramatizes the role of technical auditing and describes the type of information necessary for a sound QA methodology.

The vector of information on quality should be internal control, in recognition of the fact that QA is a vital issue to any firm. Tier-1 companies know by experience they have been right in instituting a quality authority at their auditing department. My advice is that because costs and quality correlate this audit mission needs to extend its reach into cost control and return on investment (ROI). The board should be very interested to know that *our* company is doing much better than the industry average in the 3-dimensional framework shown in Figure 11.6.

Furthermore, because a fast advancing technology makes knowledge and skills obsolescent, this 3-D frame of reference should become 4-dimensional to include *human capital* – its selection, hiring, training, and evaluation for promotion. Attracting new talent in a rewarding business environment impacts on quality results. Start-ups know this and they look at a 4-D frame for their future, while old-established businesses pay scant attention to motivation and upgrading of human capital – and to the impact this has on quality.

Quality-minded companies appreciate that the people inside must be able to attract from the outside, and they must be capable of selling a quality product at a very competitive price. This is what builds up a reputation.

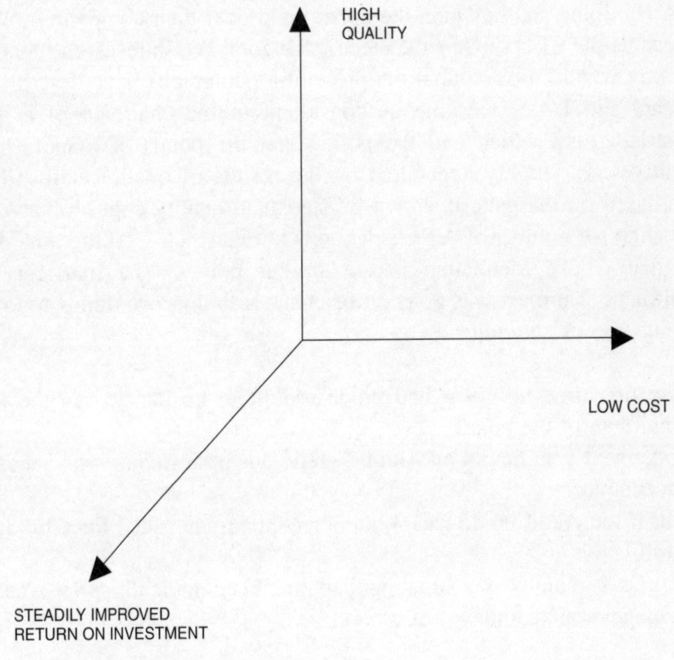

Figure 11.6 The impact of good management on competitiveness can best be appreciated in a 3-dimensional frame of reference

Speaking from personal experience, high quality is a catalyst to an attractive work environment, which also adds to reputation:

- Motivated technical talent wants to work on challenging projects.
- The quality of work one is doing tends to define self worth.

Product quality, cost containment, fast time to market, business reputation, and a challenging work environment lead to improved job performance and, in a virtuous cycle, this increases personal satisfaction. Without high quality a service economy, like ours, will be falling out of control. It is no secret that for this reason highly competitive technical companies provide:

- Challenging assignments and
- Sufficient support for success.

Successful companies are very careful to populate their work groups with people who are creative, decisive, productive, and care for quality and costs. By doing so, they gain the upper hand over their competitors. When he became the CEO of General Electric, Dr John Welsh recast the company in a way which mirrors what the preceding paragraphs have described.

Years ago I was working as consultant to the chairman of a major industrial group which had the policy that the bonus of manufacturing executives was highly dependent on the results of quality audits. These were based on the pattern shown by statistical quality control charts, like the *c* chart (of number of defects per unit) in Figure 11.7. At the time, I was told that Chase Manhattan had a similar policy. The manager of a department or project was given three chances to improve things following the outcome of an audit:

- The first time he got a bad grade (Audit 4) he had to see the Vice-Chairman of the board.
- If the next year he got an Audit 2 grade, his performance was judged as acceptable.
- But if the Audit grade was 3, the Vice-Chairman asked for a follow-up audit.
- If in six months the situation had not been radically improved, the manager was definitely out.

I would advise every company, whether a credit institution or engineering, manufacturing or merchandising concern, to adopt an approach which follows the general lines of this Chase procedure. Particularly in connection

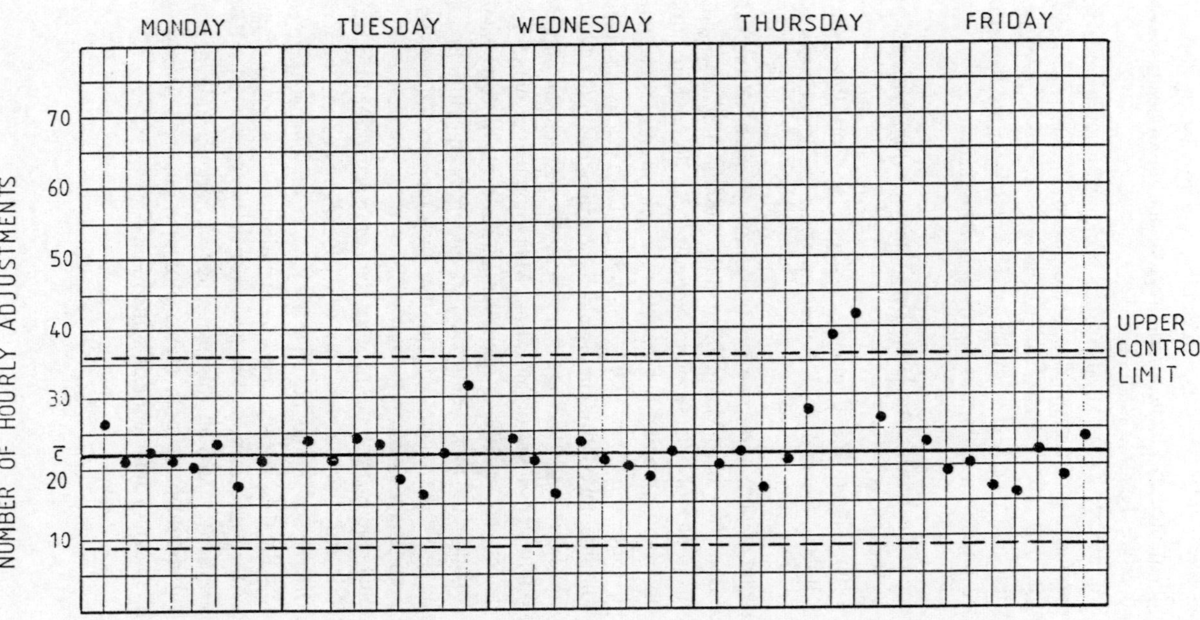

Figure 11.7 Control chart (*c* chart) for number of defects per unit and adjustments on an hourly basis, during a week

to project management, there is much to be gained if personal evaluation stresses efficiency, budgets, costs, timetables, *and* product quality. This should be implemented by means of both regular and major design reviews done in a proactive, dynamic manner.

Let me take another example, also from banking but with an evident impact on engineering. In about the same timeframe (the late 1970s) Citibank installed a minicomputer in its foreign operations department dedicated to tracking customer complaints. The people in the department were rewarded through a system of *merits* and *demerits*:

- The absence of customer complaints led to merits, while demerits were applied for complaints.
- For every complaint; the computer assigned a short time for its resolution. If the same complaint showed up again, the demerits doubled.

All this had an evident influcnce on premiums as well as on career development. Both the Chase Manhattan and the Citibank implementations are excellent examples of what a service economy can do (and should do) to protect itself from a creeping low quality and lack of care. Bureaucracy has no place in modern business. Only the best performance is acceptable.

In conclusion, internal control intelligence is so important in QA because our goal should be one of dramatic improvements in such an important performance parameter in any organization. Many companies which target reduction of defects and rework, or improvements in cycle time, try hard to locate existing data of the merits/demerits sort, and find difficulties in doing so because they have not taken due care that such data should always be available through database mining.

Organizational studies must define what data are needed for QA, which information collected at production floor or back-office is usable, how data collection and analysis should be done to have a reasonable degree of confidence, how the data streams must be exploited for maximum impact, and what databased information elements must be interactively available. Every process briefly stated in this paragraph should be audited – and internal control should bring both matter-of-course quality reporting and audited results to senior management's attention.

12 Services Provided by Information Technology to the Auditing of Internal Controls

INTRODUCTION

Technologically advanced banks appreciate that internal control is the key to keeping their house in order, and to supporting management information requirements in an able manner. There is a crying need for new, sophisticated paradigms on how to use information technology for internal control reasons. This need has been present for some years, but only today has it started to be more generally appreciated because few banks had the skill and culture necessary for implementation of rigorous solutions.

The worst a company can do in terms of supporting its internal controls through technology is to use mainframes and programs written in COBOL Both are Palaeolithic, awfully expensive, and ineffectual. The solution should be intelligent networks and deductive distributed databases supported by sophisticated software. An effective technological solution is needed to handle internal control challenges – including real-time feedback, online data capture, models, simulators, expert systems, agents, and interactive 3-dimensional visualization of obtained results.

Internal controls require the kind of solution appropriate for interactive computational finance which is based on fully distributed real-time systems. Cost-effective approaches to internal control information requirements are networked any-to-any, based on Web software and client-servers. The workstations are the clients and there is an array of database engines dedicated to tracking internal control results (see also the reference to Citibank's merits/demerits in Chapter 11).

Research which I did in the 1998–2000 timeframe on the use of computers in internal control and auditing shows that while several banks use software as aid to auditing programs few employ expert systems and interactive knowledge artefacts (agents) which serve this purpose so much better. By contrast, many institutions now use sophisticated software for risk management. For instance, the Treasury/UK Operations of Barclays Bank uses expert systems to track exposure:

- These knowledge engineering artefacts work in real-time and
- They focus on market risk, assisting the prudential management of the trading book.

This is a welcome exception to European banking where, by and large, the board and senior management ignore high technology because they are still listening to the voices of people who are dedicated mainframers and those of computer vendors with conflicts of interest. This is tantamount to continuing to live in a time when the computer was as three times as big as a refrigerator and only big companies could afford a million instructions per second (MIPS).

Today a giga instructions per second (GIPS) has become the unit of measurement. We use this power to analyze data feeds in real-time, and to highlight a pattern's most salient features. But, in a depressingly large number of cases information technology is still run by people of low MIPS. This kills efforts to radically renew the technology base. It also keeps Euroland about six years behind the United States in information technology investments, as dramatized in Figure 12.1.

Year in and year out I am surprised at the number of companies which are afraid of technology, even if they spend on an inordinate amount of money on it. Instead of leaping forward and exploiting the full potential of their investments through the most advanced solutions, they bend over backwards to use whatever had become obsolete back in the 1970s and early 1980s – a full quarter-century gap.

Some banks have the technology to move into intraday, tick-by-tick management of their exposure, but they don't use it. A senior executive said:

> We receive reports on a daily basis. The front desk could produce intraday reports, but it does not do that yet. It really depends on your status. If you are a market leader and trade in exotics you need sophisticated instruments and rapid-fire solutions.

The truth is that to remain competitive we have to use increasingly more sophisticated instruments and IT solutions commensurate with the requirements of rigorous internal control.

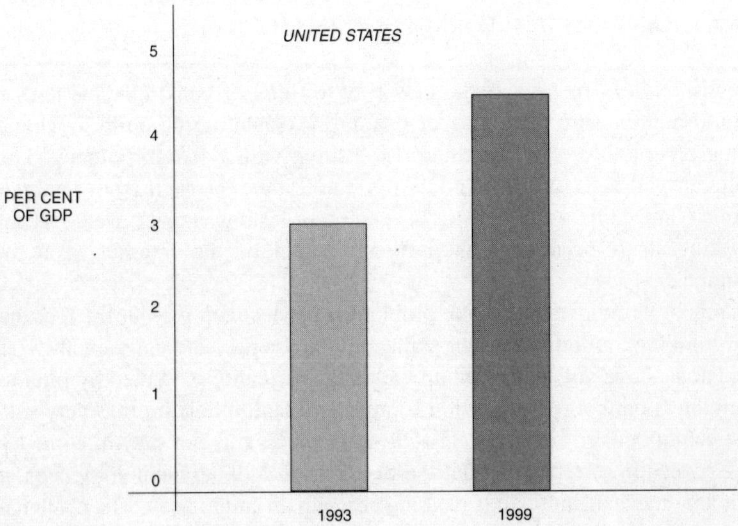

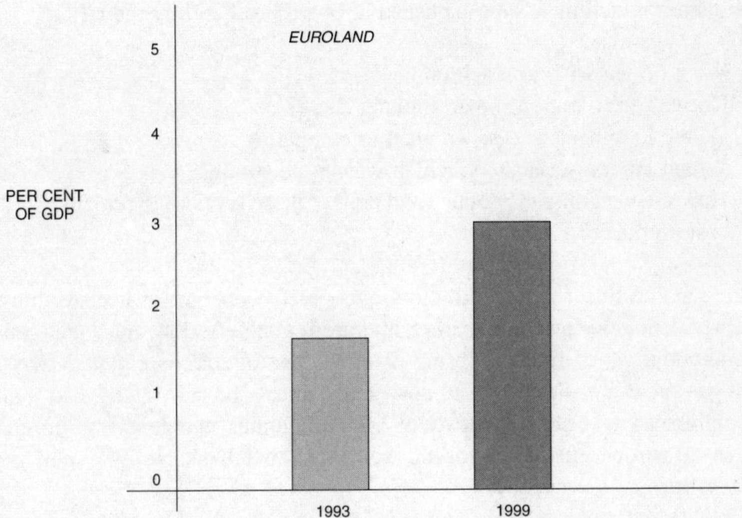

Figure 12.1 Investments in information technology: United States v. Euroland, 1993 and 1999

POSITIONING OUR INSTITUTION TO PROFIT FROM THE FACT THAT BANKING IS INFORMATION IN MOTION

'Information in motion' is the new way to think of banking. This term is identifying the shift from a paper-board, bricks and mortar outfit to what is often regarded as a virtual enterprise dealing with electronic money. This metamorphosis is as profound as the one 2500 years ago from barter to money and it is expected to have a long-lasting impact well beyond banking itself because it is part and parcel of the Internet economy (Chorafas, 1997).

Yet, in its fundamentals, the problem is not technology, but the fact that our thinking, our attitudes, our skills, our experience, and consequently our decisions, have not yet caught up with the new reality presented by Internet banking (i-banking). Adaptation is a professional obligation for every self-respecting banker, but as the last 20 years shows it is not easy to come by.

I never tire of repeating that the best way to look at technology is as an enabling mechanism to do something else, not an end in itself. The challenge in positioning our bank to capitalize on the Internet economy is that to a very substantial extent, in the financial industry today, it is pretty clear what the emerging technology is going to be. What is still a puzzle is how should we use this technology to make profits. This evidently calls for strategic guidelines which must be established at board level and by the CEO:

- What do we wish to reach online?
- Do we *really* want to be an Internet Bank?
- Where in cyberspace do we want to compete?
- Which are the services on which we can be strong?
- How are we going to produce and deliver these services to remain a low-cost producer?

There are no linear answers to these queries. To get some answer we must clearly define *our* product, market, and profit goals. And we must clear our mind about which road can bring us there. The Internet is a generic term, not a precise answer. Yet our goals must be clear, precise and comprehensive. There is no room for ambiguities and fence-sitting can have disastrous effects, as the market passes our bank by. We want get ready to force the unexpected.

What do I mean by *getting ready*? Let me answer through a practical example. On 27 October 1997, the economic crisis in East Asia and other reasons sparked stock market activity that sent trading volumes to a record high. The NASDAQ stock exchange received a record of 20 million hits in one day at its Internet trading site, <nasdaq.com.> As a result, NASDAQ urgently needed additional servers to handle this large increase:

- At NASDAQ's request Dell built and shipped eight custom-configured, fully tested server systems in just 36 hours.
- Three days later, NASDAQ was using the servers to conduct its online business without any glitches.

This rapid-action solution provided NASDAQ with a state-of-the-art system. The new information technology gear was up and running within a timeframe no other computer vendor had so far matched. The rapid turnover was achieved by a joint Dell and NASDAQ sales, procurement, and manufacturing team working together to understand, then rapidly respond to, customer requirements.

Rapid response and results-oriented action is the way in which financial institutions today must treat their customers. An example on how to apply such fast-response and deployment solutions comes from the treasury business. Treasury information both for *our* institution and for *our* important clients must be:

- Rapid
- Credible
- Easy to understand
- Simple to use.

Real-time information and associated decision support must lead to solutions which offer transparency, observe market discipline, appeal to reliable investors, are enriched with the best available technology, are flexible, and are able to handle exceptions. Able solutions target not only the automation of production but also of delivery. They provide gateways to control action and enhance the ability to handle operations at an international level.

Regulators and transnational institutions are moving along the real-time path. An effort, spearheaded by the Committee on Payment and Settlement Systems of the Bank for International Settlements (BIS), focused on moving the interbank settlement system from settling accounts overnight to an effective real-time settlement. The principle is that the faster the settlement, the faster the time supervisors can react – and, therefore, the faster the damage of defaults can be contained.

Commercial banks, investment funds, mutual funds and other institutions, too, should be highly interested in damage containment. They should also appreciate that only high technology really helps in implementing a timely and efficient service. One way I use to classify banks is by judging how they fare in the A, B, C, D classification system shown in Figure 12.2. The line representing level of sophistication rises from left (D class) to right (A class). By contrast, the number of banks in each category is high in the D class and low in the A class.

What top management often fails to appreciate is that this is a matter of 'winner takes all', and the winners are to be found in this A class. They are there not only because they are leaders in technology but also owing to the fact their management is very efficient in all business functions. This has much to do with both strategy and with tactics.

THE USE OF ADVANCED TECHNOLOGY IS NOT A FAD, BUT AN OBLIGATION

Top-tier banks epitomize the use of advanced technology as a major force in competition. They are using technology to be leaders in innovation and to push globalization faster and deeper, not just because it adds more business leverage but because it permits then to employ the best brains. This helps to re-invent the company and to reengineer the world-wide requirements of its clients.

Not only credit institutions but also other international service companies do the same. The core of their global strategy is to use advanced information technology to help customers capitalize on international markets. At the same time they appreciate that the synergy of globalization and information technology may entail more operational risks (see Chapter 2), which brings the need for better internal control – a requirement again served through high technology.

For instance, like the foremost financial institutions, companies specializing in delivery services see themselves more as an IT firm than as transporters of goods. Today, more than two- thirds of FedEx customers handle orders and delivered online. 'We decided years ago,' says chairman and CEO Frederick W. Smith, 'that the most important element in this business is information technology, and we have geared everything to that philosophy – recruitment, training, and compensation. Fail-safe precision is the key to it all' (*Business Week*, 23 March 1998).

An entity re-inventing itself through advanced technology experiences a return to fundamentals. The effective use of high technology requires board policies and the setting of milestones as well as standards. Since the early

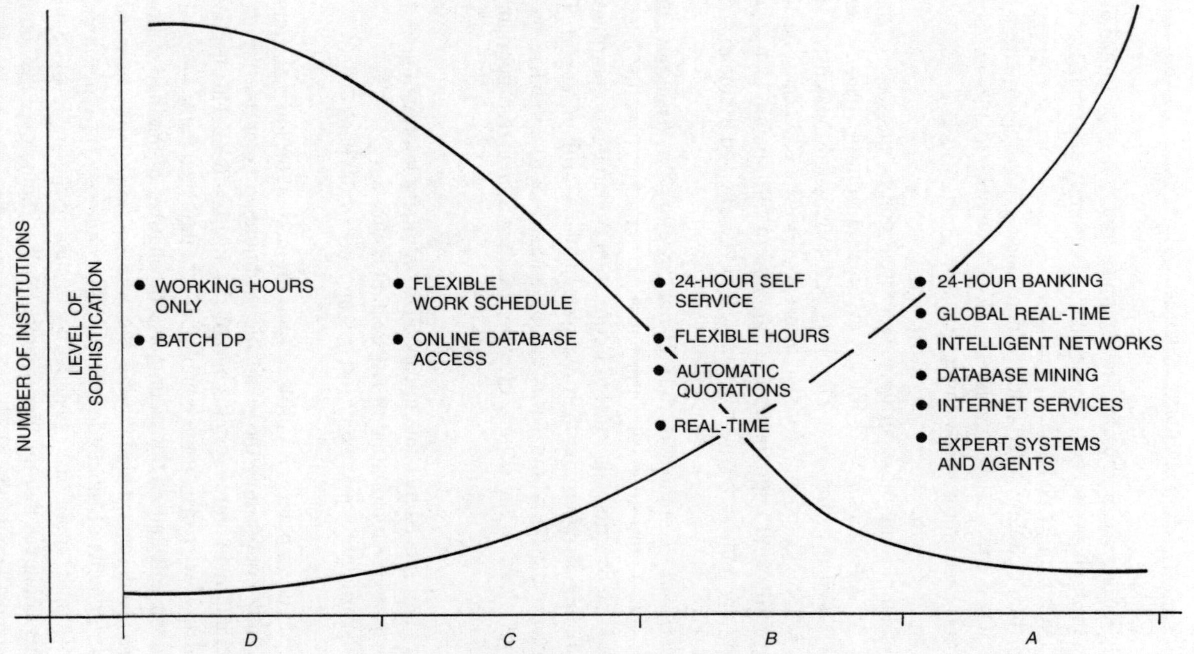

Figure 12.2 Technology supporting four different banks which offer personal banking services

1990s, following a top management decision, no IT project was undertaken at Bankers Trust that lasted more than six months. Such policy brought with it other corporate-wide norms, such as:

- The choice and use of first-class development tools which permitted them to gain the high ground because they did not currently exist in most of the bank's competitors and
- A well made architectural study which made it possible to carve out of the IT grand design smaller chunks executable in the six-month timeframe, and immediately implementable.

These examples are most pertinent in a discussion on the services to be provided by information technology to internal control, because they prove that even if a first-class IT job is demanding it is feasible, but it requires skill, precision and decision to get results. The CEO must be sure about the ability and know-how of his director of information technology in carrying out a mission whose grand design is explained by the diagram in Figure 12.3.

Commerzbank commented during our meeting in Frankfurt that, basically, the contribution of information technology towards internal controls can be described as equal to information technology's contribution towards trading activities and their requirements for real-time support. The senior executive with whom I was talking added that to capitalize on IT investments aimed at the control of exposure, it is extremely important to have in place:

- Policies and procedures able to capitalize on timely information
- An adequate documentation of risk-related issues and
- A limits structure reflective of the risk appetite of the bank.

These three bullets points also provide food for thought for internal control, since on the bottom-line the available technology is at the heart of successful internal control systems and of risk management. This becomes more evident if we consider the complexity of a universal bank's portfolio, the volume in outstanding transaction, and the number of trading locations.

Commerzbank also added during the meeting that it has invested a significant amounts of money in information technology, to bring both its market risk and credit risk systems to a state-of-the-art level. Senior management believes that this development will continue over the coming years, as banks around the globe are keen to integrate new products and market developments into their business systems.

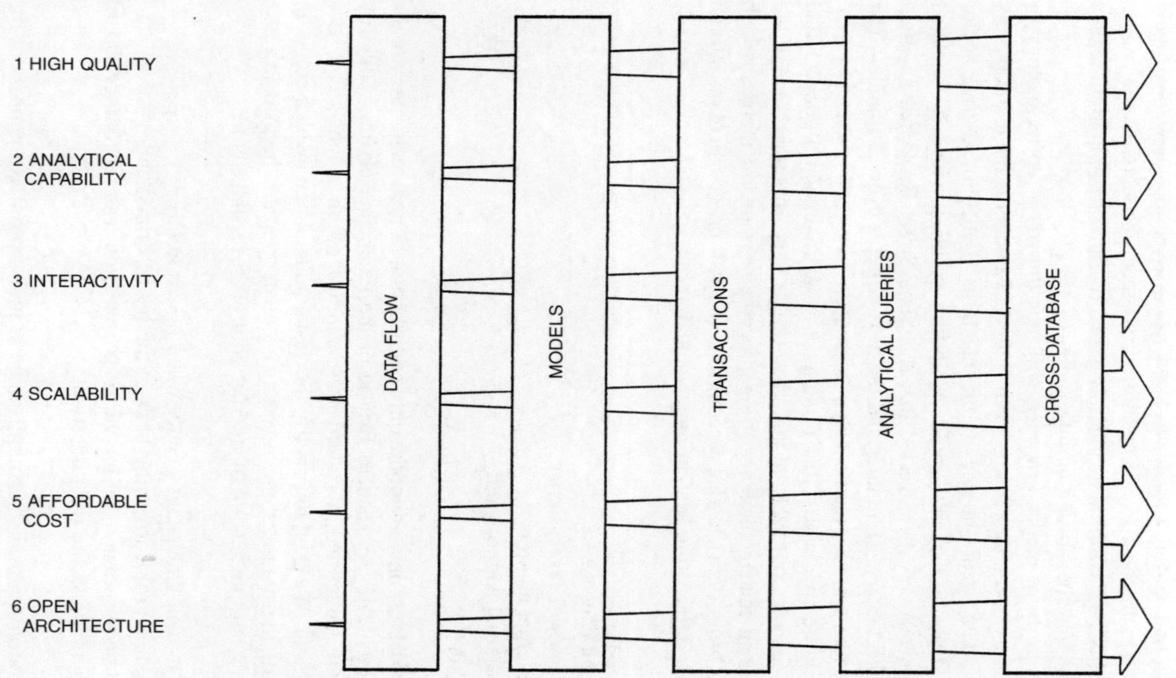

Figure 12.3 Grand design of an IT solution addressing a range of functional and operational characteristics

In one of the rare success stories in conversion procedures in the banking industry, Barclays Bank restructured its risks archives. It shut down its main customer systems for a weekend to cut over to a new distributed database accommodating 25 million customer accounts. As a major upgrade this new solution seamlessly replaced three incompatible legacy procedures and their programming support.

The majority of banks, however, still lack the advanced technology of the type I have been describing, even if their IT budget is huge and rapidly increases every year. In one of the meetings, I mentioned to a senior executive, proud that his credit institution could produce an updated balance sheet every two weeks, that the State Street Bank had a virtual balance sheet every 30 minutes and the next target is every 5 minutes. The careful reader would remember this reference.

It should be appreciated that IT support to internal control goes beyond the balance sheet and P&L, though this, too, is very important. One of the challenges in management reporting procedures is to use metrics which permit to bring both classical accounting and risk prognostication into an interactive information system understandable by:

- All board members
- All bank executives
- All classes of professionals
- The internal auditors
- The external auditors and
- The supervisors.

The speed of response is not the only contribution of high technology to the policy I advocate. As Richard Britton of the Financial Services Authority (FSA) aptly suggested, a pattern presentation through graphics can be a powerful tool. We need to simplify the vast amount of data which comes in and out of the organization. Interactive colour graphics help to increase everyone's comprehension of internal controls facts and figures:

- Management understands better when it sees trends
- Internal control alarms ring bells in the board's mind and
- By showing trends, a graphical presentation can encourage board members to ask the right questions.

High technology means accomplishments. It also prompts members of the board and senior management to be more and more demanding, because they see that their requests lead somewhere. Let us never forget that information technology is a company's infrastructure, and when the infrastructure is Palaeolithic the figures in P&L statements can be abysmal.

Added to internal management information requirements is the fact that regulators increasingly require a whole range of reports based on tight inspection procedures. An example is reporting on the specific risk of an institution, and on the way an entity positions itself to face market volatility. Interactive reporting also shows whether senior management is in control, well before the bad news hits the bottom-line.

Very few people at the top of the organizational pyramid have this concept and even fewer are inquisitive about what *more* they should ask, and should get, from information technology. This happens because the majority of these people are not computer literate. While they are very demanding in terms of performance from the bank's trading and loans departments, they are very lax in terms of deliverables from information technology.

The crevasse between internal control and technology does not end there. Four key people in the control of risk: the credit risk manager, market risk manager, the compliance officer, and the chief technology officer never seem to work together. With few notable exceptions credit managers and compliance officers depend very little on expert systems, intelligent networks, and datamining – and information technology does not know how to make software for internal control. This explains the gap between the ever-growing internal control requirements and the supports information technology is willing to provide.

ONLINE BANKING AND THE AUDITING OF FINANCIAL OPERATIONS

Although more or less each credit institution offering home banking services developed its own model for online transactions, there is an underlying general trend which can best be described through a relatively simple diagram like the one in Figure 12.4. The knowledgeable reader will appreciate that the service underpinning this presentation is today called *brick and click*: branch offices made of bricks and mortar are still in the picture, but much is done online through computers.

Electronic banking has not seen the success originally expected. Public response in the cyber age is not linear, not does a new service remain attractive forever. A US survey made in mid-1999 by Cyber Dialogue found that almost one-third of people who used online banking services subsequently dropped

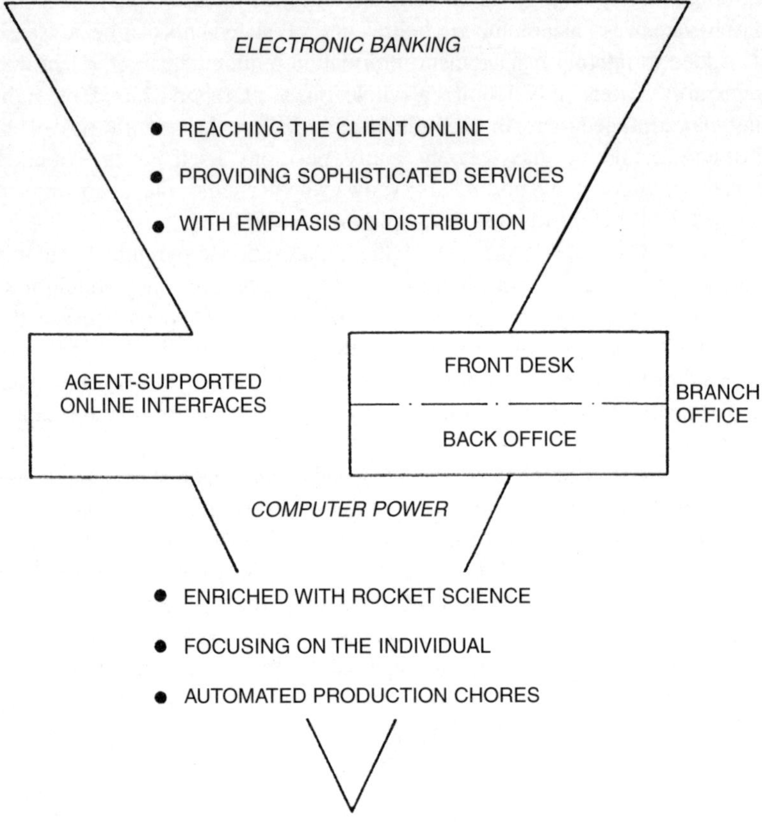

Figure 12.4 A bank's financial network and effective management of client accounts

out (*Retail Banker International*, 20 September 1999). While the number of consumers banking online rose to 6.3 million in July 1999, the study also established that only 35 per cent of online users who had discontinued were inclined to try it again.

Consumers began banking online to save time but, as these statistics indicate, a large number discontinued use because they were not convinced about security, or were dissatisfied with the level of customer service. There is, however, a silver lining. In contrast to online banking, only 3 per cent of investment traders who are online have discontinued trading online, while 85 per cent of these say that they are satisfied with their service.

Online brokerages like Schwab and E*Trade have demonstrated leadership by investing aggressively in marketing and customer service.

Retail banks, however, did not react in a way commensurate with Internet time and Internet services. Institutions who fail in moving with their time risk losing their customer relationships and therefore their reason for being. This is, in my judgement one of the first things IT auditing should investigate:

- Do we have a strategy which can assure leadership in a brick and click market?
- Is *our* bank's technology state of the art when compared to market demands and drives?

The title of this chapter addresses the services information technology should render to auditing; but this issue and what I am currently discussing correlate. What information technology can do for auditing is up to a point a reflection of what information technology can do for the bank as a whole. The common ground between information technology and banking services at large is full of requirements relating to both account management and real-time accounting in the broadest sense of the term.

The planning and control of how information technology should help the bank rests with senior management. The irony is that both senior management and the bank's professionals have been badly starved in terms of technology support, and they are not marking enough fuss. Look at the statistics in column (1) and (2) of Figure 12.5, which come from a study I did in 1990 and update practically every year:

- For the majority of companies the tragedy is that little has changed in the decade of the 1990s by way of IT support.
- On the contrary, user requirements developed a great deal, as shown in column (3) of Figure 12.5, but they remain unsatisfied.

Bread-and-butter banking functions still constitute the bulk of computer-based services. These include: account opening, account maintenance, card products maintenance (such as orders for a new card, recording loss of a card, modifying a card limit, blocking of a card, unblocking of a card); business relating to credit products (like capture of loan application details, sanction of loans, disbursement of loans, termination of loans, monitoring of loans); and so on. These are not today the cutting edge of competition.

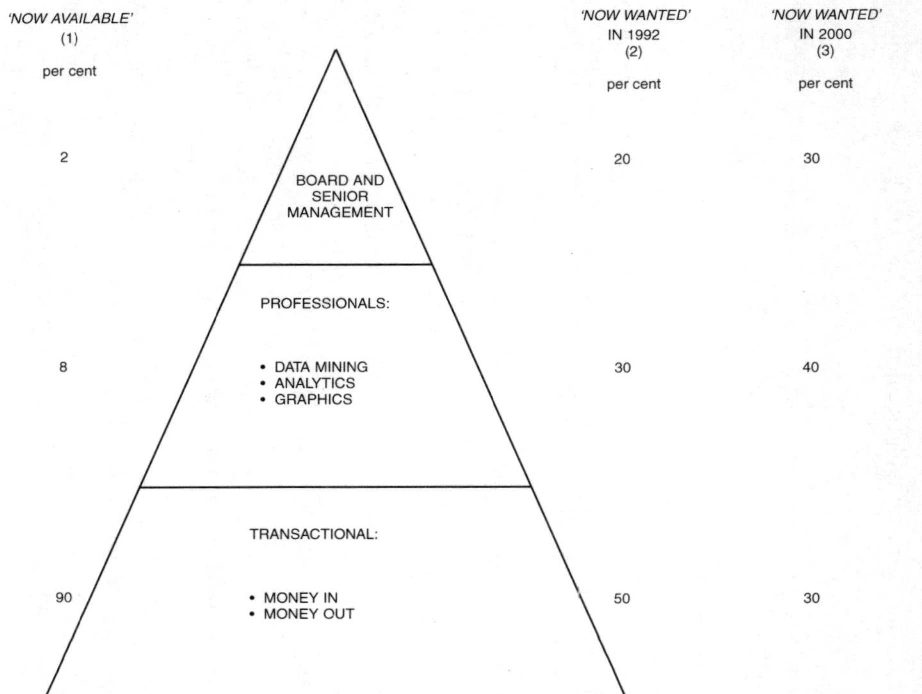

Figure 12.5 The distribution of IT investments and supported functionality is not keeping pace with end-user demands

For practically every company in any walk of life, the most important justification for spending big on information technology is that:

- Externally it supports client satisfaction and
- Internally helps in restructuring and cost-cutting.

This is where IT auditing should concentrate its examination skills. From a global perspective, a critical benefit of the cutting edge of information technology is that it makes real-time data available world-wide. Managers and professionals can communicate much more quickly with counterparts in other countries and learn what works and what does not, or investigate latent areas of major risks.

This is not doable through backwater approaches, where the major part of the budget is spent on data clearance, printed reports, and batch processing. Among the functions which should be in real-time both in the sense of client support and for agent-based auditing reasons are subscription and redemption of investment products; operations relating to capital market instruments (shares, bonds, warrants); buying, selling, and monitoring of positions relating to foreign exchange; commodities trading; derivative financial instruments; and operations relating to insurance and other ancillary services. Also the many aspects of operational risk.

Still other activities which should be online both for execution and for auditing reasons concern private investors, asset management, investment funds, investment consulting, portfolio management, corporates, and institutional services. Financial instruments at large must be handled in real-time with regard to investment strategy, portfolio type, asset allocation, and desired constraints by position.

I would be pushing at an open door (at least at top-tier institutions) to say that trade order management must be fully real-time-supported through expert systems: order entry, combining individual order to global order, and checking of liquidity position, block position, and any other constraints. The same is valid for portfolio browser and analysis, including information about asset composition, details of securities holdings and securities movements, average cost per security, and portfolio performance.

Internal control intelligence has much to gain by using agents to execute portfolio valuation, analysis of time-weighted return performance, and money-weighted return performance. Important information the computer must allow board members, the CEO, and senior management to have at their fingertips is new, custodian holdings, cost data, and a whole range of valuations such as:

- Fees earned by customer, asset value, type of portfolio, location, and so on
- Fees based on performance for institutional investors, as well as corrections of calculated fees.

Even the ablest auditors need properly delineated implementation procedures permitting them to effectively carry out top management's wishes regarding in-depth examinations and controls. Because the business environment gets more and more complex, without effective online supports the best system of controls will be nothing more than a façade.

The financial industry has seen examples of this in high-profile losses that have been reported by institutions where the existence of control systems was not questioned, but able solutions were not implemented by the organization in a global sense – a task not possible without the best technology available in the market. The absence of high technology to beef up auditing and internal control should be a warning to firms and supervisors that a weak environment may exist, which would pose significant risks to:

- An institution
- Its customers and
- Its counterparties.

Without any doubt, the quality of management can be improved by feeding critical information online into internal control. This includes a whole range of parameters, from asset statements for institutional and private investors, to other customer data and investment data; tax data by country and branch, including experimentation on tax rates for optimization reasons; and P&L statements and statements of recognized but not yet realized gains and losses. Rich databases containing these items should be available online for auditing reasons.

THE EFFECTIVE USE OF INFORMATION TECHNOLOGY FOR INTERNAL CONTROL

'There is one thing that struck us in use of information technology for risk management,' said John Welsh of the Group of Thirty, 'every time we spoke to senior executives in risk management, everyone stated categorically that the goal and objectives of his function was to measure interest rate risk, currency exchange risk and other market risks. But when we asked specifics like ''Where are you now?'' the IT piece was not in place.'

Part and parcel of this same issue is how much manual massaging is necessary to get meaningful internal control information out of the great daily data streams pouring into the bank's database or reaching senior management desks in the form of special reports. While the exact answer varies from one financial institution to another, the finding by the Group of Thirty is that:

- In the general case, it takes lots of manual massaging to obtain significant risk-oriented information and
- IT structure and computer systems are far behind when compared to the stated strategic objectives of the bank.

In a way, this is changing but not yet radically so. The big US banks and some banks in the United Kingdom do take quite seriously the need to radically upgrade their information technology. This, however, is not true of the majority of continental European banks. As a result, internal controls are at present much more at a conceptual level than a system which has bones and muscles.

Re-architecturing information technology to serve internal control needs in the best possible manner is nearly synonymous to designing big integrated systems. Big systems are not little systems that have outgrown their original size, which characterizes the state of the vast majority of information technology today available in banking. Big systems are totally different from overgrown little systems in terms of:

- Design
- Implementation
- Verification and
- Maintenance.

Batch processing is a conglomeration of little systems, each a discrete island on incompatible platforms, with obsolete software and concepts belonging to the Palaeolithic age. What is more, most batch programs grew like wild cacti. To say that this mismatch of machines and software is counterproductive is to state the obvious. It is a regrettable state of affairs which can serve neither operating requirements nor auditing.

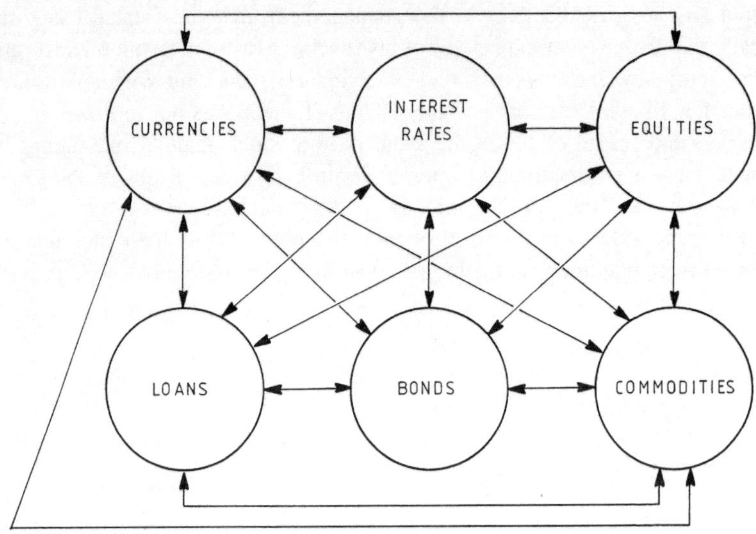

Figure 12.6 Financial instruments become complex because they can be combined in many and varied ways

Computer programs written in the 1960s and 1970s, which are still running today, paid no attention to the fact that financial instruments become complex once they would be combined in many and different ways like the example given in Figure 12.6. Let us always keep in mind that innovation does not only mean something totally new but also a novel *combination* and a novel *restructuring* of what we now have. (See also the discussion of complexity.) The permutations taking place in producing new instruments are almost endless, but to obtain something which makes sense:

- Novel financial instruments must undergo lots of experimentation in real-time and
- Their pricing must be thoroughly tested to ensure that all possible risks have been accounted for.

Not only will a modern solution be integrative both bottom up and top down, but it will also need to support in the most efficient manner intrinsic-time, high-frequency financial data (HFFD) (Chorafas, 1995c) and real-time internal control. The best bet is that agents will dominate the landscape and the models being used will be, to a large extent, non- linear.

The old computer age, often referred to as 'Electronic Data Processing' or EDP was linear, but the modern Information Age is about:

- Exponential technology
- Derivatives financial instruments and
- Increasing-return economics.

This is a Darwinian-type evolution, of survival of the best. Companies which do not take seriously the need to steadily adapt to business evolution and re-invent themselves do not survive. What I just said has been particularly true since the 1990s. Look at the roster of the 100 largest US companies in 1990. Only 16 were still in the top-100 list in 1999.

Some may argue that, to a significant degree, the wave of change started in the 1950s, not in 1990. If so, non-believers are advised to consider *Fortune* magazine's first list, published in 1956, of America's 500 biggest companies. Only 29 of its top 100 firms could still be found in the top 100 by 1992. Let me, however, bring to the reader's attention the fact that:

- From 1956 to 1992, 39 years passed, and in 1992 there were still 29 companies left in the top-100 list.
- From 1990 to 1999, there are just 9 years (one-quarter the previous figure) and only 16 are still in the top-100 list.

If this was the criterion of the pace of corporate rise and fall, then we can say that this pace has accelerated by 600 per cent. One might wonder how is it possible that so many supposedly wealthy, well managed, successful firms fail. Evidently something happened to make them unfit for their business environment. Globalization, deregulation, innovation and technology changed the rules, but not everything is due to these. More potent negative factors have been:

- Management which is not worth its salt and
- Falling behind, which made the force of technology disruptive.

In the general case, professional and trade associations think further ahead than individual companies and they appreciate better the need for internal control intelligence and advanced risk management. They also appreciate the importance of high tech. 'We see IT as more and more important to the future of the banking industry,' said Susan Hinko of the International Derivatives Dealers Association (ISDA). 'This is particularly true in derivatives. Banks have to invest in technology.'

American regulators think the same way. 'IT is an area of our biggest challenge,' said William McDonough of the Federal Reserve Bank of Boston. In his opinion, the systems people the bank employs must be expert in the *new* information technologies, and lead their institution towards sophisticated solutions which work in real-time. I subscribe 100 per cent to this notion. William McDonough also underlined the fact that while for a central bank it is not easy to assess whether the commercial banks under its jurisdiction have cutting-edge technology every effort is now made to bring the supervised banks state of the art in information technology into the picture. The way he put it was: 'Even making an assessment of state-of-the-art is complex, but we look at IT when we examine the bank's line of business.' Internal auditors and external auditors should take note.

Is the Federal Reserve Bank of Boston associating the commercial banks' level of technology with its ability to face adversity? Is it promoting the implementation of efficient internal control and managing risk? 'You rapidly get to the point where examiners have to criticise the level of technology because the bank cannot manage its risks in an able manner,' was the answer.

THE REGULATORS EMPHASIZE THE NEED TO USE TECHNOLOGY IN AN ABLE MANNER

What was stated above about the position taken by the Federal Reserve regarding the usefulness of advanced technology is not an exception, but the way in which US regulatory agencies think. The Securities and Exchange Commission (SEC) follows a very similar approach. 'We look at the whole system including IT,' said Robert A. Solazzo of SEC in New York. 'Are limits extended without authorisation? Does the system detect it? Is senior management immediately informed?'

This is the best way of looking at internal control as well as auditing. Capturing deviations and getting the facts immediately into senior management's hands is not possible without first-class technology. 'If you see a highly leveraged account, concentration and large debit balance – you know it may be trouble,' advised Solazzo. 'But the system must be sophisticated enough to flash out such facts.'

Imperceptibly, the supervisory authorities in the United States have led the commercial and investment banks towards the use of better technology than they currently have. Call reports are now executed electronically. At the beginning, some commercial banks said that they did not have the computer solution to report online – but when the regulators did not change their position, they found it.

Through their supervisory duties, the regulators have the means to push the institutions under their authority towards the right track. For instance, until January 1998 SEC was accepting reports submitted by some brokers and mutual funds on paper. Since then everything has to be done electronically, online. It is 'do it or die'. There is no alternative, and the supervised institutions have got the message.

'We emphasize that controls and systems must be commensurate with the activities the bank undertakes,' was the message given by many of the central bankers whom I met in New York, Washington, and Boston. Are they examining every facet of technology and its usage in the institutions which they supervise? 'No!' was the answer. Robert A. Solazzo put it in this way: 'We focus primarily in 4 or 5 areas:

- Trading,
- Credit,
- Liquidity and funding,
- Internal auditing.

The advances characterizing the institution's information technology as well as security issues are other areas where supervisors and their examiners pay attention. They do so at a strategic level. 'We are not computer experts,' Solazzo suggested. 'But we do our best.' This is a policy I would like to see adopted by all regulators.

To the query whether the inspection of investment banks, brokers, and mutual funds includes information technology, Edward A. Ryan, Jr of the SEC in Boston answered: 'It has to include IT. The report must say whether or not what is available today is satisfactory.' To the question how SEC examiners look at information technology, Ryan said: 'We look at what they are using and what the vendors offer. We are not sophisticated computer experts, but we can see the difference.'

The regional staff of the SEC is assisted by the fact that at its headquarters in Washington the Commission has en enforcement staff which includes computer experts and rocket scientists. Little by little, particularly after the 1996 Market Risk Amendment all regulators in G-10 countries have added rocket scientists to their staff. These people have the skills to:

- Analyze cases brought to their attention
- Model instruments and control situations with non-linear characteristics
- Track developments which lag behind the state of the art and
- Highlight conditions which are wanting in terms of compliance or other criteria.

Should investment banks use real-time systems and knowledge engineering? 'That will be an excellent opportunity for a broker,' suggested Edward A. Ryan, who then added: 'The Commission is not pushing information technology, but it watches that is made good use of it.' This is, indeed, the regulator's role.

Other supervisors have taken a similar position. To the question whether the banks under his authority should use models and real-time systems, one of them answered: 'Not if you don't mark-to-market.' But then he added: 'Since marking-to-market is today practically a requirement, this makes real-time mandatory.'

Many supervisors in the United States now look at technology as a service which does much more than helping in keeping records. They would like to see evolving a *market memory* facility which addresses the history of the world of credit, including near-failures and bankruptcies. The leading thinking is that the lessons from the turbulence the financial industry has gone through today would be lost without advanced technology to keep them in perspective:

- As a reference and
- As a case study.

Some senior central banker I talked to projected in the near future the day when models will help in analyzing and in synthesizing estimates of financial health. This approach is currently taken by certain credit institutions and investment banks for internal management control reasons, but is expected to become more generalised and to graduate as a powerful means of auditing.

Many regulators look at database mining as a good way of getting the facts at the examiners' discretion. Some believe that online datamining is a great tool for internal control, because it permits us to obtain not only figures but also trends, as well as to identify outliers and exceptions. The Federal Reserve said that, the combination of database mining and models makes possible a proactive approach to internal control an approach contrasting favourably with statistics obtained after the fact which often provide management with information that is too little, too late.

WHY AUDITING INCREASINGLY DEPENDS ON COMPUTER SYSTEMS

It is a self-evident fact that to know what is needed in computer support and understand which portions of the audit are most affected by the institution's computer environment, the auditor should be computer-literate. But while this is important, it is not enough. It is also necessary to appreciate both the status and the complexity of the bank's computer-based activities.

There are also other basic requirements for valid computer-based auditing processes. One of them is to establish the reliability of information elements in the database which will be used in the audit. Another is to appreciate the quality of the software (high or low) used for computer processing, from bread and butter accounting applications to the support of professional and managerial functions.

Seen from the auditor's viewpoint, an application may be considered to be complex when the volume of transactions is such that IT experts, the auditors themselves, and other users would find it difficult to identify and correct errors in processing. Or, the computer generates transactions or entries directly to this application that cannot be, or are not, validated independently.

A case of complexity also exists when transactions are exchanged electronically with other companies without manual review for intervening errors, proprietary screening, or reasonableness. This becomes a particularly sensitive issue in case there is a history of errors in data entry (a case I have found to exist in 90 per cent of companies). Or, data entry is affected by, or might affect, segregation of duties.

The problem I have quite often encountered in my professional practice is not only IT obsolescence and lack of tuning to real-life information requirements, but also lack of mission-critical information while relatively unimportant data is massively produced. There is a sort of decoupling between what is really needed and what is massively produced, as Figure 12.7 suggests. Typically, management information needed to do business is substandard, while a vast amount of less important data is being produced:

- The data which is urgently needed for analytical reasons and internal control activities is scarce to find, if it is available at all.
- By contrast, there is a huge amount of obsolete, inaccurate (error rates are often staggering), and to a large degree useless data.

Not only must useful information be properly identified, be fully updated and be reliable, but this process must also observe the principle of *materiality* known from general accounting principles. This states that the significance of a data element relates to the relative importance of financial statement assertions. Every auditor should appreciate this reference.

The auditor's work is much more sensitive when the process he or she is confronted with has a documentation which might be misleading, whether

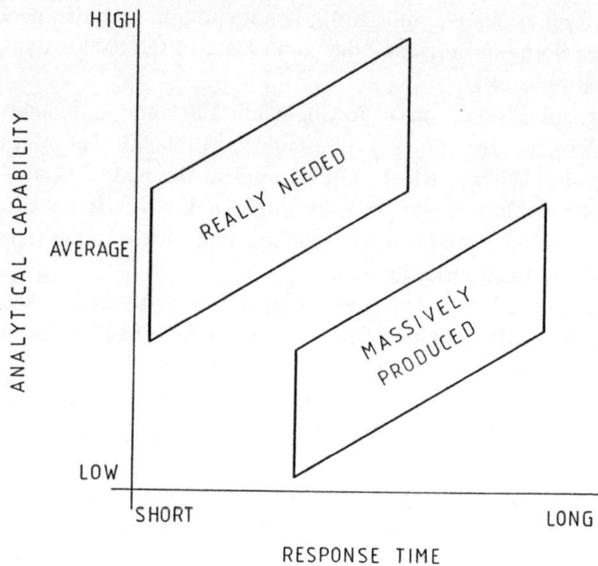

Figure 12.7 Management information needed to do business v. data which is massively produced

this is taking place intentionally or unintentionally. I have seen this happening quite often with source documents, computer files, and other evidential matter that may be required in the audit. Sometimes the evidence may exist for only a short period of time. If so, it is advisable to generate an internal reporting practice that can be useful in performing substantive tests.

Both more classical audits and computer-based audits are handicapped because of lack of transaction trails and other journal type documents. Computer-based operational routines should be implemented to assure that a complete transaction trail that is useful for audit purposes exists permanently (rather than for only a short period of time), and that it has significant detail. Where a complex application performs a large number of processing steps, there must be:

- A complete transaction trail which includes time, officer, counterparty, type of transaction, possible constraints, amount, and so on and
- Ways and means to detect in a timely manner possible massaging of an application's programs for reasons which are, in the general case, fraudulent.

Apart the risks inherent to data accuracy and software reliability, programming errors embedded in a computer-based environment may have both a pervasive effect and an account-specific consequence on material mis-statements. The source of this type of computer risk is not only intentional (for instance, for reasons of misappropriation of funds) but also the result of deficiencies in program development, program maintenance, or control over access to utility programs.

The statement made in the preceding paragraph has a dual perspective. The effort of auditors to capitalize on computer-assisted chores may be compromised because of software unreliability; and there is a steady need to audit the information technology. Program deficiencies tend to have a pervasive impact on computer applications – and, more likely than not, increase the potential for errors or fraudulent activities. At the same time malfunctioning is not uncommon in systems that:

- Must deal with many different exception conditions
- Control cash disbursements, cash transfers or other liquid assets and
- Because of their nature are susceptible to fraudulent actions by users or by computer personnel.

Ironically, technological advancements may themselves assist fraudulent activities. As new technologies emerge, they are frequently employed to build more complex computer systems that may include weak spots. An example is access to and manipulation of databases. Links between distributed databases which have been poorly conceived or are improperly administered from a security viewpoint is another example.

For all these reasons, the auditor should be extremely careful about the quality of the computer environment he deals with when designing programs and procedures to reduce auditing risk to an acceptably low level. While theoretically the auditor's specific objectives do not change whether accounting data is processed manually or by computer, the methods of applying audit procedures to gather evidence are greatly influenced by computer processing.

13 The Contribution of External Auditors to the Internal Control System

INTRODUCTION

The role of *external auditors* is important not only to the certification of accounts but also as a professional support to a company's internal audit function. Typically, external auditors are certified public accountants (CPAs, chartered accountants) who are hired by senior management for independent auditing duties. External auditors are also delegated by bank supervisors and other regulatory authorities who have the function of independent examiners. The wider description of their mission includes:

- Evaluation and certification of the work of internal auditors
- Review of the company's records and computational procedures
- Evaluation of accounting procedures for compliance reasons
- Analysis of financial reports and disclosures
- Testing of assets, liabilities, revenues, and expenses in terms of valuation
- Appraisal of internal controls and their adequacy under stress conditions.

Because they have a relative independence from the bank's management, external auditors can play an important role in account reconciliation and in the maintenance of an effective system of internal control. Indeed, in the Group of Ten (G-10) countries, many regulatory agencies are now requiring that external auditors take on the mission of assessing the internal control system of the bank they audit, beyond their more classical work of certifying the annual accounts.

External auditors resist this added responsibility because they consider it to be outside their traditional role of controlling whether a company's business has been correctly reflected in its financial statements. Also because the duty of a thorough investigation of weak links in the chain of command cannot be based on quantitative evidence like accounts reconciliation.

The existence of written procedures alone is no assurance that an adequate internal control environment exists, without additional evidence of proper implementation and verification by the board and senior management. External auditors say that if they assume responsibility for internal controls such examination must be carried at all levels, and it should also be verified if line managers are actively involved in internal controls and their frequent use.

The duties of auditing internal controls are further complicated by the fact that there exists nothing comparable to accounting standards. The procedures that need to be put in place to properly implement a system of internal controls are usually left to individual firms. Senior management, however, is responsible for creating an appropriate risk management and control structure within the company, which must be cost/effective. Therefore, the auditing of internal controls is to a large extent the auditing of senior management.

The auditing of internal controls by external auditors for regulatory reasons may become very involved, particularly if it covers any transaction in any market, with any instrument, and with any counterparty. A knowledgeable opinion I heard in several meetings in the United States, the United Kingdom, Germany, and Switzerland is that from an auditor's perspective internal control is not just financial control – even if this is the older, more classical definition. For this reason, in Britain, the Hampel Report advised adding two new areas to the internal control duties, which are shown in Figure 13.1.

In the past, external auditors were interested in a company's system of internal control only insofar as it had a role to play in the correctness of financial statements, since they needed to rely upon management controls to form their opinion of what was written in the books. We have gone a long way beyond this more limited perspective. Chartered accountants nevertheless fear that supervisory authorities continue to expand the limits of their duties. For instance, if regulators oblige them to give a written opinion on the adequacy of the internal control system as a whole, when auditing the company's annual accounts, this might lead to a sea of litigation.

VALUE-ADDED DUTIES BEYOND THOSE CLASSICALLY PERFORMED BY EXTERNAL AUDITORS

To a considerable extent, the change in policy by supervisors regarding what external auditors should provide in terms of findings and documentation, has been the aftermath of a report on 'The Audit of

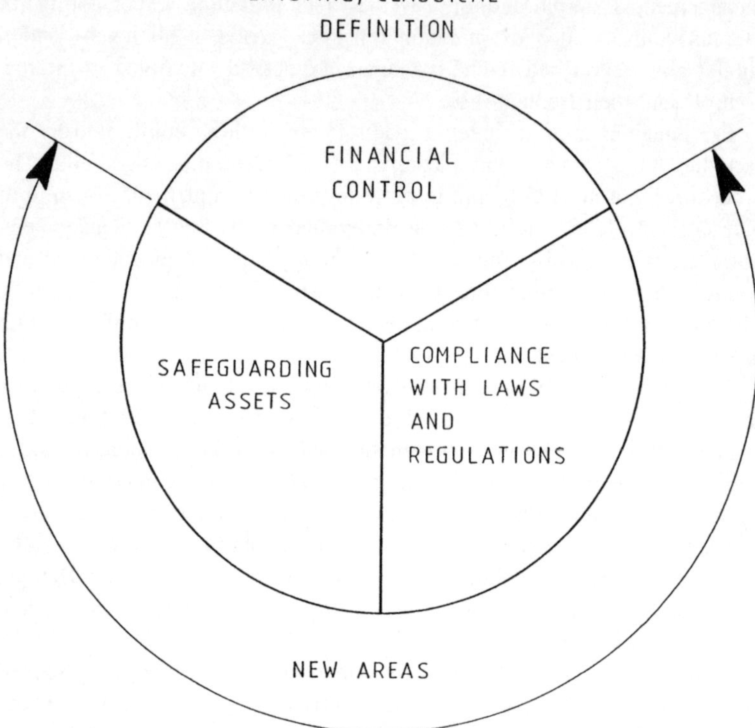

Figure 13.1 The Hampel Report recommended adding new areas to internal control

International Commercial Banks' issued in 1990 by the International Auditing Practices Committee of the International Federation of Accounts. This document was finalized after consultation with the Basle Committee on Banking Supervision.

This extension of the external auditors' mission is consistent with the fairly recent concept of ensuring the quality of internal controls through audit activities, including recommendations for necessary improvements (see Chapter 1). The value-added contribution by external auditors is that they can provide an independent feedback to senior management on the effectiveness of the bank's internal control system, such feedback reaching all the way to the regulators.

Central bankers have been quick to capitalize on the new concept of extended functions and responsibilities by external auditors. For instance, since 1998 in Germany external auditors are required by supervisory authorities to provide a specific assessment of the:

- Scope
- Adequacy and
- Effectiveness

of the bank's internal controls, including its internal auditing system. Such evaluation constitutes a specific well defined task, connected to the analysis and certification of annual accounts. The rules stipulate that while complying with the requirements of independence and competence in performing such duty, the external auditors may make use of the reports of the bank's internal auditors.

The CPAs' report concerning these two missions – certifying the annual accounts of a company and auditing its internal control system – is usually submitted to the Audit Committee (see also Chapter 1). The opinion of many cognizant people with whom I spoke on these value-added duties is that the existence of more than one goal should be welcome since, usually, one goal will support the other:

- In their traditional work, the external auditors must choose whether or not to rely on accounting documents and vouchers they are presented with.
- The value of these documents, however, greatly depends on the effectiveness of the internal control system and its dependability.

Therefore, an auditor conducting an evaluation of internal controls in order to assess the extent to which he can rely on this system, needs only to extend already existing auditing procedures. But there is also an opposite opinion expressed by other participants in this study. It says that external auditors are trained to do quantitative analysis, while the examination of internal control requires qualitative skills to a significant degree. This other school of thought also presses the point that when it comes to internal controls there is significant difference between *principles* and *practice*.

The implementation of the principles of auditing in connection with qualitative factors poses some problems at least from the CPA's viewpoint. Opponents of the idea of any extension to the classical auditing mission also suggest that external auditors tend to become subject to special supervisory requirements. This added responsibility amplifies the role external auditors used to play – both at a national and international level – as CPAs should:

- Aim to identify and document significant management control weaknesses that exist at a bank and
- Report them to senior executives and the supervisors, either as integral part of the audit or in confidential letters.

There is yet another value-added responsibility. Through the 1996 Market Risk Amendment by the Basle Committee on Banking Supervision, external auditors are included among the parties who are entrusted with the task of assuring the validation of internal models (eigenmodels) used for measuring market risk (Chorafas, 1998b). While the supervisory authorities retain the overall responsibility of approval, their functions are assisted through the analysis and certification external auditors might do:

- Internal control intelligence can be instrumental in powering models written for risk management – and, alternatively, weaknesses in risk management can be traced to the level of internal control.
- As we saw in Chapter 2, internal control and risk management correlate, and their synergy helps in identifying strengths and weaknesses of the internal control system.

One of the assessments which has shown up time and again is that because today the risk an institution takes is distributed and the worst cases which exist are often hidden from the board and senior management, the internal control system must show *risk concentration*. How this will be done depends on the specific needs and responsibilities of every member of management at any point in time.

Dr Rüdiger von Rosen, of the Deutsche Aktieninstitut, added that the No. 1 characteristic of a valid system of internal control was its ability to enssure accuracy and transparency. Both internal and external auditors must focus on this subject. Management must know every day what goes on – first in summary and then, as the need arises, in detail, because as von Rosen says: 'Personal accountability poses technological and organizational requirements. It should not be an empty word.'

'Internal control and the accounting system,' von Rosen added, 'must assure transparency not only to internal management and the regulators, but also to the public.' Reliable public information is needed for the shareholders. Secrets don't last that long any-more, and frequently they are counterprodutive. Ad hoc publicity of negative events like insider trading weights heavily on the accountability of the board.

Independent credit rating agencies expressed a similar opinion. In the words of David Beers, of Standard & Poor's, in London:

> The emphasis on the board's accountability is OK, and the same is true of real-time operations regarding internal control. But the exposure data and the failures must be known on a daily basis. The failures are breakdowns in accountability and in the information stream.

David Beers further commented that pinpointing accountability poses a very difficult problem because it really reaches the level of board members, and directors are notoriously bad in questioning senior management. 'Legislation and regulation can be of significant help in implementing accountability,' Beers said, 'In New Zealand, for example, the law sees to it that gains and losses are transparent; reporting is done daily even if the accounts the board signs are quarterly.'

In my book, this reference to legal and regulatory practices in New Zealand sums up nicely what I see as the most important value-added characteristic of the new mission given to external auditors in connection with internal control. Their responsibilities can be better fulfilled through a system view of key factors which come into play in good management and whose status should be transparent. Figure 13.2 suggests that an integrative solution should rest on four pillars which partly overlap with one another, but all four contribute to sound management.

WHAT SHOULD BE EXPECTED FROM AUDITING INTERNAL CONTROLS BY EXTERNAL AUDITORS?

Auditing by external auditors requires a mindset toward financial transactions and patterns which exist in the audited company's database. The CPA can capitalize on the fact that he or she is an outsider whose work is required both by the company's audit committee and by supervisory authorities, because the CPA is expected to take a view free of the internal organizational pressures which might influence the internal auditor's work.

Another element to keep in perspective is that the internal auditor has had for some time responsibilities beyond those classically done by the CPA, such as consulting with senior management, doing performance analysis, assisting in operational reviews, and fulfilling certain organizational duties. These activities are indirectly related to the financial area of account reconciliation and aim at providing senior management with a company-wide control picture.

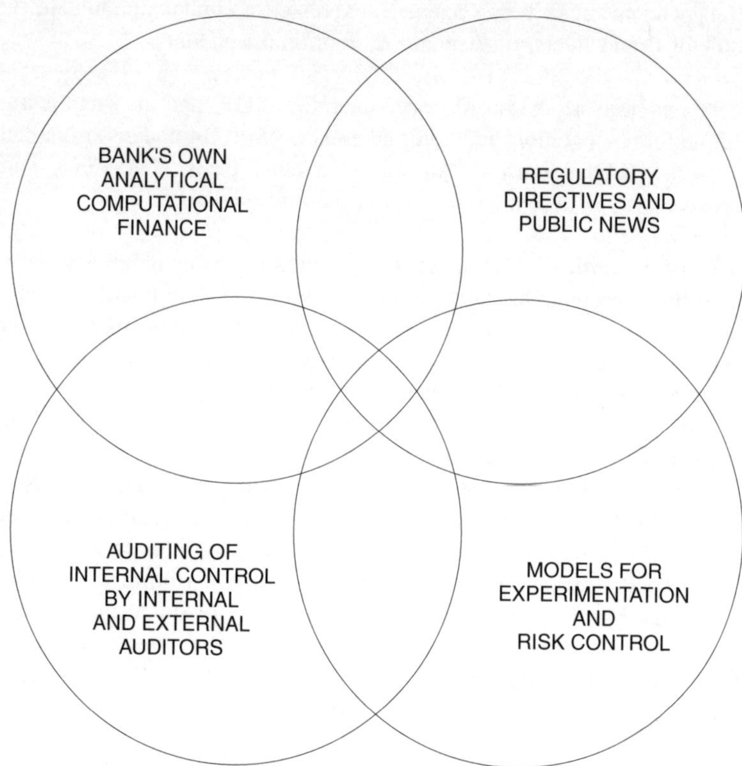

Figure 13.2 Rigorous evaluation of exposure, study of business opportunity, and analysis of business intelligence rest on four pillars

Now a similar mission falls on the external auditor, as the supervisory authorities require that he or she analyze the bank's internal control structure and reports on his findings. Some people think this will be an uphill battle because career auditors are often perceived negatively by the personnel of many companies hiring their services, one of the key reasons being that they have not done a good job of educating a company's managers and professionals on what they accomplish through their efforts.

There are also cognizant people who believe that the wave of mergers between CPAs' firms, particularly the bigger and better-known ones, is counterproductive because it reduces choice and can lead to conflicts of interest. Regulators, too, are concerned that megamergers among the top chartered accountants' firms might reduce their independence of action.

The Securities and Exchange Commission (SEC) is warning that companies should be wary of awarding too much business to the Big Five accounting firms for fear of conflict of interest.

In the background of megamergers among CPAs is the so-called 'one-stop-shopping' concept. Some companies, however, do not buy that idea 'It has some real economic synergy, but I insist on picking and choosing among an array of suppliers,' says Ameritech Chief Financial Officer Oren G. Shaffer (*Business Week*, 18 January 1999).

The counterargument is that if the CPAs audit internal control then polyvalence and maybe size would count. Concerned about new capital requirements for operational risk, some banks look favourably at auditing internal controls by external auditors. 'I would assume that if operational risk is going to attract a capital charge, the external auditors will at the same time be starting to audit the bank's internal controls,' said a senior executive of ABN–AMRO.

There is also the problem that responsibilities at board level may need to be extended and redefined. To my knowledge, so far in the majority of companies the certification of eigenmodels has not been part of the mission of the audit committee. This creates a weak spot in an organization's defensive armoury, particularly so as for over 20 years tier-1 banks have audited their IT operations. The use of modelling solutions constitutes a natural evolution of information technology. Why, then, should eigenmodels not be audited?

All this helps to show that since the market has changed and supervisory rules are in evolution, it is time to adapt organization and structure to the new conditions. It is, once more, back to fundamentals. Some of the CPA companies have figured that out; they are also aware that the classical auditing of financial statements is no more a booming market.

At Arthur Andersen, for instance, traditional financial statement auditing grew just 8 per cent in 1998 and made up only a fifth of the firm's \$6.1 billion in revenues. But consulting grew 38 per cent, to \$1.1 billion. To rejuvenate its business opportunity, Andersen is rapidly expanding the add-on services it sells to auditing clients:

- An example in the more classical side is measuring susceptibility to fraud.
- On the technology side, new products are consulting and advising on a wide range of issues.

Arthur Andersen's new business perspective focuses on IT consulting, an area where many CPAs' firms are eager to expand. On Wall Street analysts have adopted a 'wait and see' attitude because in the IT market rivals such as EDS and IBM are, respectively, about 3 times and 10 times as big as Andersen Consulting, and they have the capital to supply hardware and software not only advice. I question the wisdom of giving advice and selling supplies to the same client.

In my book, the acquisition of IT skills by external auditors is a positive development as long as there is no conflict of interest between auditing and consulting. There is no way today to leave computers out of the auditing equation; all the accounting books are databased. And it is hoped that internal control will increasingly use models, as I have so often emphasized.

Rethinking account reconciliation, reliable financial reporting, information technology, and the development and use of eigenmodels is part of the back to fundamentals policy we have been talking about. It is also proper to keep in perspective the fact that the organizational impact of internal controls has changed significantly during the last few years. As Peter Bürger, of Commerzbank, suggested, this change had a significant effect on numerous issues such as:

- More thorough internal control policies, and awareness that these policies may actually not be observed.
- Independent oversight, particularly of risk monitoring and the reporting function connected to trading units.
- Transparency of risks, leading to queries such as: What information is available? In what form is it reported?
- More rigorous measurements, including attention to the methodology being used to measure risks and analyze them.
- Timeliness and quality of information: How often is risk reported? Is the information accurate?

All five bullet points reflect much more than the initiative of one commercial bank, because the G-10 regulators have already played a major role in establishing requirements for a modern internal control methodology; now they are seeing to it that these are observed. A good example is the standard reporting methodology for the savings and loans developed by the Office of Thrift Supervision (OTS). This methodology is universally applied between savings and loans in the United States and it distinguishes between:

- Trading and
- Risk management.

Attention is paid to derivative financial instruments even if only a few thrifts have come into the derivatives market: 76 out of the 1119 supervised by OTS. 'Once in a while we find a thrift who bought a reverse floater, but the majority of the savings and loans stay out of this market,' said Timothy Stier, of OTS. External auditors could take a leaf out of OTS' book. There is much that can be learned from the way the supervisors of US thrifts have turned up their internal control inspection procedures after the S&L industry went into a tailspin in the late 1980s.

ARE CENTRAL BANK EXAMINERS BETTER POSITIONED IN STUDYING THE EFFECTIVENESS OF INTERNAL CONTROLS?

The SEC says that external auditors must provide an opinion on internal control that is documented and satisfactory. However, since as we saw above that there exist no universal evaluation criteria the different CPAs firms tend to do different types of evaluation. This underlines the need for standards and also poses the question whether both the examiners of regulatory authorities and CPAs should use the same standards in auditing a company's internal controls.

This is not an issue which can have a linear answer. First of all, regarding both the supervisors charter and CPAs' requirements, no two countries have the same concept regarding internal control audits. Then there is the fact that with the exception of the United States and of Italy, in relatively few G-10 countries does central bank and other regulatory agencies have a body of its own examiners. This is, however, changing.

- The Swiss Federal Banking Commission instituted a new department in 1998: Big Banks, with own examiners and
- The French Commission Bancaire also has a department specializing in supervision of large credit institutions.

Another fact of which to take note is that in some countries, such as the United States, there is little connection between the bank regulators and the external auditors because the examiners of regulatory agencies do the hands-on bank inspection the exception to this rule is the Federal Housing Finance Board which uses external auditors for its inspection). British and German regulators in contrast depend a great deal on the report the external

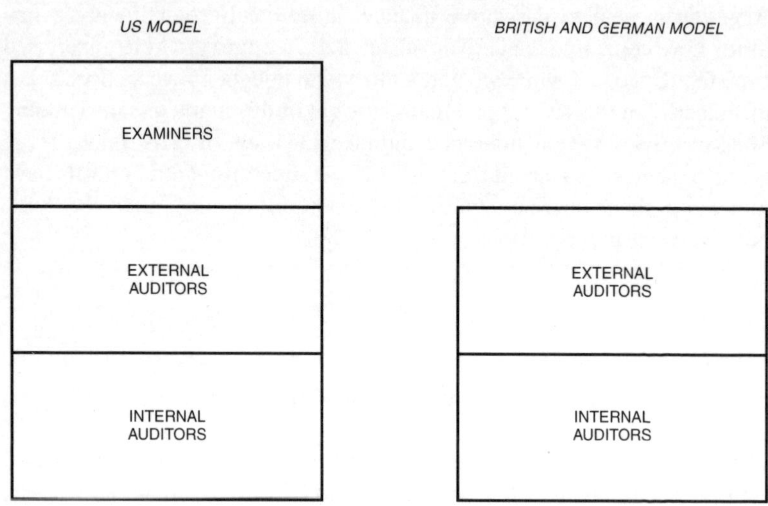

Figure 13.3 A three-tier and a two-tier model in bank supervision

auditors will make, which constitutes the basis of their examination of the bank:

- The US solution can be compared to a three-layered system of inspection, as shown in Figure 13.3.
- By contrast, in Britain and Germany the model is a two-tier system, where central banks outsource the examiners' job to external auditors.

The difference between a two-tier and a three-tier approach to supervision can be significant in terms of auditing results, particularly in connection to qualitative subjects like internal controls. The Federal Reserve, for example, is mandating more stringent requirements than those external auditors usually follow. And a central bank could establish a more rigorous training programme for its examiners – including skills in auditing internal controls – than a CPA firm is typically doing.

There is another significant difference I can see between the two- layered and the three-layered system of inspection, and it concerns the implementation of quality control principles. If the central bank's examiners find reasons to be dissatisfied with the credit institution's accounts and/or internal control, their superiors may decide to increase the frequency of auditing inspections:

- In the United States I was told of banks which were visited by the Fed's examiners quarterly or even monthly, when the situation warranted doing so.
- External auditors cannot take the sort of initiative even if they are unhappy with the books, because this can be interpreted as a way to increase their billing.

Central bank examiners can also make surprise visits for auditing credit institutions under their authority, which is not part of the CPAs' charter. Speaking of my experience as consultant to the board of Italian banks, the Auditing Department of the Bank of Italy would call on a Friday to say that starting that same evening and for a long weekend a team of its own computer experts would take over the commercial bank's computer centre for auditing purposes.

Examiners working for a supervisory authority also have a statutory right to dig deeper than CPAs. Before going further with this argument, however, it would be good to examine what are the reports external auditors submit and what can be done to improve upon these deliverables. External auditors generate different types of reports and of supporting documents. Typically these include:

- The standard audit and
- A management letter.

In the *management letter* the external auditing firm confidentially presents detailed findings and recommendations. In some cases, report(s) are also submitted from chartered accountants to regulators during the auditing period, or at the end of it. In principle, standard audits reports can be classified as:

- The *unqualified report*, or 'clean opinion' which states that financial statements are presented in accordance with rules and regulations.
- The *qualified report*, which may use the same language as the unqualified one, but will add 'except for' or some other indication of a problem.

The problem the qualified report identifies may be lack of sufficient evidential matter, restrictions imposed on the scope of the audit work, departure from accounting rules, or other issues having to do with financial statements. The 'except for' indicates that supervisors should ask additional questions of management.

Unqualified reports are, so to speak, a 'clean bill of health'. Qualified reports call for some medicine, but not necessarily a bitter one. The reader's attention should also be brought to two other reports written by independent auditors, in case their findings point to severe weaknesses prevailing in the audited company and its management:

- The *adverse report* usually concludes that the financial statements are not presented in conformity with rules and regulations.

This type of report is issued when auditors and the management cannot work out their differences. Even more serious is the case when the independent auditors issue:

- A *disclaimer*. This document expresses no opinion on the company's financial statements and their dependability.

The disclaimer is a very serious document indeed. The external auditor issues it when he has concluded that substantial doubt exists about the ability of the company to continue as a going concern for a reasonable period of time. What the disclaimer indicates is that the independent auditor is not prepared to assume the responsibility for the company's financial statements and their content.

What would be different with central bank examiners? First of all, because the external audit is a major component of supervision, many (but not all) regulatory bodies conduct their own review about the external auditor's independence. This is in a way a seal of approval of the independent external auditor as a firm, but not of each specific audit this firm is doing. By contrast, when its own examiners conduct the external audits, the central bank, or other regulatory body, stands by each one of them.

Second, and equally important, is the fact that because of an emergency supervisory agencies may decide to add to the scope of an external audit, or initiate a new procedure altogether. Starting with the Year 2000 (Y2K) problem, and the rigorous standards American bank supervisors established for preparedness, computer service bureau too came under scrutiny – because of the correct assumption that information technology is core function to a credit institution.

In conclusion, the findings of the central bank's own examiners, when they audit a supervised institution, is a different ballgame than what CPAs do. They go further and deeper, and they may also be visiting and auditing a supervised institution more frequently than the annual cycle. I was told during my research of certain credit institutions on the edge of bankruptcy which were visited almost monthly by examiners of the Federal Reserve.

Also external auditors, though in principle independent, might find themselves in some cases in a conflict of interest since the company whose books and internal controls they audit is the one which pays their fees. Central bank examiners don't have such conflict while, in contrast, they have a direct line to the regulatory authority which must take corrective steps to right the balances, if the audited institution's accounting reconciliation and internal controls are found to be wanting.

THE CONCEPT BEHIND OUTSOURCING INTERNAL AUDITING AND OTHER DUTIES

As it is to be expected, one of the issues discussed during the meetings with supervisors was whether they get involved, or will get involved, with improvements to be made to the commercial banks' internal controls. Today, there is no evidence that this is taking place at any other level than in general outline, which emphasize the importance of a strong internal control culture. But some responses I got to my queries make me think this might be changing.

Will internal control duties ever be considered for outsourcing? The regulators do not think this is wise, while in the large majority of cases commercial banks and investment banks are not prepared to outsource functions which have to do with internal control. One of the senior executives with whom I discussed this issue said: 'The bank does not outsource its internal control functions. An exception is, of course, project-related work, where we employ external consultants and information technology contractors.'

'Supervisors don't like outsourcing,' suggested Mauro Grande of the European Central Bank, 'but we have some cases particularly among small banks were internal control is outsourced.' Some credit institutions have got the message. A senior executive of a major investment bank said: 'We have never outsourced internal control and, as a matter of policy, most recently the reverse is true. We tend not to outsource information technology any more.' The thesis of the European Central Bank (ECB) is that the best way to handle internal control is through both:

- Regulation and
- Inspection.

Are central banks doing outsourcing? 'The Bundesbank is doing no outsourcing,' said Hans-Dietrich Peters and Hans Werner Voth. 'We segregate the work of the internal auditors who look after the balance sheet, and the external auditors. But other banks use external auditors to audit their balance sheet.' According to German law, every year external auditors must audit the efficiency of the Bundesbank's internal system and given an opinion on whether it is efficiently structured. The check-up of the organization is the duty of Bundesbank's:

- Auditing department and
- Controlling department.

The Controlling department has three main divisions: Budgeting and cost accounting; Balance sheet accounting; and organization. Hence, the fact that internal auditors audit the organization, just as they audit the balance sheet, make sense. The Federal Reserve Board, too, audits the 12 Federal Reserve Banks every year. For this, it uses its own examiners.

Supervisory authorities are not adverse to outsourcing certain duties because external auditors can assist regulators in their mission. 'However we do it, we will find it difficult to be resourced in a way to go into multinational companies for inspection,' said Richard Britton, of the Financial Services Authority (FSA). 'Hence, the role of external auditors increases. Now they have to write down their view of the internal controls of a bank.'

One of the crucial questions connected with the extension of mission given to chartered accountants is who pays for the added service. 'It is the audited firms,' said Richard Britton.

> The firm will either pay the external auditor or the supervisory authority. To inspect internal controls we need three times the personnel we have today as supervision. The taxpayer should not pay this bill.

Other central banks and supervisory authorities, too, depend a great deal on external auditors for the audit of the commercial banks they control. The German Federal Banking Supervision Bureau and the Swiss Federal Banking Commission (for other institutions than the Big Banks) are examples:

- The German supervisors now require external auditors also to audit the internal controls of supervised banks.

- The Swiss bank supervisors also want external auditors to check the internal controls.

So there is some scope for outsourcing certain well defined parts of the internal controls job – provided the board and CEO retain full responsibility for the results. The Austrian National Bank had this to say on the issue:

> Generally, credit institutions are free to outsource functions and, as part of their duty of diligence, the executive board is responsible for their choice of partners in this respect (culpa in eligendo). We assume that most of the outsourcing is done in connection with IT services, including but not limited to the purchase of models for risk calculation.

Other regulators, too, take a prudent approach to outsourcing and the risks this might involve in the longer run. The Federal Reserve mentioned guidance released at end of 1997 regarding the practice of outsourcing. These directive underlined the full accountability of the board and of senior management in this regard:

- The main responsibility implied by the Fed directive is that senior management must administer the outsourcing contract.
- The point was also made that outsourcing obliges the bank to have people able of evaluating the outsourcer's security and performance.

The Fed directive also implied that commercial bank's management must be comfortable with the outsourcing decision and its aftermath. It must retain all work papers, making them available for inspection, and it should assure that reasonable standards are applied for work paper preparation as well as for review.

Rules on outsourcing by the Fed also pay attention to conflicts of interest. The SEC is doing the same. If there is even a remote possibility of such conflicts, the commercial bank must refer to the SEC, which has jurisdiction in these cases. The Fed's concern is that independence might be impaired, and therefore measures must be taken to avoid it.

From the commercial bank's viewpoint, outsourcing is an issue with as many opinions as there are institutions. David Woods, of ABN–AMRO, said that his bank is not currently using outsourcing to any great extent but this is under serious review. Bernt Gyllenswärd, of Skandinaviska Enskilda Banken, suggested that his institution is thinking about outsourcing.

A CLOSER LOOK AT OUTSOURCING INTERNAL AUDITING: ITS 'PLUSES' AND 'MINUSES'

The last section has focused on outsourcing connected with the work done by external auditors and some other service providers such as IT firms. To conclude this discussion we should also consider outsourcing arrangements for internal auditing chores, which are not the darlings of regulators or of major commercial bankers but might be necessary for smaller outfits. Such arrangements are often called 'internal audit assistance' or 'extended audit services'. Those who like them say that they might be beneficial to an institution if internal auditing outsourcing is:

- Properly structured
- Carefully conducted
- Prudently managed and
- Its final responsibility rests with the board.

Because all these four prerequisites are rarely fulfilled, bank supervision agencies are concerned that the structure, scope, and management of internal audit outsourcing schemes does not contribute to the institution's safety and soundness. Therefore, the supervisors want to ensure that arrangements with an outsourcing vendors do not leave directors and senior managers with the impression that they have been relieved of their responsibility for:

- Reliable financial reporting and accounting reconciliation
- Maintaining an effective system of internal control and
- Overseeing the internal audit function of their company.

In to its fundamentals, an outsourcing arrangement of the type under discussion is a contract between the bank and a third party, a vendor which contracts to provide what should have been internal auditing services. One of the reasons why it is difficult to clearly state the 'do's' and 'don'ts' with regard to internal auditing outsourcing arrangements is that they take many forms:

- The contracted services can be limited to helping internal audit staff in an assignment for which they lack expertise.

Limited outsourcing approaches are typically under the control of the institution's management of internal auditing. In these cases, the outsourcing vendor, typically a firm of chartered accountants, reports to the internal auditing director.

- But outsourcing arrangements may also require an outsourcing vendor to perform virtually all internal audit work.

When this is the case, the bank should maintain a *manager of internal auditing* with a small internal staff. The outsourcer assists this staff in determining risks to be reviewed; recommends and performs auditing procedures as approved by the internal auditing manager; and reports its findings jointly with the internal audit manager to either the full board or its audit committee.

To help bank management appreciate its responsibilities, the US regulatory agencies have set out some characteristics of sound practices for the internal auditing function, in connection with the use of outsourcing vendors for audit activities. In addition, the regulators provide guidance on how these outsourcing arrangements may affect the Fed's examiners assessment of internal control.

For instance, if the examiner's evaluation of a given outsourcing scheme indicates that the outsourcing arrangement has diminished the quality of the institution's internal audit function, he will adjust the scope of his examination by making more rigorous. He will also:

- Bring that matter to the attention of senior management and the board of directors and
- Incorporate it in the rating he gives to the institution's management.

If I can make a contribution to this process it will be by suggesting the use of *confidence intervals connected to a rating scale*. It is always a great assistance to decision-making to be able to see a trend and also account for the fact that since any evaluation contains subjective elements there is, for example, a 95 per cent confidence interval connected to the trend line.

This is shown in Figure 13.4, which reflects the rating of an internal control service through answers provided to a questionnaire, and the two 95 per cent thresholds computed on the basis of variance in opinions (A sort of modified Delphi method (Chorafas, 2000c).) The careful reader will observe that the trend line is improving over time, but rather slowly. While it starts with a rating below 70 per cent, successive evaluations reach about 85 per cent in the rating scale, but only after a regulatory long period of time. Alternatively we can use quality control charts by variables and by attributes' such as those already discussed.

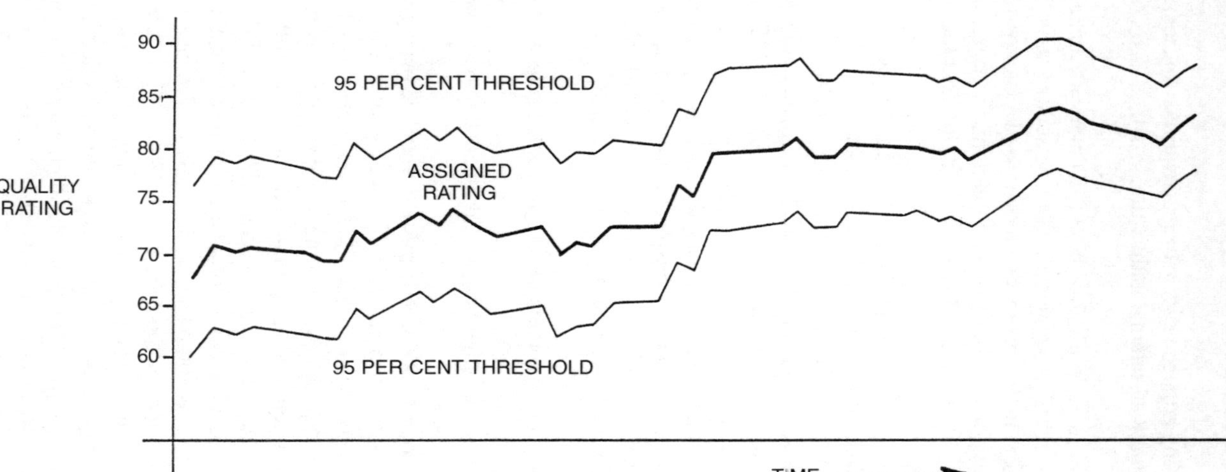

Figure 13.4 Rating the quality of internal auditing and/or outsourced services using confidence intervals

The use of quality control charts will fit well with current practice by the Fed that when an examiner's initial review of an outsourcing arrangement raises doubts about the external auditor's independence, he would ask the institution and the external auditor to demonstrate that the arrangement has not compromised the auditor's independence. If the examiner's concerns are not adequately addressed, then the regulatory agency follows up.

Let's always keep in mind that when outsourcing internal auditing functions the accountability of the board, the CEO, and senior management is being engaged. Central to top management's responsibility is the fact that when outsourcers provide internal audit services, the board of directors and senior executives of the bank must sign their report and assume personal responsibility for its contents. Therefore, when negotiating the outsourcing arrangement with a vendor, an institution should:

- Set out in clear terms the scope, frequency, and content accountability of the work to be performed
- Establish the system of reporting to senior management and directors about the contracted work and
- Elaborate the protocol for changing the terms of a service contract, if significant issues are being raised.

In any company, internal rules and regulations should see to it that all work by the outsourcing vendor is well documented and all findings of control weaknesses are promptly reported to the institution's board or auditing committee. Furthermore, prior to entering an outsourcing arrangement the institution should perform enough due diligence to satisfy itself that the outsourcer has sufficient staff qualified to perform the contracted work.

Because an outsourcing arrangement is a personal services contract, the institution's internal audit manager should have confidence in the competence of the staff assigned by the outsourcing vendor, and receive prior notice of staffing changes. In spite of this, it should be appreciated that when an institution enters into an outsourcing arrangement (or significantly changes the mix of internal and external resources used by internal auditing), it increases its operating risk.

Finally, because the arrangement might be suddenly terminated, a company should have a contingency plan to mitigate any significant discontinuity in audit coverage, particularly for high-risk areas. Planning for a successor to the prospective outsourcer should be part of negotiating the latter's service contract. Contingency planning, however, goes further than that. It requires that the bank has on hand a skeleton of internal resources able to track the outsourced functions – as outlined in the opening paragraphs of this section.

LIABILITIES WHICH MIGHT COME THE WAY OF EXTERNAL AUDITORS

The betting is that the vendor outsourcing a company's internal auditing function will be a chartered accountant. Therefore, to complete the discussion in the previous section about possible liabilities on the institution's side because of outsourcing one of its core functions, we should look at auditing liabilities issues which affect the CPAs. In the United States, such liabilities became a huge subject after the S&Ls (thrifts) meltdown of the late 1980s.

The big CPAs presently take very seriously the possible financial consequences of litigation regarding their external audits, let alone the added responsibility of outsourced internal auditing services. In England and in Luxembourg, the liquidators of BCCI claimed $8 billion from Price Waterhouse and Ernst & Young. This money was demanded because of the 1985 audit of the collapsed bank. Additional claims were filed in connection with the 1986 and 1987 audits.

In 1990, in Canada, Ernst & Young, and a predecessor of Peat Marwick Thorne, paid a major portion of a C$125 million settlement in connection with the failure of two Canadian banks. Price Waterhouse was sued in Hong Kong with regard to the bankruptcy of Peregrine Investments in early 1998, in the aftermath of the East Asia meltdown.

In the early 1990s, in Australia, KPMG settled for A$100 million in a A$1.1 billion suit resulting from the audit of Tricontinental Corporation, a government-owned merchant bank. Ernst & Young was sued for A$175 million by the liquidator of the investment bank Duke Group; this case was settled for A$35 million.

In London, a High Court judge found an accounting firm liable for negligence in permitting a loss-making Lloyd's of London syndicate to close its accounts. By implicating the syndicate's auditors, Ernst & Whinney (now part of Ernst & Young), this ruling made it easier to extract cash to finance a settlement offer to the insurance market's litigating names.

Coopers & Lybrand in the United Kingdom and in Singapore and Deloitte & Touche in Singapore have put up to £33 million ($54 million) as a 'contribution from auditors' because of alleged negligence in the Barings case. This is part of £91 million ($151 million) available to the liquidators, the next biggest sum to that of the auditors has come from a 'contribution from certain other covenants'.

Big as they may seem in absolute terms, these sums are a bargain since claims for damages in the English auditors' action have been estimated before interest, as being at least £1 billion ($1.65 billion) including goodwill; or £560 million ($930 billion) excluding goodwill. The liquidators reached this figure by considering the claim as in essence monies which went out of Barings Futures Singapore on unauthorized trades after the date at which Nick Leeson's activities should have ceased – if the audit had not been carried out in an allegedly negligent manner.

On paper, the difference between £33 million and £1 billion is tremendous, but in the world of auditor liability nothing is as cut and dried, and at that time (mid-1988) precedents were thin. It fact, executives from chartered accountants' firms suggested that the external auditor relies, in part at least, on the assurances provided by the company's management. Therefore, even if there was some misinterpretation and misrepresentation it was not all the external auditors' fault.

In the Barings case, the external auditors asserted that at the time of the collapse their firm had not signed its audit opinion and had not completed its audit work. Coopers & Lybrand maintained that it had not exhausted the audit work which could have led to the identification of Nick Leeson's alleged frauds. Hence the chartered accountants' argument concerned contributory negligence by various members of the senior management team at Barings.

There is also a matter of coverage by insurance. Coopers' insurance cover was shown to be £47.06 million ($78 million) subject to an excess which had already been exhausted. Deloitte & Touche Singapore's cover did not exceed £55 million. At the bottom line this means that whatever is not covered by insurance should be paid by the partners. In terms of capital reserves, however, accountants are not banks with minimum capital requirement established by regulators.

- CPAs do not accumulate capital reserves beyond those necessary to meet their day-to-day, operating requirements
- This carefully crafted argument is upset if a court decides that the partners are personally responsible.

All this is food for thought in terms of giving the external auditors more assignments, like the responsibility for auditing internal control and indeed for substituting themselves for a company's internal auditors. As the Barings bankruptcy case demonstrates, the normal hazards of litigation increases greatly in the case of global operations. They would grow further if internal controls were audited.

Besides this, the complexities of global internal controls and personal accountability are such that legal cases would drag on for years, with discovery after discovery being inconclusive if not outright controversial. Nor are common sense and logical thinking good guides in the sea of litigation. The life of the law is not logic but experience, as Justice Oliver Wendell Holmes once said.

Bibliography

Attali, J. (1985) *Sir Siegmund G. Warburg. Un Homme d'Influence*, Paris: Fayard.

Basle Committee on Banking Supervision (1998) 'Framework for the Evaluation of Internal Control Systems', Basle: BIS, January.

Chernow, R. (1990) *The House of Morgan*, New York: Touchstone, Simon & Schuster.

Chorafas, D.N. (1960) *Statistical Processes and Reliability Engineering*, Princeton: Van Nostrand.

——— (1968) *The Knowledge Revolution*, London and New York: Allen & Unwin and McGraw-Hill.

——— (1987) *Engineering Productivity Through CAM/CAD*, London: Butterworth.

——— (1994a) *Chaos Theory in the Financial Markets*, Chicago: Probus.

——— (1994b) *Advanced Financial Analysis*, London: Euromoney.

——— (1995a) *Financial Models and Simulation*, London: Macmillan.

——— (1995b) *How to Understand and Use Mathematics for Derivatives, 1: Understanding the Behaviour of Markets*, London: Euromoney.

——— (1995c) *How to Understand and Use Mathematics for Derivatives, 2: Advanced Modelling Methods*, London: Euromoney.

——— (1997) *Internet Financial Services: Secure Electronic Banking and Electronic Commerce?*, London and Dublin: Lafferty.

——— (1998a) *Agent Technology Handbook*, New York: McGraw-Hill.

——— (1998b) *The Market Risk Amendment. Understanding the Marking-to-Market Model and Value-at-Risk*, Burr Ridge, IL: McGraw-Hill.

——— (1999) *Setting Limits for Market Risk*, London: Euromoney.

——— (2000a) *Reliable Financial Reporting and Internal Control: A Global Implementation Guide*, New York: John Wiley.

——— (2000b) *Managing Credit Risk, 1: Analyzing, Rating and Pricing the Probability of Default*, London: Euromoney.

——— (2000c) *Managing Credit Risk, 2: The Lessons of VAR Failures and Imprudent Exposure*, London: Euromoney.

——— (2000d) *New Regulation of the Financial Industry*, London: Macmillan.

——— (2000e) *Credit Derivatives and the Management of Risk*, New York: New York Institute of Finance.

——— (2001a) *Managing Risk in the New Economy*, New York: New York Institute of Finance.

——— (2001b) *Managing Operational Risk: Risk Reduction Strategies for Investment Banks and Commercial Banks*, London: Euromoney.

Chorafas, D.N. and H. Steinmann (1991) *Expert Systems in Banking*, London: Macmillan.

——— (1992) *Do IT or Die*, London and Dublin: Lafferty.

European Monetary Institute (EMI), Banking Supervision Subcommittee (1997) 'Internal Control Systems in Banking Institutions', Frankfurt: EMI, July.

Grant, J. (1992) *Money of the Mind*, New York: Farrar, Strauss, Giroux.

IOSCO (1998) *Methodologies for Determining Minimum Capital Standards for Internationally Active Securities Firms*, May.

Lee Bailey, F. (1975) *For the Defence*, New York: New American Library/Signet.

Walton, S. (1993) *Made in America: My Story*, New York: Bantam Books.

White, M. (1997) *Isaac Newton: The Lost Sciences*, London: Fourth Estate.

Appendix of Participating Organizations

The following organizations, through their senior executives and system specialists participated in the recent research projects that led to the contents of this book and its documentation.

AUSTRIA

National Bank of Austria

Dr Martin OHMS
Finance Market Analysis Department

3, Otto Wagtner Platz
Postfach 61
A-1011 Vienna

Association of Austrian Banks and Bankers

Dr. Fritz DIWOK
Secretary General

11, Boersengasse
1013 Vienna

Bank Austria

Dr Peter FISCHER
Senior General Manager, Treasury Division
Peter GABRIEL
Deputy General Manager, Trading

2, Am Hof
1010 Vienna

Creditanstalt

Dr Wolfgang LICHTL
Market Risk Management

Julius Tandler Platz 3
A-1090 Vienna

Wiener Betriebs- and Baugesellschaft mbH

Dr Josef FRITZ
General Manager

1, Anschützstrasse
1153 Vienna

GERMANY

Deutsche Bundesbank

Hans-Dietrich PETERS
Director
Hans Werner VOTH
Director

Wilhelm-Epstein Strasse 14
60431 Frankfurt am Main

Federal Banking Supervisory Office

Hans-Joachim DOHR
Director Dept. I
Jochen KAYSER
Risk Model Examination
Ludger HANENBERG
Internal Controls

71–101 Gardeschützenweg
12203 Berlin

European Central Bank

Mauro GRANDE
Director

29 Kaiserstrasse
29th Floor
60216 Frankfurt am Main

Deutsches Aktieninstitut

Dr Rüdiger Von ROSEN
President

Biebergasse 6 bis 10
60313 Frankfurt-am-Main

Commerzbank

Peter BÜRGER
Senior Vice President, Strategy and Controlling
Markus RUMPEL
Senior Vice President, Credit Risk Management

Kaiserplatz
60261 Frankfurt am Main

Deutsche Bank

Professor Manfred TIMMERMANN
Head of Controlling
Hans VOIT
Head of Process Management, Controlling Department

12, Taunusanlage
60325 Frankfurt

Dresdner Bank

Dr Marita BALKS
Investment Bank, Risk Control
Dr Hermann HAAF
Mathematical Models for Risk Control
Claas Carsten KOHL
Financial Engineer

1, Jürgen Ponto Platz
60301 Frankfurt

GMD First – Research Institute for Computer Architecture, Software Technology and Graphics

Prof. Dr Ing. Wolfgang K. GILOI
General Manager

5, Rudower Chaussee
D-1199 Berlin

FRANCE

Banque de France

Pierre JAILLET
Director, Monetary Studies and Statistics
Yvan ORONNAL
Manager, Monetary Analyses and Statistics
G. TOURNEMIRE, Analyst, Monetary Studies

39, rue Croix des Petits Champs
75001 Paris

Secretariat Général de la Commission Bancaire – Banque de France

Didier PENY
Director, Control of Big Banks and International Banks

73, rue de Richelieu
75002 Paris

F. VISNOWSKY
Manager of International Affairs
Supervisory Policy and Research Division
Benjamin SAHEL
Market Risk Control

115, Rue Réaumur
75049 Paris Cedex 01

Ministry of Finance and the Economy, Conseil National de la Comptabilité

Alain LE BARS
Director International Relations and Cooperation

6, rue Louise Weiss
75703 Paris Cedex 13

HUNGARY

Hungarian Banking and Capital Market Supervision

Dr Janos KUN
Head, Department of Regulation and Analyses
Dr Erika VÖRÖS
Senior Economist, Department of Regulation and Analyses
Dr Géza NYIRY
Head, Section of Information Audit

Csalogany u. 9–11
H-1027 Budapest

Hungarian Academy of Sciences

Prof. Dr Tibor VAMOS
Chairman, Computer and Automation Research Institute

Nador U. 7
1051 Budapest

ICELAND

The National Bank of Iceland Ltd

Gunnar T. ANDERSEN
Managing Director
International Banking & Treasury

Laugavegur 77
155 Reykjavik

ITALY

Banca d'Italia

Eugene GAIOTTI
Research Department, Monetary and Financial Division
Ing. Dario FOCARELLI
Research Department

91, via Nazionale
00184 Rome

Instituto Bancario San Paolo di Torino

Dr Paolo CHIULENTI
Director of Budgeting
Roberto COSTA
Director of Private Banking
Pino RAVELLI
Director Bergamo Region

27, via G. Camozzi
24121 Bergamo

LUXEMBOURG

Banque Générale de Luxembourg

Prof. Dr Yves WAGNER
Director of Asset and Risk Management
Hans Jörg PARIS International Risk Manager

27, avenue Monterey
L-2951 Luxembourg

POLAND

Securities and Exchange Commission

Beata STELMACH
Secretary of the Commission

1, P1 Powstancow Warszawy
00-950 Warsaw

SWEDEN

Skandinaviska Enskilda Banken

Bernt GYLLENSWÄRD
Head of Group Audit

Box 16067
10322 Stockholm

Irdem AB

Gian MEDRI
Former Director of Research at Nordbanken

19, Flintlasvagen
S-19154 Sollentuna

SWITZERLAND

Swiss National Bank

Dr Werner HERMANN
Head of International Monetary Relations
Dr Christian WALTER
Representative to the Basle Committee
Robert FLURI
Assistant Director, Statistics Section

15 Börsenstrasse
Zurich

Federal Banking Commission

Dr Susanne BRANDENBERGER
Risk Management
Renate LISCHER
Representative to Risk Management Subgroup, Basle Committee

Marktgasse 37
3001 Bern

Bank for International Settlements

Mr. Claude SIVY
Head of Internal Audit
Herbie POENISCH
Senior Economist, Monetary and Economic Department

2, Centralplatz
4002 Basle

Bank Leu AG

Dr Urs MORGENTHALER
Member of Management
Director of Risk Control

32, Bahnhofstrasse
Zurich

Bank J. Vontobel and Vontobel Holding

Heinz FRAUCHIGER
Chief, Internal Audit Department

Tödistrasse 23
CH-8022 Zurich

Union Bank of Switzerland

Dr Heinrich STEINMANN
Member of the Executive Board (Retired)

Claridenstrasse
8021 Zurich

UNITED KINGDOM

Bank of England, and Financial Services Authority

RICHARD BRITTON
Director, Complex Groups Division, CGD Policy Department

Threadneedle Street
London EC2R 8AH

British Bankers Association

Paul CHISNALL
Assistant Director

Pinners Hall
105–108 Old Broad Street
London EC2N 1 EX

Accounting Standards Board

A.V.C. COOK
Technical Director
Sandra THOMPSON
Project Director

Holborn Hall
100 Gray's Inn Road
London WC1X 8AL

Barclays Bank Plc

Brandon DAVIES
Treasurer, Global Corporate Banking
Alan BROWN
Director, Group Risk

54 Lombard Street
London EC3P 3AH

Abbey National Treasury Services plc

John HASSON
Director of Information Technology & Treasury Operations

Abbey House
215–229 Baker Street
London NW1 6XL

ABN–AMRO Investment Bank N.V.

David WOODS
Chief Operations Officer, Global Equity Directorate

199 Bishopsgate
London EC2M 3TY

Banksgesellschaft Berlin

Stephen F. MYERS
Head of Market Risk

1 Crown Court
Cheapside,
London EC2V 6LR

Standard & Poor's

David T. BEERS
Managing Director, Sovereign Ratings

Garden House
18, Finsbury Circus
London EC2M 7BP

Moody's Investor Services

Samuel S. THEODORE
Managing Director, European Banks
David FROHRIEP
Communications Manager, Europe

2, Minster Court
Mincing Lane
London EC3R 7XB

Fitch IBCA

Charles PRESCOTT
Group Managing Director, Banks
David ANDREWS
Managing Director, Financial Institutions
Trevor PITMAN
Managing Director, Corporations
Richard FOX
Director, International Public Finance

Eldon House
2, Eldon Street
London EC2M 7UA

Merrill Lynch International

Erik BANKS
Managing Director of Risk Management

Ropemaker Place
London EC2Y 9LY

The Auditing Practices Board

Jonathan E.C. GRANT
Technical Director

Steve LEONARD
Internal Controls Project Manager

P.O. Box 433
Moorgate Place
London EC2P 2BJ

International Accounting Standards Committee

Ms Liesel KNORR
Technical Director

166 Fleet Street
London EC4A 2DY

MeesPierson ICS

Arjan P. VERKERK
Director, Market Risk

Camomile Court
23 Camomile Street
London EC3A 7PP

Charles Schwab

Dan HATTRUP
International Investment Specialist

Crosby Court
38 Bishopsgate
London EC2N 4AJ

City University Business School

Professor Elias DINENIS
Head, Department of Investment
Risk Management & Insurance
Prof. Dr John HAGNIOANNIDES
Department of Finance

Frobisher Crescent
Barbican Centre
London EC2Y 8BH

UNITED STATES

Federal Reserve System, Board of Governors

David L. ROBINSON
Deputy Director, Chief Federal Reserve Examiner
Alan H. OSTERHOLM, CIA, CISA
Manager, Financial Examinations Section
Paul W. BETTGE
Assistant Director, Division of Reserve Bank Operations
Gregory E. ELLER
Supervisory Financial Analyst, Banking
Gregory L. EVANS
Manager, Financial Accounting
Martha STALLARD
Financial Accounting, Reserve Bank Operations

20th and Constitution, NW
Washington, DC 20551

Federal Reserve Bank of Boston

William McDONOUGH
Executive Vice President
James T. NOLAN
Assistant Vice President

P.O. Box 2076
600 Atlantic Avenue
Boston, MA

Federal Reserve Bank of San Francisco

Nigel R. OGILVIE, CFA
Supervising Financial Analyst, Emerging Issues

101 Market Street
San Francisco, CA

Seattle Branch, Federal Reserve Bank of San Francisco

Jimmy F. KAMADA
Assistant Vice President
Gale P. ANSELL
Assistant Vice President, Business Development

1015, 2nd Avenue
Seattle, WA 98122-3567

Office of the Comptroller of the Currency (OCC)

Bill MORRIS
National Bank Examiner/Policy Analyst,
Core Policy Development Division
Gene GREEN
Deputy Chief Accountant
Office of the Chief Accountant

250 E Street, SW
7th Floor
Washington, DC

Federal Deposit Insurance Corporation (FDIC)

Curtis WONG
Capital Markets, Examination Support
Tanya SMITH
Examination Specialist, International Branch
Doris L. MARSH
Examination Specialist, Policy Branch

550 17th Street, NW
Washington, DC

Office of Thrift Supervision (OTS)

Timothy J. STIER
Chief Accountant

1700 G Street NW
Washington, DC, 20552

Securities and Exchange Commission, Washington DC

Robert UHL
Professional Accounting Fellow
Pascal DESROCHES
Professional Accounting Fellow
John W. ALBERT
Associate Chief Accountant
Scott BAYLESS
Associate Chief Accountant

Office of the Chief Accountant
Securities and Exchange Commission
450 Fifth Street, NW
Washington, DC, 20549

Securities and Exchange Commission, New York

Robert A. SOLLAZZO
Associate Regional Director

7 World Trade Center
12th Floor
New York, NY 10048

Securities and Exchange Commission, Boston

Edward A. RYAN, Jr.
Assistant District Administrator (Regulations)

Boston District Office
73 Tremont Street, 6th Floor
Boston, MA 02108-3912

International Monetary Fund

Alain COUNE
Assistant Director, Office of Internal Audit and Inspection

700 19th Street NW
Washington DC, 20431

Financial Accounting Standards Board

Halsey G. BULLEN
Project Manager
Jeannot BLANCHET
Project Manager
Teri L. LIST
Practice Fellow

401 Merritt
Norwalk, CN 06856

Henry Kaufman & Company

Dr Henry KAUFMAN

660 Madison Avenue
New York, NY

Soros Fund Management

George SOROS
Chairman

888 Seventh Avenue, Suite 3300
New York, NY 10106

Carnegie Corporation of New York

Armanda FAMIGLIETTI
Associate Corporate Secretary, Director of Grants Management

437 Madison Avenue
New York, NY 10022

Alfred P. Sloan Foundation

Stewart F. CAMPBELL
Financial Vice President and Secretary

630 Fifth Avenue, Suite 2550
New York, NY 10111

Rockefeller Brothers Fund

Benjamin R. SHUTE, Jr.
Secretary

437 Madison Avenue
New York, NY 10022-7001

The Foundation Center

79 Fifth Avenue
New York, NY 10003–4230

Citibank

Daniel SCHUTZER
Vice President, Director of Advanced Technology

909 Third Avenue
New York, NY 10022

Prudential–Bache Securities

Bella LOYKHTER
Senior Vice President, Information Technology
Kenneth MUSCO
First Vice President and Director,
Management Internal Control
Neil S. LERNER
Vice President, Management Internal Control

1 New York Plaza
New York, NY

Merrill Lynch

Johnn J. FOSINA
Director, Planning and Analysis
Paul J. FITZSIMMONS
Senior Vice President, District Trust Manager
David E. RADCLIFFE
Senior Vice President, National Manager Philanthropic Consulting

Corporate and Institutional Client Group
World Financial Center, North Tower
New York, NY 10281–1316

HSBC Republic

Susan G. PEARCE
Senior Vice President
Philip A. SALAZAR
Executive Director

452 Fifth Avenue, Tower 6
New York, NY 10018

International Swaps and Derivatives Association (ISDA)

Susan HINKO
Director of Policy

600 Fifth Avenue, 27th Floor, Rockefeller Center
New York, NY 10020–2302

Standard & Poor's

Clifford GRIEP
Managing Director

25 Broadway
New York, NY 10004–1064

Mary PELOQUIN-DODD
Director, Public Finance Ratings

55 Water Street
New York, NY 10041–0003

Moody's Investor Services

Lea CARTY
Director, Corporates

99 Church Street
New York, NY 10022

State Street Bank and Trust

James J. BARR
Executive Vice President, US Financial Assets Services

225 Franklin Street
Boston, MA 02105–1992

MBIA Insurance Corporation

John B. CAOUETTE
Vice Chairman

113 King Street
Armonk, NY 10504

Global Association of Risk Professionals (GARP)

Lev BORODOVSKI
Executive Director, GARP, and
Director of Risk Management, Credit Suisse First Boston (CSFB), New York
Yong LI
Director of Education, GARP, and
Vice President, Lehman Brothers, New York
Dr Frank LEIBER
Research Director, and
Assistant Director of Computational Finance,
Cornell University, Theory Center, New York
Roy NAWAL
Director of Risk Forums, GARP

980 Broadway, Suite 242
Thornwood, NY

Group of Thirty

John WALSH
Director

1990 M Street, NW
Suite 450
Washington, DC, 20036

Broadcom Corporation

Dr Henry SAMUELI
Co-Chairman of the Board, Chief Technical Officer

16215 Alton Parkway
P. O. Box 57013
Irvine, CA 92619–7013

Edward Jones

Ann FICKEN (Mrs)
Director, Internal Audit

201 Progress Parkway
Maryland Heights, MO 63043–3042

Teachers Insurance and Annuity Association/College Retirement Equities Fund (TIAA/CREF)

John W. SULLIVAN
Senior Institutional Trust Consultant
Charles S. DVORKIN
Vice President and Chief Technology Officer
Harry D. PERRIN
Assistant Vice President, Information Technology

730 Third Avenue
New York, NY 10017–3206

Grenzebach Glier & Associates, Inc.

John J. GLIER
President and Chief Executive Officer

55 West Wacker Drive
Suite 1500
Chicago, IL 60601

Massachusetts Institute of Technology

Ms Peggy CARNEY
Administrator, Graduate Office
Michael COEN, PhD Candidate,
ARPA Intelligent Environment Project

Department of Electrical Engineering
and Computer Science
Building 38, Room 444
50 Vassar Street
Cambridge, MA 02139

Henry Samueli School of Engineering and Applied Science, University of California, Los Angeles

Dean A. R. Frank WAZZAN
School of Engineering and Applied Science
Prof. Stephen E. JACOBSON
Dean of Student Affairs
Dr Les LACKMAN
Mechanical and Aerospace Engineering Department
Prof. Richard MUNTZ
Chair, Computer Science Department
Prof. Dr Leonard KLEINROCK
Telecommunications and Networks
Prof. CHIH-MING HO, PhD
Ben Rich-Lockheed Martin Professor
Mechanical and Aerospace Engineering Department
Dr GANG CHEN
Mechanical and Aerospace Engineering Department
Prof. Harold G. MONBOUQUETTE, PhD
Chemical Engineering Department
Prof. Jack W. JUDY
Electrical Engineering Department
Abeer ALWAN
Bioengineering
Prof. Greg POTTIE
Electrical Engineering Department
Prof. Lieven VANDENBERGHE
Electrical Engineering Department

Westwood Village
Los Angeles, CA 90024

Andersen Graduate School of Management, University of California, Los Angeles

Prof. John MAMER
Former Dean
Prof. Bruce MILLER

Westwood Village
Los Angeles, CA 90024

Roundtable Discussion on Engineering and Management Curriculum (2 October 2000)

Dr Henry BORENSTEIN, Honeywell
Dr F. ISSACCI, Honeywell
Dr Ray HAYNES, TRW
Dr Richard CROXALL, TRW
Dr Steven BOULEY, Boeing
Dr Derek CHEUNG, Rockwell

Westwood Village
Los Angeles, CA 90024

University of Maryland

Prof. Howard FRANK
Dean, The Robert H. Smith School of Business
Prof. Lemma W. SENBERT
Chair, Finance Department
Prof. Haluk UNAL
Associate Professor of Finance

Van Munching Hall
College Park, Maryland 20742-1815

Index